T0399441

Wealth, Power, and Authoritarian Institutions

OXFORD STUDIES IN AFRICAN POLITICS & INTERNATIONAL RELATIONS

General Editors
Nic Cheeseman, Peace Medie, and Ricardo Soares de Oliveira

Oxford Studies in African Politics and International Relations is a series for scholars and students working on African politics and International Relations and related disciplines. Volumes concentrate on contemporary developments in African political science, political economy, and International Relations, such as electoral politics, democratization, decentralization, gender and political representation, the political impact of natural resources, the dynamics and consequences of conflict, comparative political thought, and the nature of the continent's engagement with the East and West. Comparative and mixed methods work is particularly encouraged. Case studies are welcomed but should demonstrate the broader theoretical and empirical implications of the study and its wider relevance to contemporary debates. The focus of the series is on sub-Saharan Africa, although proposals that explain how the region engages with North Africa and other parts of the world are of interest.

Wealth, Power, and Authoritarian Institutions

Comparing Dominant Parties and Parliaments in Tanzania and Uganda

MICHAELA COLLORD

OXFORD
UNIVERSITY PRESS

OXFORD
UNIVERSITY PRESS

Great Clarendon Street, Oxford, OX2 6DP,
United Kingdom

Oxford University Press is a department of the University of Oxford.
It furthers the University's objective of excellence in research, scholarship,
and education by publishing worldwide. Oxford is a registered trade mark of
Oxford University Press in the UK and in certain other countries

Published in the United States of America by Oxford University Press
198 Madison Avenue, New York, NY 10016, United States of America

British Library Cataloguing in Publication Data
Data available

Library of Congress Control Number: 2023949212

ISBN 9780192855183

DOI: 10.1093/9780191945335.001.0001

Printed and bound by
CPI Group (UK) Ltd, Croydon, CR0 4YY

Preface and Acknowledgements

In writing this book, I wanted to look at why institutions matter, but not necessarily in the ways we are taught to expect. I do not talk about authoritarian parties and parliaments as a source of regime stability, nor do I present legislative institutionalization as contributing to democratization. Instead, I situate these institutions in their politico-economic context, exploring how they reflect and magnify a prevailing distribution of elite power.

While there are many sources of power, I focus on wealth. I examine how diverse trajectories of state-led capitalist development engender differing patterns of elite accumulation and contestation across regimes. These differences, in turn, influence institutional landscapes. While some ruling parties are institutionally coherent and disciplined, others are fractured across rival networks of politicians and financiers. While some legislatures are docile, others are battlegrounds, creating space for unresolved factional tensions to simmer, and sometimes explode.

Ultimately, I wanted this analysis to help makes sense not just of how institutional variation affects macro-level politics—regime survival, for instance—but of how it influences routine decision-making, the kind of decision-making that affects people's everyday lives.

What does it mean, then, if a party or legislature magnifies elite contestation? What impact does that have on distributive politics? Or on the ability of more popular interest groups to organize and influence elites? The focus on how political institutions interact with the broader political economy of a regime helps clarify in whose interests they operate, and what scope there is for more redistributive or inclusive politics. That is the aim of this book.

As with any theoretical argument, this one is the product of a series of encounters—with books, people, and their ideas. It is also rooted in place. It draws on general theory, but this is a book about and inspired by East Africa, by its political and intellectual history.

First, for his incredibly generous supervision, his encouragement and support throughout the PhD and after, I am grateful to Nic Cheeseman.

A second important influence involved a network of scholars working within a political economy tradition. This book started as a doctoral project at the University of Oxford where, through workshops and seminars, I was introduced to political settlements analysis. I grew hugely through interactions with Lindsay Whitfield, Pritish Behuria, Tom Goodfellow, Ole Therkildsen, Anne Mette Kjaer, and perhaps most especially, Hazel Gray. Many of these scholars were focused on using a political settlement approach to make sense of institutions and decision-making as they relate to development processes. Meanwhile, I was trying to make sense of political institutions—parties and legislatures. Yet the way they grounded an institutional analysis in a study of underlying power dynamics helped me revisit my earlier reading of the political science literature on authoritarian institutions. I was also encouraged to consult Catherine Boone's work, and later, was grateful for the chance to work as a researcher on her project, 'Spatial Inequalities in the Political Economy of Africa', which further informed edits to this book.

A third crucial encounter was with an older political economy literature, linked more closely to the East African region and with a particular focus on how distributions of power overlap with different post-colonial development trajectories. I have not been lucky enough to meet many of the relevant authors, so I acknowledge their work in typical academic fashion in the main text of this book. But on a more personal level, I am grateful for illuminating conversations with Chambi Chachage and for the many reading suggestions. I am also grateful for our trip to visit Lionel Cliffe's personal archive in Yorkshire, where we were kindly hosted by Margaret Sketchley and Peter Lawrence. At an institutional level, I am thankful for my affiliation to the Makerere Institute of Social Research and to the University of Dar es Salaam, both of whose libraries and seminars were an immense resource.

There are many other debts beyond these influences. For innumerable ideas and much of the empirical material, I am grateful to the many anonymous individuals who participated in my research. Thank you for your knowledge and your time. There is no book without you. I am also grateful for the access provided by the Parliaments of Tanzania and Uganda, including to their libraries. To Emma Boona, Simon Osborne, and Alexander Makulilo, thank you for hosting me. To John Mugabi, Juliet Josiah, Deo Walusimbi, Mercy Njoroge, Carol Namutosi, Will Boase, Lubega Kizza, Benjamin Sulle, Grace Minja, Cyrielle Maingraud-Martinaud, and Lucas Ndyamkama, thank you for teaching me so much and for giving me a home away. Thank you also to Wambui Wa-Ngatho, who got me learning Swahili, something many others have since helped with—and tolerated.

I am grateful to Ricardo Soares de Oliveira, Tim Power, Paul Chaisty, and again, Catherine Boone for their feedback on my thesis. For helping me rethink many things, if not for this project, then for the next one, thanks to Sabatho Nyamsenda. For reading and discussing my work, during and after my PhD, thank you to Roger Tangri, Moses Khisa, James Tumusiime, Hippo Twebaze, Michael Wahman, Yonatan Morse, Aikande Kwayu, Ben Taylor, Gerrit Krol, Thabit Jacob, Nelson Kasfir, Radha Upadhyaya, Mathew Wilson, James Giblin, Sarah Brierley, Jonathan Fisher, Emmanuel Sulle, Portia Roelofs, George Roberts, Simukai Chigudu, Sa'eed Husaini, Dan Paget, Sam Wilkins, Anne Wolf, Nicole Beardsworth, Laura Martin, Rebecca Engebretsen, Barnaby Dye, Jakob Hensing, Densua Mumford, Felicitas Becker, Ian Cooper, Danny Choi, Shana Warren, Ivan Ermakoff, Deborah Bryceson, Robert Elgie, and the participants at the ECPR Joint Sessions 2018. I am also grateful to the three anonymous reviewers of this manuscript for very thoughtful feedback, which has strengthened the book.

This project started ten years ago, and it has continued to evolve, along with my own thinking. There are changes I have incorporated, and some I could have taken further. While I am grateful to many people for their input, the mistakes are, of course, mine. I hope readers find something of interest to contribute to their own understanding and analysis.

Finally, I would like to thank Alexa Zeitz, Jamie Stern-Weiner, and Ellie Jackson for so much support over a very long time. This book is dedicated to Kate and Grace Collord.

Contents

List of Figures

List of Tables

List of Abbreviations and Acronyms

ACODE	Advocates Coalition for Development and Environment
ACT-Wazalendo	Alliance for Change and Transparency – Wazalendo
APA	Administration of Parliament Act
ASP	Afro-Shirazi Party
BDP	Botswana Democratic Party
BoT	Bank of Tanzania
BoU	Bank of Uganda
CAG	Comptroller and Auditor General
CC	Central Committee
CCM	Chama Cha Mapinduzi
CHADEMA	Chama Cha Democrasia na Maendeleo
CNU	Cameroonian National Union
CPDU	Cameroon People's Democratic Movement
CRC	Constitutional Review Committee
CSBAG	Civil Society Budget Advocacy Group
CSO	Civil Society Organisation
CUF	Civic United Front
CVL	Crystal Ventures Limited
DGF	Democratic Governance Facility
DP	Democratic Party
EPRDF	Ethiopian People's Revolutionary Democratic Front
FDC	Forum for Democratic Change
FY	Financial Year
G55.	Group of 55
GEMA	Gikuyu, Embu, and Meru Association
IFI	International Financial Institution
IMF	International Monetary Fund
IPTL	Independent Power Tanzania Ltd
KADU	Kenya African Democratic Union
KANU	Kenya African National Union
KMT	Kuomintang
KPU	Kenya People's Union
LEGCO	Legislative Council
LoP	Leader of the Opposition
MCP	Malawi Congress Party
MMD	Movement for Multi-Party Democracy
MP	Member of Parliament
MPLA	Movimento Popular de Libertação de Angola

MRND	Mouvement Révolutionnaire National pour le Développement
NAAA	National Assembly Administration Act
NAIC	NRM NEC Ad Hoc Issues Committee
NBC	National Bank of Commerce
NCCR-Mageuzi	National Convention for Construction and Reform - Mageuzi
NEC	National Executive Committee
NGO	Non-Governmental Organisation
NRA	National Resistance Army
NRC	National Resistance Council
NRM	National Resistance Movement
OGCW	Office of the Government Chief Whip
PAC	Public Accounts Committee
PAFO	Parliamentary Advocacy Forum
PAP	Pan African Power Solutions
PAP	People's Action Party
PFOG	Parliamentary Forum on Oil and Gas
POAC	Public Organisations Accounts Committee
PPI	Parliamentary Powers Index
PRI	Institutional Revolutionary Party
PS	Parti Socialiste du Sénégal
PFMB	Public Financial Management Bill
RPF	Rwandan Patriotic Front
SACCO	Savings and Credit Cooperative Organisation
TANESCO	Tanzania Electric Supply Company Ltd
TANU	Tanganyika African National Union
TIC	Tanzania Investment Centre
TPLF	Tigrayan People's Liberation Front
TPSF	Tanzania Private Sector Foundation
UMNO	United Malays National Organization
UAE	United Arab Emirates
UKAWA	Umoja wa Katiba ya Wananchi (Coalition for a People's Constitution)
UMNO	United Malays National Organization
UMWU	Uganda Medical Workers Union
UNATU	Uganda National Teachers Union
UNIP	United National Independence Party
UPC	Uganda People's Congress
UPE	Universal Primary Education
URA	Uganda Revenue Authority
USSR	Union of Soviet Socialist Republics
UVCCM	Umoja wa Vijana wa CCM
VAT	Value Added Tax
YPA	Young Parliamentary Association

1

Introduction

On 7 February 2008, then Prime Minister Edward Lowassa of Tanzania took to the floor of Parliament and, to the apparent surprise of many in the Chamber, announced his resignation. This came after a parliamentary select committee tabled a report implicating Lowassa in the so-called 'Richmond scandal'. He stood accused of intervening to secure a contract for the Houston-based Richmond Company, which promised to supply 100 megawatts of emergency power in 2006 during a severe, nationwide shortage. Yet Richmond never did produce any power, and it later transpired that the company was registered in the US as a 'printing shop and business services centre'. Parliament's intervention, under the leadership of then Speaker Samuel Sitta, united legislators from the ruling party, *Chama Cha Mapinduzi* (CCM), and opposition parties. MPs proclaimed that they were tired of being 'muzzled' and that the legislature was no longer a 'rubber stamp'. Public excitement ran high, and the media speculated about the dawn of a new, democratic era.[1]

There is another version of the Richmond story, though. Instead of recounting a victory for democratic accountability, this alternative narrative is rife with rumours, power struggles and deceit. Lowassa himself claimed shortly before resigning that Richmond was not the issue; 'The problem was the premiership ... they wanted the premiership'.[2] Observers have since alleged that Speaker Sitta, also a CCM politician, was acting on a personal vendetta. He used his authority in Parliament to frame the Prime Minister while President Jakaya Kikwete looked on, fearing Lowassa's growing popularity and political influence.[3] Within the ruling party, MPs and allied political financiers divided into rival factions, one aligned with Sitta and another with Lowassa.

The further Richmond receded into the background, the more muddied the facts became and the more grandiose the rumours. Whatever the truth of the matter, the scandal did not mark the end of the legislature's new-found vigour,

---

[1] Accessed 18 February 2017: https://wikileaks.org/plusd/cables/08DARESSALAAM98_a.html.
[2] Accessed 19 February 2017: http://www.thecitizen.co.tz/News/Richmond--Lowassa-and-the-race-to-Ikulu/1840340-2734086-bk2tpwz/index.html.
[3] Interviews with journalists and MPs, including members of the select committee tasked with investigating the Richmond contract.

Wealth, Power, and Authoritarian Institutions. Michaela Collord, Oxford University Press. © Michaela Collord (2024).
DOI: 10.1093/9780191945335.003.0001

at least not during Kikwete's presidency (2005–2015). Likewise, Lowassa was not the last of Kikwete's ministers to lose their position due to parliamentary pressure. A new trend had emerged in Tanzania, and people started talking about *Bunge lenye meno*, a parliament 'with teeth'. Kikwete's successor, President John Pombe Magufuli (2015–2021) did later reign in this newly assertive parliament, disciplining CCM MPs while repressing the opposition. Yet his actions only raise further questions about what lies behind changes in *Bunge's* strength, and indeed, in legislative assertiveness more generally. Elsewhere on the continent, for instance, in neighbouring Kenya, an assertive legislature was not a new phenomenon; even under one-party rule, Kenyan presidents had to be wary of legislative opposition and manage it carefully.[4] Meanwhile, in Uganda, another of Tanzania's neighbours, the legislature gained a reputation for its independence in the 1990s,[5] and this despite a recent history of civil conflict, then still ongoing in the north of the country. Again, given this variation both within Tanzania and across the region, we may well ask, what explains legislative strengthening in African states? And what is its political significance?

I am certainly not alone in posing these questions. After a period of neglect, African parliaments are the focus of a new wave of research.[6] The same applies more generally to 'authoritarian legislatures', that is parliaments in countries that remain under one-party or, like Tanzania and Uganda, dominant party rule.[7] Some of this work also examines ruling parties alongside legislatures, the understanding being that internal party politics directly affects how assertive the legislature may be.[8] This interest in authoritarian institutions—including both parties and parliaments—grew after early hopes attached to the 1990s 'third wave of democratization' were largely disappointed. Despite undergoing a multiparty transition, many African states remained under dominant-party rule.[9] Even where an incumbent ruling party did lose power, its defeat did not necessarily lead to improvements in civil and political rights.[10] Yet the

---

[4] Gertzel, 1970; Cheeseman, 2006; Opalo, 2019.

[5] Kasfir and Twebaze, 2009.

[6] Salih, 2005; Nijinks et al, 2006; Barkan, 2009; Lindberg, 2010; Brierley, 2012; van Vliet, 2014; Collord, 2018, 2021; Ofosu, 2019; Opalo, 2019, 2021; Demarest, 2021.

[7] For a survey of the recent literature, see: Gandhi et al., 2020.

[8] Collord, 2018, 2021; Opalo, 2019.

[9] As of 2016, the cut-off year for this study, there were 16 incumbent ruling parties in Africa that had either stayed in power since an initial multiparty transition or else won power off an incumbent in a multiparty election only to then emerge as dominant ruling parties themselves over successive electoral cycles. These countries include Angola, Burundi, Cameroon, Chad, Congo-RoC, Djibouti, Ethiopia, Gabon, Mozambique, Rwanda, Sudan, South Sudan, Tanzania, Togo, Uganda, Zimbabwe.

[10] Bleck and van de Walle find that of the 49 African states that have conducted at least some multiparty legislative and presidential elections since 1990, only nine qualify as 'Free' according to Freedom House ratings while 20 are rated 'partly free' and 20 'not free'. Even countries like Kenya or Zambia, which have experienced multiple presidential successions and party alternations, remain in the 'partly free' category. See Bleck and van de Walle, 2018: 50–51.

persistence of authoritarian or semi-authoritarian regimes does not mean that these states operate uniformly, or even in particularly similar fashions. In some cases, authoritarian leaders exercise relatively close control over party elites, ruling parties are cohesive, and the legislature marginalized. In other cases, by contrast, ruling parties are internally divided across rival factions, and parliament—at least at times—challenges a would-be dominant executive.

In seeking to explain institutional variation, this book diverges from the existing literature in several ways. It eschews the normative emphasis of a democratization literature preoccupied by how parliaments *could or should* deepen democracy.[11] It also avoids the functionalist analysis central to some authoritarian politics research, which claims that dictators 'choose' to institute a strong party or legislature to achieve regime stability.[12] Drawing instead on a mix of political economy and historical institutionalist literature,[13] the book examines how authoritarian political institutions reflect—and to some extent, magnify—elite power dynamics. These institutions are a 'terrain of contest',[14] an arena where power is tested, negotiated, and in some cases, re-ordered.

While there are many sources of elite power, and indeed, many kinds of 'elites',[15] the analysis aims to distil how the *socio-economic foundations* of a regime affect access to *material* sources of power in ways that, in turn, impact the institutional landscape. It focuses, first, on *divergent patterns of wealth accumulation*, which are themselves rooted in contrasting trajectories of state-led capitalist development. It then considers the *institutional consequences*. Where a class of private wealth accumulators expands, rival patron–client factions—comprising political financiers, politicians, as well as party and government officials—can more easily form, thereby leading to heightened contestation within ruling parties. These factional rivalries then erode party discipline while encouraging greater legislative institutional strengthening and assertiveness.

---

[11] Barkan, 2009.

[12] Gandhi, 2008; Opalo, 2019.

[13] Shivji, 1976; Thelen, 1999; Pierson, 2000; Rodan and Jayasuriya, 2012; Khan, 2018.

[14] Mandaza, 1994.

[15] Depending on one's focus, the term elites can encompass a diverse array of religious leaders, traditional leaders, elected politicians, wealthy individuals, university graduates, celebrities, and more. As discussed further in Chapter 2 and in the subsequent empirical chapters, this book focuses mainly on political and economic elites, namely politicians, political financiers, as well as party and state officials. The assumption is not that these actors wield equal power or are equally 'elite'; rather, the analysis explores how they organize together, forming part of the same factional networks and institutional power structures. I also do not want to overlook other, e.g. religious elites, but I tend to discuss them only in so far as they also integrate the power structures that are the focus of the book. Overall, this analysis aligns with what Lentz (2016: 40) identifies as 'functional elites' approaches in the study of African politics, 'understanding elites as individuals in leading positions in the political sphere or other societal fields with regular influence on decision-making that affects larger groups'.

Beyond explaining the emergence of an undisciplined party or an assertive parliament, what political significance do they have? Thinking back to the Richmond scandal, the legislature may appear as an empowered watchdog, checking executive corruption, or it may be a forum for factional score-settling. Or both. Again, rather than foreground a normative assessment, this book emphasizes how legislative outcomes—whether normatively desirable or not—reflect an underlying power distribution. As such, a strong legislature provides a platform for elite rivals to pursue their political ambitions and, where required, challenge and expose each other. There are also opportunities for less powerful actors—including collective organizations like unions, farmers' associations, cooperatives, and advocacy groups—to advance their political interests. However, the political economy of Africa's authoritarian regimes is such that these opportunities remain relatively rare, and the organizations involved politically vulnerable. Thus, a core argument of the book is that, rather than broadly representative, even relatively assertive parliaments remain elite-dominated institutions. As in, the legislature is principally a tool in the service of elite interests and, only secondarily, allows for a more broadly accountable politics.

The theory laid out in this book does not pretend to explain all sources of elite power and motivations. Nor does it explain all institutional variation across Africa; rather, it identifies *one* set of mechanisms, *among others*, that can guide our analysis of real-world authoritarian politics. Ultimately, this politics needs to be studied 'in all its messy complexity'.[16] Yet the hope is that the theory developed here—however partial—can help make sense of some of that complexity. In what follows, I present a longer summary of my argument and its significance. I then elaborate on its contribution to the wider literature. Third, I present my methods and my rationale for selecting Tanzania and Uganda as my main cases, albeit with further reference to Rwanda and Kenya. Finally, I outline the plan of the book.

1.1 The Argument

This book presents a theory of party and legislative strength and its significance under authoritarian rule. I focus on 'authoritarian' contexts where either a single or dominant party holds power. For the theory to apply, this ruling party must also conduct routine elections; these elections are either *within*

---

[16] Cooper, 2014: xi.

the ruling party in the case of one-party rule,[17] or where multiparty, they are manipulated to favour the incumbent ruling party and, thus, widely recognized as unfair. When identifying regime types, some literature would not apply the same 'authoritarian' label to both one-party and dominant party regimes; it would instead distinguish, referring to the latter with terms like 'competitive authoritarian', 'semi-authoritarian', or 'hybrid'.[18] Yet former single parties often survive multiparty transitions, and in these instances, how power is contested within an authoritarian coalition may not change dramatically.[19] As such, I do not assume a sharp conceptual distinction between regime type pre- and post-multiparty transition. Instead, I explore the authoritarian continuities from single to dominant party rule. Beyond labels, I am interested in how power is contested and how institutions actually work in these contexts.

As elaborated in the next chapter,[20] I assess differing levels of legislative strength along two dimensions: first, in terms of the *institutional changes* that enhance the legislature's *potential* to influence the executive;[21] and second, in relation to parliament's *actual performance*, how it challenges the executive through legislative, budgetary, and scrutiny activities. To then *explain* variation in legislative strength, I follow several other scholars in positing an *interdependent relationship between authoritarian party and legislative institutions*. I argue that, where an authoritarian party is institutionally strong and disciplined, intra-elite contestation is effectively contained within the party and, consequently, the legislature remains marginal. Conversely, where a party is institutionally weak and vulnerable to internal division, elite contestation can spill over into the legislature. This elite bargaining, in turn, leads both to legislative institutional strengthening and greater assertiveness. By way of illustration, we can revisit the story of how the Richmond scandal played out in Tanzania's *Bunge*. The legislature grew 'teeth' seemingly because of the elite rivalries pitting Prime Minister Lowassa, Speaker Sitta, and their respective factions against each other. These same rivalries also undermined President Kikwete's power to enforce discipline within the legislature.

This analysis of the relative strength of ruling parties versus parliaments says something about *how power is ordered in a regime*. In other words, a stronger

---

[17] They may involve some version of party primaries as has happened across many one-party African regimes.

[18] Levitsky and Way, 2010.

[19] Scholars including Magaloni and Kricheli (2010) make a similar point. For studies that emphasize these authoritarian continuities, see: Ajulu, 1999; Morse, 2019; Opalo, 2019.

[20] Please see Chapter 2 for references to the works inspiring this argument.

[21] These institutional changes could involve legal reforms to legislative powers, but they are more often subtler, for instance, involving changes to the Standing Orders and make-up of the committee system, which then enhance oversight capacity.

ruling party implies that top leaders are better able to control an authoritarian coalition; conversely, a more assertive legislature suggests decision-making is more contested across a fragmented elite. Yet the analysis does not clarify *why* power is ordered in these differing ways. Is it the mere presence of a strong ruling party that helps centralize power? Why do some parties contain elite contestation and ensure parliament's marginalization? Why are others fractious and undisciplined, enabling legislative strengthening?

This is where my analysis diverges from the existing literature, offering an alternative framework. I do not start by emphasizing how different party institutional configurations influence the organization of power in a regime; rather, I first highlight the *socio-economic foundations* of elite power, which I argue, help determine the strength of authoritarian party institutions. As in, it is not, in the first instance, institutions that order power; rather, an underlying elite power distribution orders institutions. That said, these institutions are *not* then mere epiphenomena, simply reflecting a power distribution. Drawing on historical institutionalist analyses, I stress the *mutual relationship* between informal power dynamics and formal institutions. Ultimately, institutions not only reflect *but can also further entrench* a particular power distribution.

My analysis begins with the initial process of regime consolidation, which I identify as a critical juncture. This designation applies because during the period immediately following an authoritarian party's accession to power, the strategic choices of party leaders are likely to 'trigger a path-dependent process that constrains future choices'.[22] I isolate two sets of choices, *economic* and *institutional*, which I maintain regime leaders routinely confront early in their tenure. The first choice relates to their preferred approach to state-led capitalist developments. The second then hinges on whether to invest in a strong party institutional apparatus. Leaders' decisions on these issues affect which of *two ideal types* an emerging authoritarian party is most likely to approximate, and consequently, what prospects there are for legislative strengthening (see Figure 1.1).

A first party type, an 'institutionalized coalition', emerges where authoritarian leaders choose to concentrate control over wealth accumulation; they limit the scope for a private economic elite to expand while encouraging state- and party-ownership. A range of ideological factors may inform this choice, but regardless of myriad possible motivations, this strategy of 'politicized accumulation' also serves to *centralize power* within the authoritarian coalition. Indeed, without strong private entrepreneurs to act as political financiers,

---

[22] Capoccia and Kelemen, 2007: 348.

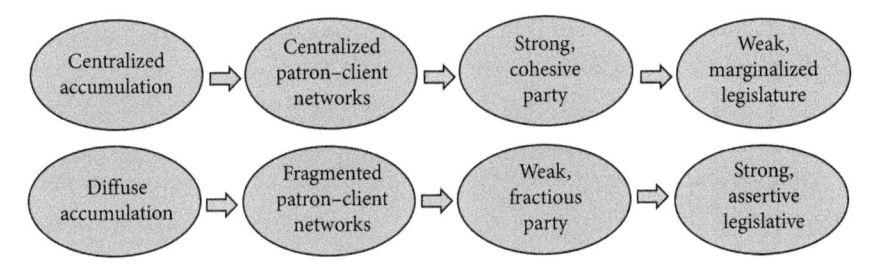

Figure 1.1 Party and legislative institutional variation

patron–client networks remain more centralized,[23] largely controlled by the top party leadership. When authoritarian leaders combine this centralized control with an active investment in strengthening party structures, this further consolidates the ruling party as an 'institutionalized coalition'. Finally, the strength of the ruling party ensures top leaders can enforce discipline, preventing elite rivalries from surfacing in the legislature, which remains a marginal institution.

By contrast, a more fractious party—or what I call a 'bargained coalition'— takes shape where authoritarian leaders encourage the expansion of a private class of accumulators, albeit one largely composed of political allies. This alternative 'strategy of politicized accumulation' then enables patron–client factions to multiply, bankrolled by elite rivals turned political financiers. Meanwhile, by virtue of their preferred economic strategy, authoritarian leaders party-building options are already limited; factional tensions would likely undermine formal party structures even if regime leaders did invest in party-building. Ultimately, weak party discipline means that elite rivalries are likely to spill into the legislature as well. These tensions then enable institutional reforms, the aim being—at least *partly*[24]—to turn parliament into a more effective tool for pursuing personal and factional advantages. These same elite rivalries also propel more direct legislative interventions, challenging the executive. Together, then, the weak ruling party and stronger legislature magnify the influence of contending factions while eroding the central control of the President and other top leaders.

---

[23] See the next chapter for further conceptualization of 'clientelism', patron–client networks, and how they manifest. I also highlight their relevance both in developing country contexts and in advanced industrialized countries with established democracies.

[24] As discussed further at other points in this book, normative reformist goals also guide the actions of some activist MPs; as in, the claim is not that MPs' motivations are reducible to material ones alone. The point, however, is to highlight how material conditions help structure broad patterns of elite contestation and institutional change.

The above analysis accounts for the *origins* of party and legislative strength, but how might these institutions *evolve* after the initial period of regime consolidation? I argue that they undergo a process of institutional 'lock-in', which encourages a degree of 'path dependence'. However, this continuity also depends on prevailing patterns of wealth accumulation and patronage distribution. In an 'institutionalized coalition', if the party leaders can no longer maintain their centralized control over wealth accumulation, for instance, following an economic crisis or liberalizing reform, then rival patron–client factions will multiply. Factional contestation will, in turn, undermine party institutions. This leaves room for the legislature to become a more important channel for elite bargaining. As such, a change in the political economy of the regime will lead to changes in its institutional landscape as well. *However*, an 'institutionalized coalition' is unlikely to simply collapse and assume all the characteristics of a 'bargained coalition'. Rather, the legacy of a strong party apparatus slows the process of institutional erosion. For instance, political actors, when seeking to extend their informal patronage networks, are still compelled to work around existing party structures, navigating internal party elections and candidate selection procedures. Given these constraining factors and thus the gradual pace of party institutional decay, legislative institutionalization will also be halting, and liable to reversal.

Regarding a 'bargained coalition', the extent of economic change may be more minimal. Indeed, it is doubtful that regime leaders could switch to more centralized state- or party-ownership, although over time, wealth can become more concentrated in the hands of a narrower regime elite. Yet even so, it becomes progressively more difficult—not to say impossible—for party leaders to belatedly invest in party-building. Political elites, notably parliamentarians and their allied financiers, will have invested in informal patronage networks and personalized ties to a local political base. With time, these same elites will also grow accustomed—along with the mass electorate—to a system in which political actors mobilize through informal patronage organizations. They will therefore continue to coordinate their actions as before, ignoring injunctions to respect party rules. For instance, aspiring candidates, if defeated in internal party primaries, will routinely dismiss the results and contest elections as Independents. The enduring, fractious nature of internal party politics then ensures the continued *unpredictability* of the legislature. Factional tensions resurge, motivating continued investment in legislative institutionalization as well as more routine executive–legislative clashes.

Finally, while I have theorized how party and legislative institutions form and evolve over time, why does this change matter, if at all? I argue that we can better explain the significance of a strong legislature once we have understood how legislative outcomes reflect factional rivalries amongst a political and economic elite. In studying legislative activity, I focus especially on its distributive implications, theorizing through what mechanisms legislative activity may impact distributive outcomes. The literature on this topic generally suggests that stronger parliaments lead to more popular accountability and more *progressive* redistribution. However, I propose an alternative set of causal mechanisms, which point towards contrasting distributive outcomes. Given that elite contestation drives legislative interventions, it follows that much of this activity would cater for elite interests, and with largely *regressive* distributive implications.

More bottom-up pressures may *occasionally* produce progressive distributive outcomes, but these are likely the exception to a dominant trend. Where they occur, two conditions can play an important enabling role: one, a mix of 'mass-based' and more middle-class advocacy groups can help galvanize legislative action; and two, the constellation of factional divisions within parliaments means that a sufficient number of legislators are motivated to leverage this outside agenda to gain an advantage over elite rivals. In other words, where the prevailing elite power structure offers an opening, otherwise marginalized groups can use legislative channels to influence political decisions, thereby encouraging more progressive redistributive outcomes. Even if exceptional, instances of effective bottom-up pressure driving legislative interventions deserve more attention; they reveal how a diverse array of actors—elite and non-elite—contest for power and influence within a context of top-down authoritarian dominance.

1.2 Contributions of the Argument

This book makes several contributions. First, it adds a novel argument to the comparative and more specifically Africanist literatures on authoritarian institutions. Second, it combines often distinct institutionalist and political economy analyses, opening new avenues for research. Third, it challenges conventional assumptions about the everyday practice of authoritarian rule and expectations of democratization.

As detailed further in the next chapter, the book builds on recent studies of authoritarian and dominant parties while also offering several new contributions. First, it makes an original conceptual distinction, identifying contrasting 'types' of ruling or dominant party based on an analysis of their patronage structure and institutional make-up. By contrast, many comparativists have tended to posit one 'modal' dominant party institutional form, thereby ignoring important differences.[25] The Africanist literature, in particular, has tended to present authoritarian party institutions as weak and personalized, dominated by 'Big Men' politicians.[26] Recent scholarship has started to differentiate across authoritarian parties, for instance, based on institutional strength, internal organization, and durability.[27] Yet while my analysis echoes this appreciation of party variation, my conceptualization of party types is distinct.

This then brings me to the book's second contribution, which is its novel political economy explanation of parties' institutional origins, their evolution over time and, ultimately, how they help to order power within an authoritarian coalition. As detailed above, this book systematically analyses the relationship between, one, the distribution of power and wealth within an authoritarian coalition and, two, how this relates to ruling parties' institutional make-up. I acknowledge from the outset that the relationship between power and party institutions is an *endogenous* one, but it does not follow that party institutions are insignificant, mere epiphenomena. Rather, I clarify how party institutions both reflect and *reinforce* a prevailing power distribution; as in, more centralized accumulation and a consolidation of patron–client factions enable leaders to maintain strong party structures that further consolidate their decision-making power and their control over patronage resources.

Regarding the study of parliaments, this book is part of a recent wave of literature that has begun to examine the inner workings of authoritarian legislatures, including institutional reform processes and more routine legislative activity.[28] This work descends from the bird's eye perspective of earlier, large-N comparative analyses focused on the presence or absence of an authoritarian legislature.[29] It also differs from some Africanist discussions of parliaments, which after the 1990s multiparty transition, adopted a normative focus; as in, they explore whether and how MPs are accountable to popular demands or in what ways the legislature *could* serve as a democratic check on the executive.[30] This book, instead, examines how elite contestation drives legislative activity and the ways in which the legislature further amplifies

---

[25] This is common in large-N studies focused on the presence or absence of a ruling party, for instance: Svolik, 2012; Boix and Svolik, 2013. It is also a feature of single case study analyses, for instance: Magaloni, 2006; Greene, 2007; Reuter, 2017. For a more comprehensive review and critique, see Meng, 2020.

[26] Van de Walle, 2003; Manning, 2005; Arriola, 2013.

[27] Riedl, 2014; Morse, 2019; Opalo, 2019; Meng, 2020, 2021.

[28] Opalo, 2019; Gandhi et al., 2020; Noble, 2020; Truex, 2020; Collord, 2021; Demarest, 2021; Opalo, 2022.

[29] Gandhi and Przeworski, 2006; Gandhi, 2008; Boix and Svolik, 2013; Wilson and Wright, 2015.

[30] Salih, 2005; Barkan, 2009; Humphreys and Weinstein, 2012; Ibn Zackaria and Appiah-Marfo, 2022.

these elite power dynamics. While some recent studies also examine the link between elite contestation and legislative outcomes,[31] this book delves into the politico-economic foundations of this elite bargaining. It examines how contrasting trajectories of state-led capitalist development shape the distribution of power within an authoritarian coalition and how elite contestation then affects party and legislative institutional outcomes.

This brings us to another contribution of the book. In developing my political economy analysis, I draw on an older Africanist literature, which examined post-colonial private and state accumulation and how it affected political institutions.[32] I also draw on more recent 'political settlements' literature, inspired by the work of Mushtaq Khan.[33] However, whereas this political settlements work focuses primarily on how the power distribution within a regime affects economic outcomes, my book is concerned with how it affects political institutions and their outcomes. The book can, therefore, help build a bridge between recent political economy and institutionalist analyses, encouraging more cross-fertilization in future.

Finally, the book helps rethink the relationship between would-be democratic institutions, authoritarian politics, and democratization. First, it pushes the study of authoritarian political institutions beyond a focus on often *distant* political outcomes, like regime collapse.[34] Rather, this book refocuses on questions of political *process*, on *how* routine authoritarian politics works, and especially, on how diverse actors—both elite and non-elite—navigate various opportunities and constraints to influence decision-making. In this way, it provides a more fine-grained study of the political and institutional changes *ongoing* under authoritarian rule, changes that profoundly affect people's everyday lives. Second, the book diverges from the democratization literature. It avoids the above-mentioned normative preoccupation with stronger legislatures leading to stronger democracies. Instead, the analysis underscores the varied experiences of political contestation and participation[35] *within authoritarian regimes*. It looks beyond categories of 'authoritarian' versus 'democratic' and beyond teleological assumptions about a transition from one to the other.[36] Through a study of power and political institutions, it directly

---

[31] Opalo, 2019; Noble, 2020; Collord, 2021; Demarest, 2021; Opalo, 2022.

[32] Sklar, 1963; Gertzel, 1970; Hyden and Leys, 1972; Shivji, 1976; Jorgensen, 1981.

[33] Khan, 2010; Whitfield et al., 2015; Gray, 2018.

[34] Critics of the authoritarian institutions literature have advocated a similar change of dependent variable for some time. See Pepinsky, 2014.

[35] Robert Dahl's (1971) classic dimensions for identifying democracies.

[36] For a similar critique, see, for instance: Rodan and Jayasuriya, 2012.

examines what room there is to contest rival interests, whose interests are included, whose are marginalized, and with what consequences.

1.3 Research Design

To test my causal argument, I employ a combination of cross-case and within-case comparison. While each type of comparison presents unique advantages, the strongest inferences are drawn by integrating the two as 'partners in the iterative task of causal investigation.'[37] For the cross-case comparison, I adopt a 'most similar' comparative method; 'background conditions' are similar across the chosen cases, but the relevant independent variables and potentially the dependent variable identified in the theoretical model differ.[38] There are several advantages to this approach. Given the fixed nature of the 'background conditions', it may be assumed that the presence or absence of the independent variables of interest is what causes variation in the dependent variable.[39] This advantage is especially significant for scholars analysing critical junctures and historical path dependence.[40] For the purposes of this study, it helps confirm that, despite facing similar challenges during early periods of regime consolidation, leaders' had multiple strategic options to choose from and that, as a result of their differing decisions, contrasting historical paths ensued.

There are nevertheless limitations to this cross-case comparison, not least that real-world cases only ever approximate the conditions of a 'most similar' design. Moreover, to confirm that a theorized causal pathway is in fact present in a given case, we need to supplement cross-case with within-case comparison. For this, I apply a process tracing method to each of my case studies, which involves theorizing and then testing a causal mechanism, i.e. a series of steps or 'entities that undertake activities' that together are 'what transmits causal force through a mechanism.'[41] Testing a causal mechanism involves determining whether its 'observable manifestations' are present in a case,[42] thereby increasing our confidence the mechanism operates as theorized, at least within that single case. With this approach in mind, the empirical chapters are organized such that each one addresses a particular link in the theorized causal chain.

Regarding my case selection, the study centres on authoritarian single and dominant party regimes in Africa, although many of the insights could apply

---

[37] Gerring, 2007: 83. See also: Capoccia and Kelemen, 2007.
[38] Gerring, 2007: 88.
[39] Seawright and Gerring, 2008: 304.
[40] Capoccia and Kelemen, 2007. See Chapter 3 for more discussion.
[41] Beach and Pedersen, 2013: 29.
[42] Ibid., 15.

elsewhere. This focus encompasses regimes that consolidated immediately after independence from colonial rule in the 1960s and 1970s and generally formed one-party states. It also includes a cohort of dominant party regimes, which took power after Independence from minority white rule in the 1980s and 1990, and finally, a group of regimes that emerged after military coups and civil conflict, particularly in the 1980s and 1990s. Within this broad universe of cases, regimes differ markedly along the major independent variables of interest, namely pattern of wealth accumulation and party institutional strength. Figure 1.2 contains a sub-set of the total case universe, showing roughly where different authoritarian parties—historical and contemporary— fall in relation to these two dimensions.[43] The clustering of parties in the upper right and lower left quadrants nevertheless offers a provisional illustration of the theorized relationship between patterns of wealth accumulation and party institutional strength. By contrast, the upper left quadrant is largely unpopulated, except by more highly institutionalized parties that shift left after economic changes lead to a decentralization of wealth accumulation,[44] again in keeping with my above-outlined argument. Finally, parties occupying the

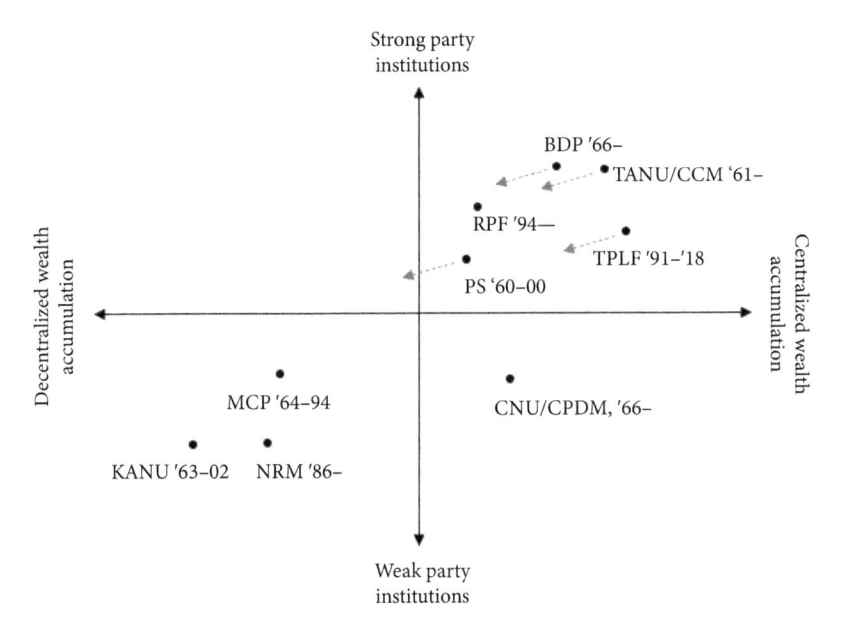

Figure 1.2 Variation across authoritarian parties

[43] The case placement is an illustrative approximation based on a review of secondary literature.

[44] The absence of arrows indicating change over time for parties in the lower left quadrant does not mean that these parties remained politically static; for instance, the factional power base in KANU reordered after President Moi succeeded Kenyatta. However, there are no arrows because these parties did not experience changes that would alter in a significant or sustained way their positions along the two axes included in this model, which is again only broadly illustrative.

lower right quadrant are few and are notable in so far as they hold power in countries where petroleum exports provide a centralized source of wealth accumulation.

For my two main cases, I chose one case from each of the upper right and lower left quadrant. The selected cases therefore differ on the independent variables of interest, and as it happens, the dependent variable too. As discussed below, they also count as 'most similar' in that they resemble each other on relevant 'background conditions', although given the nature of real-world case studies, this remains an approximation. The two main cases selected are Tanzania under the Tanganyika African National Union (TANU), which became Chama Cha Mapinduzi (CCM) in 1977 after a merger with Zanzibar's Afro-Shirazi Party, and Uganda under the National Resistance Movement (NRM). I also refer to the Kenya African National Union (KANU) and the Rwandan Patriotic Front (RPF), as clarified below. I analyse my two main cases from the period of regime consolidation up through the 2015 election for Tanzania and the 2016 election for Uganda, albeit with further discussion of some significant later developments in the conclusion of this book. I here briefly summarize what patterns of cross-case and within-case variation they present.

First, these cases differ in that the Tanzanian ruling party, TANU, first consolidated as an 'institutionalized coalition' while its Ugandan counterpart, the NRM, formed a 'bargained coalition'. At independence, the TANU leadership sought to implement a 'socialist' or *Ujamaa* economic approach, which included a range of interventions to ensure centralized control of wealth accumulation and thus patronage. The leadership simultaneously invested in TANU and later CCM's institutional strength, turning the party into one of the most highly institutionalized on the continent.[45] By contrast, the NRM leadership—after leading a rebel insurgency to victory in 1986—adopted a series of policies favouring private sector expansion, albeit within certain politically circumscribed bounds. NRM leaders simultaneously opted for a so-called 'no-party' system of governance, which constituted a de facto one-party state but with minimal investment in party institutions.[46]

Cross-case variation aside, Tanzania and Uganda also present valuable within case variation. This allows me to test for my theorized causal mechanisms as well as evaluate the nature and extent of institutional path dependence. Regarding Tanzania, economic liberalization starting in the 1980s led to

---

[45] On the relative institutional strength of CCM, see Chapters 3–4. See also: Basedau and Stroh, 2008; Morse, 2019.

[46] On the institutional weakness of the NRM, see Chapters 3–4. See also: Carbone, 2008; Makara et al., 2009; Collord, 2016; Wilkins, 2021.

a decentralization of wealth accumulation and fragmentation of patron–client networks, which partially subverted CCM's formal institutions. However, this institutional erosion was gradual, and when contrasted with the ruling party in Uganda, CCM still appears relatively strong. Moreover, as discussed in the conclusion to this book, the party discipline revived after John Magufuli became President in 2015. As such, we see how a form of institutional lock-in, borne out of TANU's early strength as an 'institutionalized coalition', meant that the party's decline proved only relative and at least partly reversible. Uganda under the NRM witnessed an inverse dynamic. Patterns of wealth accumulation remained relatively consistent, yet despite party leaders' efforts to strengthen the NRM's formal structures and procedures, the party remained locked into its own path-dependent trajectory, meaning it stayed fractious and institutionally incoherent.

Finally, the selection of Tanzania and Uganda for a cross-case and within-case comparison is appropriate in that the two cases differ not only on the relevant independent variables but also on the dependent variable, legislative institutional strength and assertiveness. The Tanzanian legislature has remained weak by regional standards,[47] only beginning to strengthen amidst CCM's institutional erosion.[48] The Ugandan parliament, by contrast, has been identified as one of the more assertive in the region.[49] This is, I should reiterate, *relative* to other parliaments. Uganda's legislature—particularly when studied alone and not comparatively—is also decried for its many failures to stand up to an authoritarian executive.[50] However, this book does not aim to demonstrate that the Tanzanian or Ugandan legislatures are 'strong' by some standard conventionally applied to parliaments in more democratic settings;[51] rather, it explores whether and how these institutions help magnify elite contestation, creating uncertainty in executive–legislative relations and compelling authoritarian leaders to accommodate legislative challenges at least some of the time. I elaborate on this approach to studying legislative strength in later empirical chapters. The key point, though, is that the historical weakness of the Tanzanian legislature when contrasted with the Ugandan parliament provides the causal leverage for a cross-case comparison. Within-case comparison enables me to test whether my theory explains change over time, namely a gradual strengthening of the Tanzanian parliament and continuity for the Ugandan legislature.

[47] Kjekshus, 1974.
[48] Collord, 2018.
[49] Kasfir and Twebaze, 2009; Collord, 2016, 2021.
[50] Tripp, 2010.
[51] A classic legislative studies literature also queries whether 'democratic' parliaments reliably achieve a particular standard: Blondel, 1970; King, 1976.

This brings us to the issue of whether Uganda and Tanzania do, in fact, present similar 'background conditions', thereby qualifying as 'most similar' cases. This assessment is also an opportunity to review *alternative arguments*; it is especially important that any variables of direct theoretical relevance not be markedly dissimilar across the two cases. I now briefly address several such variables, although I return to a discussion of alternative arguments and relevant background conditions in the empirical chapters.

A first background condition of interest is the type of electoral system as this may affect party cohesion and discipline. A first-past-the-post system, for instance, is thought to encourage more personal voting while proportional representation confers more authority on the party leadership, particularly where there is a closed list.[52] Tanzania and Uganda, however, both use primarily a first-past-the-post electoral system,[53] so this variable cannot account for differences between the two.

A second variable of interest is the level of multiparty competition, which is theoretically relevant in that some scholars argue parliament strengthens as competition intensifies. In so far as this argument holds, meaning party competition is a significant background variable, Tanzania and Uganda do count as 'most similar'. From the multiparty transition to my 2015 and 2016 cut-off years, Tanzania's CCM averaged 79 per cent of the legislative vote share and Uganda's NRM 69.5 per cent.[54] Even if CCM outperformed the NRM, both parties retained a hegemonic vote share. More fundamentally, though, there are reasons to question whether increased party competition leads to legislative strengthening. Scholars present two arguments to explain this supposed relationship. First, they theorize that, where competition is greater, MPs are more accountable to their electorate and, therefore, more likely to challenge the executive in voters' interests. Second, scholars suggest that opposition MPs are more likely to have the individual qualities of a 'reformer',[55] and thus are more likely to challenge the executive.[56] Evidence in support of the first hypothesis is lacking,[57] and indeed, some studies show that more intense competition actually increases party discipline, discouraging legislative interventions.[58]

---

[52] Carey and Shugart, 1995.

[53] Tanzania does use a version of proportional representation for women's 'special seats' in Parliament but not for the majority of elected members. See Chapter 5 for more discussion.

[54] Figures from Appendix A, Morse, 2019.

[55] Weghorst, 2022.

[56] Barkan, 2009.

[57] Studies examining whether increased competition among elected officials encourages greater accountability find that, while it may lead to more investment in constituency service, it does not result in more interventions in local councils or national assemblies. Grossman and Michelitch, 2018; Ofosu, 2019.

[58] Killian, 2004; Brierley, 2012.

These findings imply a more complex relationship between party competition and legislative autonomy.[59] Regarding the second, 'reformer' hypothesis, the argument advanced in this book is that, where the ruling party dominates the legislature, the success of reformist MPs—whatever party they hail from—depends on ruling party discipline. Ultimately, outcomes of reformist efforts depend on the internal politics of the incumbent party.

A third variable of interest relates to variation in the political salience of ethnicity across the two countries. This is potentially more relevant for a 'most similar' case comparison. Scholars have, for instance, related CCM's cohesion to the limited politicization of ethnicity in Tanzania,[60] although this analysis arguably overlooks the significance of ethnicity in more localized political competition.[61] Meanwhile, Uganda has a history of ethnic divisions fuelling party fragmentation and instability.[62] There are nevertheless several reasons why this apparent difference does not pose a significant challenge to cross-case comparison. One, *elite contestation* within their respective authoritarian coalitions *does not track neatly along ethnic lines.* In this vein, the NRM initially cultivated a more multi-ethnic coalition than earlier regimes in post-colonial Uganda.[63] While the party's self-proclaimed 'broad base' narrowed with time,[64] contestation within the NRM still occurs among elites *of the same ethnic group* as well as between elites of differing ethnicities,[65] raising questions about the importance of ethnicity per se. Relatedly, NRM party primaries in erstwhile peaceful constituency can turn violent not because of ethnic composition but rather because it has become the focus of a 'proxy wars' whereby 'competition between local candidates is reinforced by a conflict among central-level elites'.[66] A second reason why it is still useful to compare Tanzania and Uganda is that the *politicization of ethnicity is itself intertwined with politico-economic dynamics* that are the focus of this book, notably the control of economic resources and the configuration of patron–client networks.[67] For instance, differences in land tenure regime—and with it, opportunities for private land ownership and accumulation—have seemingly reduced the political salience

---

[59] The comparative literature on democratic regimes has long emphasized this complexity. See King, 1976.
[60] See Green (2011) for a review of arguments in this vein.
[61] Martin, 1988; Bavu, 1990. Author interviews with CCM parliamentary candidates.
[62] Mutibwa, 1992.
[63] Low, 1988. The major exception throughout the first two decades of NRM rule was the Northern Acholi sub-region still ravaged by civil war, although this too was—at least provisionally—integrated into the NRM fold following the cessation of conflict. Omach, 2014.
[64] Oloka-Onyango, 2000; Lindemann, 2011.
[65] Carbone, 2008; Kjaer and Katusiimeh, 2021; Wilkins, 2021.
[66] Kjaer and Katusiimeh, 2021: 177.
[67] Berman, 1998; Ajulu, 1999; Boone, 2014; Boone et al., 2022.

of ethnicity in Tanzania while exaggerating it in Uganda.[68] Meanwhile, the analysis of 'proxy wars' suggest it is factional rivalries that may periodically politicize ethnicity rather than ethnicity fuelling elite rivalries.[69] In sum, we cannot ignore the varying political salience of ethnicity in Tanzania and Uganda; however, ethnicity per se is not a compelling alternative reason for differences in elite contestation across the two countries.

On a related point, Tanzania and Uganda also vary when it comes to the political prominence of local, 'traditional' elites and their relations with the national leadership. This variation is theoretically relevant in so far as some scholars, notably Riedl, argue that the decision of national leaders to incorporate local, traditional elites in the ruling coalition leads to stronger, more durable ruling party institutions. Conversely, the attempted 'substitution' of local elites with formal party structures results in a less cohesive, institutionally weaker ruling party.[70] The difference between Tanzania and Uganda on this point would be problematic except that the outcomes are the reverse of what Riedl's theory would lead us to expect. TANU—later CCM—sought to 'substitute' traditional elites and is the far stronger party.[71] Meanwhile, the NRM has somewhat inconsistently sought to align with traditional elites, notably restoring Uganda's kingdoms,[72] yet the party is relatively fractious. Thus, Riedl's alternative argument does not account for party outcomes in these two cases and, consequently, does not compete with the explanation advanced in this book.[73]

A final 'background condition' worth considering is whether Uganda and Tanzania's ruling parties faced strong opposition when coming to power. The relevant theory, in this instance, suggests that confrontation with a 'strong and well-organized opposition' during the period of regime consolidation leads to the formation of more cohesive and durable ruling parties or 'organizational weapons'.[74] Again, there are clear differences on this point between Tanzania and Uganda, yet the relative institutional strength of the two ruling parties is also the opposite of what we would expect. TANU had a comparatively peaceful rise to power and developed into a strong party while the NRM fought a five-year rebel insurgency and later consolidated as an institutionally weak party.

---

[68] Boone, 2014; Boone and Nyeme, 2015.

[69] This analysis aligns with various constructivist and instrumentalist accounts of ethnicity. Jorgensen, 1981; Berman, 1998; Lynch, 2006; Reuss and Titeca, 2017.

[70] Riedl, 2014.

[71] For a discussion of why Riedl's argument does not apply in Tanzania, see: Paget, 2019.

[72] Doornbos and Mwesigye, 1995.

[73] This is not to say that variation in local–national elite relations is insignificant. For an analysis of its political consequences, see for instance: Boone, 2003; Koter, 2013.

[74] Smith, 2005; Levitsky and Way, 2012.

Even so, the contrasting ways by which the NRM and TANU attained power—as well as the different time periods and conditions under which this took place—deserve further attention. These are obvious points on which the two cases differ in their 'background conditions'. I address this issue by referring to two additional shadow cases in this book, particularly when analysing the 'critical juncture' period. I contrast TANU's regime consolidation with that of its geographical neighbour and immediate contemporary, the Kenyan African National Union (KANU), which consolidated as a 'bargained coalition' in the 1960s. I then contrast the NRM with the Rwandan Patriotic Front (RPF), which took power eight years after the NRM also following a protracted civil war as well as a genocide. I show how the RPF, in contrast to the NRM, consolidated as an 'institutionalized coalition'. These additional case comparisons, albeit less developed, help confirm the validity of the main arguments of the book.[75] Extending my analysis to cover different time periods and conditions of regime consolidation is also valuable in its own right, despite the additional comparative challenges. I can demonstrate how similar logics govern authoritarian party consolidation through space and time, thereby affirming the relevance of my theory to a wider case universe. This runs counter to a comparative historical literature in African studies which tends to root the discussion of authoritarian trajectories in the immediate post-colonial period.[76]

To conduct the above-outlined within-case and cross-case analysis, I rely primarily on qualitative data gathered from a variety of sources. Over a cumulative 15 months of field work in Uganda and Tanzania, I conducted 158 elite interviews and accompanied six MPs to their constituencies. I attended parliamentary committee meetings, seminars, and workshops; observed internal party meetings and public rallies; conducted archival research including in both the Ugandan and Tanzanian parliamentary archives as well as the East Africana archive at the University of Dar es Salaam; visited the personal archives of academics and former government officials; and collected documentation from party headquarters, NGO offices, and the archives of various media houses. The archival research involved both English and Swahili sources. In addition to these primary sources, I also rely on secondary literature, particularly for the historical discussion of the early periods of regime consolidation. I compliment this qualitative data with quantitative measures, notably relating to parliamentary business (e.g., the number of bills passed).

---

[75] These comparisons are also useful in that TANU and KANU inherited from Britain—the departing colonial power—a similar legislative blueprint, building on the colonial-era Legislative Councils (LEGCOs). Meanwhile the NRM and RPF both rebuilt legislative institutions post-conflict.
[76] Arriola, 2013; Riedl, 2014.

I also draw surveys data on MPs self-reported expenses, which I accessed through the Uganda country office of the National Democratic Institute.

I mainly use data from interviews and archival material to provide 'account evidence', which covers various aspects of a process, including how and why it unfolded as it did.[77] I also use this data to derive 'sequence evidence', that is, information on the precise sequences of events. Both types of evidence are essential for process tracing analysis.[78] They also influenced my sampling methodology when conducting elite interviews. I aimed for a broadly representative sample of MPs from different parties, whose assertions I could then triangulate with interviews from an array party officials, journalists, and activists from advocacy organizations, among other interviewees. However, in addition to ensuring a representative sample, I also sought out interviews with specific individuals who I knew were directly involved in an event of interest, for instance, the enactment of legislative institutional reform, party constitutional change, and the like. I identified these key informants by using secondary literature, media coverage, and snowballing techniques.

1.4 Plan of the Book

Chapter 2 of this book elaborates on the theoretical framework and where it sits in the literature. It thus lays the foundations for the four subsequent empirical chapters, each addressing a key step in the argument. One focuses on authoritarian party consolidation, a second on party continuity and change, a third on legislative institutional strengthening, and a fourth on legislative performance, as in, when and how parliament intervenes to challenge the executive. Each empirical chapter itself comprises three main sections. The first section reviews the argument and methods for the relevant portion of the causal analysis. This involves further discussion of alternative arguments, how these will be tested, and with what evidence. The next two sections then address the Tanzanian and Ugandan cases in turn, the exception being Chapter 3, which pays equal attention to Kenya and Rwanda as well.

To clarify, Chapter 3 sets out how authoritarian leaders' strategic decisions during an early period of regime consolidation influence what 'type' of ruling party is likely to emerge, an 'institutionalized coalition' or a 'bargained coalition'. Given this theoretical focus, the empirical analysis centres on the initial

---

[77] On different kinds of evidence and their use in process tracing, see Beach and Pedersen, 2013.
[78] Ibid.

period when TANU first consolidated power in Tanzania, forming an 'insti-tutionalized coalition', and when the NRM took power in Uganda, forming a 'bargained coalition'. It also incorporates details from Kenya and Rwanda to offer additional causal leverage. For each case, it first traces the decision-making process that resulted in leaders choosing one strategy of 'politicized accumulation' over another and then does the same for leaders' choice of party-building strategy.

Chapter 4 examines institutional continuity and change in authoritarian parties, demonstrating its theoretical argument through the comparison of TANU/CCM and the NRM. It identifies dynamics of *institutional path dependence* in each case, following on from the initial critical juncture of regime consolidation. Yet it also shows how party institutional trajectories remain *sensitive to shifts in a country's wider political economy*. The analysis adopts the selection process for parliamentary and presidential candidates within each party as a strategic focus. It uses this to show how economic liberalization in Tanzania from the 1980s and the associated fragmentation of patron–client networks undermined formal candidate selection procedures in CCM up through the 2015 elections. Even so, the legacy of strong party structures still slowed the organization of rival factions and limited their autonomy. Regarding Uganda's NRM, by contrast, the party's candidate selection was from the start poorly institutionalized, undermined by informal pressure and patronage expenditure. Despite the NRM leadership repeatedly attempting to enforce formal discipline, particularly following the 2005 return to multi-party politics, these efforts failed, and this due to the continued prevalence of private political finance and fragmented patron–client networks.

Whereas the two preceding chapters explain variation in party institutional strength over space and time, Chapters 5 and 6 shift focus, showing how the political economy of authoritarian parties helps explain variation in legislative strength. I use legislative strength or 'institutionalization' to refer both to *institutional strength* and to *actual performance*. Chapter 5 focuses on institutional strength, indicating how a legislative institutional reform process may begin where private accumulation is less controlled, patron–client factions more fragmented, and ruling party discipline weak. The chapter first details how and why Tanzania's legislature weakened from the late 1960s through the 1970s amidst the consolidation of TANU/ CCM as a strong 'institutionalized coalition'. It then examines how this trend reversed from the 1980s onwards amidst the gradual institutional erosion and growing factionalism of CCM. The chapter then explores how in Uganda, by contrast, legislative institutional strengthening occurred early under the NRM, a 'bargained coalition'. The level of legislative institutional strength, moreover, remained largely stable, despite repeated efforts by the executive to reduce it.

While Chapter 5 examines legislative institutional strength, which enhances the *potential* for legislative assertiveness, Chapter 6 centres on *actual* performance. Again, it shows how the strength of legislative challenges to the executive depend on the political economy of the ruling party and related dynamics of intra-elite bargaining. As with legislative institutional strength, it finds that the Tanzanian parliament, while marginal when TANU was at its most cohesive and institutionally strong, became a more significant channel for elite contestation and, consequently, more assertive after CCM party institutions began to erode and factional competition increased. The Ugandan Parliament, by contrast, proved a consistent platform for elite bargaining and periodic challenges to the executive, reflecting and magnifying elite contestation within the ruling party. Beyond a simple study of performance, though, the chapter probes the significance of an assertive legislature for distributive politics. Through analysis of specific legislative interventions, it demonstrates how legislators extract material and political benefits for themselves and allied politico-economic elites, suggesting the regressive redistributive implications of an assertive parliament. The chapter also explores under what conditions legislators may intervene to favour progressive redistributive measure, highlighting the galvanizing effects of more bottom-up organized pressure.

The conclusion reviews the main contributions of this book before engaging with three additional areas of inquiry. First, it expands on an earlier discussion of *authoritarian discontinuities*, examining the significance of John Magufuli's presidency in Tanzania (2015–2021) and the political reversals it caused, including increased party discipline and legislative marginalization. Moving beyond the focus on dominant party regimes, it next engages with the implications of *more competitive multiparty politics* for legislative strengthening. Finally, it reflects more broadly on the relationship between legislative strengthening and *democratization*. It engages with critical debates about democracy and development as well as the significance of institutions. Ultimately, it calls for a shift in focus, arguing that more energy could be invested in understanding the intersection between would-be democratic institutions and the underlying political organization that determines in whose interests they operate. Of central importance here is the organization of otherwise marginalized groups—small farmers and traders, transport workers, residents of underserved informal settlements, and professionals providing key social services, like health workers and teachers, among others. These actors are organizing to leverage what space is available for contestation and change within contexts where the distribution of power and resources remains highly unequal. Understanding when and how they organize—including on occasion through the legislature—remains an important goal for future research.

2

Wealth, Power, and Authoritarian Institutions

It is necessary from the very nature of things that power should be a check to power.

—Montesquieu, *The Spirit of the Laws*, Book XI

The post-colonial state remains the terrain of contest, particularly between the various factions and fractions of the petty bourgeoisie.

—Mandaza, 1994

Formal political institutions in authoritarian regimes have long been dismissed as weak and largely insignificant, particularly in the African context.[1] A newer literature has, however, begun to shift focus. It asserts that authoritarian institutions do 'matter', notably in the management of elite contestation. It also highlights considerable institutional variation across regimes. Building on this work, I here outline a theory to better explain party and legislative institutional variation. Why is it that ruling parties in some countries are institutionally strong, featuring well-defined formal structures and procedures and a relatively high level of discipline? Why are ruling parties elsewhere weak and internally divided? Similarly, why are some legislatures more institutionalized and assertive, routinely challenging the executive? Why are legislatures elsewhere more marginal? And ultimately, why does this institutional variation matter, if at all? Is a more assertive legislature a 'democratic' check on the executive? How do parties and legislatures affect the broader balance of power in an authoritarian regime? Whose interests are served and whose suppressed?

In answering these questions, the chapter diverges from much of the recent comparative politics literature on authoritarian institutions. It does not take

---

[1] The Africanist and broader comparative politics literature has tended to present ruling parties as personalized, subject to the whims of authoritarian 'Big Men'. Meanwhile, the legislature was dismissed as a 'rubber stamp' or 'sideshow'. Zolberg, 1966; Mezey, 1989; Van de Walle, 2003; Manin, 2005; Arriola, 2013; Mozaffar and Scarrit, 2005; Randall and Svasand, 2002a; Booth and Golooba-Mutebi, 2012.

political institutions themselves as the starting point but rather prioritizes an analysis of institutional origins and ongoing evolution. More specifically, it emphasizes how these institutional structures emerge out of a prevailing societal *distribution of power and corresponding elite power dynamics*. While there are many sources of power, I examine how differing patterns of accumulation affect the structure of patron–client networks within an authoritarian party, and ultimately, the strength of both party and legislative institutions. The theory, while presented in a straightforward, declarative manner for the sake of clarity, offers a necessarily *partial* explanation. It may *guide* the analysis of specific contexts, but individual cases will inevitably present complexities that go beyond what this theoretical framework proposes.

In brief, the argument goes as follows. Where strategies of state-led capitalist development result in *more expansive private accumulation*, wealthy elites emerge as prominent political financiers and bankroll rival patron–client factions. The resultant factional tensions undermine ruling party cohesion and subvert formal party structures. Elite contestation then spills over into the legislature, which serves as an institutional platform from which legislative elites and their allies can pursue factional interests. As such, these same elites have an incentive to invest in an institutional reform agenda in so far as this provides fresh opportunities to challenge rival elites from within the legislature.

This explanation of legislative strength also helps clarify its *significance*. Drawing, on insights from historical institutionalism, the idea is that differing levels of party and legislative institutional strength both reflect and further *reinforce* the prevailing distribution of power within a regime; they provide elite factions with different sets of institutional tools to entrench their political position and further marginalize their rivals. As such, they also shape the scope for political participation, how varied a range of actors are involved— both elite and less elite—and, thus, who can influence decision-making processes.

As hinted earlier, this emphasis on the *mutual relationship* between elite power dynamics and institutional outcomes helps dispel certain problematic assumptions in the literature. For one, my analysis indicates a strong legislature is more normatively ambivalent than much of the democratization literature would suggest. Similarly, it goes beyond the functionalist analysis still prevalent in the authoritarian institutions literature; rather than claim that dictators create strong legislatures to ensure regime survival, I instead delve into how parties and parliaments mediate more day-to-day elite contestation and decision-making processes. As such, I ascribe a more modest role to the legislature than some other scholars. Yet, I aim to clarify how parties and legislatures fit into a routine authoritarian politics, plus what opportunities they provide diverse actors seeking political influence.

In what follows, I first situate my analysis within the wider literature on authoritarian institutions. I identify recent advances in this research, note remaining gaps, and outline how I address these gaps through my alternative political economy approach. I then present my theory in more depth, detailing how it furthers our understanding of authoritarian institutions, their interaction with elite power dynamics, and their significance.

2.1 Towards an Analysis of Authoritarian Institutions

A growing body of comparative research refocuses attention on how political institutions, including parties and legislatures, operate within authoritarian regimes.[2] I begin by reviewing the important contributions of this work as well as some remaining limitations. To address these limitations, I draw key insights from two alternative literatures, a 'critical' political economy literature and an historical institutionalist literature. I use these insights to suggest how political institutions evolve to reflect and magnify an underlying distribution of wealth and power in authoritarian contexts.

2.1.1 Authoritarian Institutions in Comparative Research

Since the early 2000s, scholarly interest in authoritarian parties and legislatures has intensified. With time, this work has gained in sophistication, advancing from what I refer to as a first wave literature focussed principally on regime survival into a second wave of more nuanced analysis. Among other advances, the recent literature highlights the complex interaction between elite contestation, parties, and parliaments. Theoretical ambiguities nevertheless remain. Which forms of elite contestation are significant? What explains variation in elite power dynamics? Does this variation determine institutional outcomes, or is it institutions that reshape the power balance in authoritarian regimes? In what follows, I expand this review of the authoritarian institutions literature. I then briefly engage with a separate literature on political institutions and democratization. This work raises similar questions about the

---

[2] Note here that I refer to as 'authoritarian' both single and dominant party regimes. This study focuses on both one-party regimes, albeit with elections, and 'competitive authoritarian' regimes, i.e., regimes with multiparty politics but where the ruling party dominates elections that may be free (parties can compete) but not fair (there is no level playing field) (Levitsky and Way, 2010).

relationship between power and institutions, namely, about whether power orders institutions or institutions order power.

The first wave of authoritarian institutions literature comprised a mix of large-N and some smaller-N case study analyses. The large-N comparisons identified a simplified independent variable, namely, the presence or absence of an authoritarian party or legislature.[3] The smaller-N comparisons did sometimes pay more attention to variation in institutional strength,[4] although just as often presented their case study of interest as emblematic of authoritarian parties writ large.[5] Both kinds of study tended to adopt the same outcomes of interest, arguing that the presence of (strong) authoritarian institutions led to greater regime stability or better economic outcomes.[6] This result was because both parties and legislatures could, scholars maintained, facilitate elite co-optation and power-sharing.

Despite the agenda-setting contribution of this early research, there are several limitations. One concern is that these analyses do not adequately explain the *origins of institutions* themselves and what factors shape their continued evolution.[7] As noted by Thomas Pepinsky, without a prior analysis of institutional formation and change, scholars cannot be certain that the outcomes attributed to parties and legislatures (B) are actually a consequence of these institutions and not, instead, the result of some underlying factor that shaped both institutions (A) and the outcome of interest (C) (see Figure 2.1).[8] Relatedly, scholars tended to claim that a 'dictator' would 'choose' to create a party or legislature to control elite contestation, but these scholars would then explain the collapse of these same institutions as resulting from uncontrolled elite division within the ruling coalition. How is it that an institution can both independently regulate elite conflict and be undermined by that very same conflict?[9] Can we be sure that these institutions 'matter', i.e. that they can independently influence political outcomes of interest? Where does power actually lie?

---

[3] Gandhi and Przeworksi, 2006; Gandhi, 2008; Svolik, 2012; Boix and Svolik, 2013; Wilson and Wright, 2015.

[4] Brownlee, 2007.

[5] Magaloni, 2006; Greene, 2007.

[6] See also: Geddes, 1999; Lust-Okar, 2006; Levitsky and Way, 2010, who are also interested in whether autocratic breakdown leads to democratization; Gehlbach and Keefer, 2011. For a recent study that links high levels of party institutionalization—in both authoritarian and more democratic settings—with better 'state performance', see Sigman, 2023.

[7] Pepinsky, 2014.

[8] Figure adapted from Pepinsky, 2014.

[9] These are issues affecting the authoritarian institutions literature but, more generally, that also affect rational choice institutionalist analyses. See: Riker, 1980; Mahoney and Thelen, 2009.

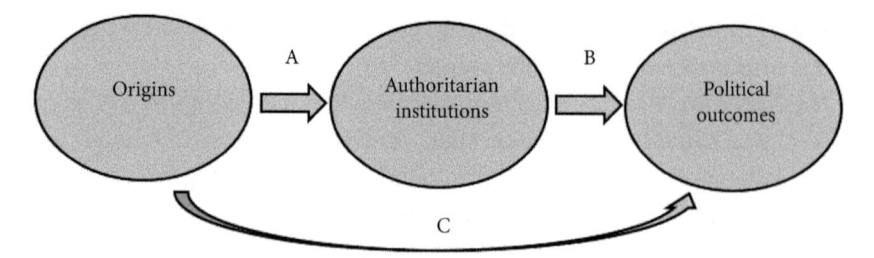

Figure 2.1 From institutional origins to political outcomes

Partly in response to this challenge, scholars have reoriented their analysis in several important ways. Some studies have begun to trace institutional origins more closely,[10] to assess institutional variation and not just a 'crude measure' of presence or absence,[11] and to make more use of small-N case studies to better test specific causal mechanisms.[12] Building on all this work, scholars have also moved away from a preoccupation with regime survival to examine more routine politics, 'quotidian, rather than existential, questions'.[13] Research on legislatures, for instance, explores the role of authoritarian parliaments in shaping policymaking.[14]

Alongside its shift in focus and approach, this recent literature has made several important contributions, both theoretical and empirical. While valuable, these contributions also draw attention to remaining gaps. Beginning with the literature on authoritarian legislatures, one key theme to emerge is the *significance of elite contestation* in shaping legislative activity; factional divisions within a ruling coalition turn the legislature into an 'arena for elite bargaining', thereby influencing both legislative institutional change and performance.[15] This is a crucial observation, but it leaves open questions about what forms of elite contestation matter and what factors underlie surface-level elite divisions.[16]

I further review and critique different ways of addressing these questions in Section 2.1.2. For now, one key—if still partial—answer involves studying

---

[10] Lebas, 2011; Riedl, 2014; Opalo, 2019.

[11] Lebas, 2011; Riedl, 2014; Morse, 2019; Opalo, 2019; Gandhi et al., 2020: 9; Meng, 2020; Krol, 2021.

[12] Lebas, 2011; Riedl, 2014; Morse, 2019; Opalo, 2019, 2021; Meng, 2020; Truex, 2020; Noble, 2020; Lu et al., 2020; Collord, 2021; Demarest, 2021; Wolf, 2023.

[13] Collord, 2021; Gandhi et al., 2020, 16; Lu et al., 2020; Noble, 2020; Truex, 2020; Demarest, 2021; Opalo, 2022.

[14] Collord, 2021; Lu et al., 2020; Noble, 2020; Schuler, 2020; Truex, 2020; Demarest, 2021; Opalo, 2022.

[15] Ibid.; Opalo, 2019.

[16] Williamson and Magaloni (2020) raise this concern in a review article, suggesting that scholars should examine, for instance, whether 'regime type may provide one source of variation relevant to these questions' (14).

how elite contestation channels through ruling parties plus how this party politics can then impact the legislature. For several reasons, this is a fairly obvious analytical step to take. First, the broader legislative studies literature underscores how low party cohesion can encourage legislative assertiveness;[17] where parties are institutionally weaker and more divided, the lack of discipline makes it harder for the executive to control party representatives in the legislature, leading to more legislative challenges to the executive. There is also a noteworthy recent study of authoritarian legislatures that adapts these same insights.[18] In his excellent historical comparison of the Zambian and Kenyan legislatures, Ken Opalo notes that there is an inverse relationship between strong authoritarian parties and strong legislatures. Where a ruling party is strong, as in Zambia post-Independence, it offers a vehicle through which authoritarian leaders co-opt fellow elites, ensuring greater party discipline and, consequently, marginalizing the legislature. Conversely, where the ruling party is weak, as in Kenya, the legislature becomes an important 'arena for elite bargaining', strengthening institutionally as a result.

However, even as Opalo clarifies the relationship between authoritarian parties and legislatures, his analysis moves the analytical question down a level. Variation in party institutional strength and discipline may help explain whether elite contestation surfaces in the legislature, but what then explains the variation in party strength? Here Opalo's explanation arguably reflects a broader issue in the authoritarian institutions literature. He echoes a functionalist logic, arguing that whether elite contestation is contained within a strong ruling party or, alternatively, is managed through the legislature largely depends on a dictator's 'choice' of favoured institution; however, this choice itself depends on whether the leader is *strong enough* to effectively balance fellow elites'.[19] We are left wondering what work the notion of 'choice' is doing if the would-be free decision ultimately depends on a dictator's strength. Relatedly, if it is this strength that conditions the dictator's choice of party or legislature, what autonomy do the resultant institutions have from the underlying power distribution that helped shape them?

A similar ambiguity surfaces when it comes to Opalo's analysis of how party and legislative institutions influence political outcomes, specifically the balance of power between a legislative and executive elite. For instance, he argues that in Kenya, where the founding President chose to manage elite bargaining through the legislature, parliament then became a channel for rent

---

[17] King, 1976; Olson, 1994; Chaisty et al., 2014.
[18] Opalo, 2019.
[19] Opalo, 2019, 81 (emphasis in the original).

distribution. Over time, this arrangement empowered a legislative elite as MPs could better secure resources from the executive, including to cultivate their own electoral base and political autonomy. This analysis is compelling up to a point; yet, while it maintains that institutions shape elite power dynamics, we could just as soon reverse the causal arrow, applying a Pepinsky-style critique (see Figure 2.1). For instance, rather than a stronger legislature being a source of power, enabling a parliamentary elite in Kenya to access state resources, what if this elite had access to power and patronage through other sources? What if, to preface my own argument, they could access political finance from a class of at least semi-autonomous private accumulators? What if they could then invest in legislative strengthening to gain advantage over factional rivals? It is not necessarily an either-or situation; stronger elites can invest in building up legislative institutions that then further magnify their power, including by helping them access executive patronage, as Opalo deftly demonstrates.

In brief, this authoritarian institutions literature has become more sophisticated with time. Important recent findings include the recognition that elite contestation drives legislative activity and that authoritarian parties mediate whether and how elite factional tensions surface in the legislature. Questions remain, though, about how to conceptualize and study sources of elite power, about the precise interaction between elite power and institutional outcomes, and about the broader significance of these outcomes. We will return to these questions in the next section (Section 2.1.2).

Before proceeding, though, it is important to acknowledge that, whereas the above discussion engages with the literature on authoritarian institutions, there is a separate strand of research that links strong political institutions with democratization.[20] Work on authoritarian institutions stresses their role in securing regime survival and in mediating authoritarian decision-making; by contrast, theorists of democratic consolidation suggest that these very same institutions are, by definition, at odds with authoritarian rule and that their gradual strengthening paves the way for democracy.[21] The core contention, then, is that the gap in political development between industrialized democracies and authoritarian or 'hybrid' regimes stems from differences in their institutional infrastructure. Countries democratize as they acquire the requisite institutional trappings, including a strong legislature, judiciary, and political

---

[20] Linz and Stepan, 1996; Bratton and van de Walle, 1997; Schedler, 1998: 99–101; Diamond, 1999; Fish, 2006; Barkan, 2009, 2013.
[21] Bratton and van de Walle, 1997; Diamond, 1999.

parties.[22] Applying this analytical lens to African politics, Bratton and van de Walle argue that the continent's 'neo-patrimonial' regimes—characterized by presidential dominance, pervasive clientelism, and abuse of state resources—will democratize where key political institutions 'gain organizational strength and win popular acceptance'.[23] Barkan echoes this analysis in his influential study of African parliaments, stressing the importance of legislative strengthening as a basis for overcoming enduring 'neo-patrimonial' tendencies and for providing a necessary check on executive power.[24]

Despite the contrasting assumptions of the authoritarian institutions and democratization literatures, they do share a conviction that political institutions 'matter', that they shape elite power dynamics and, consequently, political outcomes of interest. By the same token, the democratization literature is also vulnerable to a Pepinsky-esque critique; it attributes causal power to political institutions without adequately accounting for what shapes those very same institutions. Bratton and van de Walle, for instance, offer a strangely circular but not altogether unusual analysis, stating that, 'The less democracy is undergoing consolidation, the more unlikely it will survive at all and the more likely it will suffer reversal. Put another way, [...] the process of consolidation [will begin] when the democratic phase leads to some institutionalization and legitimation of democratic rule'.[25] They effectively equate democratization with institutionalization while also seeking to explain democratization in terms of institutional strengthening.[26] Regarding legislative institutions specifically, Barkan notes that a 'coalition for change' uniting 'reformist' and more 'opportunist' legislators can lead to institutional reforms that bolster the autonomy of the legislature vis-à-vis the executive. He, however, provides only a cursory explanation of what factors lead to the initial formation of a 'coalition for change', thereby leaving his analysis incomplete.

Ultimately, addressing the shortcomings of both the authoritarian institutions and the democratization literature requires a deeper analysis of what

---

[22] Bratton and van de Walle, 1997; Diamond, 1999. See also Linz and Stepan, 1996. On democratization by elections, see: Schedler, 2002; Lindberg, 2006, 2009.

[23] Bratton and van de Walle, 1997: 236.

[24] Fish, 2006; Barkan, 2009, 2013.

[25] Bratton and van de Walle, 1997: 237.

[26] There is a wider literature that embraces the idea of a 'virtuous circle' connecting institutional strengthening and democratization. Literature on the supposed process of democratization by elections has provided some of the more widely cited recent analysis in this vein. It has, however, also prompted numerous reflections seeking either to challenge or moderate its main conclusions, including the argument from Morgenbesser and Pepinsky (2019: 3) that 'in Southeast Asia, elections are almost always the culmination rather than the cause of democratization', which originates with an elite split within an authoritarian coalition. See also: Schedler, 2002; Lindberg, 2006, 2009; Levitsky and Way, 2010; Edgell et al., 2018.

underlying factors shape party and legislative institutions. Section 2.1.2 outlines an alternative analytical approach, which begins not with a study of institutions but with an examination of divergent patterns of elite contestation and their significance.

2.1.2 An Alternative Political Economy Approach

To conceptualize elite power and to understand how it shapes political institutions, I draw on an alternative political economy literature. This work refocuses attention on the socio-economic underpinnings of elite contestation within an authoritarian coalition as well as the impact of this contestation on institutional formation and change. If then the wider socio-economic context shapes authoritarian institutions, the question nevertheless remains, do these institutions have any independent effect of their own? To answer, I draw a second set of insights from an historical institutionalist tradition. The core idea, adapted to an authoritarian context, is that institutions do not independently regulate processes of elite co-optation or power-sharing; however, they can *magnify* an existing pattern of elite contestation, and where the elite power balance shifts, they can help *slow down* this process, presenting obstacles to new forms of political organization. The next two sub-sections develop each of these points in turn.

2.1.2.1 Elite Contestation, Patron–Client Factions, and Institutions

First, how do we conceptualize elite power and its influence on authoritarian institutions? As noted earlier, the recent authoritarian institutions literature emphasizes the importance of elite contestation in shaping legislative outcomes; however, the *nature and origins* of this elite contestation remain ambiguous. Some of this literature focuses on bureaucratic or inter-ministerial differences in policy-preferences and how these then play out in the legislature.[27] In a study of China's National People's Congress, Rory Truex acknowledges that other forms of elite division matter, including ideological and 'factional', but adds that these are often too 'opaque' to study.[28] Other scholars, notably a recent cohort of researchers focused on Africa, do explore this more 'opaque' politics, highlighting the effects of *informal patronage networks* on legislative activity.[29] This is promising work, but it introduces the fresh question, namely, *what structures these patronage networks? How are they organized?*

---

[27] Lü et al., 2020; Noble, 2020; Truex, 2020.
[28] Truex, 2020: 29.
[29] Collord, 2018, 2021; Demarest, 2021; Opalo, 2022.

Even as it provides key insights, the Africanist literature also highlights the challenges of finding satisfactory answers to these questions. Both older analyses of Africa's 'neo-patrimonial' politics and more recent institutionalist studies present patronage resources as largely concentrated within the state.[30] As such, formal institutions—for instance, the bureaucracy, ruling parties, and the legislature—play an important role in shaping the structure of patron–client networks; these institutions serve as channels through which to access state resources and, thus, provide a scaffolding around which to organize patron–client factions.[31] This is a vital point; however, it is not the whole story. First, in so far as recent scholarship argues that patronage networks are both shaped by and—as noted earlier—themselves shape institutions, we again risk adopting a circular logic. Moreover, there is little discussion of alternative sources of power that might be organized—at least partially—outside authoritarian institutional frameworks. Opalo suggests that—unliked in the history of European legislative development—there were no powerful societal actors in post-colonial African states capable of buttressing the legislature to check a dominant President.[32] Meanwhile, in a study of Nigeria's National Assembly, Leila Demarest maintains that the parliament has become more assertive thanks to patronage networks linking legislators to bureaucrats and politicians heading key government bodies.[33] She presents a fascinating analysis, but again, it fixates on the state as a source of power and patronage. She notes that she is unsure how MPs access public revenue outside the president's control, which she suggests is 'atypical in African countries', but speculates that it may be because military rule in Nigeria 'strengthened the bureaucracy'.[34]

An alternative political economy literature offers a different explanation both of what structures elite patron–client factions and of how these networks relate to institutions. It examines how patron–client networks evolve through the interaction between state and societal actors,[35] including a *class of semi-autonomous accumulators*. This literature recognizes that the state in low-income, post-colonial contexts remains a dominant economic actor; yet

---

[30] Much of the authoritarian institutions literature shares this assumption. Magaloni, 2006; Greene, 2007.

[31] Allen, 1995; Bratton and van de Walle, 1997; van de Walle, 2001, 2003; Manning, 2005; Cheeseman, 2006; Barkan, 2009; Opalo, 2019; Demarest, 2021.

[32] Opalo contrasts legislative development in Europe, which 'reflected the existing balance of power between the monarch and the nobility within the realm', and legislative development in post-colonial, low-income states where the chief executive did not need fellow elites to support his rule, as in Europe, but rather 'controlled the flow of patronage to fellow elites' (Opalo, 2019: 18–19).

[33] Demarest, 2021.

[34] Ibid., 697.

[35] This is *not* to suggest that neo-patrimonial and institutionalist analyses more generally ignore the interaction between state and societal actors; only that they see the state as the overriding source of patronage resources without taking seriously how variation in economic structure—particularly patterns of accumulation—can affect the distribution of wealth and patronage. For recent literature on party institutions—rather than legislatures—that shares these assumptions, see Sigman, 2023.

this work also emphasizes that the wealth and political influence of a private sector elite, even if closely bound up with the state, varies considerably across countries. This variation is due notably to contrasting trajectories of state-led capitalist development and, relatedly, to authoritarian leaders' diverging strategies of 'politicized accumulation',[36] as in, their varying *economic strategies* for managing the distribution of wealth and power within a regime. Depending on this distribution, patron–client networks may be relatively cohesive or fragmented. Rather than formal institutions shaping patronage networks, the causal arrow tends to point the other way; as in, the *distribution of wealth and power across patron–client networks* shapes what kind of institutions can form and endure over time.

This political economy literature is itself varied. In highlighting the above-outlined points, I draw on two strands of research, both with a strong Africa focus. I also draw on a third, more cross-regional body of comparative political economy work, which applies this analytical approach to the study of authoritarian parties. First, recent Africanist research using a 'political settlements' framework maintains that the distribution of power—both within and beyond a ruling coalition—directly impacts what formal institutions emerge and how they operate; where institutions produce benefits that do not align with the prevailing distribution of power, then groups will mobilize to change those institutional structures.[37] How then is power organized? There are varied means, but the idea is that *clientelist* political organizing dominates in low-income countries.[38] The study of clientelism generally invites a more materialist focus, although scholars elaborating a political settlements framework stress that economic capabilities are not the only factor defining the power of clientelist factions. Power also depends on coercive capabilities, ideology, leadership skill, and more.[39]

This is an important point, and one to which I will return. Nevertheless, the second—and older—Africanist political economy literature I draw on is more preoccupied by cross-country differences in post-colonial economic structure

---

[36] I borrow this term from Boone, 1992. See also: Shivji, 1976; Soares de Oliveira, 2015; Ajulu, 2021.

[37] Behuria et al., 2017; Khan, 2018. For studies that apply and elaborate this approach, see especially: Whitfield et al., 2015; Gray, 2018; Goodfellow, 2022.

[38] According to Khan, this is because profits from investment are limited, sectoral interests weakly defined, and the state's fiscal resources are insufficient to maintain more impersonal state institutions and inclusive welfare provision. However, it is worth noting that a growing political sociology literature also explores the prevalence of elite networks, essentially elite patron–client relations, in high-income capitalist countries as well, including established democracies. See: Domhoff, 2007; Hacker and Pierson, 2010. For a lengthier discussion of clientelism, its conceptualisation and significance, see Section 2.2.1.

[39] Behuria et al., 2017; Gray, 2018; Khan, 2018: 5.

and the effects on patronage politics and institutions.[40] Taken together, this work suggests that, while newly independent African states generally had a small domestic capitalist elite, their political leaders went on to develop very different strategies for accommodating economic and political interests.[41] This resulted in the expansion of a private sector elite in some countries and its relative marginalization in others. Contrasting patterns of private accumulation then influenced—or more accurately, were mutually shaped by—diverse institutional and political outcomes. These varied outcomes included: the consolidation of strong ties between political financiers and politicians in some countries;[42] in others, the marginalization of personalized patron-client factions and the emergence of a 'bureaucratic bourgeoisie';[43] across the region, contrasting forms of party organization with differing levels of internal cohesion and discipline;[44] within a shared one-party context, very different electoral politics;[45] and although somewhat less studied, variation in legislative strength and executive–legislative relations.[46]

Finally, recent comparative political economy research offers further insights, specifically regarding the organization of ruling coalitions and parties. Similar to the Africanist literature, this work emphasizes how political institutions reflect differing 'patterns of ownership and control in the economy'.[47] More specifically, scholars argue that differing authoritarian economic strategies—and related forms of state-led capitalist development—influence authoritarian party strength and cohesion.[48] For instance, in post-colonial Malaysia, the United Malays National Organization (UMNO) nurtured a new entrepreneurial class, a politically supportive Malay elite capable of rivalling the economic strength of more oppositional Chinese Malaysians. This strategy of maintaining close ties to a privileged economic elite, while ensuring regime stability for a period, came under pressure after the 1997 Asian financial crisis.[49] The economic downturn produced an intra-elite rupture that compelled UMNO leaders to curb non-transparent patronage distribution and to open up political space to ruling party opponents. In contrast to the UMNO's political reliance on Malay entrepreneurs, Singapore's People's Action Party (PAP)

---

[40] The political settlements literature also draws on this earlier work.
[41] Iliffe, 1983.
[42] Swainson, 1977; Ajulu, 2021.
[43] Shivji, 1976.
[44] Sklar, 1963; Jorgensen, 1981.
[45] Hyden and Leys, 1972; Kiondo, 1994; Mmuya, 1994.
[46] Gertzel, 1970; Tordoff, 1977.
[47] Rodan and Jayasuriya, 2012: 181.
[48] Sangmpam, 2007; Rodan and Jayasuriya, 2012; Pepinsky, 2014.
[49] Rodan and Jayasuriya, 2012: 184–185.

dealt with political challenges by rendering many Singaporeans economically dependent on the state and ruling party. In the absence of economic and social bases from which would-be rivals could mount a political challenge, PAP has retained its organizational strength and avoided destabilizing intra-elite tensions that might loosen its hold on power. The two parties' diverging trajectories illustrate how differing authoritarian economic strategies can lead to varying degrees of party cohesion and regime stability.

Taken together then, the Africanist political economy literature and comparative literature from other regions highlight the socio-economic underpinnings of different patronage structures, which in turn shape the institutional landscape in authoritarian regimes. To reiterate, this political economy analysis diverges sharply from studies that suggest formal institutions shape patron–client structures or that assume a narrower focus on state patronage, even discounting the significance of other sources of wealth in society.[50]

Before concluding this section, it is worth flagging that there are important studies of authoritarian institutions and party politics—including within the Africanist literature—that also adopt a version of political economy analysis; however, this analysis differs from the approach advocated here, which is sometimes referred to broadly as 'critical' political economy.[51] The chief difference is that, while this other work explores the political implications of economic reforms, it focuses on a relatively limited set of state interventions and fairly straightforward causal mechanisms, often involving either more or less state patronage and state control of the economy. It does not address 'the mutual and historical constitution of states, markets and classes',[52] the ongoing interaction between state and societal actors as they contest the distribution of power and wealth within authoritarian regimes.

Beatriz Magaloni and Kenneth Greene, for instance, both explain authoritarian party rule through a study of the 'political economy of dominance'.[53] Magaloni argues that for a dominant party equilibrium to endure, economic growth must remain high enough to provide sufficient resources for ruling parties to co-opt both voters and elites. Greene adds that 'privatization weakens dominant parties because it limits their access to public funds, and without these funds, well-greased patronage networks run dry [...]'.[54] Both analyses use the case study of Mexico's long-ruling Institutional Revolutionary Party

---

[50] Opalo, 2019: 18–19; van de Walle, 2001: 120.
[51] Pepinsky, 2014; Beinin, 2021.
[52] Beinin, 2021: 1.
[53] Magaloni, 2006; Greene, 2007.
[54] Greene, 2007: 34.

(PRI). However, they oversimplify the implications of economic changes in Mexico through the 1980s and 1990s, and consequently, in other dominant party regimes to which they claim to generalize. Their focus is on how fluctuating access to public sector spoils affects elite incentives to defect from the ruling party. Even Greene, with his interest in privatization, does not acknowledge the impact of these changes beyond a reference to the PRI's declining 'resource advantage'. Yet an alternative reading, focused not just on state resources but on a broader societal distribution of wealth and power, would stress how privatization fundamentally altered the PRI's initial strategy of state-led capitalist management and intra-elite bargaining, exposing the party to new internal tensions. Privatization gave rise to an expanded semi-autonomous accumulating class whose demands the ruling party struggled to satisfy. This new economic elite ultimately spurred the opposition's 2000 election victory after a faction of wealthy businessmen defected from the ruling party to finance a rival presidential candidate.[55] Without looking at the changing dynamics of capitalist development and its impact on the distribution of power in this way, an explanation of the PRI's defeat is incomplete.

Another important political economy analysis that differs from my own is Leonardo Arriola's thesis that financial liberalization helps explain the success of multi-ethnic coalitions in ousting authoritarian party incumbents. He points in an interesting direction with his argument that liberalization can help encourage would-be political financiers to bankroll an opposition coalition without fear of financial reprisals. This emphasis recognizes the threat a more autonomous economic elite can pose to the survival of an authoritarian regime. However, again, Arriola may not adequately engage with the particular structure of power and ownership and the capitalist history of the country cases he examines. For instance, commenting on his treatment of the Kenyan case, Upadhyaya and Totolo conclude that 'historical patterns of wealth accumulation are more important than the level of liberalization of the financial system when it comes to the political effects of the financial system'.[56] They observe that the political financiers—many of Kikuyu ethnicity—who backed opposition elites from 1998 until the opposition victory in 2002 could act as effective financiers because Kenya's first president 'oversaw the consolidation of an independent Kikuyu-dominated entrepreneurial elite'; as a

---

[55] Greene (2007) even describes this process in his empirical analysis but without linking it into a more fine-tuned theoretical framework.

[56] Upadhyaya and Totolo, 2020: 479.

result, by the 1990s, this same elite 'had already developed the resources needed to contribute significant sums towards a [co-ethic] opposition leader's campaign'.[57]

The earlier-outlined 'critical' political economy approach thus diverges from the wider literature on authoritarian institutions, including many existing efforts to analyse the impact of economic change on authoritarian politics. The approach advanced in this book first focuses attention on the historically defined structures of elite wealth accumulation and political domination. It then uses this analysis to explain differences in authoritarian institutional landscapes, examining both parties and legislatures. The question nevertheless remains, if the make-up of institutions depends on the societal distribution of wealth and power, what independent role—if any—do these institutions play in politics? Whose interests do they serve? Why do they matter?

2.1.2.2 Institutions Matter

While scholars adopting a critical political economy approach generally accept that institutions, once created, *do* exert some influence on actors' behaviour, they often do not specify how.[58] Historical institutionalists offer some helpful insights here, enriching our understanding of how institutions—once formed—can affect political outcomes, i.e. why they *matter*.

Rational choice institutionalism, which inspires much of the authoritarian institutions literature,[59] emphasizes how institutional rules 'structure social interactions and produce equilibrium outcomes, that is outcomes that no one has an incentive to alter'.[60] By contrast, an historical institutionalist approach, rather than focus on equilibrium, presents institutions as 'objects of ongoing *skirmishes*'; this is because 'actors try to achieve advantage by interpreting or redirecting institutions in pursuit of their goals, or by subverting or circumventing rules that clash with their interests'.[61] It follows that institutions change along with a changing distribution of power, which strengthens some actors over others in the 'ongoing skirmish'. However, rather than simply mirroring this changing power distribution, institutions have *their own distributional effects*. As suggested in the above quotation, powerful actors alter institutions to better suit their interests, creating new institutional tools, new resources that help 'reproduce and *magnify*' their own political influence.[62] This point

---

[57] Ibid.
[58] Sangmpam, 2007: 204; Rodan and Jayasuriya, 2012.
[59] Magaloni, 2006, 2008; Gandhi, 2008; Boix and Svolik, 2013.
[60] Levi, 2009: 128.
[61] Streeck and Thelen, 2005: 19.
[62] Thelen, 1999: 384.

is crucial. In effect, institutions become a source of power in their own right; they 'actively facilitate the organization and empowerment of certain groups while actively disarticulating and marginalising others'.[63]

Through this analysis, an historical institutionalist approach also captures how institutions can engender their own 'path dependent' trajectories. The idea is that, once a path is set, 'institutions continue to evolve in response to changing environmental conditions and ongoing political manoeuvring'; however, this evolution occurs *in ways that are constrained by past trajectories*.[64] One consequence of this is that, even where an underlying power distribution begins to shift, institutional path dependence can moderate and slow down what might otherwise be a more dramatic political change. There is a fine balance between institutional continuity, which is a legacy of an earlier founding moment, and institutional change, which is a process linked to ongoing political struggle.

Applying this historical institutionalist approach to the study of authoritarian parties and legislatures allows for a fresh analysis of how these institutions both evolve alongside a changing socio-economic context and, crucially, also help amplify prevailing patterns of elite conflict, offering additional channels through which dominant actors seek to assert their power within an authoritarian coalition. Combined with a political economy analysis, this approach helps integrate a study of, one, the origins of elite contestation and its effects on authoritarian institutions and, two, how these institutions then mediate and amplify elite power dynamics. While the above discussion identifies the general approach to institutional change, I now specify a theorical framework to explain party and legislative change and why, ultimately, it matters, whose interest are served, with what political and distributional consequences.

2.2 A Theory of Political Institutions in Africa

In what follows, I first identify two authoritarian party ideal types, linking different distributions of elite wealth and power with variation in party institutional strength and cohesion. I then specify the contrasting trajectories of party formation and change characteristic of each party type, linking these to contrasting paths of capitalist development across post-colonial African states. Third, I relate these party trajectories to different legislative outcomes, indicating how the strength and cohesion of an authoritarian party influences both

---

[63] Ibid. See: Pierson, 2000.
[64] Thelen, 1999: 384; Pierson, 2000, my emphasis.

the level of legislative institutional strength and performance. In the process, I reflect on what this analysis tells us about whose interests are served by a more assertive parliament, who can participate in legislative activity, contest for influence, and affect important political and economic outcomes.

The purpose of this theoretical framework is to highlight the oft-neglected relationship between, on the one hand, authoritarian economic interventions and resultant patterns of 'politicized accumulation' and, on the other hand, the institutional order within a regime.

2.2.1 Two Authoritarian Party Ideal Types

Authoritarian parties can vary along two interrelated dimensions: one, the distribution of wealth and patronage within an authoritarian regime; and, two, the institutional strength and cohesion of the ruling party.

Regarding the first dimension, the distribution of wealth and prevailing pattern of accumulation within a regime can be more or less centralized, which in turn, affects the opportunity for rival patronage networks to organize. Where there is a larger class of private accumulators, particularly where a semi-autonomous private sector expands, this creates opportunities for rival elites to mobilize resources—either their own money or that of prominent political financiers. They thereby form their own patron–client factions, leading to a more fragmented distribution of power within the ruling coalition. Conversely, where ownership and accumulation are concentrated under state and party control, and where the private sector is subject to greater regulation, this limits the potential for rival factions to emerge. Instead, the authoritarian leader and close allies are in a stronger position to control both accumulation and patronage distribution. This distribution occurs as per the leader's specifications down a chain of political dependents occupying lower-level positions in the party, thereby centralizing power within the regime.

I define the second dimension, party institutional strength, by creating an amalgamation of Angelo Panebianco and Samuel Huntington's influential criteria. My definition takes into account: one, the strength of a party's central bureaucracy; two, the degree of 'complexity' or differentiation amongst a party's organizational sub-units; three, the degree of internal 'coherence' and clear organizational 'boundaries', which I assess in terms of the 'degree of correspondence between a party's statutory norms and its "actual power structures"'; and four, a party's 'adaptability', which I narrow here to refer to an organization's 'generational age' or the number of peaceful successions from one set of leaders to another.[65] This last indicator is especially relevant to authoritarian parties in developing countries given the extensive literature documenting the destabilizing effects, in particular, of presidential succession battles.[66] While this operationalization of party strength, which I elaborate on in subsequent chapters, does not encompass all key institutional features, it is more detailed than what we find in much of the authoritarian parties literature. This level of detail is important, though, if we are to understand the specific ways party structures and rules become 'objects of skirmishes' and thereby help mediate and reinforce a particular elite power distribution.

Ultimately, these two dimensions—the distribution of wealth and patronage plus party institutional strength—combine to define two authoritarian party ideal types (see Figure 2.2). A first type, what I call a 'bargained coalition', features decentralized accumulation and patronage distribution, on the one hand, and an institutionally weak party, on the other. A second type, an 'institutionalized coalition', has the reverse characteristics, namely more centralized control over accumulation and patronage resources plus a strong institutional apparatus.

To clarify, the expectation is that where patterns of accumulation become more diffuse, and thus where patron–client factions are more fragmented, the institutional make-up of an authoritarian party will evolve to reflect that change; rival actors will mobilize to reform or simply to subvert party structures and procedures that favour central control. For instance, they will infiltrate and undermine the authority of a party's would-be impartial bureaucratic structures such that paid party officials show allegiance to a variety of factions and less to the party leader. Conversely, where accumulation becomes more centralized and a party's top leaders work to consolidate factional networks, they are also likely to introduce—or to revive—party institutions that further amplify their hold on power. For instance, they may reform the central bureaucracy, ensuring that they can use this structure to project their authority throughout the party.

In theorizing these two ideal types, I draw on the above-reviewed political economy literature as well as and on an older literature on clientelism and

---

[65] Huntington, 1968: 17–22; Panebianco, 1988: 58.

[66] See for instance: Magaloni, 2006; Cheeseman and Hinfelaar, 2009; Cooper, 2017.

Note that I do not use Huntington and Panebianco's 'autonomy' indicator, which references a party's independence from external actors, because I argue it is a cause rather than a marker of party institutional strength. Similarly, I do not include Panebianco's indicator regarding the nature of party finance, although I share his view about its significance.

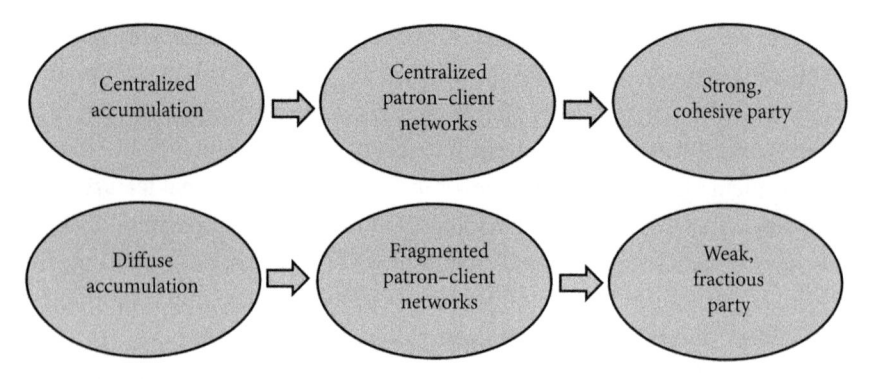

Figure 2.2 Two party ideal types

party politics.[67] However, my biggest inspiration is the political settlements literature. This work is particularly instructive when linking the dimensions of patronage structure and party institutional make-up, leaving aside the analysis of wealth accumulation for now. It is worth expounding on two points here. First, the political settlements work helps clarify the link between power, patronage structures, and institutions. Formal institutions reflect an underlying power distribution, but crucially the exercise of power in developing countries is itself 'based on informal organizations, typically patron–client organisations'.[68] Hence, formal institutions evolve in line with an underlying *structure* of patron–client networks.

Second, political settlements analysis helps guide an analysis of power and patronage structures, which it maps along two axes, *horizontal and vertical*. Elaborating on Khan's political settlements framework, Lindsay Whitfield and co-authors assess the 'horizontal distribution [of power] *among ruling elites*' in terms of how 'fragmented or cohesive' these ruling elites are.[69] Where power is more 'dispersed' along a horizontal axis, elites 'become focused on jockeying for power among themselves because power is relatively equal and a large number believe they have a good chance of gaining the top political position'.[70] This jockeying, in turn, makes it difficult for government leaders to manage

---

[67] Khan, 2005, 2010; Rodan and Jayasuriya, 2012. Regarding the older literature on clientelism, notably focused on African politics, it emphasizes the value of studying patron–client networks or 'factions' to make sense of elite contestation. See, for example: Lemarchand and Legg, 1972; Sandbrook, 1972. Regarding the political parties literature, I draw on a tradition that similarly stresses the link between, on the one hand, different forms of party finance and more or less personalized exchange and, on the other, party strength and cohesion. Michels, 2001; Panebianco, 1988.

[68] Khan, 2005, 2010: 5, 46.

[69] Whitfield et al., 2015: 98.

[70] Ibid.

'rent-seeking opportunities' as factional rivalries escape their control.[71] Meanwhile, I analyse the distribution of power along a *vertical* axis in terms of the strength of top-level ruling elite vis-à-vis lower-level factions within the same ruling party.[72] These low-level factions encompass smaller, more geographically localized patron–client networks. They are then amalgamated, where a horizontal power distribution is more centralized, into a bigger patron–client faction, or where the horizontal distribution is dispersed, into *multiple factions* spearheaded by rival segments of the ruling elite.

To recap, I have now identified two party ideal types and reflected on the links between patronage structure and party institutions. It nevertheless remains to be seen, how can we explain the origins of these institutions and their variation over time? This question invites a more probing analysis of wealth accumulation and how its varying patterns shape relations between economic and political elites.

2.2.2 Capitalist Development, 'Politicized Accumulation', and Party Trajectories

I argue that the initial consolidation of an authoritarian party—and the type of party to emerge—is closely bound up with the party leadership's preferred strategy for managing capitalist development. As illustrated through the examples of Malaysia's UMNO and Singapore's PAP, party leaders can—through their economic interventions—help reshape patterns of accumulation and party organization in a regime. I build on this insight by systematically relating different economic interventions to the emergence of contrasting structures of accumulation and patronage and, hence, contrasting party institutional outcomes. I then adopt an historical institutionalist frame to account for change over time. I outline the initial 'critical juncture' period of regime consolidation and then the diverging 'path dependent' trajectories of different party types.

---

[71] Ibid.
  This discussion of clientelist ties among regime elites and of a 'horizontal' power distribution is somewhat unconventional, given that the relationship between patron and client is often assumed to be hierarchical (Stokes et al., 2013: 13). The analysis is, however, by no means unique. In a classic conceptual study of political clientelism and development, Lemarchand and Legg observe that clientelist relations can be 'found among the political and economic elite' even if 'the near status equality of the participants may make it difficult to separate the roles of client and patron' (1972: 168–169). Moreover, while individual patron–client factions may resemble a more conventional pyramid structure (Barkan, 1979; van de Walle, 2001), headed by a cluster of ruling elites who then dominate lower-level actors, competition across these factions complicates the overall picture (Sandbrook, 1972). As Whitfield et al. note, even a would-be dominant President may struggle to discipline this intra-elite jockeying.
[72] Khan, 2010: 61.

2.2.2.1 African Leaders, State-led Capitalist Development, and 'Politicized Accumulation'

First, to appreciate the significance of leaders' different economic interventions, we need to recognize that state-led capitalist development has varied across African countries and, in turn, has led to different patterns of accumulation and patronage distribution. An emphasis on variation in economic structure across Africa—and specifically, on variation in the extent of private accumulation—is somewhat controversial. As briefly alluded to before, Africanist scholars who identify the state as *the* key source of patronage have downplayed the relevance of private accumulators as potential patrons. Bratton and van de Walle, for instance, argue that the exploitation of state resources in Africa post-Independence has led to a distinctive pattern of 'presidentialism', or 'the systematic concentration of power in the hands of one individual'.[73] While the President serves as patron-in-chief, the majority of clients remain 'completely or partly dependent on the state for their income and welfare', resulting in the 'absence of a powerful indigenous private sector'.[74]

Countering this view, an Africanist political economy literature maintains that patterns of accumulation and patronage distribution did vary across the region. It goes on to detail how and why, highlighting a series of important political factors. First, while recognizing the influence of colonial legacies on post-colonial power structures, this literature nevertheless characterizes the period of regime consolidation immediately post-Independence as a moment of great political contingency; *choices* made by nationalist leaders affected whether a regime would survive and, if it did, what sort of coalition would emerge out of the 'heterogeneous' independence elite.[75] Central to this process were leaders' strategies of state intervention in the economy, which led to politically determined patterns of wealth accumulation. These differing forms of '*politicized accumulation*', in turn, shaped class formation and patronage structures in African states.[76]

In his volume, *The Emergence of African Capitalism*, John Iliffe identifies three general patterns of accumulation post-independence, all of which

[73] Bratton and van de Walle, 1997: 63.

[74] Van de Walle, 2001: 120. Regarding the immediate post-Independence period, see also Opalo, 2019: 18–19.

[75] Sklar, 1979: 537; Hartmann, 1983; Boone, 1992: 23–26; Mutibwa, 1992.

[76] On 'politicized accumulation', see Boone, 1992. See also: Shivji, 1976; Rodney, 1980; Jorgensen, 1981. While I take inspiration from these earlier studies, I do not achieve the careful analysis of class formation that some pursue. I instead highlight fairly broad cross-country distinctions in patterns of wealth accumulation and patronage distribution, plus examine the factional networks to which they give rise. Some recent comparative work on authoritarian political economy revisits issues of class conflict within the state, which is a promising direction for future work. See, for example, Karas and Donmez, 2023.

depended on the size and strength of the domestic private sector.[77] First, fearing the political consequences, some leaders 'sought to prevent the emergence of private African capitalists in any form'.[78] For instance, Kwame Nkrumah of Ghana feared, according to a senior advisor, 'that if he permitted business to grow, it will grow to the extent of becoming a rival power to his and the party's prestige'.[79] In a second set of cases, leaders used state power to 'acquire property and business interests so that holders of office are also owners of property'.[80] This could be managed in different ways with varying implications for the structure of patron–client networks. Leopold Senghor in Senegal used the state to ensure that the 'growing Senegalese business community was tied to a party-bureaucratic political machine and, consequently, did not emerge as an independent political force'.[81] By contrast, Mobutu Sese Seko in Zaire was less concerned with finding a stable means of 'channelling local private accumulation', as in Senegal;[82] instead, loyalty to him, as 'the patron of patrons', was 'the ultimate requirement for entry and continued membership' of a relatively 'fluid' and factional ruling elite.[83] Finally, a third category of nationalist leaders—notably in Nigeria, Kenya, and arguably Cote d'Ivoire—oversaw the emergence of a capitalist elite who could control 'substantial areas of enterprise'.[84] In the process, this group gained a degree of economic independence from the state or, at least, were able to mobilize in rival patron–client factions to compete for privileged access to the state.[85]

Nationalist leaders could define the contours of 'politicized accumulation' and engender such variable results, in part, due to the dependence upon the state of an 'historically weak domestic capitalist class', whose weakness resulted in turn from 'the limited development of agrarian and industrial capitalism during the precolonial and colonial periods'.[86] Early post-Independence leaders also benefitted from the institutional inheritance of an economically interventionist colonial state, which had developed the tools—albeit to varying degrees—to regulate and reform sectors capable of generating significant

---

[77] Iliffe, 1983: chapter 4.
[78] Ibid., 77.
[79] Ibid.
[80] Ibid.
[81] Boone, 1990: 433.
[82] Boone, 1990: 433.
[83] Callaghy, 1987: 101.
[84] Ibid.; Iliffe, 1983: 77.
[85] Ibid.; Schatz, 1977; Lubeck, 1987; Upadhyaya and Totolo, 2020.
[86] Iliffe, 1983; Whitfield et al., 2015: 95. Even if the size and wealth of an African capitalist elite varied somewhat across states, it remained principally reliant on low value-added agricultural production and small-scale trade, themes discussed more in subsequent chapters. See: Shivji, 1976; Swainson, 1977; Iliffe, 1979.

rents.[87] This ability to use the power of the state to reshape patterns of domestic accumulation was not, however, restricted to Africa's post-Independence leaders alone. Rather, regimes that came to power in the 1980s and 1990s, notably following a period of civil war, have also proved remarkably adept at moulding the economy to suit their political interests, and this despite implementing donor-backed liberalizing economic reforms.[88]

For instance, the Rwanda Patriotic Front (RPF), a former rebel outfit which came to power in 1994, has cultivated party and military investment groups, which have helped the leadership retain 'centralized control over the distribution of rents while dispersing power among several elites whose loyalty and performance remains in check'.[89] The party and military continue to dominate strategic holdings while many private investors are foreign or else loyal capitalist partners to the regime.[90] As a result, there are few elites with the economic base either to pose a threat to the RPF's hold on power or, less ambitiously, to foment factional infighting within the ruling party. Uganda's National Resistance Movement (NRM),[91] meanwhile, offers a counter example. Under President Museveni, the economic elite has expanded markedly, buoyed by a combination of rent-seeking and private investment. While entrepreneurs remain politically vulnerable should they choose to oppose Museveni's rule directly, the extent of private wealth accumulation by politicians and allied financiers has fuelled factional tensions within the NRM, from the very top down to the lowest levels.[92]

Thus, patterns of wealth accumulation do indeed vary across African states in keeping with differing, politically motivated strategies of state-led capitalist development. This variation then gives rise to contrasting patronage structures, some centralized and others more fragmented. As indicated earlier, differences in the configuration of patron–client networks directly affect the extent of party strengthening. Some of the Africanist literature hints at this relationship. For instance, it is implied through the above-cited emphasis on the need to prevent private wealth becoming a rival to 'party prestige' or

---

[87] Cooper, 2002; Young, 2012; Whitfield et al., 2015; Lewis, 2019. For more on the powers of market intervention in post-colonial states, this time in the Middle East, see: Malik and Awadallah, 2013. The next chapters detail these state powers of market-intervention, i.e., the tools authoritarian leaders use to pursue varying strategies of 'politicized accumulation'.

[88] Amidst ongoing changes in many African economies, for instance, the expansion of the service sector relative to agriculture, authoritarian leaders have retained the ability to use varying strategies of 'politicized accumulation' to their advantage, as discussed more in subsequent chapters. For related analysis, see: Goodfellow 2018.

[89] Behuria, 2016: 6.

[90] Ibid.; see also Behuria and Goofellow, 2016.

[91] The NRM took power in 1986 after a five-year civil war.

[92] Tangri and Mwenda, 2013; Tangri and Mwenda, 2019; see Chapters 3 and 4, this volume.

'party-bureaucratic political machines'.[93] There are also individual case studies that make the link between governments' preferred strategies of economic intervention and the organizational make-up of ruling parties.[94] The literature in this area is nevertheless sparse and does not offer a systematic analysis of the link between accumulation, patronage, and party organization. What's more, some of the work that goes furthest in illustrating variation in economic strategy and patronage regimes ignores its implications for party institutional configurations, assuming a weak party and 'Big Man' politics everywhere.[95]

This then leaves the question, how do we link an analysis of varying accumulation and patronage structures with the study of party institutional consolidation and change over time? For this, I pursue an historical institutionalist approach, identifying an initial 'critical juncture' phase as well as subsequent dynamics of institutional continuity and change.[96]

2.2.2.2 The Critical Juncture

I identify the early period of authoritarian regime consolidation as a moment of contingency during which leading political actors confront a series of 'critical decisions'; that is, although constrained by 'antecedent conditions', these leaders are nevertheless presented with strategic choices whose consequences can *reshape the structural parameters within which future political decisions are made*.[97] As discussed above, newly instated authoritarian leaders make a 'critical decision' when they choose their preferred strategy of 'politicized accumulation', informed by a mix of political expediency and ideology.[98] I argue that, through this choice of strategy, they influence both the structure of accumulation and patronage distribution in a regime and the long-term prospects for authoritarian party institutional strengthening.

---

[93] Iliffe, 1983: 77; Boone, 1990: 433.

[94] Okumu and Holmquist, 1984.

[95] Arriola, 2013.

[96] I elaborate on these steps, including the relevant hypotheses and hypothesis-testing strategies at the start of the empirical chapters, each of which addresses a different element in the hypothesized causal mechanism.

[97] My analysis here is most influenced by Capoccia and Keleman's (2007) characterization of a critical juncture as a 'situation in which the structural (that is, economic, cultural, ideological and organizational) influences on political action are significantly relaxed for a relatively short period, with two main consequences: the range of plausible choices open to powerful political actors expands substantially and the consequences of their decisions for the outcome of interest are potentially much more momentous' (343). Building on Capoccia and Keleman, Ermakoff (2017) 'grounds the analysis of open-ended conjunctures in the concept of "critical decisions", that is, decisions that actors know are highly consequential for other people, entail individual risk, and substantially alter the cost structure of subsequent options once the decision is made.' Identifying a critical juncture empirically thus becomes a matter of confirming when actors are confronted by '*critical decisions*', as discussed further in the next chapter.

[98] See Chapter 3 for more discussion.

Where leaders allow for a more decentralized pattern of accumulation and thus a more fragmented patron–client structure, notably where political-cum-entrepreneurial elite achieve some measure of economic independence, party institutionalization likely remains low and a 'bargained coalition' takes shape. By contrast, where leaders either insist on greater state economic control or otherwise constrain private accumulation, prospects for party insti-tutionalization improve. However, institutional strengthening is by no means guaranteed; rather, an 'institutionalized coalition' emerges where authori-tarian leaders *combine* the centralization of accumulation and patron–client networks with concerted party-building efforts. Whether to invest in party-building thus constitutes a *second* 'critical decision', albeit one that hinges, in part, on the first (Figure 2.3).

2.2.2.3 Institutional reproduction

In keeping with theories that link institutional forms to an underlying distri-bution of power, I argue that the reproduction of authoritarian party types depends, first and foremost, on the endurance of early patterns of accu-mulation and patronage distribution. In a 'bargained coalition', the more decentralized character of patron–client networks requires that party leaders employ a range of political and economic tools to maintain or renegotiate the original elite 'bargain', cultivating factional allies while selectively disciplin-ing any would-be challengers whose wealth and power becomes a threat. The party organization, meanwhile, remains weakly institutionalized as a loose confederation of political elites and financiers concentrate on building up

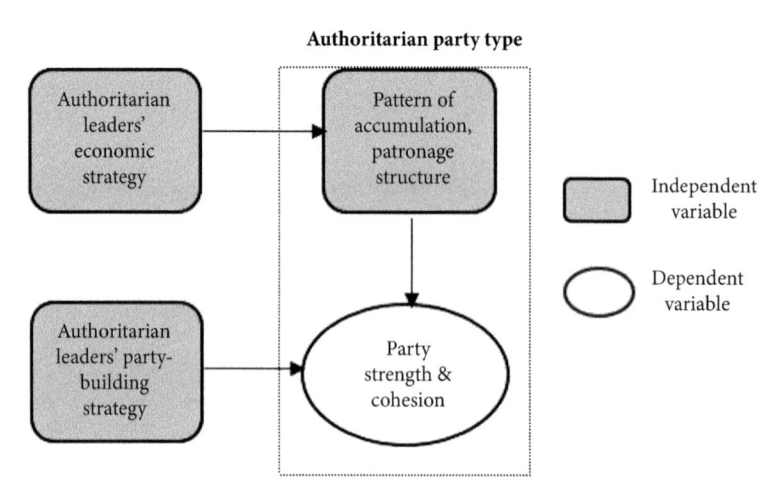

Figure 2.3 Authoritarian party type

local political machines. In the case of an 'institutionalized coalition', by contrast, leaders must ensure the continued centralization of accumulation and patronage to maintain and further consolidate a strong party organization.

The underlying distribution of wealth and patronage is not, however, the only factor contributing to institutional reproduction. As noted earlier, party institutions generate their own set of distributional effects, which while initially a reflection of the prevailing balance of power, may diverge over time.[99] Pierson's concept of 'increasing returns' helps clarify this point; in short, new institutions cause individuals to commit to particular forms of political organization and mobilization, which means their subsequent 'cost of exit from established arrangements rises dramatically.'[100] This dynamic of 'increasing returns' then means that an established party institutional form can persist even when the underlying structure of accumulation and patronage distribution begins to change.

The trajectory of a 'bargained coalition' is the more straightforward of the two party ideal types (Figure 2.4). It is unlikely that the party leadership could muster the political momentum and material resources required to dramatically recentralize control over accumulation and patronage without jeopardizing regime survival.[101] Under the circumstances, it is even less likely that the party leadership could succeed in a belated party strengthening effort.

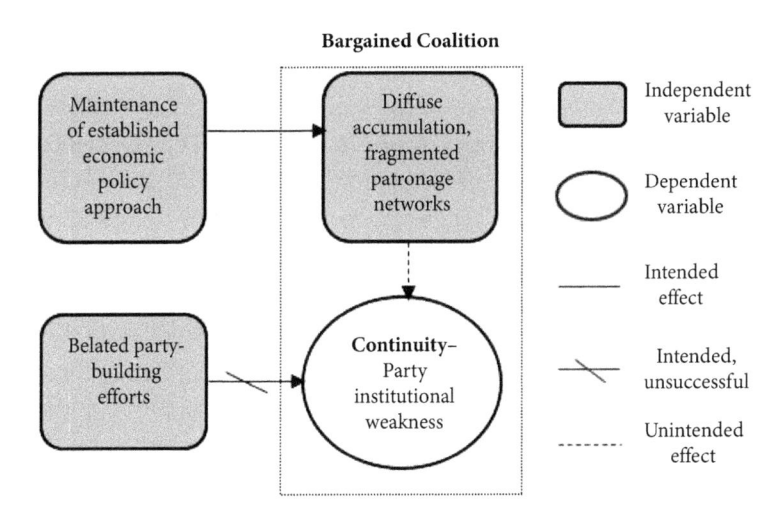

Figure 2.4 Trajectory of a bargained coalition

---

[99] Thelen, 1999; Pierson, 2000. See Chapter 3 for elaboration.
[100] Pierson, 2000: 259.
[101] Boone, 1992: 25–26. Unlikely is not to say impossible, as explored further in the conclusion of this volume.

Institutionalized Coalition

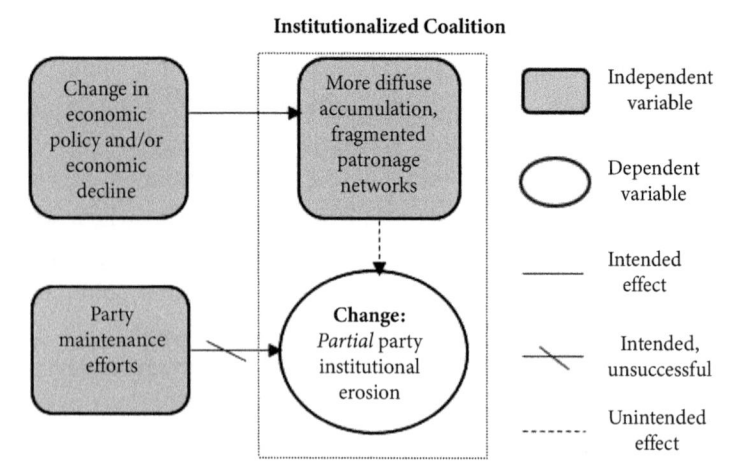

Figure 2.5 Trajectory of an institutionalized coalition

Instead, political mobilization will continue to centre on individual patrons, their local fiefdoms and allied patronage networks.

More interesting because less obvious is the fate of 'institutionalized coalitions' (Figure 2.5). The leadership's centralized control over wealth accumulation can erode for a variety of reasons, including the failure of party-owned enterprises, an expanding informal sector, external pressures to implement structural adjustment, and related liberalizing economic reforms.[102] The emergence of new sources of political finance then enables elites to invest in a personal political base while simultaneously exacerbating factional rivalries. These developments are likely to engender a process of party de-institutionalization as centralized authority structures and binding procedural rules are contested. However, an 'institutionalized coalition' does not simply revert to a 'bargained coalition'. The process of institutional decay will be gradual and potentially reversible in the short- to medium-term, and this is due to the dynamics by which party institutions themselves become a barrier to change. These institutions, along with the forms of political organization and mobilization they help sustain, will persist, at least temporarily, in the face of a changing distribution of power.

As emphasized at the start, real world cases can only approximate the two ideal types set out in the above model. But the point is not to explain away all relevant institutional variation. What I identify are a set of underappreciated analytical dimensions and historical processes that, I argue, can help guide the in-depth study of authoritarian parties, each with its own idiosyncrasies. This

---

[102] See, for instance Thioub, Diop and Boone, 1998.

discussion of party trajectories, also provides the foundation from which to build a theory of legislative institutional change under authoritarian rule.

2.2.3 From Party to Parliament

How does variation across authoritarian parties influence legislative strength? How does it affect whether and how parliament emerges as an 'arena for elite bargaining'? In what follows, I briefly define legislative strength, which I relate both to *institutional strength* and *actual performance*. I then assess, first, how different party types—and associated differences in levels of elite contestation—influence institutional change in parliament, producing different outcomes in terms of legislative institutional strength. Second, I detail how party type and legislative institutional strength *jointly* influence legislative performance, plus to what ends. Who is 'represented'? Whose interests are served?

2.2.3.1 Legislative Institutionalization

I equate legislative strength with the degree of 'institutionalization' achieved. The concept of institutionalization can be slippery, however, engendering seemingly intractable debates over definition and measurement. Drawing on Cooper and Brady, I define it in relation to both legislative institutional form and performance.[103] The idea is that a stronger or more 'institutionalized' legislature will have certain institutional features that help ensure the independence and efficacy of legislators in challenging an executive agenda. However, these institutional features, while they may *facilitate* legislative activity, do not *guarantee* a more assertive legislature. Hence the value of also assessing actual legislative performance.

I elaborate further in Chapters 4 and 5, but as regards legislative institutions, I assess their strength in terms of the 'complexity' and 'coherence' or 'boundedness' of the legislature's organization and procedures.[104] This involves examining the make-up of the committee system, the rules for electing parliamentary leaders, and control over the legislative budget, among other features. Regarding performance, I use a simplified quantitative measure,[105] namely the share of executive bills passed relative to the number tabled and

---

[103] Cooper and Brady, 1981: 988–1006.
[104] This is keeping with a seminal article by Polsby (1968), who draws inspiration from Huntington (1968).
[105] There is no straightforward quantitative measure. Blondel, 1970, 1973; Arter, 2006.

the proportion of private members' bills relative to government legislation.[106] I then examine a series of case studies—legislative review of government bills, amendments to the national budget and corruption probes. Each case constitutes a 'power drama', an executive-legislative clash that, while arguably an exception to the usually more mundane parliamentary routine, nevertheless helps reveal how intra-elite bargaining is channelled through the legislatures and the extent to which this parliamentary assertiveness can force changes to an executive agenda.

2.2.3.2 Party Variation and Legislative Institutional Change

My argument is that, where the ruling party in an authoritarian regime resembles a 'bargained coalition', the legislature is likely to undergo a process of institutionalization. By contrast, where the ruling party is an 'institutionalized coalition', the legislature is likely to remain institutionally weak. However, if an 'institutionalized coalition' begins to erode, losing some of its organizational cohesion, the legislature will gain in prominence and strength. This process is gradual, however, and the legislature is unlikely to acquire the same degree of autonomy as it otherwise might under a 'bargained coalition'.

Why exactly, though, is there this relationship between a 'bargained coalition' and legislative institutional strengthening? Or between an 'institutionalized coalition' and legislative marginalization? Here, it is important to link the *structural analysis* of 'politicized accumulation' and ruling party politics to a micro-level analysis of the *individual actors* directly involved in legislative reform, namely MPs and their factional backers. This means examining the incentive structures they face as well as the more *contingent* ways the organization of patronage networks impacts on their behaviour.

In the case of an 'institutionalized coalition', as in, a regime where accumulation and patronage are more centralized plus the ruling party relatively strong and cohesive, individual legislators have little opportunity to cultivate their own political networks and instead must appeal to the party leadership. Elected MPs therefore have little reason to risk offending the leadership by supporting a legislative reform agenda. Similarly, ambitious politicians will not be able to use parliamentary leadership positions, for instance the Speakership, to develop a personal profile or to challenge the executive.

By contrast, in a 'bargained coalition', so a regime where accumulation is relatively diffuse, patron–client factions more fragmented, and party strength

---

[106] Saiegh, 2014.

and discipline low, we can expect more MPs to adopt an assertive stance in parliament. To advance their political interests outside the legislature, MPs must
both foster a political base in their constituency and cultivate the support of
elite factional networks, which they need to access campaign funds and the
like. When it comes to politics *inside* parliament, MPs' factional alliances mean
they are less constrained by party discipline. What's more, given their extra-
parliamentary ties, they have a positive incentive to back institutional reforms
that enhance their own patronage power, namely, that amplify the material
advantages and political influence associated with their legislative office.[107]
They can, for instance, use improved budgetary and legislative oversight powers either to satisfy constituency demands or to cater to the interests of their
political financiers, not to mention their own personal interests.[108] Ambitious
political financiers may also actively participate in organizing MPs within the
legislature to pursue a particular agenda, although this is more likely to relate
to an ad hoc issue rather than to a broader institutional reform effort.

Rank-and-file MPs aside, legislative leaders—notably the Speaker—have
similar incentives to strengthen parliament where a 'bargained coalition' is
in power. Again, these leaders can use an institutionally stronger legislature
to help advance their political careers. They also play a *crucial* coordinating
role in any reform agenda. On this point, it is important to stress that the
translation of underlying structural conditions into actual clientelist organizing and institutional change is not automatic; rather, returning to an insight
from the political settlements literature, the power of patron–client factions
depends notably on 'the capacity of their *leadership* to mobilize and enthuse'.[109]
Skilled and ambitious leaders thus play an important role both in determining whether and *when* powerful patron–client factions organize as well as
how they affect institutional change. In the case of the legislature, key leaders
include the Speaker of Parliament and committee chairs but, also, particularly
enterprising political financiers, ministers, and the President.[110] The stronger
the factional rivalries among these different actors, the more likely these elite
tensions are to spill over into the legislature, turning it into an arena of elite
contestation and helping to motivate a process of institutional strengthening.

How does this analysis then compare with alternative explanations? On a
surface level, it aligns with at least some of the above-reviewed literature on

---

[107] On the material advantages that MPs gain from office, see: Eggers and Hanmueller, 2009; Truex,
2014; Koter, 2017.

[108] Samuels, 2002.

[109] Khan, 2010: 5.

[110] On the institution-building influence of an ambitious Speaker, aided by enabling extra-
parliamentary conditions: Sheingate, 2009.

authoritarian and democratic legislatures. Both bodies of work highlight the interdependent relationship of party and legislative institutions. Where ruling parties are organizationally strong and cohesive, this discourages legislative institutionalization; where they are weak and disunited, this engenders legislative strengthening.[111] My analysis nevertheless furthers our understanding in ways that clarify when legislative reform takes place, the motivations that drive political actors to pursue this reform, and the significance of these changes.

First, responding to the authoritarian institutions literature, I stress that rulers do not simply 'choose' to introduce a strong party or parliament, using these institutions to manage their coalition.[112] While there is an element of choice early on, this relates as much or more to leaders' preferred strategies of 'politicized accumulation'. Moreover, party and legislative institutions remain the focus of ongoing struggle, which often *escapes the leader's control*. Where a legislature undergoes institutional strengthening, this does not signal that a dictator has made a concerted *choice* but rather that rival elites have gained the upper hand and are moulding the legislature to better advance their interests.

Second, while individual legislators do play a role in driving reforms, as per the literature on democratic parliaments,[113] their reformist ambitions are conditioned by the extra-parliamentary context. Moreover, in studying this wider political context, scholars cannot limit their analysis to the ruling party and its strength or weakness; also of immediate significance are the structures of accumulation and patronage that determine this party strength. This broader focus helps reveal how it is not just legislators' ambitions that matter but also the elite rivalries of political financiers, whose interests MPs then channel into legislative activity.

Third, this view of external patronage politics and its effects on legislative strength directly contradicts much of the Africanist literature on democratization and legislative strengthening. As discussed previously, scholars like van de Walle and Barkan argued that a strong legislature could help counter 'neo-patrimonial' or clientelist politics.[114] By contrast, I argue that it is *differences in patronage structures*—not their presence or absence—that account for contrasting institutional outcomes. Somewhat paradoxically, it is where contestation across factional networks is more pronounced that legislative institutional strengthening is most likely to occur.

---

[111] Olson, 1994; Cheeseman, 2006; Gandhi, 2008; Opalo, 2019.
[112] Gandhi and Przeworski, 2006; Brownlee, 2007; Gandhi, 2008; Magaloni, 2008; Magaloni and Kricheli, 2010.
[113] Barkan, 2009.
[114] Bratton and van de Walle, 1997; Barkan, 2009.

Finally, it is important to clarify that normative reformist goals also guide the actions of some activist MPs; as in, the claim is not that MPs' motivations are reducible to material ones alone. Rather, the point is to highlight how material conditions help structure broad patterns of elite contestation and institutional change. Returning to Barkan's earlier-referenced argument about legislative 'coalitions for change', the analysis here can elucidate when and why a majority of more 'opportunist' MPs might unite with 'reformists', who will themselves have a variety of motivations, some material, some normative. Among the more normatively motivated MPs, there are also individuals who make considerable personal sacrifices, whether in relative isolation or with the passive support of opportunist colleagues. Again, my attention to the ways legislative activity reflects and magnifies external power struggles is not meant to diminish these individual efforts, but to set them in context.

There is a tradition in legislative studies, from which I draw inspiration, that is far more attuned to the ways legislative institutional change relates to external power struggles. Histories of Western parliaments, for instance, associate their gradual consolidation with the shifting balance of power between a monarch and a group of influential notables.[115] Leaping ahead in time, some analyses of institutional change in the United States Congress reject a tendency to study its institutional history in 'isolation'; instead, they link this history to 'broader contextual features of American politics'.[116] For instance, Brady and Epstein argue that as industrialization blurred the urban–rural partisan divide in the late nineteenth century, legislators from the two main parties came to represent a far more heterogenous and overlapping set of interests. This then led to a decline in partisan decision-making and a decentralization of power away from party leaders within Congress.[117]

An older literature on legislatures in Africa pursued a similar analysis. Scholars interested in post-Independence regime consolidation identified the legislature as an important arena within which the struggle for control played out. In states where a strong party took power, parliament was quickly marginalized, supplanted by the ruling party 'as the centre of debate'.[118] In other cases, ruling parties atrophied and the legislature became a site of elite contestation.[119] Crucially, these accounts tended to relate legislative politics and the

---

[115] On Montesquieu and the fragility of constitutional liberty without the "moderating power of the nobility", see: Hont, 2005: 105–107. See also Maddicott, 2010.
[116] Sheingate, 2009: 198.
[117] Brady and Epstein, 1997.
[118] Lee, 1963: 384–385. See also Kjekshus, 1974; Tordoff and Molteno, 1974.
[119] Gertzel, 1970.

degree of party control to *divergent patterns of 'class' formation*.[120] In one fascinating account, Tordoff suggests that the emergence of a more prominent entrepreneurial class in Zambia 'played a role in a more vocal parliament' following the 1973 elections.[121] He then speculates that, 'if the business class becomes less dependent on the state, the standing and powers of Parliament would at least be altered and might be enhanced with bourgeois politicians providing a check on the executive'.[122] While Tordoff did not carry his analysis any further, the following chapters demonstrate the truth in his passing remarks.

2.2.3.3 Legislative Performance and Its Significance

While elite contestation can help drive legislative institutional reform, what of the legislature's actual performance? When is the legislature more assertive? Whose interests are served?

As noted earlier, legislative institutionalization relates both to the institutional strength of parliament and its actual performance. These two features are related in that, where legislative institutions strengthen, these changes also enhance the potential assertiveness of parliament. For instance, the introduction of new, more powerful legislative committees—like, for instance, a Budget Committee to strengthen budgetary oversight—provides rival factions with new institutional channels through which to pursue their competing interests. The institutional make-up of the legislature does not guarantee heightened performance, though. Legislative assertiveness also depends on the constellation of elite factions at a given point in time, and how factional tensions cut across the executive and legislature. It follows that, just as legislative institutions are more likely to strengthen where the ruling party is a 'bargained coalition', the legislature is also likely to be more assertive. However, where the ruling party is an 'institutionalized coalition' *in decline*, particularly where centralized control over wealth accumulation has begun to erode, emerging patron–client factions may also fuel executive-legislative tensions.

Beyond studying legislative assertiveness, though, it is also worth engaging with the wider significance of these challenges to the executive. I forego the normative and functionalist expectations of some earlier literature on both authoritarian and would-be democratic legislatures.[123] The more recent research in this field has begun to examine policymaking in more depth, plus

---

[120] Holmquist, 1984.
[121] Tordoff, 1977.
[122] Ibid.
[123] Bratton and van de Walle, 1997; Gandhi and Przeworksi, 2006; Fish, 2006; Gandhi, 2008; Barkan, 2009; Svolik, 2012; Boix and Svolik, 2013.

how the dynamics of elite contestation may influence legislative interventions.[124] I build on this work, expanding my analysis of *what processes drive legislative interventions* to then better understand *whose interests are served*. I focus especially on a set of classic questions relating to the *distributive* implications of a more assertive parliament, namely 'who gets what, when and how?'

My argument here is two-fold. First, if more assertive legislative interventions often coincide with factional jockeying, as theorized above, it follows that this legislative activity has *regressive* distributive implications; politicians focus their legislative activity on directing material rewards towards themselves and elite backers within their patron–client factions. However, in suggesting that legislators are largely preoccupied by intra-elite bargaining, I do not mean that they ignore their voters or that there is no prospect for more progressive redistribution. To understand when and why legislators might challenge the executive in favour of progressive policy outcomes, I draw on Jacob Hacker and Paul Pierson's analysis of 'the politics of organized combat'.[125] Along with other scholars,[126] they emphasize the role organized interests play in shaping policy and, consequently, distributive outcomes. In the case of MPs, they may be accountable to voters, but I suggest voter pressure is likely insufficient to motivate more progressive legislative interventions. Indeed, MPs also face more targeted pressures from their party leadership, the President, elite factions to which they belong, and less elite groups as well. Determining what interests are likely to win out in 'the politics of organized combat' then requires a contextually sensitive analysis to establish which groups are best able to influence legislative decisions.

This then brings me to my second argument. While more elite-dominated factional interests are likely to drive much of the legislative agenda, less elite organized groups can—at least sometimes—motivate more progressive policy interventions. For instance, where they consolidate their organization and build their membership base, trade unions, farmers' associations, cooperatives, faith groups, and the like do shape politicians' behaviour, including in policymaking.[127] While these groups may not comprise the most marginalized of society, they do rely on *relatively* egalitarian strategies of collective action, and at least some of the time, their specific interest group objectives align with the concerns of other more disadvantaged groups. For instance, pressure from

---

[124] Noble, 2020; Truex, 2020; Collord, 2021; Demarest, 2021; Opalo, 2022.
[125] Hacker and Pierson, 2010.
[126] Khan, 2005; Domhoff, 2007.
[127] For examples from the African context, see: Titeca and Vervisch, 2008; Okafor, 2009; Martiniello and Nyamsenda, 2018.

public-sector unions for a salary increase may align with a popular preference for improved social services.

Regarding how I pursue this analysis, I do not try to replicate studies in the field of distributive politics that focus on the aggregate distributive effects of stronger democratic institutions, including legislatures. This work has tended to claim that these institutions favour progressive redistribution, and this because they ostensibly encourage greater accountability and responsiveness to the median voter.[128] The findings nevertheless remain inconclusive, particularly when it comes to the effects on actual policymaking.[129] I refocus, instead, on case studies of actual legislative policy interventions. By examining specific interventions, all with clear fiscal implications,[130] I can better identify what pressures—and therefore whose interests—legislators are responding to when they seek to alter an executive agenda. I can then revisit mainstream assumptions and identify alternative mechanisms through which legislative activity may influence distribution outcomes, ones that may then be amenable to testing at the aggregate level in future work.

2.3 Conclusion

What explains variation across authoritarian parties and parliaments? Why are some parties strong and cohesive while others are institutionally weak and fractious? Why are some parliaments marginalized and others more assertive? Why, if at all, do these differences matter? Who is able to participate in party and legislative politics and whose interests are served?

In answering these questions, I draw on an alternative political economy analysis, both Africanist and more broadly comparative, to develop a fresh argument about how wealth, power and political institutions interrelate in the context of Africa's single and dominant party regimes. In brief, the argument goes as follows. Variation in legislative institutionalization, across both space and time, is a function of the cohesion and institutional strength of ruling parties. I offer a 'path dependence' analysis of authoritarian party trajectories, beginning with an initial period of regime consolidation. During these founding moments, authoritarian parties evolve to approximate one of two ideal types. The outcome depends on the strategic decisions of the party leadership regarding, first, their preferred strategy of state-led capitalist development and,

---

[128] For a review and critique, see Golden and Min, 2013.

[129] Ibid.; Khan, 2005; Nel, 2005; Ross, 2006; De Kadt and Lieberman, 2020; Grossman and Michelitch, 2018; Ofosu, 2019.

[130] For instance, changes to the national budget and amendments to some legislation, e.g. tax legislation.

second, whether to invest in party-building. Where the prevailing strategy of economic management leads to more diffuse pattern of wealth accumulation and consequently more decentralized patron–client networks, prospects for party-building are limited and the party forms a 'bargained coalition'. Where leaders, by contrast, centralize control over wealth creation and, consequently, also over patronage networks and where they *also* invest in party institutions, an 'institutionalized coalition' emerges.

In light of the institutional weakness and factionalism characteristic of a 'bargained coalition', the legislature in this case is more likely to emerge as a significant arena of intra-elite bargaining. This, in turn helps ensure its gradual institutionalization. Under an 'institutionalized coalition', by contrast, the greater degree of party strength and cohesion means that the legislature remains a marginal institution and undergoes very little by way of institutional reforms.

Once formed, it is very unlikely that a 'bargained coalition' will see any significant change in either the structure of patronage networks or the party's institutional strength. There is, by contrast, a possibility of within-case variation where an 'institutionalized coalition' begins to decay. This occurs as a result of economic changes, which weaken the party leadership's ability to maintain its centralized control over wealth accumulation and patronage distribution. As more fragmented patronage networks begin to form within the party, its institutional coherence will also suffer. Under such circumstances, the legislature gains in prominence as it becomes a forum within which to negotiate across newly empowered factions.

Finally, this analysis of what processes help account for a stronger legislature also sheds fresh light on what the significance of this institution may be. I argue that, given the prominence of elite-dominated factions in driving legislative interventions, it is their interests that will be most often served. However, there is room for a more expansive study of the 'politics of organized combat' that involves other interest groups—including trade unions, cooperatives, and the like—that can, at least occasionally, leverage elite divisions to advance more progressive, redistributive goals.

I test the various steps in my causal chain in the four proceeding empirical chapters. I begin in the next chapter with my analysis of the early period of authoritarian party consolidation, move on to discuss continuity and change in party strength, then consider the impact of contrasting party trajectories on legislative *institutional* strength. In a final empirical chapter, I examine the impact of party politics on actual legislative performance and its distributive implications.

3

Authoritarian Party Consolidation

A Critical Juncture

> [T]he people who anxiously watch to see whether we will become 'Communist' or 'Western Democrats' will both be disconcerted. We do not have to be either. We shall grope forward, and it may be that we shall create a new synthesis [...].
>
> —Julius Nyerere, July 1961[1]

> Clearly, we needed some outside help. Accordingly, in 1986 we began debating among ourselves, the International Monetary Fund and the World Bank on how best to tackle these problems. We did not, however, reach an agreement until 1987. We had to resolve some conceptual problems [...]. Hence we spent the year sorting out those conceptual problems within the cabinet and the caucuses of the movement, and between ourselves and the international financial institutions.
>
> —Yoweri Museveni, 1997[2]

Periods of regime consolidation are marked by uncertainty, debate, and political struggle. Their outcomes are shaped by the decisions of key actors as they experiment with and finally settle on a new political order.

The above citations from two newly instated leaders speak to one aspect of this early period of heightened uncertainty, namely the choice of economic policy orientation. Julius Nyerere, Tanzania's founding President, speaks of 'groping forward', searching for a 'new synthesis' between East and West, between 'Communist' and Capitalist, or 'Western Democrats'. Intervening at a very different historical juncture, with the Eastern bloc in decline and an externally imposed Structural Adjustment agenda as the new norm, Uganda's

---

[1] Nyerere, Julius. 'Groping Forward' speech at Kivukoni College inauguration. Reprinted in Nyerere, 1967.

[2] Museveni, 1997: 183–184.

Wealth, Power, and Authoritarian Institutions. Michaela Collord, Oxford University Press. © Michaela Collord (2024). DOI: 10.1093/9780191945335.003.0003

President Yoweri Museveni still talks of a contested process requiring the resolution of 'conceptual problems' both internally and with outside creditors.

It may seem that, with fewer external economic and ideological constraints, Nyerere was in a better position to deliver his 'new synthesis'. In what follows, though, I demonstrate how both leaders—working within a wider elite coalition—exercised a high degree of agency in tailoring their preferred economic strategy. I then show the significance of this elite agency in shaping not only patterns of 'politicized accumulation' but also the institutional strength and cohesion of ruling parties. In this way, I argue, leaders' early actions contribute to defining the structural parameters within which subsequent regime politics play out.

I should add that, in focusing on logics of regime consolidation and control, both economic and political, my aim is not to downplay the seriousness of the ideological dilemmas in play. As in, I do not discount the substance of these 'conceptual problems' nor the relevance—in some instances, the vital importance—of normative as well as material considerations. While I return to these concerns at various points in this volume, I remain grateful to others for emphasising a history of ideas and their impact.[3]

The chapter begins with a more in-depth review of the relevant theoretical argument and the method used to study party origins. I then move on to my empirical analysis, which involves my main cases—Tanzania and Uganda—as well as a more minor case comparison with Kenya and Rwanda. As explained, I pair these cases so as, first, to analyse *post-independence* authoritarian regime consolidation, involving TANU and KANU, and next, to analyse *post-conflict* regime consolidation, involving the NRM and RPF.

3.1 Argument and Methods

The period of regime consolidation constitutes a critical juncture during which leaders make two sets of key strategic decisions (Figure 3.1).[4] A first, more fundamental decision relates to leaders' preferred strategy of 'politicized accumulation'. A second concerns whether to invest in strengthening ruling party institutions. The two decisions are not independent of each other. Indeed, where leaders' economic interventions favour more decentralized wealth accumulation, and thus more fragmented patronage networks, this choice makes

---

[3] See, for instance: Mkandawire, 2001; Gray, 2018; Getachew, 2019; Shivji et al., 2020; Roberts, 2022.
[4] See Chapter 2 for a full theoretical discussion.

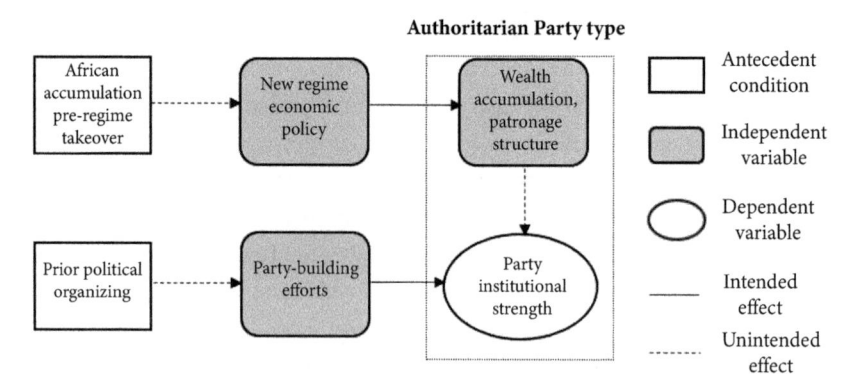

Figure 3.1 Authoritarian party formation

investment in party strengthening difficult, thereby leading to weak party institutions and the emergence of a 'bargained coalition'. Conversely, where leaders' economic decisions favour the centralization of wealth accumulation and thus patronage networks, this outcome is compatible with party institutional strengthening. Such strengthening is not inevitable, however. Rather, an 'institutionalized coalition' emerges where nationalist leaders combine the centralization of wealth accumulation with *concerted* party-building efforts.

Leaders' decisions regarding both economic policy and party strengthening are also influenced by 'antecedent conditions', notably the patterns of indigenous wealth accumulation and political organizing that existed before they took power. For instance, more indigenous accumulation could predispose leaders to favour more decentralized patterns of wealth accumulation. Similarly, a more unified pattern of political organization could encourage authoritarian party strengthening. Yet the decisions of newly instated leaders on these issues are not a foregone conclusion, which if true, would negate the notion that regime consolidation constitutes a critical juncture. Indeed, applying a critical juncture analysis comes with certain methodological exigencies.

A critical juncture is a moment of heightened contingency during which powerful actors are confronted with a series of 'critical decisions'. These are decisions whose consequences have the potential to reshape the structural parameters within which future political action is pursued.[5] When identifying critical junctures, process-tracing techniques capture both the importance of actors' decisions as well as the presence of alternative options, that is, the *contingency* of the moment.[6]

---

[5] Capoccia and Kelemen, 2007; Ermakoff, 2017: 131. See Chapter 2 for further discussion.
[6] Capoccia and Kelemen, 2007.

With this in mind, I elaborate two parallel theory-guided narratives to compare historical processes across my main cases, Tanzania and Uganda. I further strengthen the comparative research design for the critical juncture period by adding two shadow cases, Kenya and Rwanda. I directly compare the consolidation of Tanzania's TANU party as an 'institutionalized coalition' with that of the Kenya African National Union (KANU), a 'bargained coalition'. I do the same for Uganda's NRM, a 'bargained coalition', and the Rwandan Patriotic Front (RPF), an 'institutionalized coalition'.

There are several reasons for the shadow cases. First, although Tanzania and Uganda approximate 'most similar' cases,[7] there are still theoretically significant differences in their 'background conditions', most notably regarding the *timing* and *manner* of the ruling parties' ascent to power. As previously noted, the fact that TANU consolidated in the 1960s–1970s while the NRM came to power in the 1980s might seem to account for the differences in patterns of accumulation; faced with economic crisis and externally imposed structural adjustment, perhaps NRM leaders had little choice but to adopt policies favouring private sector expansion and thus more decentralized accumulation. I nevertheless demonstrate that this difference in timing is not significant, at least in so far as leaders in both periods still exercised a degree of agency. I show this through the pair-wise comparison of TANU and KANU, which both emerged in the 1960s yet cultivated very different strategies of 'politicized accumulation'. I then compare the NRM and RPF, which took power in 1986 and 1994 respectively but *also* favoured starkly contrasting patterns of politicized accumulation.[8]

Regarding the *manner* by which each party took power, TANU experienced a relatively smooth handover from the departing British colonial administration while the NRM fought its way into government through a five-year insurgency. Some scholars maintain that, when a party gains power through violent means and in the face of strong opposition, this encourages the development of stronger party organizations.[9] Such arguments do not hold for the NRM, which I present as an example of a party with a weak organization, despite its history of armed struggle. I offer, however, a more robust rejection of the violence-equals-party-strength hypothesis by showing variation in party strength both between parties that assumed power peacefully (TANU and KANU) and through civil war as rebel insurgencies (NRM and

---

[7] For a full justification, see Chapter 1.
[8] See also Pitcher (2012) on variation across Africa's democracies in post-structural adjustment privatization processes and related institutional reforms.
[9] Smith, 2005; Levitsky and Way, 2012.

Table 3.1 Variation in party type and background conditions

		Party type	
		Institutionalized Coalition	Bargained Coalition
Background Conditions	1960s No insurgency victory	TANU(Main case)	KANU(Shadow case)
	1980s–1990s Insurgency victory	RPF(Shadow case)	NRM(Main case)

RPF).[10] Ultimately, by adding the two shadow cases, I show the strength of the theoretical model while confirming that seemingly important differences in 'background conditions' are of little significance in explaining divergent economic or institutional outcomes (Table 3.1).

More generally, my cross-case comparison is well suited to meet the demands of a critical juncture analysis as it helps evaluate the *importance of leaders' contrasting decisions*, i.e. the contingency of the moment. This is because cross-case analysis helps demonstrate that alternative options were available—as in, they were adopted in one case but not the other—plus what the consequences of these alternative paths could be.[11] Strengthening the 'most similar' quality of the case comparison with the two shadow cases also helps to contrast leaders' decisions with more specificity and thus offers a more persuasive illustration of the counterfactual. Of particular significance is that, even as the overarching strategies remained the same, the specific economic policy options available to leaders varied between the post-Independence regimes of the 1960s and the post-conflict governments of the 1980s and 1990s. As such, the shadow cases help to demonstrate in more granular detail and with a more direct comparison of like with like the implications of leaders choosing one policy over another.

In what follows, I first develop a theory-guided narrative for the post-independence authoritarian parties, TANU and KANU. I then do the same for the post-conflict parties, the NRM and the RPF. For each case, I examine the decision-making process surrounding the preferred strategy of 'politicized

---

[10] Arguably Mau Mau and the 1950s Emergency in Kenya belie this 'peaceful transition' label. But key KANU leaders, and certainly Kenyatta, were not actually involved in or particularly sympathetic to Mau Mau. Moreover, if the theory that violence leads to strong party institutions holds, then we would expect KANU to develop robust party institutions whereas the opposite occurred. Finally, like TANU, KANU took power through negotiations with colonial authorities and elections, which contrasts sharply with the violence of the NRM and RPF insurgencies.

[11] Capoccia and Kelemen, 2007: 359.

accumulation'. I then ascertain whether the party leaders invested or not in party-building and how these efforts were indirectly affected by prevailing patterns of wealth accumulation. As detailed in Chapter 2, I evaluate the extent of party-strengthening based on: (1) the strength of a party's central bureaucracy; (2) the degree of 'complexity' or differentiation among a party's organizational sub-units; and (3) the degree of internal 'coherence', assessed based on the degree of congruence between statutory rules and actual practice. I do not, at this stage, include the fourth indicator of party institutional strength, namely 'adaptability' or 'generational age', as it is too early to be relevant. Across the four cases, I expect to find that, where leaders favoured more centralized accumulation, this allowed for more control over patron–client networks, thereby enabling greater internal party discipline and effective party-building efforts. By contrast, where leaders favoured more decentralized accumulation, the resultant fragmentation of patron–client networks eroded party discipline and, even where leaders *attempted* to engage in party-building, these efforts were unsuccessful.

3.2 Post-Independence Regimes

In the heady political atmosphere of the 1960s, newly instated nationalist governments were under pressure to deliver the 'fruits of independence', but also to shore up their ruling coalition. They had considerable choice in how they approached these tasks, not only because of the prominence of both left- and right-wing ideologies but also because of the defining structural features of African economies and state institutions at the time. An indigenous capitalist private sector was only beginning to emerge across much of the continent. Meanwhile, independent African states inherited a range of colonial-era tools to actively mould the emerging capitalist economy as per the preferences of the ruling elite.[12]

Among other strategic decisions, governments could choose: whether to favour the dominance of state-owned enterprise through extensive nationalization; whether to, instead, support private sector expansion, notably through improved access to credit, procurement contracts, and a more lenient regulatory regime;[13] whether to favour more direct state control over land or to support individualized ownership and the accumulation of capital surpluses

---

[12] Iliffe, 1983: 77; Whitfield et al., 2015: 26. See also: Kennedy, 1988; Cooper, 2002; Young, 2012.
[13] For a succinct review of the tools available to African governments, see: Kennedy, 1988: 64–65. See also: Swainson, 1980; Lubeck, 1987.

through agriculture;[14] and, whether to favour or discourage 'straddling', a trend in many countries whereby public officials used their salaries to invest in the private sector and thereby join a class of capital accumulators.[15] Although this is by no means an exhaustive list of policy options, leaders' orientation across these strategic areas contributed to the divergence between more centralized, state-centric versus decentralized, private sector-promoting patterns of wealth accumulation in independent African states (see Table 3.2).

In what follows, I focus less on the significance of these early interventions in determining economic outcomes—a separate topic to the one covered in this book—but rather on how divergent patterns of 'politicized accumulation' fed into logics of authoritarian party institutional consolidation. I show how the

Table 3.2 Policy orientation and accumulation patterns of post-Independence regimes

| | | Pattern of wealth accumulation | |
		Centralized	Decentralized
Key areas of economic decision-making	Private v. public investment focus	Preference for public sector expansion, including through nationalization, preferential allocation of credit to state-owned enterprise, and increased public sector capital investment; parallel restrictions on private sector expansion, including limits on access to credit and regulatory constraints (e.g. regarding tax, licensing, etc.).	Preference for private sector expansion, including through additional facilities to improve private sector access to credit, public subsidies, and a more permissive regulatory environment; limited nationalization and public-sector investment.
	Land tenure system	Restrictions on freehold land tenure; may involve State control over land through leasehold land tenure and State administrative control over customary land.	Support for expansion of freehold land tenure, i.e. individualization of land ownership and growth in the private land market.
	Attitude towards 'straddling'	Limits on public employees and elected officials' ability to engage in private enterprise, controls on corruption as a means of personal enrichment.	Support for public employees and elected officials investing in private enterprise, limited or weak control over corruption.

[14] Swainson, 1987.
[15] Kennedy, 1988: 53–54. See also: Iliffe, 1983.

Tanzanian regime cultivated a more centralized pattern of wealth accumulation while the Kenyan regime a more decentralized pattern. For each country, I examine how these divergent patterns emerged, emphasizing the significance of uncertainty, debate, and political struggle during the initial 'critical juncture' period. I then consider the wider institutional context, evaluating the ruling elites' attitude towards party strengthening and how the success of their efforts (or lack thereof) was influenced by the prevailing patterns of accumulation.

3.2.1 Tanzania—Consolidation of an 'Institutionalized Coalition'

After Independence in 1961, the *Tanganyika African National Union* (TANU)—which became *Chama Cha Mapinduzi* (CCM) in 1977 after it merged with Zanzibar's *Afro-Shirazi Party*—consolidated as an 'institutionalized coalition'; it featured relatively centralized control over wealth accumulation and patronage combined with a robust party institutional apparatus. 'Antecedent conditions' linked to Tanzania's experience under colonial rule influenced what strategic decisions were available to TANU leaders as they sought to mould the party's post-Independence trajectory. Yet TANU only consolidated as an 'institutionalized coalition' after a period of policy experimentation, debate, and political struggle, which lasted throughout much of the 1960s.

3.2.1.1 Economic Policy
The TANU-led government eventually adopted a package of policies that, together, discouraged private wealth accumulation and favoured state-led economic expansion. This package combined, most notably: a commitment to curbing 'straddling' practices through a strict Leadership Code; limited support for private enterprise in favour of public sector growth; and the abolition of freehold land tenure coupled with an emphasis on state-led agricultural production.

Certainly, pre-Independence patterns of indigenous accumulation helped ensure the political space needed for TANU, once in power, to pursue a statist economic strategy. For a variety of reasons, the British colonial administration in mainland Tanzania—then Tanganyika[16]—did not invest heavily in promoting capitalist expansion and even less in the emergence of African

---

[16] Mainland Tanzania, which is the focus of this book, was referred to as Tanganyika until it formed a union with Zanzibar in 1964.

capitalists.[17] Partly as a result, the nationalist coalition in Tanzania comprised mainly teachers, traders, unionists, and clerks, among others.[18] Some scholars conclude that subsequent government policies owed 'much to the fact that those who took control of the state in 1961 were not capitalists.'[19]

An emphasis on the significance of this colonial legacy nevertheless paints too simplistic a picture of Tanzania's post-colonial development trajectory and the considerable level of *uncertainty* involved. For one, small as it was, we cannot entirely disregard an emerging African capitalist elite nor its economic and political significance. Particularly in the cash-crop growing regions of the north-east and Lake Zone, more affluent farmers and traders pioneered new forms of economic and political organization under colonial rule, including Tanganyika's first tribal associations and cooperative unions.[20] Later on, the wealth of these leading agricultural regions helped give a 'new' elite the incentives and political exposure to back nationalist politics.[21] As such, alongside Dar es Salaam, these areas formed TANU's first organizational strongholds.[22] While the interests of the 'new' elite did not ultimately dominate the nationalist coalition, their political demands and economic contribution still influenced the post-Independence government, at least for a time.

Partly due to conflicting ideological and political pressures, the immediate post-Independence period was one of policy contradictions and overall *private-led capitalist expansion.*[23] Through the early to mid-1960s, official government policy, heavily influenced by World Bank-drafted development plans, aimed to encourage growth in commercial farming and thus agricultural exports. While these policy interventions met with mixed results, agricultural production did expand, partly due to the *private* efforts of Tanzania's African capitalist farmers. Yet, even as the government encouraged commercial growth, actors within TANU reaffirmed the party's long-held socialist or *Ujamaa* principles, albeit in a somewhat inconsistent fashion. For one, the party—then dominated by its National Executive Committee (NEC)—reiterated calls for an end to freehold land tenure and the resettlement of peasants into planned villages. Some re-settlement of largely *subsistence* farmers did occur, but this did not affect production in the more affluent food and

---

[17] See, for instance: Shivji, 1976; Iliffe, 1979; Mueller, 1981; Hartmann, 1983; Kimei, 1987; Makoba, 1998.

[18] Mueller, 1981: 459; Coulson, 1982: 108.

[19] Coulson, 1982: 108. See also: Shivji, 1976; Mueller, 1981.

[20] Hyden, 1977: 187; Iliffe, 1979; Mtei, 2009; Fisher, 2012.

[21] For this designation of a 'new' elite, see Hyden, 1977.

[22] Iliffe, 1979: 486.

[23] Pratt, 1976; Coulson, 1982; Hartmann, 1983, especially chapters 2–3; Makoba, 1998, chapter 2; Chachage, 2018.

cash-crop growing regions. Party members also issued a more conventional set of demands for the 'fruits of independence', including for the Africanization of the public service and private enterprise. Somewhat contrary to the aims of *Ujamaa*, this process would entail a large-scale redistribution of wealth from the predominantly Asian commercial elite into private, African hands.[24] Finally, caught between the government and party position, President Julius Nyerere—Tanzania's pre-eminent nationalist leader—alternated between the two. He was still 'groping forward', searching for a suitable development strategy.[25]

Several factors eventually compelled Nyerere to adopt a more uncompromising socialist agenda, one which was then owned by the party and—with more reticence—accepted by the President's cabinet ministers and government.[26] Nyerere was preoccupied by the growing class stratification in Tanzania, including by the increased prominence of African capitalist farmers.[27] In urban areas too, industry expanded rapidly as did construction. This trend was especially pronounced in Dar es Salaam where senior politicians and civil servants were using their more generous government salaries to invest in real estate.[28] Two unanticipated events also fed Nyerere's malaise, notably a diplomatic row with Britain and West Germany, which resulted in the suspension of financial assistance from both countries, followed by a politically fraught strike by university students demanding exemption from National Service requirements.[29] Nyerere saw the strike as a dangerous assertion of the class privilege of a rising elite and worked to suppress it.

He ultimately intervened with what later became known as the Arusha Declaration, a speech delivered at a meeting of the TANU NEC in January 1967.[30] Drafted by Nyerere himself, the Declaration committed the Party and Government to a far stricter policy of 'socialism and self-reliance'.[31] It presented a vision of development rooted in agriculture and reliant on the mobilization of peasant labour. Crucially, the Declaration also introduced a Leadership Code, which greatly limited prospects for 'straddling' and thus for private

[24] Iliffe, 1979: 573–575; Hartmann, 1983.
[25] Pratt, 1976: 2; Hartmann, 1983.
[26] Joan Wicken, Nyerere's long-time personal assistant and speech writer, recalled: 'If we had been as democratic as all that, we would never have got the Arusha Declaration, not because of the people's lack of support, but because of the leadership. Nyerere had to fight that every inch of the way' (cited in Tripp, 2023: 47–48). See also: Hartmann, 1983; Masha, 2011.
[27] Van de Laar, 1972: 109; Pratt, 1976: 216–225.
[28] Coulson, 2013: 221–222 and 235.
[29] Hartmann, 1983: 164–169; Makoba, 1998: 160; Coulson, 2013: 221–223.
[30] The speech was not on any NEC meeting agenda and was introduced at the meeting by Nyerere. See, Mwansasu, 1979: 184.
[31] Masha, 2011.

accumulation by TANU officials and politicians. TANU leaders were barred from engaging in 'practices of Capitalism or Feudalism', including holding company shares or directorships in any privately owned enterprise, receiving two or more salaries, or renting out property.[32]

It took time for the effects of the Arusha Declaration to become clear and for a policy agenda to crystallize, and this due to continued debate and political jostling.[33] The socialist agenda gradually gathered momentum, though, leading to the consolidation of a distinctly statist economic strategy and a more centralized pattern of wealth accumulation.[34] These macro-outcomes came about as a result of a constellation of different policy interventions.

One element of the Declaration that Nyerere was adamant should be implemented immediately was the Leadership Code. He emphasized its urgency for reshaping private accumulation, noting, 'Had we delayed, you would discover two years from now that our leadership has become rather entrenched in the accumulation of personal property.'[35] Somewhat predictably, the Code proved a bitter pill to swallow, eliciting the strongest opposition of all the provisions in the Declaration,[36] but Nyerere made only minor concessions in response.[37] The material impact of the Code, meanwhile, was immediately apparent as its enforcement prompted a collapse in the Dar es Salaam real estate market, which as noted earlier, had been booming largely due to investments by politicians and public servants.[38]

The effective enforcement of the Code would likely not have been possible, however, without further statist interventions.[39] Of particular note was the dramatic post-Arusha Declaration expansion of public enterprise. Even here, though, the process took time to accelerate as policy debate and experimentation continued. While the Arusha Declaration gave way to an early wave of nationalization, this was short-lived and restricted to foreign capital, notably banks and external trading firms.[40] Nyerere was quick to call an end to the nationalization drive, though, insisting that private investors were still welcome.[41] The halt proved temporary. After first heeding the warnings of several

---

[32] Nyerere, 1967.

[33] See Hartmann (1983), chapter 5 on the Arusha Declaration as a process rather than a one-off, triggering event.

[34] For a general assessment, see: Mueller, 1981; Hartmann, 1983; Tripp, 1997; Makoba, 1998; Coulson, 2013; Gray, 2018.

[35] Transcript from press conference, March 1967, cited in Pratt, 1976: 236.

[36] Hartmann, 1983: 202–203.

[37] See: 'The Arusha Declaration: Answers to Questions', 1967.

[38] Ibid.

[39] For examples of states where Leadership Codes were introduced but with little impact, see Zambia under Kaunda and Uganda under Obote, Baylies, and Szeftel, 1984.

[40] See: 'Public ownership in Tanzania', first published in the *Sunday News*, 12 February 1967.

[41] Ibid.

cabinet ministers, in 1969 Nyerere ceded to pressure from the party and parliament to proceed with a rapid nationalization of domestic capital, mostly at the expense of Tanzanian Asians.[42] In 1970, wholesale trade was nationalized. This move was later followed by the nationalization of citizen-owned industries and rented properties.[43] Another blow to private entrepreneurs came in 1976 with *Operation Maduka* (shops). All private shops in collectivized *Ujamaa* villages (discussed below), on state farms, or near state-owned industries were to close and be replaced by cooperative shops run by residents and workers.[44]

Nationalization aside, government development planning and credit provision further favoured public enterprise as 'the major agent of development and accumulation of capital' while 'downgrading' private capital.[45] The Second Five-Year Development Plan (1969–1974) assigned the bulk of new development projects to the public sector.[46] The National Development Corporation, created in 1964 to help attract foreign capital investment, was repurposed post-Arusha Declaration to '[establish] new companies plus [to expand] existing ones within the parastatal sector'.[47] Meanwhile, publicly owned banks favoured parastatals, leaving private sector entrepreneurs to struggle.[48] Industrial and import licences were also difficult to secure and were given out on a discretionary basis to a select few private firms. These were largely Asian-owned companies while African entrepreneurs—and the majority of less politically favoured Asian entrepreneurs—remained marginalized.[49]

The effects of the Tanzanian government's emphasis on parastatal growth, achieved at the expense of private sector expansion, can be measured using a range of indicators. The number of parastatals rose rapidly from 64 in 1967 to over 400 by the 1980s.[50] Lending to the public sector continued to dwarf lending to private enterprise such that, by 1980, the public sector received 90.7 per cent of total credit and the private sector just 9.3 per cent, leaving aside informal financial markets.[51] Investment trends, meanwhile, reversed after 1967 with the public sector replacing the private sector as the leader in gross fixed capital formation (Figure 3.2).[52] Employment patterns reflected the shifting

[42] Hartmann, 1983: 203, 206.
[43] Ibid., 244–245.
[44] Makoba, 1998: 198; accessed 19 July 2017: https://www.tzaffairs.org/1976/07/.
[45] Hartmann, 1983: 262; Mwapachu, 2005; Coulson, 2013: 245.
[46] Makoba, 1998: 316.
[47] Ibid., 309.
[48] Nyagetera, 1992; Kimei, 1987; Makoba, 1998; Mwapachu, 2005: 377–378.
[49] Mwapachu, 2005: 377–378.
[50] Makoba, 1998: 303; Pitcher, 2012: 51.
[51] Kimei, 1987: 213; Nyagetera, 1992: 78.
[52] Ndulu and Mutalemwa, 2002: 124–125.

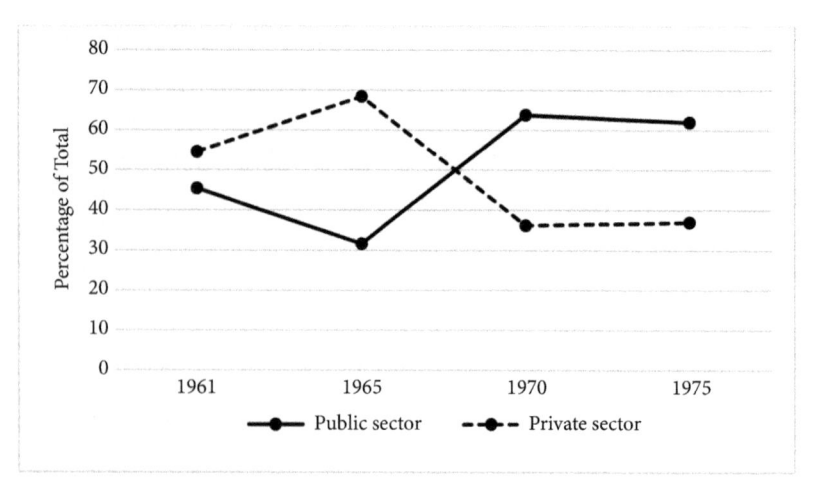

Figure 3.2 Tanzania—gross fixed capital formation by the public and private sectors, 1961–1975

balance with private sector employment stagnating between 1969 and 1974 even as employment in the parastatal sector doubled.[53] The impact on private accumulation was also clear as the pre-tax incomes of 'capitalist entrepreneurs' reportedly fell by 47 per cent between 1969 and 1975.[54]

While there were clearly normative motivations behind the socialist turn as well, the preference for public sector growth ultimately dovetailed with a general trend towards the centralization of patronage distribution and the entrenchment of a relatively narrow, party-aligned bureaucratic elite. The post-Arusha Declaration period marked a new phase in the Africanization process, which after the first wave of nationalization, encompassed managerial positions in erstwhile foreign-owned multinationals.[55] As the appointing authority of parastatal CEOs and board members, President Nyerere invariably favoured CCM cadres and in particular a narrow group of top government officials, primarily ministers, principal secretaries, and technocrats.[56] Meanwhile, the growth of African capitalist traders—who had begun to emerge alongside the somewhat more numerous African capitalist farmers—stalled in the 1970s while there was a total absence of African industrialists.[57] The private sector elite, such as it was, had no collective lobbying power as 'government

---

[53] Coulson, 2013: 327–328.
[54] Ibid., 239–240.
[55] Makoba, 1998: 193–194.
[56] Shivji, 1976: 89; Makoba, 1998: 196–197, 199; Chijoriga, 1999: 21.
[57] Makoba, 1998: 198; Mwapachu, 2005: 376.

was able, through the instrumentality of discretionary resource allocation, to divide the business sector and deal with it on a company-by-company basis.'[58] As mentioned above, this approach favoured a select group of firms owned by Asian Tanzanians who were careful to cultivate a low political profile.[59] Unsurprisingly, very few members of Tanzania's capitalist elite were represented in the TANU NEC, Cabinet, or Parliament.[60] In his influential volume on Tanzania's political economy, Issa Shivji concluded that the post-Arusha Declaration period saw the consolidation of a 'bureaucratic bourgeoisie', a ruling class dependent on the state and ruling party for its reproduction.[61]

Despite the significance of parastatal enterprise, perhaps most fundamental to TANU's statist control of wealth accumulation—given Tanzania's primarily agrarian economy—was its rejection of freehold land tenure and its preference for state-led agricultural production. Nyerere and the TANU NEC opposed the individualization of customary land tenure, believing it would lead to the consolidation of a landed bourgeoisie.[62] Even though government policy in the early 1960s favoured capitalist farmers,[63] the Cabinet pushed through—at Nyerere's behest—legislation 'nationalizing' land, i.e. converting all freehold land titles into 90-year leases and ensuring direct state administrative control over customary land.[64] By eliminating freehold land tenure, the government effectively prevented farmers from mortgaging their land, an important means of accessing capital.[65]

However, the full significance of these reforms only became apparent post-Arusha Declaration as export-oriented capitalist agricultural policies were eclipsed by renewed efforts to introduce collectivized or *Ujamaa* villages. After early, abortive attempts at 'villagization', Nyerere called in 1969 for a stronger push while directing government to discriminate against commercial farmers, denying them access to credit and agricultural inputs.[66] Then, in late 1973, TANU resolved that the whole rural population should live in collective villages by the end of 1976.[67] The ensuing forced resettlement and expropriation

[58] Mwapachu, 2005: 376.
[59] Ibid.; Balachandran, 1981: 322.
[60] Makoba, 1998: 198.
[61] Shivji, 1976.
[62] Ibid., 51; Mueller, 1981: 468, 477.
[63] Iliffe, 1979: 574–575. See also Hartmann, 1983; Coulson, 2013.
[64] Coulson, 2013: 182; Boone and Nyeme, 2015: 71.
[65] Kimei, 1987; BOT report.
[66] Coulson, 2013: 201, 256–259.
[67] Ibid., 296.

of African-held landholdings affected about half of Tanzania's rural population as people were relocated into 8,000 new villages.[68] Any remaining rural economic power bases, notably concentrated around large-scale farmers, were further eroded in 1976 with the nationalization of the Cooperative Unions—generally dominated by more established farmers—and their replacement with government corporations.[69] The combined effect of these measures was to ensure that the nuclei of rural capitalism, which expanded in the 1960s, disappeared or saw their development forestalled in the 1970s.[70] There were exceptions; some rich farmers turned villagization to their advantage while party and state officials leveraged their positions for personal gain as small-scale agrarian capitalists.[71] But this only yielded a relatively unproductive capitalism 'stunted in its most backward form'.[72]

In sum, during the early period of regime consolidation, the TANU government favoured statist economic interventions, nurturing a centralized pattern of 'politicized accumulation' and patronage distribution. Yet as the immediate post-Independence period of policy contradictions and capitalist expansion suggests, this outcome was not inevitable. It took a concerted effort by President Nyerere—backed by sympathetic TANU leaders—to engineer a reversal in the late 1960s, setting the TANU regime on a new developmental path. Admittedly, the results of TANU's efforts fell short of outcomes achieved by richer socialist regimes in Eastern Europe and the USSR, and the Party never managed—or truly sought—to quash all independent capitalist enterprise.[73] Even so, the effects of its interventionist measures were significant. Taking stock of the Party's progress following the 1976 cooperative nationalization, one observer noted, 'In less than ten years from the Arusha Declaration, the state had taken a controlling interest in virtually all productive institutions that could easily be nationalized.'[74] Meanwhile, Nyerere himself declared in 1977 that the previous decade of reforms had 'stopped and reversed a national drift towards the growth of class society', meaning a capitalist society with its characteristic concentration of wealth amongst bourgeois accumulators.[75]

---

[68] Boone and Nyeme, 2015: 71.
[69] Samoff, 1989.
[70] Iliffe, 1983: 79.
[71] Von Freyhold, 1979: 120; Mueller, 1981: 494–496; Makoba, 1998: 209–210. Villagization was also pursued more aggressively in Tanzania's poorer regions such that, while it did slow the growth of agrarian capitalists in affluent regions, it also further entrenched existing regional inequalities. See: Coulson, 1982; Silwal, 2016.
[72] Mueller, 1981: 496.
[73] Bienen, 1970; Gray, 2018, chapter 4.
[74] Coulson, 2013: 209.
[75] Cited in Iliffe, 1983: 79.

3.2.1.2 Party Strengthening Efforts

As was true of its statist economic strategy, the success of TANU's party-building was by no means a foregone conclusion, although again, there were favourable 'antecedent conditions'. Immediately after Independence, TANU went through a period of institutional erosion, which only later gave way to a concerted party strengthening effort. Crucially, given the theory advanced in this book, state-control of wealth accumulation and patronage distribution directly reinforced the party-building project. The paucity—not to mention strict regulation—of private political finance prevented the emergence of strong local patrons even as party and administrative control over access to key resources reinforced the strength of formal institutional structures.

In the latter days of British colonial rule, TANU was undoubtedly in a better position than many other nationalist parties to organize and extend its territorial reach. This was due to the relatively 'yielding' attitude of the colonial administration.[76] TANU leadership also appreciated the significance of coupling mass support with 'minute organization' and pushed for the creation of branches and the bureaucratization of the party with paid officers at national and local levels.[77] Even so, TANU was not a 'mass party'; it did not have a 'hard-core party bureaucracy' nor a stable source of finance before Independence.[78] The party's weakness only seemed to increase after 1961 as it struggled to collect vital membership dues and as many of its most able officers went into government.[79] As one close observer noted, 'It is hard to exaggerate the disorganization and incompetence that existed in the central offices of the party by 1965.'[80]

Despite TANU's weakness in the early 1960s, leaders introduced a range of formal changes to its structures and authority, many of which proved highly significant later on. Local government reforms introduced in 1962 provided the first opportunity to strengthen the party bureaucracy through a fusion with local government administration.[81] Native Authorities were abolished and replaced by Regional and Area Commissioners, who automatically became regional and district TANU secretaries while also assuming ex officio membership of the TANU National Conference and NEC.[82] An army mutiny

---

[76] Bienen, 1970: 52–53. Iliffe, 1979: 552–554.
[77] Iliffe, 1979: 557–558.
[78] Bienen, 1970: 61–62.
[79] Ibid., 65; Pratt, 1976: 210.
[80] Pratt, 1976: 210.
[81] Cliffe, 1967b: 14.
[82] Velzen and Sterkenburg, 1972a: 261; Bienen, 1970: 67–68; Van Cranenburgh, 1990: 106. On "state-party fusion" in general, see: Makulilo, 2008.

and the revolution in Zanzibar in 1964 provided further impetus for party strengthening, motivating the reinvigoration of the TANU youth league plus the introduction of party cells.[83] These cells formed the basic unit of the party, comprising just 10 households responsible for electing their cell leader. Finally, TANU saw its de jure strength further reinforced with the adoption of the 1965 Interim Constitution, which turned Tanzania into a one-party state. It also elevated the authority of TANU party organs, particularly the NEC, which acquired a status on a par with the National Assembly.[84]

While these early reforms laid important groundwork, it was only in the latter half of the 1960s, and particularly after the Arusha Declaration in 1967, that 'quietly but effectively the party's competence as an organization was greatly strengthened'.[85] This party strengthening process depended on combining *formal* party changes with parallel efforts to centralize wealth accumulation and patronage distribution as per TANU's *Ujamaa* commitment. The dual-track process allowed for the de facto distribution of power to reinforce the ruling party's de jure structures and authority.

Additional reforms to party's structures and functions post-1967 included: the more 'systemic' and top-down creation of party cell units and the re-election of cell leaders;[86] the formalization of the candidate nomination process ahead of internal party elections (1969);[87] the establishment of TANU branches in public sector work-places and ujamaa villages (1969);[88] the reduction in the size of the Central Committee and its division into sub-committees 'charged with supervising the activities of a set of ministries and their parastatals' (1969);[89] the parallel reorganization of the party Headquarters into departments to service the sub-committees;[90] the further bureaucratization of the party and its fusion with the state administration;[91] a constitutional amendment adopted in 1975 transforming TANU's de facto hegemony into de jure supremacy over all state organs;[92] and, the replacement in 1977 of the 1965 Interim Constitution with a permanent constitution, which further reinforced the supremacy of the ruling party. A final raft of bureaucratic reforms conducted in 1982 brought CCM to what one scholar referred to as the Party's

---

[83] Cliffe, 1967: 14; Bienen, 1970: 375; Van Cranenburgh, 1990: 106.
[84] Van Cranenburgh, 1990: 75.
[85] Pratt, 1976: 259.
[86] Levine, 1972; Bienen, 1974: 443.
[87] Pratt, 1976: 259; Mwansasu, 1979: 184.
[88] Mwansasu, 1979: 180; Hartmann, 1983: 231.
[89] The number of these sub-committees rose from four in 1969 to seven in 1974.
[90] Mwansasu, 1979: 180; Hartmann, 1983: 231.
[91] Tordoff, 1977: 36; Mwansasu, 1979: 181–182; Msekwa, 2012: 35–36; Coulson, 2013: 300–301.
[92] Mwansasu, 1979: 172–179; Mlimuki and Kabudi, 1986: 73.

'apogee.'[93] The reforms ensured that the various departments of the CCM Secretariat could 'compete' with 'every bureaucracy' of the government and elevated the party Secretary General to number three in the State hierarchy.[94]

These formal changes became effective in practice as TANU leaders used a combination of disciplinary measures and centralized patronage resources to rebalance power between, on the one hand, appointed party and government officials and, on the other, elected political representatives and local-level party leaders. Through various means, elected leaders' *informal* patronage roles were minimized, leaving the party and government to dominate. One key source of tension was the relationship between Regional Commissioners as party-cum-administrative officials and elected Members of Parliament (MPs). Both claimed to play a development role at the local level. MPs surveyed in the early 1960s saw themselves as local patrons, their job being 'to get something from the government for the people.'[95] Regional Commissioners, meanwhile, presided over Regional Development Committees responsible for allocating important development funds.[96] They also helped administer land following the previously mentioned abolition of Native Authorities.[97]

Disagreement over the exact remit of MPs versus Commissioners came to a head shortly after the Arusha Declaration. Two MPs from the West Lake region—one of the more affluent cash crop growing areas—clashed with their local RCs over plans to introduce collectivized villages, part of the newly reinvigorated *Ujamaa* agenda. Following this incident, the MPs were subjected to an internal party enquiry, which concluded that legislators should not 'interfere with leadership', a formula which observers noted was 'vague enough to condemn any further opposition by an MP to the Regional Commissioner or other TANU functionaries.'[98] The two MPs were later expelled from TANU along with five of their parliamentary colleagues, all of whom were deemed to have 'grossly violated the Party creed.'[99] This episode set a powerful precedent; it effectively marginalized MPs as local development actors while further discouraging opposition by elected leaders to appointed Commissioners.[100]

Over the subsequent decade, state and party officials—the two often being indistinguishable—continued to assert their authority in overseeing local

[93] Martin, 1988: 89.
[94] Mlimuki and Kabudi, 1986: 80; Van Cranenburgh, 1990: 119–120.
[95] Hopkins, 1971: 165–166.
[96] Velzen and Sterkenburg, 1972: 261.
[97] Boone and Nyeme, 2015: 71.
[98] Velzen and Sterkenhurg, 1972: 261.
[99] Ibid.
[100] Ibid. See also Martin, 1988.

development efforts and distributing centrally sourced patronage. A dramatic increase in the TANU budget helped fund a growing number of salaried officials, turning party jobs into a popular career choice for university graduates.[101] The so-called 'decentralization' reforms of 1972, meanwhile, 'meant that [elected] local government was replaced in each region and district by an arm of the central civil service', which was further supervised by Party Officials.[102] Starting in 1976, salaried 'village managers' assumed more powers than elected village chairmen since they could influence and elicit funds from party and government officials in the district and regional offices.[103] The result was that, 'By the end of the 1970s, in almost every sector of life in Tanzania, power resided with officials.'[104] Elected representatives were themselves drawn into the expanding sphere of officialdom. For instance, by the 1980s, the 'most notable extra-parliamentary function' fulfilled by MPs was membership on the boards of Tanzania's parastatals.[105] These positions certainly added to legislators' personal incomes, but as appointed officials, it also encouraged them to 'speak with the voice of government' while leaving 'little room' to access or distribute patronage.[106]

The parliamentary nomination and election process within TANU offers a final indication of the balance of power between a party-state bureaucracy and elected politicians. The party took the lead in managing electoral campaigns while legislators' own mobilization efforts were proscribed. In 1965, ahead of the first one-party election, TANU adopted a system whereby various party organs from local to national level were tasked with nominating two candidates who then ran against each other in the general election.[107] Already in 1965, the party used public funds to finance all campaign meetings while banning unofficial campaigning by candidates, particularly the use private resources to influence voters.[108] Enforcement of these restrictions strengthened with time. In the 1970 election, the first after the Arusha Declaration, there was a 'fervent campaign to bar the business community from entering the race.'[109] Some unofficial campaigning did persist, but it was kept to

---

[101] Bienen, 1974: 440; Mlimuki and Kabudi, 1976: 72; Nyang'oro, 2011.
[102] Msekwa, 2012: 35–36; Coulson, 2013: 300.
[103] Coulson, 2013: 323–324.
[104] Ibid.
[105] Van Donge and Liviga, 1986: 237.
[106] Ibid.
[107] For detailed descriptions of the parliamentary selection process see: Harris, 1967; Bienen, 1970; Hyden and Leys, 1972; Mwansasu, 1974; McHenry, 1983.
[108] Ibid. See also: Mpangala, 1994.
[109] Kiondo, 1994: 72.

a minimum.[110] The party leadership, meanwhile, ensured it retained ultimate control over candidates. The TANU NEC, which had powers to veto nominees suggested by lower-level party organs, increasingly used these powers to reject would-be candidates.[111] The Party and especially the Party leadership also controlled the official campaign message.[112] Campaigns thus served as an opportunity for the party—rather than individual politicians—to broadcast its own organizational strength and development agenda to voters.[113]

In emphasizing the preponderance of the centrally funded party-state bureaucracy, it is nevertheless important not to exaggerate its strength. Scarcity of state resources prevented TANU's consolidation as a 'disciplined organizational juggernaut';[114] communication between the national and local levels was not always smooth; and the performance of various party duties by local officials remained inconsistent.[115] This administrative weakness was further aggravated by the persistence of low-level factionalism among contending local elites.[116] But what the TANU leadership was able to ensure, despite these deficiencies, was the *relative* strength of its bureaucratic structures vis-à-vis elected politicians. Even if centralized patronage resources remained limited, so long as a state-led form of capitalist expansion dominated, the superior authority of TANU's bureaucracy could endure.

The above analysis outlines how TANU consolidated as an 'institutionalized coalition' featuring more centralized wealth accumulation and patronage distribution alongside a relatively strong party institutional apparatus. This outcome was not determined solely by 'antecedent conditions'; rather, it was arrived at following an early period of experimentation and political realignment. The TANU leadership's eventual commitment to a statist centralization of wealth accumulation was essential in enabling the success of its parallel, party-building efforts, notably by consolidating the flow of patronage distribution within the party bureaucratic channels while marginalizing would-be local 'big men'. To fully appreciate this point, and to provide a concrete illustration of the counterfactual, we now turn to an analysis of the Kenyan case.

---

[110] Ibid.; see also Hyden and Leys, 1972.
[111] McHenry, 1983: 339.
[112] Cited in McHenry, 1983: 339
[113] On a similar point, see Harris, 1967: 30.
[114] Bienen, 1970: 445. See also: Martin, 1988.
[115] Ibid.
[116] Martin, 1988.

3.2.2 Kenya—Consolidation of a 'Bargained Coalition'

As was true or TANU in Tanzania, 'antecedent conditions' in Kenya influenced KANU's post-Independence trajectory, encouraging in this case to the consolidation of a 'bargained coalition'. The foregoing analysis nevertheless shows the extent of debate and political contestation that informed what were ultimately *contingent* decisions made by Kenya's leaders both to favour a pattern of decentralized wealth accumulation and to largely forego party-building efforts, which were in any event undermined by KANU's more fractious patronage networks. The discussion of Kenya, as a shadow case, is less extensive than the treatment of Tanzania, the main aim being to highlight the contrast between the two. In so doing, the analysis lays bare the consequences of alternative decisions made by leaders when faced with a similar set of strategic choices.

3.2.2.1 Economic Policy

Post-Independence, the KANU-led government in Kenya opted for a set of economic policies that, despite certain statist elements, nevertheless favoured the expansion of an African capitalist elite and, thus, a more decentralized patter of wealth accumulation. Through a series of decisions diametrically opposed to those of their Tanzanian counterparts, the ruling elite in Kenya undertook the following measures: crucially, they encouraged individualization of land tenure, thereby favouring the growth of capitalist farmers; they pursued a less extensive nationalization process than in Tanzania while actively assisting private sector expansion; and, they encouraged 'straddling', hiking public sector salaries and funnelling patronage resources through individual politicians, who were *explicitly told* to cultivate their private wealth.

First, regarding 'antecedent conditions', some scholars contend that even before Independence in 1963, 'the economic and political weight of the indigenous owners of capital was already decisive'.[117] Much more so than in neighbouring Tanganyika, a class of African accumulators had started to coalesce under colonial rule.[118] Its growth was the result notably of British efforts to promote commercial agriculture through the provision of individual land titles to African farmers.[119] Concentrated in Kenya's Kikuyu-dominated Central Province, many of these early accumulators also took up leading positions in Kikuyu organizations involved in the nationalist movement.[120] With a

---

[117] Leys, 1978: 249.
[118] See: Shivji, 1976; Mueller, 1981; Kennedy, 1988.
[119] Gertzel, 1970: 47–48.
[120] Kennedy, 1988: 93–94.

Kikuyu Prime Minister and later President, Jomo Kenyatta, leading Kenya at Independence, it did indeed look as though an 'effective "power bloc" under the hegemony of the Kikuyu bourgeoisie' was poised to take 'strategic control over the post-colonial political re-alignments needed for the next phase of accumulation'.[121]

It is too simplistic, however, to suggest that the mere presence of an indigenous bourgeoisie predestined the post-colonial Kenyan state to adopt policies consistent with further capitalist expansion. For one, there are examples of other states, such as Ghana under Nkrumah, where a landowning capitalist class began to consolidate under colonial rule yet saw its growth stymied by the policies of the post-Independence government.[122] Moreover, Kenya's own post-colonial economic trajectory was the focus of intense debate and political struggle throughout the 1960s and into the 1970s. By 1965, how to manage land—and thus the distribution of agricultural surpluses—was perhaps *the* key source of disagreement dividing both the KANU parliamentary caucus and the Cabinet.[123] A 'conservative' faction favoured the Government's settlement policies, which involved selling off land, particularly in the formerly scheduled (i.e. European settler) areas. An opposing faction of 'radicals' instead advocated a more equitable distribution or cooperative management of land by the landless African masses. These critics were concerned that prevailing settlement policy would further concentrate land in the hands of a few wealthy individuals; it would, meanwhile, exclude the majority, who had participated in the nationalist struggle on the assumption that they too would benefit from Independence.[124]

Ultimately the conservatives retained the upper hand, although not without a political fight. Their dominance within KANU was reinforced after the party absorbed its only opposition rival post-Independence, the *Kenya African Democratic Union* (KADU).[125] President Kenyatta 'bought in' KADU notably by using the settlement scheme to redistribute land in areas populated by the minority ethnic communities from which the opposition party leaders drew their support.[126] Yet the merger with KADU presented Kenyatta with a fresh political challenge as tensions intensified within KANU itself.[127] The power struggle culminated in the KANU Vice President, Oginga Odinga, being

[121] Leys, 1978: 50.
[122] Iliffe, 1983: 77; Kennedy, 1988: 94–95; Boone, 1992: 25.
[123] Ghai, 1965; Gertzel, 1970: 32–54.
[124] Gertzel, 1970: 45–49.
[125] Ibid., 54.
[126] Bienen, 1974: 69, 146–149; Throup and Hornsby, 1998: 12.
[127] Gertzel, 1970: 55–72; Bienen, 1974: 68–69.

stripped of his position in 1966 and subsequently leading a faction of radicals to defect and form the opposition *Kenya People's Union* (KPU). Kenyatta and the KANU leadership responded by clamping down on dissent within KANU while repressing and, in 1969, banning KPU.

The political victory of the conservatives paved the way for Kenyatta's Government to adopt a more comprehensive strategy of 'politicized accumulation' favouring the further expansion of an indigenous bourgeoisie. On the land issue, the Government continued to favour individual ownership and the occupation of former European settler areas. This arrangement, coupled with enabling agricultural policies,[128] allowed for the expansion of commercial agriculture and provided the primary means of accumulation by an African elite through agricultural surpluses.[129] Additional policies favouring further private sector growth included preferential licensing for African entrepreneurs, privileged access to credit, and the take-over of Asian-owned businesses. Together, these measures spurred the diversification of African capitalist enterprise and its expansion into commerce, real estate, and, by the end of the 1970s, manufacturing.[130] Despite losing out to 'Kenyanization' policies, the remnants of the Asian community in Kenya also prospered, adding to the ranks of capitalist traders and industrialists.[131]

One indicator of overall private sector growth during the 1960s and into the 1970s is the domestic credit to the private sector as a percentage of GDP, which rose sharply from 13.2 per cent at Independence in 1963 to a pre-crisis high of 21.8 in 1980.[132] Meanwhile, nationalization and public sector expansion was less extensive in Kenya than in Tanzania. One crude measure of this is the number of state-owned enterprises, which by the 1980s figured 240 in Kenya versus 425 in Tanzania, nearly twice as many despite Tanzania's far smaller economy.[133] The end result was that the private sector contributed a significant share to overall processes of capitalist expansion and wealth accumulation in Kenya even as the public sector remained *relatively* small by regional standards.

While actively fostering a capitalist elite, government ensured—through support of 'straddling' practices—that this business elite directly reinforced

---

[128] Bates, 2014.
[129] Swainson, 1977, 1987.
[130] Swainson, 1977, 1987; Leys, 1978; Balachandran, 1981.
[131] Balachandran, 1981: 321.
[132] Accessed 20 July 2017: http://data.worldbank.org/indicator/FD.AST.PRVT.GD.ZS?locations= KE-TZ-UG-RW.
Note that similar data is not available for Tanzania until 1988, when it started to be collected as part of the financial liberalization process.
[133] Pitcher, 2012: 51.

and indeed overlapped with the KANU political and administrative elite. Instead of driving a wedge between politics and business, as happened in Tanzania, the KANU leadership nurtured well-connected politico-business factions within the ruling coalition. Civil servants were allowed and even encouraged to use their salaries to invest in private business interests.[134] Whereas Nyerere insisted he would 'slash the damned salaries in this country',[135] Kenyatta condoned MPs' lavish pay and special access to bank loans. He even endorsed their use of public office for private gain.[136] In a similar vein, the KANU Government set few restrictions on entrepreneurs who were keen to cultivate political ties in exchange for preferential access to credit and other benefits.[137] Indeed, these politico-business relations were expressly organized. For instance, the Gikuyu, Embu, and Meru Association (GEMA) was formed in 1971 'largely as a political and economic vehicle for the most powerful sections of the indigenous bourgeoisie.'[138] Long-time government ministers were among those to head GEMA.[139] Finally, Kenyatta encouraged *Harambee*, 'self-help' projects managed by politicians, who used personal and public funds to support constituency development. As observed by Widner, '*Harambee* contributions by the president, vice president, senior ministers and spokesmen for ethnic groups provided the currency to build coalitions and compensate groups for losses in representation or share of resources.'[140]

In sum, faced with a similar set of choices regarding land, private-sector promotion, and regulation of political finance, KANU leaders made decisions that contrasted sharply with those of their Tanzanian counterparts. The cumulative effect was the entrenchment of more decentralized wealth accumulation favouring the further consolidation of an African politico-cum-entrepreneurial elite.

3.2.2.2 Party Strengthening Efforts

The flip side of KANU leaders' strategy of 'politicized accumulation' was a willingness to forego party institutional strengthening. Where a degree of party-building *was* attempted, the effort proved unsuccessful due to factional infighting.

[134] Swainson, 1977: 43.
[135] Coulson, 2013: 221
[136] Cheeseman, 2006: 158.
[137] Bienen, 1974: 146–149. See also Shivji, 1976.
[138] Swainson, 1987: 155.
[139] Ibid.
[140] Widner, 1992: 34; see also Cheeseman, 2006.

Again, regarding 'antecedent conditions', some argue that KANU's institutional weakness can be explained 'as a legacy of colonial policy which tried to prevent the construction of a united national party' and instead restricted political organizing to the district level.[141] Even so, scholars maintain that the colonial legacy was 'not the only factor that made for maintenance of a district base in Kenyan politics'.[142] Other significant factors included Jomo Kenyatta's seeming distaste for party-building in the post-Independence period as he preferred to rely on the civil service alone 'as an instrument of rule'.[143] He therefore 'never appeared to take seriously the prospect of ruling through the party'.[144]

The 'benign neglect' of party institutions aside,[145] their strength and coherence was further undermined by the fractious patronage politics within KANU as politicians and allied financiers poured cash into building district-level political machines. The significance of this political finance was revealed notably during party primaries, which from 1969 replaced multiparty general elections.[146] With no limits set on the number of candidates per constituency, on average four contested each parliamentary seat with some constituencies contested by upwards of 10 candidates.[147] Who ultimately won these internal party contests was, to a significant degree, a function of candidates' ability to outbid their rivals, funnelling their own resources into campaigns while also marshalling the support of more far-reaching factional alliances and private sector backers.[148] Any official party presence, by contrast, was minimal if not entirely absent.

Given the lack of a cohesive and disciplined party organization, coalition maintenance under KANU hinged on the skilful management of 'politicized accumulation', patronage distribution and, where all else failed, coercive measures. Until his death in 1978, Kenyatta deflected any latent political threat—not least from newly enriched local 'Big Men'[149]—through a roughly proportional national redistribution of patronage, although he favoured an inner circle of Kikuyu elites most closely linked to his home district of Kiambu. The primary platform—both economic and political—for this Kiambu faction was the above-mentioned GEMA. The GEMA Holdings Company developed its economic interests in agriculture, real estate, commerce, banking,

---

[141] Gertzel, 1970: 9; Bienen, 1974: 85–86.
[142] Bienen, 1974: 87.
[143] Okumu and Holmquist, 1984: 50.
[144] Bienen, 1974: 79.
[145] Okumu and Holmquist, 1984: 50.
[146] Hyden and Leys, 1972; Okumu and Holmquist, 1984.
[147] Hyden and Leys, 1972: 397.
[148] Ibid., 404.
[149] Throup and Hornsby, 1998: Ajulu, 1999; Cheeseman, 2006: 166.

and manufacturing.[150] At the same time, the Association acted as a 'substitute' for the 'defunct' KANU party, mobilizing funds and fielding election candidates.[151] The Kiambu elite had to tolerate certain degree of compromise so as to preserve the wider KANU coalition. Where directly challenged, though, particularly from within its own Kikuyu ethnic bastion, it resorted to repression and, in at least three instances, assassination.[152]

This apparent preference for informal as opposed to formal political organization within KANU did not go unquestioned; the costs incurred as a result of ad hoc elite bargaining prompted repeated 'injunctions to KANU to be better organized and disciplined'.[153] Belated party-building attempts nevertheless proved unsuccessful. Kenyatta appointed a special KANU committee in 1970 to make recommendations on how best to 'reorganize, reactive and revitalize KANU', thereby ensuring the Party stayed 'attuned to the aspirations of the people'.[154] Somewhat unsurprisingly, the Committee's report observed that 'instead of the [KANU] Constitution ruling the Party, this was replaced by personality cult and individuals gave directives far removed from the constitution only to bring about dissatisfaction and disillusions [...]'.[155] To address these concerns, the report called for a 'thorough overhaul of the structure of the Party'. Recommended reforms were later approved by a meeting of the KANU National Governing Council, during which Kenyatta condemned the corrosive effects of 'corruption and bribery'.[156] The belated 'overhaul' proved no match, though, when confronted with the 'corruption and bribery' it sought to tame. KANU's Organizing Secretary, John Keen, described the party's organization by the mid-1970s as 'appalling'.[157] To the extent that there was a national party system under KANU in the 1960s and early 70s, it remained 'one of patron–client ties built around individuals who cross[ed] into each other's districts or organizations'.[158]

To recap, this section accounts for KANU's consolidation as a 'bargained coalition' featuring relatively decentralized patron–client networks competing within the loosest of institutional frameworks. While influenced by the legacy of colonial rule, this outcome was nevertheless the product of a critical juncture. An early period of political struggle and debate in post-colonial Kenya

---

[150] Swainson, 1987: 155–156.
[151] Ibid.
[152] Throup and Hornsby, 1998: 19–20; Cheeseman, 2006: 166–170.
[153] Bienen, 1974: 79.
[154] KANU (1970), 'Report by the KANU Re-Organizing Committee'.
[155] Ibid.
[156] KANU (1971), 'Meeting of the KANU National Governing Council'.
[157] Throup and Hornsby, 1998: 18.
[158] Bienen, 1974: 99.

culminated, unlike in neighbouring Tanzania, in a decision by KANU leaders to favour a relatively decentralized pattern of accumulation while foregoing party-building. Once entrenched, Kenya's more diffuse wealth accumulation and patronage distribution ensured that subsequent, half-hearted efforts to strengthen the party came to naught. The contrasting outcomes in Tanzania and Kenya ultimately indicate the ability of post-Independence leaders, when faced with similar economic policy and party-building options, to pursue starkly contrasting paths, each leading to very different forms of party consolidation.

With regards to post-Independence regimes, it is worth noting that the labels of 'socialist'—applied to the likes of Tanzania, Ghana under Nkrumah, and Zambia, among others—or 'capitalist'—applied, for instance, to Kenya and Nigeria—are not a reliable indicator of leaders' policy orientation and associated strategy of 'politicized accumulation'. For instance, Zambia's Kenneth Kaunda seemingly espoused a modified socialism and was undoubtedly influenced by Nyerere in Tanzania. Yet he also found it politically expedient to allow for 'indigenization' and the growth of an African entrepreneurial elite. The more decentralized pattern of wealth accumulation then allowed for the fragmentation of patronage networks within Zambia's ruling United National Independence Party, eroding its institutional strength and ultimately contributing to its defeat by the Movement for Multiparty Democracy in 1991.[159] As such, the Zambian case indicates the need for careful empirical analysis of *actual economic policy and its effects*, rather than a reliance on ideological labels, if we are to understand authoritarian party consolidation.

3.3 Post-'Liberation' Regimes

Following Africa's initial wave of decolonization, subsequent regimes differed from their 1960s counterparts in that they generally gained power through violent means: after a belated and more conflictual Independence struggle;[160] after a military coup;[161] or starting with Uganda in 1986, on the back of an armed insurgency.[162] These later regimes also faced a transformed economic and geopolitical environment. By the 1980s, the economic crisis sweeping

---

[159] Baylies and Szeftel, 1984; Makoba, 1998.
[160] These include the Portuguese colonies as well as countries under white minority rule.
[161] For instance, the *People's Revolutionary Party of Benin* (1975–1990).
[162] These include the *National Resistance Movement* of Uganda (1986), the *Eritrean People's Liberation Front* (1991), the *Ethiopian People's Revolutionary Democratic Front* (1991), and the *Rwandan Patriotic Front* (1994).

across the region and the International Financial Institutions' (IFIs) new insistence on structural adjustment reforms narrowed the range of economic policy options available to ruling elites. The collapse of the Soviet Union by the 1990s further limited what policies remained on the table.

As mentioned at the start of this chapter, the changed circumstances of these later regimes might be expected to have influenced both their economic and institutional consolidation. The IFIs emphasis on 'curbing corruption' through 'less government' and private sector-led growth suggests ruling elites would no longer be free to pursue their preferred strategies of 'politicized accumulation'.[163] At the same time, a more violent struggle to gain power is thought to encourage the consolidation of 'organizational weapons' and, subsequently, stronger ruling party institutions.[164] In reality, though, the determinants of authoritarian regime consolidation in the 1980s and 1990s were similar to those informing regime outcomes in the post-Independence period.

First, newly instated ruling elites still exercised high levels of agency in moulding patterns of 'politicized accumulation' to their advantage. As one observer noted of the EPRDF regime after it formed a government in 1991, 'Ethiopian state-building was driven less by world-historical forces, and more by the energies and capabilities of [President Meles] who briefly succeeded, through intellectual power and political skill, in centralizing control over rent in his office'.[165] To achieve their desired ends, leaders deployed many of *the same* strategies of politicized accumulation as before, including: discretionary enforcement of regulatory and tax requirements, to determine the size and make-up of a private accumulating class; diverse strategies of managing land ownership, despite IFI-backed efforts to promote freehold tenure;[166] and both 'straddling' practices and more predatory forms of accumulation through siphoning public resources, again despite the IFIs' anti-corruption drive. African leaders did have to abandon large-scale nationalization efforts, though, as donors demanded the privatization of state-owned enterprises. Yet not all regimes complied with this privatization agenda equally,[167] and new regimes found alternative ways of centralizing wealth accumulation, such as through party- and military-owned enterprises (Table 3.3).

Besides pursuing contrasting strategies of 'politicized accumulation', regimes consolidating in the 1980s and 1990s also formed contrasting party institutions. Despite their shared experience of violent confrontation, ruling

[163] World Bank, 1989: 55, 61.
[164] Smith, 2005; Levitsky and Way, 2012.
[165] De Waal, 2015: 12.
[166] Boone, 2007.
[167] Pitcher, 2012.

Table 3.3 Policy orientation and accumulation patterns of post-liberation regimes

		Pattern of wealth accumulation	
		Centralized	Decentralized
Key areas of economic decision-making	Promotion of private entrepreneurs or party- and military-owned enterprise	Preference for party- and military-owned enterprise, which benefit from access to credit, procurement contracts and other financial benefits that the state can still control; parallel restrictions on the strength and autonomy of private entrepreneurs.	Preference for private entrepreneurs, albeit favouring a regime-aligned business constituency. Absence of notable party- or military-owned firms.
	Land tenure system	As before.	As before.
	Attitude towards 'straddling'	As before.	As before.

elites allowed for weak party organizations in some cases and built up strong ones in others. As before, these contrasting institutional outcomes were informed by differences in underlying patterns of wealth accumulation.

The ensuing analysis illustrates these points through a comparison of Uganda and Rwanda. It demonstrates how the newly instated ruling elites in the 1980s and 1990s pursued contrasting strategies of 'politicized accumulation', and this even as both governments acquired reputations as 'donor darlings' for seemingly embracing IFI-backed economic reforms. The contrasting outcomes of these 'politicized accumulation' strategies—leading in Uganda to decentralized and in Rwanda to more centralized wealth accumulation—then informed the extent of party-strengthening. This institutional variation came about despite both the Ugandan and Rwandan regimes pursuing a violent path to power.

3.3.1 Uganda—Consolidation of a 'Bargained Coalition'

After taking power in 1986, the *National Resistance Movement* (NRM) consolidated as a 'bargained coalition', featuring a relatively diffuse pattern of wealth accumulation and fragmented patronage structure as well as low levels of party institutional strength. This outcome, although influenced by both antecedent conditions as well a domestic and external constraints, was decisively shaped by a set of *strategic decisions made by the NRM leadership*. I address these in turn, analysing first the choice of economic policies and then the preference for a more personalized machine politics over the institution of formal party structures.

3.3.1.1 Economic Policy

NRM leaders favoured a more decentralized pattern of politicized accumulation. Yet while their strategy enabled private accumulation, it tended to ensure the continued political vulnerability and dependence of this emerging accumulating class. NRM leaders achieved this outcome by using a range of interventions to favour foreign and Asian entrepreneurs and an elite strata of regime loyalists all while neglecting or actively discouraged domestic entrepreneurs, particularly those deemed politically hostile.

Regarding 'antecedent conditions', the tendency to prefer foreign and Asian capital alongside close regime allies is not without precedent in Uganda. The country's first post-Independence President, Milton Obote, hailed from the economically marginalized northern region. After political relations soured with the more affluent Buganda Kingdom in central Uganda,[168] Obote pushed a controversial 'Ugandanization' policy that favoured notably Ugandan citizens of Asian origin while side-lining a Baganda entrepreneurial elite.[169] This Asian commercial and industrial elite, in turn, helped finance Obote's *Uganda People's Congress* (UPC).[170] Obote also sought to secure the loyalty of the fractious UPC elite by allowing ministers, party officials and parliamentarians to siphon public funds.[171] Following the 1971 coup, Idi Amin responded to popular disaffection with a perceived Asian elite by overseeing the mass expulsion of Asians in 1972. Expropriated Asian properties were then redistributed to regime supporters, a process of appropriation and redistribution repeated after Amin's 1979 overthrow and Obote's return to power in 1980.[172]

When the NRM, under the leadership of Yoweri Museveni, took power in 1986, there was nothing predetermined about what economic strategy it would adopt; rather, it embarked on a period of experimentation. It first sought to implement an avowedly socialist economic agenda, engaging in barter trade with Cuba and the Soviet Union, but the leadership did a U-turn in late 1986 amidst fears that a worsening economic crisis would erode the NRM's as-yet fragile popular support.[173] Museveni's government reached a first agreement

---

[168] Twaddle and Hansen, 1998: 12.
[169] Jorgensen, 1981: 248–252; Mamdani, 1995: 35.
[170] Jorgensen, 1981: 249.
[171] Ibid., 252.
[172] Mamdani, 1988: 1161–1162; Hansen, 2013.
[173] Mugyenyi, 1991: 69–70.

with the IMF in 1987. While efforts on the part of the Ugandan government to stall implementation of IMF conditionalities continued for another year, a sharp increase in inflation prompted the NRM government to commit to a donor-backed reform package in 1988.[174] As one NRM official from the time recalls, 'We went from extreme left ideas to extreme right.'[175] But as President Museveni also insists in his autobiography, 'We did not adopt market economics as a consequence of pressure, but because we were convinced it was the correct thing to do for our country.'[176]

This apparent conversion to a 'free market economy'[177]—a move many observers saw as inevitable given the dire economic situation[178]—was not the end of the story, though. Indeed, what followed was further experimentation, debate, and political struggle. This experimentation included various forays down what proved to be blind allies. The NRM dabbled, for instance, in a variety of military- and party-owned enterprises. Shortly after coming to power, the then *National Resistance Army*, the military wing of the NRM, created the National Enterprise Corporation, which Museveni declared would 'train, organize and utilize the army personnel to develop and carry out scientific, technological, industrial, construction and contracted service activities on a commercial basis.'[179] The Corporation continues to operate but is of negligible significance to the wider Ugandan economy.[180] Two attempts at starting party-owned enterprises, meanwhile, turned into nothing more than pre-election efforts to raise funds for NRM campaigns, ultimately through fraudulent means.[181]

Given the NRM's failure to develop its own entrepreneurial interests, President Museveni and his inner circle focused their attention instead on a series of initiatives that, far from approximating the IFI-championed 'free market' ideal, favoured the consolidation of a politically dependent class of entrepreneurs and non-productive accumulators. A first key intervention concerned the decision to return expropriated property to its original Asian owners. This move had both an economic and political rationale. Asians re-investing in

---

[174] Ibid., 73; Ochieng, 1991: 58.
[175] Interview with NRM MP, Kampala, November 2014.
[176] Museveni, 1997: 181.
[177] Ibid., 182.
[178] Southall, 1988: 67; Mugyenyi, 1991: 75.
[179] Mudoola, 1991: 241.
[180] In the 2010s, the Corporation was tasked with catalysing a transition to commercial farming through a costly yet ultimately ineffective tractor hire scheme. This example suggests the Corporation may be little more than a means of channelling patronage through the military. Accessed 24 April 2017: http://www.sunrise.ug/news/analysis/201406/can-the-army-feed-uganda-when-it-can-t-feed-itself.html.
[181] Tangri and Mwenda, 2013: 107–108.

the Ugandan economy promised to boost growth and to increase government revenues.[182] Meanwhile, their return heralded the re-emergence of a politically non-threatening, even dependent entrepreneurial elite. While various accounts suggest that a policy to return expropriated properties was first pushed as one of the IMF conditionalities,[183] President Museveni soon became the chief defender of the move. Faced with considerable opposition within the NRM government, he recalls personally chairing the Cabinet meetings and the sitting of the National Resistance Council (NRC)—the then legislative body—to see through the initiative.[184]

Ultimately a small minority of some 8,000 expelled Asians sought to repossess their properties, mostly the former owners of large-scale industrial, commercial, and residential assets.[185] The Asian presence nevertheless soon became pronounced across all major sectors of the economy, including commercial agriculture and processing, trade, manufacturing, banking, and forex, among others.[186] Some of the most prominent family names from the colonial and immediate post-colonial period, such as the Madhvani and Mehta families, were 'rejuvenated'.[187] Others, like the Ruparelia family rose to new heights.[188] Meanwhile, President Museveni and his ministers also sought to attract new Asian investors, promising tax holidays and an attractive investment code.[189]

These incentives were not matched by parallel efforts to support indigenous entrepreneurs, despite growing concern over 'Indian domination' and 'control of [the] economy'.[190] For instance, although tax reforms in the early 1990s were ostensibly aimed at reducing tax exemptions, the number of exemptions awarded to foreign- and jointly-owned large firms in fact *increased* by the end of the decade, leaving mostly Ugandan-owned medium-sized firms to shoulder a disproportionate share of the tax burden.[191] The NRM government also did little to reduce interest rates and ease access to credit, even as small- and medium-sized firms continued to cite these as 'major obstacles' accounting for their low rate of investment relative to larger firms.[192] As one long-time analyst

---

[182] Abidi, 1996: 45; Tangri and Mwenda, 2019.
[183] Mamdani, 1995: 87; Himbara, 1997: 16.
[184] Museveni, 1997: 181–182.
[185] Mamdani, 1995: 87.
[186] Abidi, 1996: 54–55.
[187] Ibid.; Himbara, 1997: 16–17.
[188] Tangri and Mwenda, 2019.
[189] Abidi, 1996: 53, 57–58.
[190] Abidi, 1996: 57; Tangri, 2015.
[191] Gauthier and Reinikka, 2006.
[192] Reinikka and Svensson, 2001: 213–214, 221.

of Uganda's political economy concludes, 'President Museveni seems wary of wealthy Ugandan entrepreneurs who emerge outside his ambit and who could potentially challenge his authority.'[193] Meanwhile, prominent Asian later began donating generously to President Museveni's presidential re-election campaigns, even as they receive substantial tax breaks and capital subsidies, among other favours.[194]

Leaving aside the return of Asian properties, a second significant area of economic decision-making relates to land reform. This remains an enduring source of controversy. President Museveni and the NRM leadership have sought to institute a land tenure system favouring freehold tenure, the idea being that this is more conducive to commercial farming; however, they have also tried to increase the power of the central government—and thus the NRM elite—over the allocation and administration of land. The net result is to favour private accumulation through land but in a manner that can be policed to favour a privileged elite.

Two emblematic political struggles over land flared during the sitting of Constituent Assembly (1994–1995), tasked with approving the 1995 Constitution, and have remained live issues ever since.[195] The first concerned the *mailo* land system peculiar to the Buganda Kingdom.[196] The NRM regime early on tried to consolidate its support within Buganda, not least by answering calls the return of the King or *Kabaka*, first exiled under Obote in 1966. However, the NRM leadership was primarily from Western Uganda and were careful to limit the powers it granted the Kingdom, which was meant to be a 'cultural' and not a political institution.[197] Control of land was central to curbing Buganda's real political as well as economic heft. Whereas the Kabaka and other Kingdom leaders lobbied the Constituent Assembly to vest powers over land administration within a regional land board with the Kabaka as trustee, this arrangement was strongly resisted by the informal NRM caucus in the Assembly, which ultimately called for more comprehensive land reform

---

[193] Mwenda, 2008; Tangri and Mwenda, 2019: 688.

[194] Tangri and Mwenda, 2013: 111. See also Chapter 8, 'Corruption in Political Finance'. On funding of Museveni's 2016 presidential campaign, see: Alliance of Campaign Finance Monitoring Final Report, 2016.

[195] Marquardt and Sebina-Zziwa, 1998: 182–183.
Interview with former Constituent Assembly member and later UPC MP, Kampala, January 2015.
Interview with former Constituent Assembly member and later FDC MP, Kampala, January 2015.

[196] Mailo land refers to the parcelling out of land by the British in the early twentieth century to the King of Buganda, the Kabaka, and Baganda Chiefs. This land allocation set the stage for what evolved into a deadlock over land rights opposing landowners 'who possessed de jure freehold over the parcels' and tenants who came to '[enjoy] de facto freehold' (Marquardt and Sebina-Zziwa, 1988: 177).

[197] Doornbos and Mwesigye, 1995: 61–64.

legislation to be introduced.[198] This call led to the 1998 Land Act, which went counter to Buganda demands, leaving the central state to administer *mailo* land while privileging the land rights of land occupants over owners, thereby disadvantaging the Buganda aristocracy.[199] This outcome further consolidated the political power of the central state over Buganda and clipped the wings of a would-be commercial-cum-political Baganda elite.

The second land-related issue to rock the Constituent Assembly related to the state's power to acquire land compulsorily for investment purposes.[200] As one former member of the Constituent Assembly recalled, 'The President kept saying, "I want land to give to my investors. I want land to give to my investors."' These repeated calls, however, fed an 'underlying suspicion' as 'people started to wonder, "Who are these investors?"'[201] Many within the Constituent Assembly concluded, 'This man wanted land for his own use, to give to his cohorts.'[202] Ultimately, Constituent Assembly members, including several high-ranking ministers in Museveni's Cabinet, 'revolted', refusing to grant the state such wide-ranging powers. As another former member recalled, when Museveni addressed the Constituent Assembly following the adoption of the 1995 Constitution, he made clear, 'You have made a beautiful constitution, but I am unhappy with two areas.'[203] One of them was land.

Despite these setbacks, Museveni's government has repeatedly tried to strengthen the state's power to acquire land, including for investment purposes.[204] Pending a legal solution on this issue, Museveni has resorted to giving away publicly owned land to investors, not least the Madhvanhi and Mehta groups.[205] There is also growing concern about state-sanctioned land-grabbing and speculative purchasing of land by politically connected elites, particularly in the post-conflict northern and oil-rich western regions.[206] Referring to these practices, one of the former Constituent Assembly members concluded wryly,

---

[198] Constituent Assembly members formed several informal groupings, which included the government aligned NRM caucus, a Buganda caucus and a caucus in favour of returning to multiparty competition.

[199] Coldham, 2000; Green, 2006; Boone, 2007.

[200] Marquardt and Sebina-Zziwa, 1998: 177, 182–183; Interview, January 2015; Interview, former Constituent Assembly member, January 2015.

[201] Interview, former Constituent Assembly member, January 2015.

[202] Ibid. See also interview, former Constituent Assembly member, January 2015.

[203] Interview, former Constituent Assembly member, January 2015.

[204] 'Government White Paper on: (1) The Report of the Commission of Inquiry (Constitutional Review); (2) Government Proposals not addressed by the report of the Commission of Inquiry (Constitutional Review)', 2004.

'Uganda will face lengthy battle over land acquisition', *Oxford Analytica*, 28 September 2017.

[205] Tangri and Mwenda, 2013: 111.

[206] Mabikke, 2011; Interview with NRM MP, Kampala, February 2015.

Accessed 23 July 2017: http://www.monitor.co.ug/SpecialReports/Government-treads-slippery-path-Madhvani-Amuru-land-saga/688342-3862718-ahoanq/index.html.

'There is a small group of either politicians or business people who have miles, square miles of land in this country. So maybe we were not wrong to be suspicious.'[207] Regime-backed efforts to redistribute land, whether through a de jure process or de facto give-aways, has thus contributed to a pattern of private wealth accumulation favouring a well-connected politico-business (and military) elite.

The handling of a third controversial issue—namely privatization— provides a final focal point by which to illustrate the NRM leadership's strategy of 'politicized accumulation'. While privatization was, again, a policy initially pushed by the IFIs, Museveni soon embraced the initiative.[208] Faced with mounting opposition both within his Cabinet and the National Resistance Council, he personally intervened to chair a debate over the Divestiture Statute, ultimately passed in August 1993.[209] Two years later, he issued a presidential directive to expedite the process, which remained mired in controversy. The initial concern was that privatization was 'designed to attract foreign investment', a 'cornerstone of NRM government economic policy'.[210] There was little interest on the part of government, by contrast, in compensating for the 'lack of domestic capital to facilitate the privatization policy', which effectively 'ignored broadening of ownership'.[211]

As the privatization process went ahead, picking up speed in the second half of the 1990s, an additional set of concerns rose to the fore, namely endemic 'corruption and cronyism', which fits a wider pattern of predatory accumulation under NRM rule.[212] Among the chief beneficiaries of privatization were family and close friends of Museveni and his wife, Janet, as well as prominent ministers. The firms they acquired were then conspicuous contributors to the NRM's 2001 election campaigns.[213] As the prominent Ugandan journalist, Charles Onyango-Obbo summarized, 'Top leaders in government chose to use privatization as a political support-building project [...]. When the enterprises were being sold to Ugandans, most went to ruling Movement members. [...]. The aim was to create a pro-regime business constituency.'[214] The

---

Accessed 23 July 2017: http://www.monitor.co.ug/SpecialReports/Combating-land-grabbing-in-the-oil-rich-districts/688342-3503598-t12is4z/index.html.

[207] Interview, former Constituent Assembly member, January 2015.
[208] See especially Chapter 5; Tukahebwa, 1998; Tangri and Mwenda, 2013.
[209] Museveni, 1997: 182; Nyirinkindi and Opagi, 2010: 360.
[210] Tukahebwa, 1998: 67.
[211] Ibid., 65–66, 71; Nyirinkindi and Opagi, 2010: 370; see also Tangri and Mwenda, 2013.
[212] Tangri and Mwenda, 2013.
[213] Ibid., 112.
[214] Cited in Tangri and Mwenda, 2013: 67.

privatization process was ultimately wound up in 2006 shortly after the World Bank suspended funds to the government's Privatization Unit citing political interference and lack of transparency.[215]

More generally, be it through the return of Asian properties, the preferential allocation of land, or the politicized privatization process, the NRM regime has ensured that political connections 'matter a great deal with regard to the profitability of businesses', enabling a minority to benefit disproportionately.[216] This has only grown more pronounced as labour-intensive agriculture has decline as a share of GDP to be replaced by capital-intensive service sector and some manufacturing activities. Business in these expanding sectors—be it commercial exporters, miners, firms producing for the domestic market, or service providers in transport, hospitality, and telecommunications—remain dominated by relatively few well-connected actors. Big firms have often relied since their inception on particularistic deals struck with President Museveni's inner circle and continue to offer large donations to the ruling party and various NRM elite.[217]

Very often the political inner circle and the top business elite are, in fact, one and the same, part of a revolving door between politics and business. As noted earlier with regards to privatization, Museveni's own family benefited significantly. Meanwhile, far from any Nyerere-esque Leadership Code, many government officials and politicians, including MPs, use their political stature to ensure preferential treatment by the Uganda Revenue Authority and other government actors.[218] The granting of high salaries and allowances to civil servants and elected politicians, especially parliamentarians, has also served to quell dissent and to encourage a perception of public office as an avenue to personal enrichment.[219] In keeping with the logic of 'straddling', MPs interviewed for this book recounted their plans to reinvest their salaries in real estate and farming as part of a strategy to turn political office into a basis for long-term financial gain. Finally, there have also been ample opportunities for accumulation by the military elite, another crucial pillar of Museveni's regime.[220]

In sum, following a largely inconsequential experiment with military- and party-owned enterprise, the NRM leadership pursued a strategy of 'politicized

[215] Accessed 23 July 2017: http://allafrica.com/stories/200603140706.html.
[216] Kjaer and Katusiimeh, 2012; Tangri and Mwenda, 2013, 2019; Bukenya and Hickey, 2017: 202.
[217] Bukenya and Hickey, 2017; Tangri and Mwenda, 2019.
[218] Bukenya and Hickey, 2017.
[219] Collord, 2016.
[220] Tangri and Mwenda, 2003; Vlassenroot et al., 2012; Khisa, 2016 & 2020.

accumulation' favouring the expansion of a private accumulating class. This elite came to be dominated by a politico-business elite supportive of—and largely dependent on—continued NRM rule. The leadership achieved this outcome through its backing of foreign and Asian investment, its manipulation of land reform and acquisition, and its exploitation of the privatization process. More generally, it continues to favour particularistic exchange relations between a relatively narrow set of business elites and Museveni's inner circle, trading financial contributions for political favours. Political office, too, serves as a route towards financial enrichment, or at least is perceived as such, even if—as discussed more later—it is also a major source of indebtedness and financial precarity. In any event, Museveni has endeavoured to build up an elite coalition that sees its participation within the NRM regime—and particularly its loyalty to the President—as key to further economic empowerment.

3.3.1.2 Party Strengthening Efforts

During the initial period of regime consolidation, the NRM leaders' preference for private accumulation and a more diffuse pattern of wealth accumulation, albeit one favouring regime-aligned elites, encouraged a form of political organization based on loose factional alliances. There was, meanwhile, little by way of formal party-building. As ever, this outcome was in part informed by 'antecedent conditions', yet even so, there was considerable debate and uncertainty regarding what organizational form the NRM should assume after taking power in 1986. Amidst ongoing political tensions, a de facto resolution emerged as rival patron–client networks took hold, thereby entrenching a largely personalized and fractious form of political organization within the NRM with little by way of formal structures.

Prior to the NRM regime, Uganda did not have a history of strong party institutions. Early efforts at nationalist organizing foundered in the 1950s, and break away parties—including Obote's *Uganda People's Congress* (UPC)—did not invest in party-building.[221] The UPC amounted to no more than a 'national confederation of locally powerful political notables',[222] a party defined by its 'patron–client nature'.[223] As Obote struggled to keep his coalition together, he found himself negotiating with a range of different power-brokers, thereby forming a succession of 'composed majorities'.[224]

---

[221] Sathyamurthy, 1975; Jorgensen, 1981; Low, 1988.
[222] Jorgensen, 1981: 221–222. See also Sathyamurthy, 1975; Mudoola, 1988: 286.
[223] Mudoola, 1988: 288–289.
[224] Low, 1988.

When Museveni's NRM first took power, one of its core promises was to break with Uganda's fraught history of party politics, which apart from the weak organization of the individual parties, had exacerbated both ethnic and religious tensions. NRM leaders proposed to transcend this troubled past through the introduction of a 'Movement' or 'no-party' system rooted in mass participation and electoral competition based on the principle of 'individual merit'.[225] What the Movement would look like in practice was unclear and remained the subject of intense debate. Of particular concern was whether and when Uganda would return to multiparty politics, given that the 'Movement' system was first announced as an interim arrangement. A related question was what organizational form the NRM should itself assume.

The question of Movement versus multiparty politics was at first put to one side after Museveni committed to forming a 'broad based' government, which included several ministers from the *Democratic Party* (DP), long-time rival of the ousted UPC. This government was meant to last the duration of an initial four-year transition period, which was indefinitely extended in 1989 pending the conclusion of a constitutional review process. Relations with the DP, meanwhile, deteriorated as the party began to fracture, divided between those who demanded an immediate return to multiparty politics and those leaders still committed to maintaining their Cabinet seats and working with the NRM.[226] Then, in 1995, the Constituent Assembly enshrined the Movement system within Uganda's Constitution. This decision came despite fierce opposition from 'Multiparty-ists' within the Assembly, who denounced the move as tantamount to the creation of a one-party state.[227] Indeed, the new constitution did effectively mark the end of any pretence of broad-based government.

The shift towards a de facto one-party state nevertheless left open the second question, namely how the NRM itself should organize politically. Throughout the late 1980s and into the 1990s, debate over the preferred organizational form persisted, albeit in 'hushed' tones.[228] One option considered was to allow the armed wing of the NRM, the National Resistance Army (NRA), to continue providing institutional leadership. Certainly, the High Command and Army Council retained a considerable degree of influence over key decisions while military officers also held a large proportion of seats in the National Resistance Council, the legislative body until the 1995 Constitution

---

[225] Carbone, 2008. See the introduction.
[226] Kasfir, 1991: 254–255; Mamdani, 1995.
[227] Mamdani, 1995; Kasfir, 2000; Oloka-Onyango, 2000.
[228] Mamdani, 1988: 1174.

introduced the National Assembly.[229] The army was also involved in grassroots level mobilizing, notably through the *mchakamchaka*[230] ideology and training initiatives for civilians and NRM cadres.[231]

Even so, it is not enough to focus on the army when explaining political organization under the NRM regime. A second contender as the locus of NRM organizing was its own bureaucratic structures. After taking Uganda's capital Kampala in 1986, the NRM established a Secretariat, which began to work 'as though a new organisation was about to be established'.[232] Over the ensuing years, though, the Secretariat retained only a small budget and few powerful officials amongst its staff, thus ensuring its influence was dwarfed by competing institutions.[233]

A final major organizational focus was the system of Resistance Councils (RCs), which first emerged as civilian village committees in NRM 'safe zones' during the 1981–1986 civil war. In the early years of the NRM government, the RCs were presented as the basic organizational units of the new, supposedly more participatory form of Movement governance. The idealized picture never matched reality, though, as the RCs first arose out of military expediency, the aim being to secure civilian support for the NRM, and relied more on the mobilization of key local notables than popular consensus.[234] After 1986, moreover, a 'bureaucratic view' quickly took hold, and the RCs were transformed into 'appendages of the civil service created to implement government policy'.[235]

Even as debate continued over what organizational form the NRM should adopt, an informal pattern of factional organizing began to emerge, spurred notably by the first elections conducted under the 'Movement' system. An inaugural *indirect* election to the NRC was held in 1989 and was followed by a direct election to the Constituent Assembly in 1994. Parliamentary and presidential elections were then held every five years starting in 1996. The 1989 'snap' election was called on very short notice and overseen by the Ministry of Local Government and the National Political Commissar, the head of the NRM Secretariat.[236] The intention was seemingly to hold an election

---

[229] Mudoola, 1991: 235.
[230] Marching or jogging in Swahili.
[231] Interview, NRM MP, November 2014.
[232] Mamdani, 1988: 1175.
[233] Kasfir, 1991: 255–256; Mamdani, 1988: 1175.
[234] Kasfir, 2005: 284.
[235] Mamdani, 1988: 1176.
[236] Kasfir, 1991: 259–260.

according to similar principles as elections under TANU in Tanzania.[237] Of particular note was the focus on sanctioned meetings organized through the local council system as well as the ban on private campaigning. 'Quiet' campaigning did persist in the sidelines but was kept to a minimum. This was partly because of the limited time to mobilize due to the short notice.[238] Some observers saw this as an intended consequence given fears that established local notables and politicians affiliated to old parties—especially the DP and UPC—could activate their networks and raise enough money to outperform candidates sympathetic to the NRM and its leaders.[239]

The somewhat muted campaigns of 1989 gave way to a more aggressive—and expensive—form of electioneering in 1994. The Constituent Assembly elections were marked by lavish spending.[240] One newspaper article acknowledged, 'We all know that the Constituent Assembly elections have been [...] in most [areas] influenced by booze, eating, money and other inducements.'[241] One winning candidate allegedly hired a plane to drop leaflets in his constituency while another handed out cows worth Ush30-40 million in areas that gave him majorities. NRM officials appeared to be the primary source of this largesse. They denied providing funding to candidates, yet top leaders—including Museveni, Vice President, Solomon Kisekka, and NRM Vice Chairman, Moses Kigongo—campaigned publicly for NRM candidates. It did not matter that many of these favourites were running against other NRM-sympathizing candidates.[242]

The 1996 general elections witnessed even higher spending and more intense factional rivalries. The NRM kept up the pretence of a TANU-style campaign with all candidates travelling together to address voters. But top NRM cadres and prominent business elites—often one and the same—intervened to sway elections.[243] Reflecting on the 1996 campaigns in his autobiography, Museveni was frank about the electoral significance of Uganda's new class of accumulators; he nevertheless sought to distinguish between the illegitimate 'parasites' supporting the opposition, which mobilized informally despite a ban on party activities, and the more virtuous 'businessmen' backing

---

[237] Museveni admired Nyerere and sought to emulate aspects of the TANU organizational approach. See: Museveni, 1997.
[238] Kasfir, 1991: 267–268.
[239] Ibid., 68.
[240] Geist, 1995; Kasfir, 1995.
[241] Citing *New Vision*, Kasfir, 1995: 165.
[242] Ibid., 175.
[243] Individuals involved in the 1996 recalled heavy spending during a series of workshops on campaign finance reform convened by the *National Democratic Institute* in Kampala between 2015 and 2016.

the NRM.[244] The opposition supposedly relied on the corrupt beneficiaries of past state patronage, or as Museveni rather colourfully described them, 'the *mafuta mingi*',[245] people 'who had received businesses stolen from the Asians expelled during Amin's time [...] and the political elites of former regimes who sat like vultures making merry over the carcasses of cows killed by an epidemic.'[246] Meanwhile, Museveni cast the NRM's 'natural constituency' as 'the real producers who have factories and farms [...].'[247] He even praised prominent entrepreneurs on the campaign trail, for instance, citing the Madhvani family by name when addressing a rally.[248]

Museveni's spin aside, other observers offered a more circumspect view of the emerging trend in campaign finance. Major Peter Rabwoni Okwiri, a long-serving soldier, attacked NRM bigshots for 'undermining the electoral process', adding, 'The injection of money into the campaigns by some leading figures in the movement is turning politics into a business.'[249] By the 2001 election, any effort to organize common campaign caravans or to limit private campaigning was abandoned. Instead, 'personal campaign machines' became the norm, funded with the contributions from NRM top cadres in highly competitive parliamentary elections averaging four candidates per constituency.[250] NRM-leaning candidates seen as too critical of the government or else at odds with one of the NRM top leaders were actively 'de-campaigned', a word used in Uganda to designate the mix of money and coercion used to undermine candidates.[251]

In sum, post-1986, Uganda's NRM consolidated as a 'bargained coalition' combining a relatively diffuse pattern of wealth accumulation—albeit favouring a pro-regime business constituency—and an ill-defined, mostly informal approach to political organizing under a de facto one-party system. The NRM leaders' preferred strategy of 'politicized accumulation', one little hampered by ongoing IFI and donor oversight, fed into what became the default mode of ad hoc mobilizing around patron–client networks. Efforts to build a more formal party-like organization foundered, overshadowed by the factional jostling of wealthy NRM cadres and business elites.

---

[244] Museveni, 1997: 209–210.
[245] The literal translation from Swahili is 'much oil', but this expression is used in Uganda to mean 'fat cats', referring especially to a predatory, regime-aligned elite, including people who might have received political cover to smuggle oil.
[246] Museveni, 1997: 209–210.
[247] Ibid.
[248] Aibidi, 1996: 45.
[249] Cited in Oloka-Onyango, 2000: 59.
[250] Carbone, 2008: 149–152.
[251] Ibid. Interviews with multiple former MPs.

3.3.2 Rwanda—Consolidation of an 'Institutionalized Coalition'

The Tutsi dominated Rwandan Patriotic Front (RPF), like Uganda's NRM, started as a rebel insurgency. In successfully ousted President Habyarimana's Hutu government in 1994 after a four-year civil war, culminating in a genocide during which government-backed Hutu extremists targeted the minority Tutsi population. Under the leadership of President Paul Kagame, the RPF regime went on to oversee what many have referred to as a 'development miracle'. Again, as was true in neighbouring Uganda, Rwanda's economic turnaround was greatly assisted by its 'donor darling' status and the attendant influx of foreign aid. Unlike Uganda, however, the RPF regime oversaw the centralization of wealth accumulation and patronage, which enabled the institutional consolidation of a strong party-administrative apparatus. Regime consolidation under the RPF in Rwanda thus offers an important counterpoint, demonstrating how one ruling elite could exercise its agency to cultivate an 'institutionalized coalition' even as its immediate contemporary and neighbour opted for an alternative strategy, building a 'bargained coalition'.

3.3.2.1 Economic Policy

Although the RPF government embraced a rhetoric of 'private sector-led growth', thereby appealing to donors and foreign investors alike, it adopted a range of measures enabling the centralization of wealth accumulation under the control of the RPF leadership, which also formed the military top brass.

First, it is hard to see 'antecedent conditions', i.e. an inherited political-economic structure, as playing any direct role in shaping the RPF's post-genocide strategy of 'politicized accumulation'. While it is true that the Habyarimana regime that preceded the RPF take-over relied on a relatively narrow class of accumulators, the ruling elite became more fractious and competition over patronage intensified amidst the economic decline of the late 1980s and early 1990s.[252] The combination of the war and then genocide, moreover, left Rwanda at economic 'ground zero'; reacting to the profound devastation, one observer concluded, 'A state wasn't reconstructed after 1994—it was imported.'[253]

The RPF's subsequent centralization of wealth accumulation was achieved notably through the cultivation of party- and later military-owned enterprises. This focus started with Tri-Star Investment, a holding company that grew

---

[252] Prunier, 1995: 87; Uvin, 2002: 20–21.
[253] Jones, 2014: 201. See also Booth and Golooba-Mutebi, 2012: 385–387; Jones, 2012.

out of the 'production department' of the RPF during the 1990–1994 war.[254] Whereas the previously mentioned equivalent in Uganda, the National Enterprise Corporation, foundered, Tri-Star expanded rapidly after the RPF took power. Amidst the initial post-genocide economic crisis, the company was thought to offer an additional source of State revenue. Later on, its profits either went to the RPF as dividends or were reinvested, enabling Tri-Star to expand its operations into a range of sectors, including trade, road construction, housing, building materials, food processing, mobile telephony, printing, furniture imports, and security services.[255] Tri-Star—later rebranded Crystal Ventures Limited (CVL)—was joined in 2007 by a similar holding company, Horizon Group. Both entities retain private sector legal status despite being fully owned by the RPF and military respectively.[256] While the National Executive Committee of the RPF decides on how to invest dividends from CVL, Horizon Group is run by a private firm whose CEO is nevertheless on secondment from the army.[257] Together, they have enabled the centralization of accumulation while the appointment of managing officers to the various subsidiaries provides a means of 'dispersing power among several elites whose loyalty and performance remain in check'.[258]

This centralization of accumulation is maintained through several parallel efforts. First and foremost, the RPF regime has retained a strict, 'zero tolerance' attitude towards corruption or elite predation.[259] One example of this, which again provides a useful contrast with Uganda, relates to the RPF regime's handling of mineral extraction from Eastern Congo in the late 1990s. While both the Ugandan and Rwandan militaries were active in Eastern Congo at the time, and while both forces took the opportunity to seize and export valuable minerals, the distribution of rents was very different in each case. Ugandan military officers took advantage of the operation to line their own pockets whereas resource extraction by the Rwandan military was centrally controlled with profits channelled through the 'Congo Desk' in Kigali.[260]

A second, albeit hotly debated, strategy deployed by the RPF to ensure centralization of accumulation involves curbing—or at least actively shaping—the success of independent Rwandan capitalists. Some scholars suggest that

---

[254] Gokgur, 2012: 18.
[255] Booth and Golooba-Mutebi, 2012: 393–394; Jones, 2014: 199. See also: Gokgur, 2012; Behuria, 2016.
[256] Jones, 2014: 197.
[257] Booth and Golooba-Mutebi, 2012: 393–394; Jones, 2014: 197.
[258] Behuria, 2016: 6. On the centralization of rents, see also: Ansoms and Rostagno, 2012; Booth and Golooba-Mutebi, 2012; Gokgur, 2012; Jones, 2014; Mann and Berry, 2016.
[259] Jones, 2014: 201.
[260] Jones, 2012: 241–242; Vlassenroot et al., 2012.

Rwanda's party-owned enterprises help 'crowd in'—as opposed to 'crowding out'—other private sector actors, breaking into new sectors and then leaving independent entrepreneurs to follow suit.[261] Other observers are far more circumspect, though, pointing to a range of ways by which RPF leaders curb private wealth accumulation whilst swiftly targeting Rwandan capitalists who fall out with the regime.[262] Gokgur stresses how, within Rwanda's modern formal sector, 'competition is effectively limited to larger firms and new conglomerates already in operation and expanding.'[263] Small players are, meanwhile, 'confronted with tax regulations that disproportionately favour their larger counterparts' while the RPF government also stands accused of directing procurement contracts towards its 'party-statals'.[264] Where such indirect means of containing the wealth, power and thus the potential political threat of private Rwandan accumulators prove insufficient, the RPF government has resorted to arresting wealthy businessmen or else driving them into exile.[265]

Leaving aside large-scale accumulators, the RPF Government has also adopted a series of policies that limit the success of more petty accumulators. It has imposed strict regulations on Rwanda's large, labour-absorbing informal economy, thereby controlling informal activities and cutting into profit margins in an already intensely competitive sector.[266] Regarding rural production, the RPF has largely achieved a transition to official land titling. This intervention favours large-scale investors while marginalizing peasant household, many of which have already seen their livelihoods eroded due to the RPF's strategy of resettlement or 'villagization'.[267]

In sum, the RPF regime has adopted a variety of measures to ensure the centralization of rents in Rwanda. Its overarching strategy of 'politicized accumulation' hinges on its careful management of party- and military-owned enterprise or 'party-statals', which despite operating in the age of structural adjustment, still proved a viable alternative to the more conventional 'parastatals'.[268]

---

[261] Booth and Golooba-Mutebi, 2012; Golooba-Mutebi and Booth, 2013.
[262] Ansoms and Rostagno, 2012; Gokgur, 2012; Behuria, 2016; Mann and Berry, 2016.
[263] Gokgur (2011) cited in Ansoms and Rostagno, 2012: 434.
[264] Ibid. See also: Gogkur, 2012; Jones, 2014: 193; Behuria, 2016: 14; Mann and Berry, 2016.
[265] Jones, 2014: 197–201; Behuria, 2016.
[266] Ansoms and Rostagno, 2012: 431–432.
[267] Ibid., 437.
[268] That said, Rwanda also retained many of its state-owned enterprises after pursuing only a partial privatization process. See Gogkur, 2012.

3.3.2.2 Party Strengthening Efforts

Centralization of wealth accumulation and patronage has supported the RPF's parallel efforts to build up a strong, top-down party-administrative organization.

There was certainly a precedent for this form of organization as Habyarimana's Mouvement Révolutionnaire National pour le Développement (MRND) evolved into a 'truly totalitarian party', which had a presence 'everywhere' while 'administrative control was probably the tightest in the world among non-communist countries'.[269] The MRND was, however, erased from Rwanda's political map after the 1994 genocide and RPF victory, leaving the new regime to establish its own organizational base.

In the immediate post-war period, the RPF leaders joined together with opposition parties in a 'broad-based' government not entirely dissimilar from its Ugandan counterpart under the NRM. The RPF was clearly dominant from the start, though, and used its position to further sideline opposition parties. By imposing a ban on all local party meetings and branch-level organizing, the RPF leaders effectively constrained party activity to narrow elite circles in Kigali such that the primary objective of opposition leaders became to gain positions within government.[270] At the same time, the RPF adopted an electoral system that left little room for its own national level politicians to develop any kind of patronage base. National Assembly elections, for instance, are conducted using proportional representation while control over who appears on the list is highly centralized and the choice entirely non-transparent.[271] In addition to these institutional barriers, wealthy individuals interested in using their resources for political ends have seen their efforts swiftly curtailed. Indeed, as mentioned earlier, Rwandan capitalists who have sought to challenge the government—usually by defecting to the opposition—have been heavily sanctioned, and this through a combination of financial and coercive means.

The national level aside, the RPF has also used its centralized control over patronage to maintain a fused party-administrative apparatus reaching down to the village level.[272] As was true in Tanzania, this system favours an administrative and technocratic elite whilst downgrading the influence and accountability of elected officials. The effort to create 'a giant patronage grid' has been realized through a succession of nominally decentralizing

---

[269] Prunier, 1995: 76–77.
[270] Jones, 2014: 149–150.
[271] Ibid., 159–160.
[272] Jones 2012, 2014; Verhoeven, 2012; Chemouni, 2014.

reforms.[273] Beginning with the 2000 National Decentralization Policy and culminating with a final redesign of local government in 2006, the RPF created 'opportunities to expand, rather than transfer or devolve, its power and influence.'[274] The decentralized government structures go from the coordinators of 10 house units at the village level through the cell, sector, district, province and finally central state levels. The only direct elections are for 10 house Coordinators and Cell Committee members. Members of the Sector Committee and District Councils are elected indirectly by members of the lower level bodies while the District Mayor and Vice Mayor are elected by the District Council members.[275] The indirect nature of elections coupled with the ban on party mobilizing at local level serves to depoliticize as much as possible local level elections while also depriving elected officials of any genuine electoral base.[276] The would-be powers of local elected officials are further diminished as a result of their limited executive responsibilities coupled with the top-down distribution of development finance. At the cell and sector levels, it is *paid* Executive Secretaries—appointed centrally—who wield executive powers as opposed to *unpaid* elected committee members.[277] Executive secretaries also double as RPF mobilizers, engaging in party political activities such as organizing rallies, campaigning for candidates, and the like.[278] At district level, the Mayor and Vice Mayor have executive powers, although they are bound to meet performance targets largely dictated from above while failure to do so jeopardizes their chances of re-selection and election.[279]

The approach to decentralization in Rwanda is reminiscent of local government reforms in Tanzania in the 1960s and 1970s, which similarly extended and empowered 'officialdom' over elected would-be patrons. The Rwandan case, meanwhile, contrasts sharply with Uganda where decentralizing reforms are associated with the extension of clientelist networks, thereby expanding the regime coalition but also creating new arenas within which factional politics are fought.[280]

In sum, the RPF leadership has managed the process of post-conflict reconstruction and regime consolidation to ensure a centralized pattern of

---

[273] Jones, 2014: 162–163.
[274] Citing Sommers (2012), Chemouni, 2014: 247.
[275] Jones, 2014: 163–164; Chemouni, 2014.
[276] Chemouni, 2014: 253; Jones, 2014.
[277] Jones, 2014: 164; Chemouni, 2014: 253.
[278] Jones, 2014: 163.
[279] Chemouni, 2014: 250.
[280] Green, 2010.

'politicized accumulation' while also ensuring the monopoly of a controlling, party-administrative institutional apparatus. These core components of an 'institutionalized coalition' are absent in neighbouring Uganda where, faced with a similar post-conflict reconstruction challenge and donor-imposed policy constraints, the NRM elite adopted a strategy consistent with the emergence of a 'bargained coalition', allowing for relatively decentralized wealth accumulation and political organizing dominated by informal, patron–client organization.

3.4 Conclusion

This chapter began with Julius Nyerere's speech in which he promises, 'We shall grope forward...' This was meant as a hopeful phrase, heralding a future of new possibilities and creative self-determination. It also speaks, though, to the profound uncertainties that confront emerging regimes. Leaders are compelled to make a series of contingent decisions as they look for a strategy that can enable them, first, to consolidate power and then, if they so choose, to pursue other, normative goals.

The paired comparisons of post-independence regimes in Tanzania and Kenya and post-'liberation' regimes in Uganda and Rwanda illustrate the varying solutions arrived at by leaders during the initial critical juncture of regime consolidation. In all four cases, contrasting strategies of 'politicized accumulation' and party-building efforts determined the strength of authoritarian party institutions. Where leaders centralized wealth accumulation, as in post-Independence Tanzania and post-genocide Rwanda, they could also effectively invest in party or party-administrative strengthening. By contrast, where leaders preferred a more diffuse pattern of wealth accumulation, as in Kenya and Uganda, party-building efforts—if pursued—remained largely ineffective. The comparison of regimes that were immediate contemporaries as well as cases over time further illustrates the significance of leaders' varied strategies of politicized accumulation, even when faced with very different political and economic constraints.

This analysis of authoritarian party consolidation nevertheless leaves open the question of what happens next. What dynamics influence the evolution of authoritarian party institutions? Does the early period of institutional consolidation affect subsequent patterns of institutional change? What residual powers do leaders have to influence institutional outcomes? It is to these questions that I now turn.

4

Authoritarian Party Trajectories

Continuity and Change

At some point, CCM started to doze. We let go of our united character, which made us drunk and careless.
—Julius Nyerere, 1987

People should forget the past, all-inclusive and individual merit politics and get reminded that Uganda is now under a multiparty system where party interests should be thought about before one thinks of his own interests.
—Hope Mwesigye, Minister and NRM cadre, 2006[1]

I would like the NRM-Organization to become the CCM [of] Uganda, like CCM of Tanzania.
—Gilbert Bukenya, Vice President of Uganda[2]

Party organizations cannot always be managed as per the desires of their leaders. The above citations speak to this basic fact, albeit from opposing vantage points. Addressing the party faithful at the 10th anniversary of CCM,[3] former President Julius Nyerere of Tanzania warned of a strong party in decline. He communicated a dire message of institutional decay and internal conflict and called for a renewed commitment to CCM's organizational integrity and socialist principles. Hope Mwesigye, then a close lieutenant of Uganda's President Museveni,[4] alluded to a contrasting organizational conundrum following Uganda's return to multiparty politics. Instead of a strong party in decline, the NRM was a weak party or 'Movement', which its leaders hoped to imbue with new-found organizational discipline. Or as Vice President Bukenya saw

---

[1] Muhereza, Robert. 'Mwesigye warns undisciplined NRM leaders', *The Daily Monitor*, 2 August 2006, 9.
[2] Cited in Kiiza, Svasand, and Tabora, 2008: 227.
[3] Recall, CCM originated in 1977 out of the merger of TANU and Zanzibar's ASP.
[4] At the time when she made the above-quoted statement, she was serving as State Minister for Local Government and as NRM Chairperson for Kabale District.

Wealth, Power, and Authoritarian Institutions. Michaela Collord, Oxford University Press. © Michaela Collord (2024).
DOI: 10.1093/9780191945335.003.0004

it, the NRM should mimic its neighbour to the South and become 'the CCM of Uganda'.

As both sets of leaders were soon to discover, there are limits to the extent that even powerful political actors can manipulate authoritarian party trajectories, be it to prevent a strong party from becoming weak or to make a weak party strong. This chapter begins with a recap of the relevant argument and methods used to study authoritarian party change over time. I then present a theory-guided analysis of the Tanzanian case followed by the Ugandan case.

4.1 Argument and Methods

While the last chapter examined the 'critical juncture' period of regime consolidation, this chapter explores authoritarian parties' subsequent path dependent trajectories. Parties 'continue to evolve in response to changing environmental conditions and ongoing political manoeuvring *but in ways that are constrained by past trajectories*'.[5] This section first details an argument about different party trajectories, the conditions for institutional continuity and change. Second, it presents the methods used to illustrate this argument through the empirical analysis of Tanzania's CCM and Uganda's NRM.

To recap, two forms of ideal typical authoritarian party may emerge from an initial 'critical juncture' of regime consolidation. An 'institutionalized coalition', comprised of more centralized patronage networks and relatively strong party institutions, takes shape where party leaders combine a strategy of 'politicized accumulation' favouring more concentrated wealth accumulation with concerted party-building efforts. By contrast, a 'bargained coalition', made up of more fractious patronage networks and weak party institutions, coalesces where party leaders favour decentralized wealth accumulation and neglect party-building or are otherwise unsuccessful.

Once consolidated, each party type endures in its established form so long as the prevailing pattern of wealth accumulation and patronage distribution remains unaltered. Parties may begin to change, though, where economic conditions change. Yet even so, a form of institutional 'lock in' limits this party transformation. As theorized by Pierson, institutions—once created—produce 'increasing returns'.[6] In this instance, formal party structures and procedures generate a combination of 'set up costs', 'coordination effects', 'learning effects', and 'adaptive expectations' that help ensure the party's institutional

---

[5] Ibid., my emphasis.
[6] Pierson, 2000; this book, Chapter 2.

reproduction, even when the conditions underlying its initial formation alter. Crucially, then, each party type is likely to follow a different trajectory, defined *both by the underlying distribution of power and the party's own institutional inheritance*. Party leaders, meanwhile, have only limited ability to manipulate these outcomes.

To clarify, an 'institutionalized coalition' may begin a process of institutional erosion where patterns of wealth accumulation become more diffuse and patronage networks fragment (Figure 4.1). Party leaders' efforts to limit this institutional decay through direct party-strengthening will be largely ineffectual so long as there is no parallel attempt to recentralize wealth accumulation. An 'institutionalized coalition' nevertheless *does not* simply collapse into an alternative, 'bargained coalition' party type; rather, it weakens *relative* to its past institutional strength. The party's institutional inheritance, i.e. the effects associated with 'increasing returns' on past institutional investments, limit the corrosive consequences of more fractious patron–client networks. Politicians and their allied factions are compelled to continue organizing through formal party institutions rather than substituting them entirely with their own patronage machines. This need to navigate established party institutions *delays* the consolidation of factional networks. It also renders them more *fragile* because they are enmeshed within formal party structures and thus lack a fully autonomous organizational base.

Contrary to an 'institutionalized coalition', a 'bargained coalition' is unlikely to undergo a significant process of institutional change, even if the party

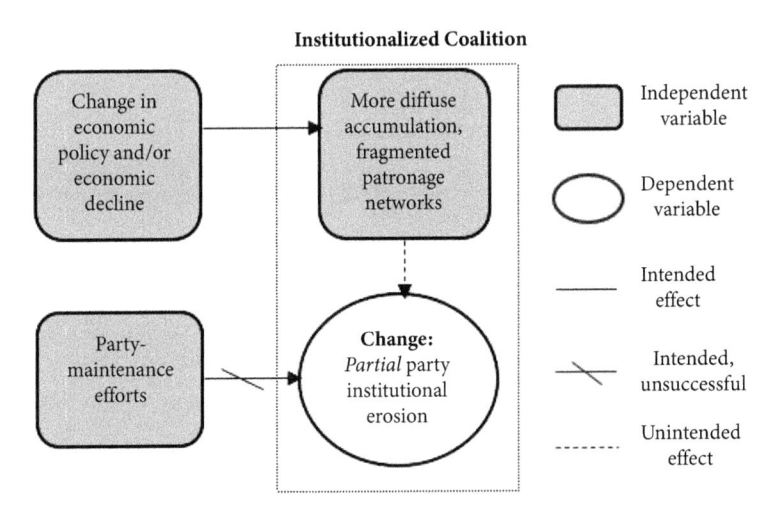

Figure 4.1 Trajectory of an institutionalized coalition

leaders belatedly decide to invest in party-building (Figure 4.2). The reasons for this institutional continuity are again two-fold. First, it is doubtful that leaders of a 'bargained coalition' could recentralize control over wealth accumulation—the key condition for effective party-building—without jeopardizing their own hold on power.[7] As such, accumulation patterns are unlikely to change significantly. Secondly, the dynamics of 'increasing returns' will, in this instance, serve to further entrench *informal* patterns of political organizing. Institutional weakness becomes self-reinforcing as personalized fiefdoms and extended patronage networks dominate while formal party structures and procedures garner little recognition or respect.

The ensuing empirical analysis combines within-case and cross-case comparison to show how an 'institutionalized coalition' and 'bargained coalition' evolve over time. Unlike the last chapter, which incorporated two shadow cases, this chapter focuses on Tanzania's CCM and Uganda's NRM with only passing reference to KANU and the RPF. It traces party developments up through the 2015 elections in Tanzania and the 2016 elections in Uganda. It does not probe changes within CCM during the presidency of John Magufuli (2015–2021), although the conclusion of this book does. Suffice it to say here that Magufuli's leadership is instructive as it suggests the potential to reverse the gradual erosion of an 'institutionalized coalition'. His tenure also

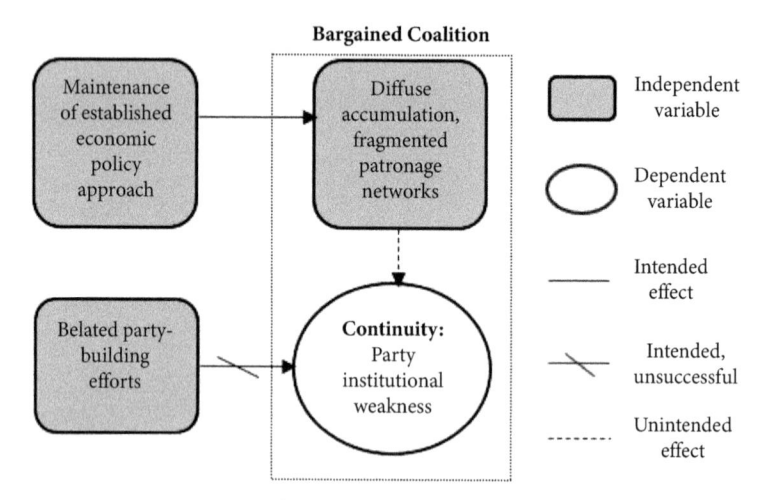

Figure 4.2 Trajectory of a bargained coalition

<hr>

[7] See Boone, 1992: 25–26.

underscores the importance of both economic and institutional tools when authoritarian leaders seek to recentralize power.

In evaluating party institutional change, this chapter supplements a general assessment of party strength—as offered in the last chapter—with a focused examination of the parliamentary nomination process. There are two reasons for this emphasis. First, concentrating on one aspect of party organization provides a consistent benchmark against which to track institutional change. Nominations are also a *strategic* focus given that candidate selection is both a *core function* of any political party and a powerful indicator of *who is in control*.[8] As noted by Schattshneider, 'He who can make the nominations is the owner of the party. This is therefore one of the best points at which to observe the distribution of power within the party.'[9] Kent, meanwhile, argues that a party organization 'can lose its candidates time after time in the general election without greatly diminishing its strength or losing the grip of its leaders. . . . But [. . .] any organization that cannot carry the primary election is a defunct organization.'[10]

I evaluate the candidate selection process, first, using the same four indicators as for party strength generally. I look at the extent to which a strong *party bureaucracy* effectively oversees nominations. I assess the '*complexity*' of the selection procedure, namely how active and varied a role a party's organizational sub-units play in the process. I also consider its '*coherence*', examining whether formal rules are respected in the face of informal pressures. Finally, unlike in the previous chapter, I also include the '*adaptability*' measure of party institutional strength, which here refers to 'generational age' or the number of smooth successions from one set of party leaders to another. Whereas for the other three indicators, my analysis focuses on parliamentary candidate selection, I examine institutional 'adaptability' through a brief study of presidential candidate selection, and specifically, of whether a party has an institutionalized mechanism to ensure a smooth succession from one president to another, bearing in mind that presidents almost invariably double as party leaders.

In addition to these four indicators, I also evaluate party strength based on a dimension specific to candidate selection, namely the 'inclusiveness' of the nomination process. Inclusiveness here refers to who is making nomination decisions, or who comprises the 'selectorate' within the party.[11] The degree of inclusiveness ranges from the extremely exclusive—a single party

---

[8] Rahat and Hazan, 2001.
[9] Schattshneider, 1942: 624.
[10] Kent, 1924: 11.
[11] Rahat and Hazan, 2001. See also Field and Siavelis, 2008.

leader appoints all candidates, to the extremely inclusive—all party members or even all eligible voters can vote on their preferred candidate. A more inclusive selection procedure implies that *more power is diverted* from the party leadership to wider array of local party elites or even rank-and-file members.

In the context of authoritarian ruling parties, I argue that the adoption of a more inclusive selection procedure, notably the introduction of open primaries in which all party members can participate, is a symptom of institutional weakness, often signalling reduced *complexity* and *coherence*. The idea is that party leaders resort to open primaries where they can no longer hope to adjudicate peacefully among rival patronage networks. Where formal rules become all but meaningless, with candidates bribing their way through the nominations, more inclusive selection procedures—cutting out any electoral college system or other party sub-units—can become a means to defuse conflict, or at least to deflect it away from the party leadership. As such, the same factors that cause party weakening in general also underpin a shift towards a more inclusive nomination process.

This interpretation varies from some more established explanations of why authoritarian parties adopt open primaries, and thus of what accounts for party institutional change more generally. An increasingly widespread view in the comparative literature holds that parties use primaries when inter-party competition intensifies. The idea is that where the opposition starts to pose a genuine electoral threat, the incumbent party introduces primaries to ensure the selection of the most popular candidate with the best chance of winning in the general election.[12] The scholarship on primaries in African parties tends to contradict this analysis, though.[13] There is also a small literature on authoritarian parties that supports my own interpretation of primaries and their significance. Referring to the decision of Taiwan's Kuomintang (KMT) to adopt more inclusive nomination procedures in the 1990s, Wu dismisses the official reasons given for the reforms, which invoked the need to enhance the party's legitimacy and electoral strength. He instead stresses that 'keen observers with access to the party's inner workings' saw an 'ulterior motive', namely, to weaken the influence of local patronage networks.[14]

In what follows, I demonstrate the validity of the two hypothesized causal chains outlined at the start of this section by tracing shifts in patterns of accumulation and party strength, first in Tanzania's 'institutionalized coalition'

---

[12] Langston, 2006; Wuhs, 2006; Martz, 2013.
[13] Ichino and Nathan (2012) observe that Ghanaian parties, which adjust their selection procedures depending on the constituency, are more likely to use primaries in 'safe seats'. For a focus on intra- rather than inter-party competition and nominations, see also: Seeberg et al., 2018; Kjaer and Katusiimeh, 2021.
[14] Wu, 2001: 111–112.

and then Uganda's 'bargained coalition'. This analysis nevertheless leaves open an important question: what would it take to disprove my core argument? What evidence is needed to assess the alternative hypothesis that party institutional change, and specifically the adoption of inclusive selection procedures, results from rising inter-party competition? If this hypothesis were true, then we would expect an erosion in the incumbent party's vote share to prompt the adoption of more inclusive nominations. I show instead that it is changes in *intra-party* competition, not rising inter-party competition, that directly motivate reforms to selection procedures. This analysis is in tension with a body of literature on democratization, which presents the transition to multiparty politics as itself a key watershed, driving the transformation of political institutions. Yet the argument here is that, to understand institutional change, including within an incumbent authoritarian party, we need to engage with broader shifts in the political economy of a regime.

4.2 Chama Cha Mapinduzi, a Strong Party in Decline

The previous chapter analysed how TANU—later CCM—consolidated as an institutionalized coalition, featuring more centralized control over wealth accumulation and concerted party-building efforts. Yet starting in the late 1970s, Tanzania began to witness the gradual decentralization of accumulation and, relatedly, the partial erosion of ruling party institutions. In what follows, I address each of these developments in turn, using parliamentary selection as a benchmark for institutional change. I then zero in on the presidential succession process, which I use to showcase the contradictory trends within CCM. On the one hand, battles over presidential nominations have catalysed the most profound factional divisions within the party; on the other hand, its strong institutional inheritance has helped contain the fallout from these internal struggles. In a final section, I consider the significance of inter-party competition on institutional change within CCM, noting its more marginal impact.

4.2.1 Changing Patterns of Wealth Accumulation

By the late 1970s, the efforts of CCM leaders to retain centralized control over wealth accumulation—always difficult given the economic weakness of the Tanzanian State—began to unravel, and this due to a combination of economic decline, growing informalization, corruption, and ultimately, economic liberalization. Tanzania's changing economy saw CCM leaders adapting a new strategy of 'politicized accumulation', one characterized by ad hoc deals brokered between an expanded private sector elite and various party officials and elected leaders. The initial transition was heavily contested and, as a result, somewhat delayed. Subsequent corruption scandals and a lingering ideological commitment to *Ujamaa* and to Nyerere's legacy have prompted repeated efforts to turn back the clock. Yet, these remained largely unsuccessful, with the arguable exception of John Magufuli's presidency (2015–2021).

The economic crisis confronting Tanzania in the late 1970s was a consequence, in part, of domestic policy errors and public sector mismanagement.[15] These domestic challenges were then greatly magnified by a range of external factors, including the second oil price shock in 1979 and a costly war to overthrown Idi Amin in Uganda.[16] These combined pressures put the formal planning system under serious strain while the informal sector expanded rapidly. Due to the collapsing real value of public sector wages, it became a matter of necessity for civil servants and other government and party officials to invest in private side 'projects'.[17] Meanwhile, the better-connected public officials engaged in a range of more lucrative informal economic activities, both licit and illicit.[18]

Deciding how to respond to the crisis proved a source of considerable tension within CCM. While still in power, President Nyerere and allies within the government and party first sought to reign in corruption and private accumulation by 'economic saboteurs'.[19] Nyerere also resisted external reform pressures. As such, it was not until his successor, Ali Hassan Mwinyi, became President in 1985 that the Tanzanian government adopted a new policy direction.[20] A first phase of economic adjustment began with the approval of an IMF and World Bank-supported Structural Adjustment Programme in 1986, which included plans for currency devaluation, fiscal retrenchment, and partial price and trade liberalization, among other measures. It was followed in 1989 and then 1993 by a second and third phase of reform involving further liberalization of foreign investment, banking and foreign exchange markets as well as fiscal retrenchment and privatization.[21]

From 1985 to 1990, Nyerere stayed on as party Chairman, meaning that Tanzania was a country with 'two leaders'.[22] The party acted as 'a restraint'

---

[15] Gibbon, 1995: 10–11; Tripp, 1997; Chachage, 2003: 19.
[16] Tripp, 1997: 63–67; Kelsall, 2002, 2003; Chachage, 2003: 19–20.
[17] Tripp, 1997: 80.
[18] Ibid., 185.
[19] Shivji et al., 2020: chapter 11.
[20] Ibid.; Gibbon, 1995: 10–12; Tripp, 1997.
[21] Gibbon, 1995: 12–14.
[22] Othman, 1994.

on the government, slowing the pace of reform.[23] Perhaps most emblematic of the two sides' conflicting views was the struggle over CCM's Leadership Code. The Code was, according to Nyerere, the most important element of the original Arusha Declaration.[24] By restricting public officials from engaging in a range of profit-making activities, it had discouraged the emergence of a domestic capitalist elite.[25] Yet throughout the 1980s, enforcement of the Code grew weaker.[26] While Nyerere continued to insist on its necessity, warning against the misleading influence of 'capitalists',[27] Mwinyi adopted a far more permissive attitude. Indeed, he actively encouraged public servants to pursue side projects to help make ends meet, and in 1991, shortly after Nyerere stepped down as CCM Chairman, he scrapped the Code altogether.[28]

The cumulative effects of liberalizing reforms and the abandonment of the Code were striking. From the mid-1980s, private sector growth accelerated rapidly.[29] This period witnessed the consolidation of an already established Asian entrepreneurial elite as well as the emergence of a more prominent African business class, including the first large-scale African industrialists.[30] Investment trends reflected this change in private sector fortunes. As indicated in Figure 4.3,[31] the public sector share of gross fixed capital formation (GFCF) fell behind private investment in the late 1970s and early 1980s, although this initial decline was largely due to a fall in government spending following the second oil price shock and a temporary withdrawal of donor support. The public share of investment again briefly overtook private investment in the late 1980s following the resumption of donor assistance; however, starting in the 1990s and amidst the government's ongoing privatization programme, private overtook public investment, giving way to a new and stable trend of private sector expansion.[32] This trend is also reflected in the increase of domestic credit to the private sector as a percentage of GDP, which rose steadily from the mid-1990s as the process of financial liberalization unfolded.[33]

---

[23] Tripp, 1997: 171.
[24] Nyerere, 1987.
[25] See Chapter 3.
[26] Oda van Cranenburgh, 1990; Tripp, 1997.
[27] Nyerere, 1987; Tripp, 1997: chapter 4. Nyerere's own views on domestic capitalists evolved throughout the 1980s, but he continued to advocate a separation between business and politics. Chachage, 2018: 236.
[28] Tripp, 1997: 187–189.
[29] Nyagetera, 1992; Tripp, 1997: chapter 7; Mwapachu, 2005: chapter 24.
[30] Tripp, 1997: 95; Mengi, 2018; Mwapachu, 2005: 376–377; Aminzade, 2013: 337; Gray, 2018.
[31] Ndulu and Mutalemwa, 2002: 124–125.
[32] Ndulu and Mutalemwa, 2002: 124–125.
[33] 'Domestic credit to private sector (% of GDP) – Tanzania'. World Bank. Accessed 24 July 2017: http://data.worldbank.org/indicator/FS.AST.PRVT.GD.ZS?locations=TZ.

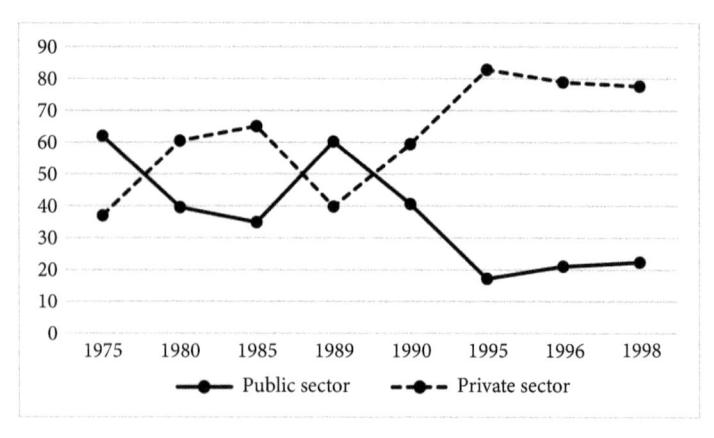

Figure 4.3 Tanzania—gross fixed capital formation by the public and private sectors, 1975–1998

While this private sector expansion came in the wake of Mwinyi's liberalizing reforms, it was not simply the product of newly unleashed market forces, as idealized by the IMF; rather, it was intimately bound up with CCM's new strategy of 'politicized accumulation'. As in, the routine exchange of favours between economic and political elites now mediated the formation of ad hoc factional alliances within the ruling party. Gibbon argues that a form of 'wild capitalism' was emerging in post-reform Tanzania.[34] Patterns of 'rent-seeking behaviour' condemned in the pre-adjustment period were now reappearing 'in free market guises, and on a larger and less controlled scale'.[35] The government faced significant revenue shortfalls due to the non-collection of import duties and taxes, corporate tax evasion as well as unpaid personal income tax bills.[36] Land-grabbing, meanwhile, grew more widespread. The state's ultimate control over land titling, which previously helped further the socialist villagization agenda and discourage rural capitalist development,[37] now enabled government to grant land to investors 'for patronage reasons'.[38] In Tanzania's lucrative mining sector, the 'merchantization of production' saw well-connected investors—including many bureaucrats and ex-bureaucrats—acting as commercial middlemen, extracting rents without contributing to productive activity.[39] Unsurprisingly, urban and

---

[34] Mmuya and Chaliga, 1994; Gibbon, 1995: 16; Gray, 2018.
[35] Ibid.
[36] Ibid.; Therkildsen and Bourguin, 2012: 45.
[37] Mueller, 1981: 491.
[38] Kelsall, 2003: 67; Therkildsen and Bourguin, 2012: 26 & 34.
[39] Chachage, 1995.

rural inequalities—antithetical to the vision of an egalitarian *Ujamaa* society—grew more acute amidst this accelerated scramble for resources. Preference for large-scale investors undercut the incomes of smallholder peasants, many of whom were dispossessed of their land and livelihood and forced to move into trading and artisanal mining activities.[40]

By the end of Mwinyi's presidency in 1995, Tanzania's new 'politicized accumulation' was causing a legitimacy crisis for the CCM government. Benjamin Mkapa, Mwinyi's successor, responded by launching a 'war on corruption'. A presidential commission charged with leading this effort reported that politicians had aligned themselves with 'rich and corrupt businessmen', giving rise to a politics driven by '[e]xcessive lust for money and wealth'.[41] Mkapa's early zeal did not last, however, and the Commission's recommendations went largely unheeded. No prosecutions of named, high-ranking officials or politicians took place. Meanwhile, Mkapa himself became entangled in several grand corruption scandals linked to the ongoing privatization process as well as lucrative investments in power generation and procurement.[42] President Kikwete, who took over in 2005, promised to renew the anti-corruption campaign, yet his presidency also foundered amidst repeated scandals and factional infighting.[43]

CCM leaders' dependence on private financiers and, thus, their active support for the new, untamed 'politicized accumulation' was exacerbated by the Party's failure to cultivate any significant source of independent revenue. After Tanzania's multiparty transition, CCM retained some access to public funding as the Political Parties Act (1992) ensures parties receive a subsidy proportionate to their electoral support, a formula that greatly favours CCM.[44] Even so, Party leaders have repeatedly emphasized that this subsidy is insufficient. In his 2016 farewell speech as outgoing CCM Chairman, Kikwete noted that it only covered salaries of party officials but that there was no reliable income to pay for meetings, trips, election campaigns, and other initiatives necessary to ensure 'the life of the party'.[45] Membership dues from CCM's alleged 8.8m members were also little help due to poor collection rates.[46] Ideas for additional revenue generation included talk of creating party-owned enterprises,[47]

---

[40] Bryceson, 2002; Bryceson et al., 2012; Fisher, 2012; Matotay, 2014; Sulle, 2017.
[41] Cited in Kelsall, 2003: 70.
[42] Ibid.; Gray, 2015.
[43] Cooksey, 2012; Therkildsen and Bourguin, 2012: 31; Gray, 2015.
[44] Therkildsen and Bourguin, 2012: 39–40.
[45] Jakaya Kikwete, 'Hotuba ya Mhe. Jakaya Mrisho Kikwete, Mwenyekiti wa Chama Cha Mapinduzi, Wakati wa Mkutano Mkuu wa CCM', Dodoma, 23 July 2016.
[46] Ibid.
[47] 'CCM is to invest in private firms', *The Citizen*, 28 May 2012.

again with little success.[48] CCM does own a range of potentially lucrative assets, including prime real estate in major cities, sports arenas and the Swahili newspaper *Uhuru*. However, the management of these assets has followed the general trend with, in this case, a de facto privatization of party wealth. Kikwete thus lamented that 'people have already taken for themselves or sold off' properties that could otherwise support the party.[49] As such, by the end of Kikwete's tenure, CCM remained in hock to an expanding network of private business interests.[50]

In sum, whereas prior to the 1980s, private sector expansion was limited and the ruling Party—through the State—retained a high degree of centralized control over wealth accumulation, this pattern later reversed. Economic decline, informalization, and liberalization helped reinvigorate private sector growth. However, what then took hold was a 'type of primitive accumulation associated with corruption in public finance', which 'mainly led to unequal processes of individual enrichment'.[51] This 'wild capitalism' privileged an emerging politico-business elite, now freed from the constraints of CCM's Leadership Code and socialist policy framework. Through to the end of Kikwete's presidency in 2015, efforts to resist this trend failed.[52]

4.2.2 CCM's Institutional Erosion

The transition to a more decentralized wealth accumulation and the resultant fragmentation of patron–client networks within CCM contributed directly to its institutional erosion. Private sector financiers, part of Tanzania's expanded entrepreneurial elite, allied with prospective candidates to advance their mutual economic and political interests. These competing factional networks then undermined the central party *bureaucracy*. They also subverted formal structures and procedures, thereby undermining the *coherence* and *complexity* of party institutions. I illustrate this trend, first, by examining the factional take-over of the party's bureaucratic structures and, second, by examining changes to CCM parliamentary nomination procedure. In both instances, party leaders' efforts to limit the corrosive effects of informal patronage pressures largely failed.

[48] 'SUKITA's assets on auction', *Indian Ocean Newsletter*, 3 January 1998; Shivji et al., 2020: 360–361.
[49] Kikwete, 2016. See also incoming Party Chairman, John Pombe Magufuli, 'Hotuba ya Mhe. Dkt. John Pombe Magufuli, Rais wa Jamhuri ya Muungano wa Tanzania na Mwenyekiti wa Chama cha Mapinduzi Kwenye Mkutano Mkuu wa Taifa wa CCM', Dodoma, 23 July 2016.
[50] This point was further emphasized in interviews with CCM MPs and journalists.
[51] Gray, 2015: 400. See also: Cooksey, 2012; Aminzade, 2013; Languille, 2015.
[52] See Chapter 7 for discussion of Magufuli's post-2015 efforts.

Although CCM began a process of institutional erosion in the 1980s,[53] this process accelerated in the 1990s. The replacement of Nyerere with Mwinyi as CCM Chairman in 1990 had an immediate effect on CCM's *bureaucratic strength* and autonomy from outside influence. In 1991, the new Chairman oversaw a radical reform of the central administrative apparatus, cutting funding and personnel.[54] To compensate for the reduced funding, Mwinyi appointed CCM cadres already elected to paid positions, notably MPs, to double as party officials at regional and district levels.[55] Independently wealthy businesspeople were also brought into the fold. After a 1992 amendment to CCM's constitution, which previously restricted party membership to workers and peasants,[56] many prominent private sector actors were appointed to high-ranking positions within the party and government.[57]

Ultimately, these changes meant rival factions—linking party officials and the rapidly expanding private sector elite—could mobilize through the party secretariat and top organs. By the time President Kikwete took over as party Chairman from Mkapa in 2006, these factional tensions were clearly compromising the institutional integrity of CCM bureaucracy. Immediately after assuming office, Kikwete removed the previous Secretary General, who had supported one of Kikwete's rivals as presidential nominee. Kikwete replaced him with Yusuf Makamba, who was reportedly not chosen 'on merit' but was the father of a key member of Kikwete's campaign team.[58] Kikwete also appointed as CCM Treasurer a leading businessman and financier of his campaign, Rostam Aziz, who was also close to Makamba. Aziz was compelled to quit in 2007, however, following an outcry over undue private sector influence at the top of the party.[59] Makamba meanwhile was accused of fuelling internal Party disputes.[60]

After his re-election in 2010, Kikwete reshuffled the top levels of CCM reportedly 'to forestall faction-fighting'.[61] Makamba was replaced by someone close to him, Wilson Mukama, who later launched an anti-corruption campaign, *kujivua gamba*, or sloughing off, like a snake shedding skin. After this initiative failed amidst aggravated tensions within the party, Kikwete swapped

---

[53] For more, see the discussion below on the multiparty transition.
[54] Mmuya and Chaligha, 1994; Tripp, 1997.
[55] Mmuya, 1998.
[56] Shivji et al., 2020: 359.
[57] Mmuya and Chaligha, 1994: 130–131.
[58] Interview with researcher and CCM activist, Dar es Salaam, August 2015.
[59] Ibid. 'The Gang's all here', *Africa Confidential*, 16 January 2008.
[60] Interview with a researcher and CCM activist, August 2015. Interview with a journalist, Dodoma, February 2016.
[61] 'New brooms, old handles', *Africa Confidential*, 29 April 2011.

Secretary Generals yet again, this time bringing in Abdulrahman Kinana. A veteran presidential campaign manager, Kinana had his own network of ties in the party plus controversial economic interests, including alleged links to elephant poaching.[62] Yet Kinana as well as then Publicity Secretary, Nape Nnauye, were cast as leaders of integrity. Kinana later undertook a series of highly mediatized country-wide tours to reinvigorate the local party structures, an explicit throwback to similar tours Nyerere's undertook in the late 1980s.[63] Even so, Kinana was accused of engaging in factional battles when he called for closer party oversight of government ministers, some of whom he controversially referred to as *mzigo*, a burden, due to their allegedly corrupt activities.[64]

At the same time, the Publicity Secretary, Nape, was not an impartial actor in CCM's factional fights. He had fallen out with Edward Lowassa, a key ally of Rostam Aziz and one-time backer of Kikwete. While a senior cadre in CCM's youth league, *Umoja wa Vijana wa CCM* (UVCCM), Nape had accused Lowassa, the then chair of the UVCCM Board of Trustees, of entering into a fraudulent deal with a construction company tasked with developing land owned by UVCCM and located along a major road in Dar es Salaam.[65] While Lowassa had attempted to engineer Nape's expulsion from UVCCM, backed by then Secretary General Makamba, Kikwete had intervened, appointing Nape a District Commissioner and, later, CCM Publicity Secretary.

The above discussion gives only a flavour of the factional dynamics at the very highest levels of the CCM bureaucracy. It nevertheless indicates how CCM's bureaucratic structures were compromised, entangled in a complex web of alliances linking politicians, paid party staff, and business leaders. A similar situation also developed within lower-level party structures.[66] Yet leaving aside the party bureaucracy, the increasingly fraught process of parliamentary candidate selection offers a further insight into the nature and causes of CCM's institutional erosion.

The formal pre-selection and election procedure used during the one-party era, briefly introduced in the last chapter, provides a benchmark against which to gauge the extent of subsequent institutional flux. The selection procedure

---

[62] 'Corrupt officials ensure the battle against poaching remains futile', *amaBhungane*, 8 August 2013. Accessed 15 November 2021: https://amabhungane.org/stories/corrupt-officials-ensure-the-battle-against-poaching-remains-futile/.

[63] Aikande Kwayu analysed these tours in fascinating detail on her blog, no longer available online following the introduction of restrictive new regulations for online content under Magufuli.

[64] Interview with a researcher and CCM activist, August 2015. Interview with a journalist, February 2016.

[65] 'Nape in familiar territory after his exit from Cabinet', *The Citizen*, 24 March 2017.

[66] Kelsall, 2000.

was first introduced within TANU ahead of the 1965 elections and endured largely unchanged until the 1990s.[67] This nomination process was notable for its clear, hierarchical ordering. It began with a *kura ya maoni* or 'opinion poll' of candidates in a special Annual District Conference. These candidates proceeding for further vetting by the District and Regional Political Committees and by the Central Committee (CC) before the National Executive Committee (NEC) gave its final approval to two nominees. Come the elections themselves, paid officials oversaw party-organized campaigns during which left little opportunity for candidates to articulate a personal message.

This relatively controlled process began to change amidst the economic upheaval of the 1980s. As paid employment in the public service and party became less attractive due to fiscal retrenchment, competition over parliamentary seats grew.[68] Rising competition also resulted from the emergence of new economic actors whose conflicting interests and desire for influence drew them into electoral politics.[69] Already in the 1985 elections, businesspersons started to play a more prominent role as political financiers.[70] Certain particularly volatile constituency-level contests were harbingers of a new trend. For instance, the rival parliamentary candidates for Rombo constituency in the historic cash-crop producing Kilimanjaro region were each backed by well-endowed entrepreneurial elites; one candidate aligned with local agricultural interests while the other represented Dar es Salaam-based traders.[71] The contestants themselves spent little money on campaigning, but their 'shadows' disbursed an estimated five times more than the official Rombo district party organizers.[72]

In the 1990 elections, there were repeats of this 'fight of the giants', notably in the same relatively affluent Kilimanjaro region.[73] Poorer regions were less affected by this emerging factional dynamic; yet Tanzania's variable political geography during this period arguably helps confirm the overarching point, namely that new economic interests were driving local factionalism within CCM. In this vein, Max Mmuya argues that the 1990 elections in the economically marginalized Mtwara region were relatively calm because the 'low

---

[67] See Chapter 3 for detail.
[68] Van Donge and Liviga, 1990; Kiondo, 1994; Kelsall, 2003.
[69] See below discussion. See also: Munishi and Mtengeti-Migiro, 1990; Kiondo, 1994; Mmuya, 1994; Gibbon, 2001; Ponte, 2004.
[70] Van Donge and Liviga, 1990; Kiondo, 1994: 74–75; Mpangala, 1994: 43–44.
[71] Munishi and Mtengeti-Migiro, 1990. See also Kiondo, 1994.
[72] Munishi and Mtengeti-Migiro, 1990: 199.
[73] Kiondo, 1994: 79–82.

employment levels' and *absence of strong vested* interests meant that there was 'hardly any political organisation of significance'.[74]

More generally, while Nyerere was still CCM Chairman, changes in the parliamentary nominations process were limited. Long-time party and state officials continued to dominate the field of candidates;[75] the party NEC vetoed the only two prominent businessmen who did make it through nominations;[76] and the volume of private finance, while rising, was still far less than in neighbouring Kenya or Zambia.[77] The real watershed moment came when Nyerere relinquished his Chairmanship after the 1990 elections. Businessmen of Asian origin won two out of four by-elections between 1992 and 1995, an unprecedented occurrence in Tanzania.[78] Come the 1995 general elections, Tanzania's first since its multi-party transition, a newly assertive business elite flocked to contest for parliamentary seats on the CCM ticket. Relatedly, private campaign spending during primaries rocketed, reportedly exceeding the amount spent in the general elections.[79] CCM primaries—in 1995 as well as subsequent elections—also featured intensified clashes between rival aspirants fronting for different economic interests, including in the recently liberalized agricultural, trade, and extractive sectors.[80]

This growth in private campaign finance and informal patronage politics quickly undermined the formal procedures that had long governed the CCM nomination process. Party leaders responded with a succession of institutional reform efforts. After barely changing for 30 years, the parliamentary nomination process changed ahead of every election from 1995 through to 2010. The reforms mainly affected the *inclusiveness* of primaries, yo-yoing from more inclusive to more restrictive to more inclusive again. A review of the successive procedural changes illustrates how the new factional politicking within CCM both *motivated* the reforms and *undermined* them, ensuring none were effective in taming informal pressures.

First, after the 1995 polls, there was a shift to *more inclusive* ward-level primaries ahead of the 2000 elections. This was, in part, a response to allegations

---

[74] Mmuya, 1994: 240.

[75] Van Donge and Liviga, 1990.

[76] Kiondo, 1994: 82–84. The vetoed aspirants were John Cheyo, with business interests in Swaziland as well as Tanzania, and Wilfrem Mwakitwange, who previously served as a TANU MP until his expulsion in 1968. See Chapter 5 for more details about his expulsion.

[77] Baylies and Szeftel, 1992; Ajulu, 1999.

[78] Mmuya and Chaligha, 1994.

[79] TEMCO, 1997; Babeiya, 2011. Interviews, CCM MP, Dodoma, June 2015 and January 2016.

[80] Chachage, 1995; Gibbon, 2001. While often concentrated within CCM, these rivalries also cut across CCM and the new opposition parties. For an example from Bukoba's liberalizing coffee sector, see: Ponte, 2004.

of bribery in the District Conference, which had affected the legitimacy of the nomination outcomes in 1995.[81] Holding primaries at ward level was no better, though, as this procedural fix only seemed to displace the vote-buying while involving a larger portion of the CCM membership in bruising political disputes.[82] Factional struggles divided local party officials, communities, and even the state administration and security forces. There were also widespread rumours involving prominent national-level politicians out to protect their local political and economic interests.

One fraught incident from Simanjiro constituency in Manyara region, home to the world's only Tanzanite mines, illustrates this emerging trend.[83] The competition in Simanjiro pitted the incumbent MP Vincent Kone, who was also the district CCM Ideology Secretary, against Christopher Ole Sendeka, the CCM district Chairman. The situation degenerated amidst bribery accusations, and counteraccusations during the ward-level primaries. Large-scale Tanzinite miners and traders were accused of bankrolling the bribery while Ole Sendeka resolved to boycott the primaries, and over 70 CCM members and local party officials protested outside the party Regional Headquarters. When allegations spread that Ole Sendeka's car was shot at and police controversially claimed that a tire simply burst in the sun, people began to argue that the corruption reached from district to national level, where there were interested parties out to protect their preferred faction.

President Benjamin Mkapa, Mwinyi's successor, added his voice to the general outcry surrounding the 2000 CCM nominations. He warned that a growing number of business elites were using their financial muscle to sway the primary outcomes, effectively 'privatizing' the party.[84] CCM was at a 'crossroads', its core principles threatened by a 'wave' of wealthy Tanzanians now vying for parliamentary seats.[85] Principled concerns aside, Mkapa allegedly also feared the growing influence of a business elite who had backed his then chief rival, Kikwete, in the 1995 presidential nomination.[86] Whatever the precise reasons, the CCM NEC went on to block the nominations of several Tanzanians of Asian origin while 40 incumbent MPs were also banned from

---

[81] Interview with the former Speaker and CCM NEC Member, Dar es Salaam, March 2016; Interview, CCM MP, June 2015 and January 2016.
[82] Ibid. Interview, former CCM MP, former CCM MP, Dodoma, January 2016.
[83] See press coverage: 'Mgombea ubunge CCM ashambuliwa kwa risasi', *Mtanzania*, 4 August 2000. 'Vurugu kura za maoni CCM—Wananchama waandama', *Majira*, 5 August 2000. 'Kushambuliwa kwa gari la Mgombea ubunge Simanjiro', *Majira*, 7 August 2000. 'Taarifa za wagombea ubunge kuenda NEC', *Majira*, 9 August 2000.
[84] 'Waogopeni wanaotaka kubinafsisha CCM—Mkapa', *Mtanzania*, 3 August 2000.
[85] 'CCM haiuzwi—Mkapa', *Mtanzania*, 14 August 2000.
[86] 'CCM kufuta kura za maoni', *Majira*, 26 August 2000.

the 2000 elections due to their 'violation of party ethics and regulations'.[87] Mkapa then declared that CCM would again change the method for conducting parliamentary primaries to prevent factional divisions from further compromising the process.[88]

This commitment explains the 2005 return to a *more exclusive* primary procedure conducted within the Constituency Conference. The rationale for this change was that it would be easier to supervise the voting process if it were held over the course of a single day and involved only a small group of people.[89] This logic was misguided, though, as the smaller number of delegates proved even easier to bribe. Amidst a cascade of complains there were, for instance, allegations of entire constituency delegations being taken to luxury hotels by certain parliamentary aspirants.[90]

Following this furore, the nomination procedure was changed ahead of the 2010 elections, this time with the introduction of *highly inclusive open primaries*.[91] The aim, yet again, was to undercut the influence of money flooding campaigns, the assumption being that no candidate could effectively bribe *en masse* thousands of voters. In this way, the party could de facto restore some integrity to the selection process.[92] However, as was arguably true of President Mkapa in 2000, President Kikwete—Mkapa's former rival turned successor— also had personal motivations for intervening in primaries. His aim was to dilute the influence of his own factional opponent, Edward Lowassa.[93] Yet widespread bribery of voters and party officials persisted in 2010, and if anything, the rule change made the nomination process even more expensive. Candidates now had to budget for additional agents at polling stations across their constituencies to guard against the potentially corrupt manoeuvring of their adversaries.[94] This points to a costly privatization of the supervisory role previously carried out by the party bureaucratic infrastructure.

After 2010, and despite these failings, the party leadership was out of new tricks. The highly inclusive open primaries were retained in 2015. The only new development was that, *for the first time since Independence*, the party NEC

---

[87] 'Kikao cha kamati kuu CCM—Adamjee, Manji, Rage nje!', *Mtanzania*, 13 August 2000.

[88] 'CCM kufuta kura za maoni', *Majira*, 26 August 2000.

[89] Interview, CCM MP, Dodoma, June 2015 and January 2016; Interview with former CCM MP, former CCM Publicity Secretary and Deputy Secretary, March 2016.

[90] Ibid. Interview, former CCM MP, Dodoma, January 2016.

[91] Interview, CCM MP, January 2016; Interview, former CCM Publicity Secretary and Deputy Secretary, March 2016; TEMCO report, 2005.

[92] Interview, former Speaker and CCM NEC member, Dar es Salaam, March 2016; Interview, CCM MP, Dodoma, January 2016; Interview, former CCM Publicity Secretary and Deputy Secretary, Dar es Salaam, March 2016.

[93] Therkildsen and Bourguin, 2012: 15.

[94] Interview, CCM MPs, Dodoma, January 2016.

did not veto a single candidate. As such, the CCM leadership further relinquished formal control in a process over which it had already lost its de facto influence.

In sum, changes in Tanzania's political economy contributed to the ruling party's institutional erosion. This process began in the 1980s before accelerating in 1990 after Nyerere stepped down as CCM Chairman. From Mwinyi's tenure through Kiwkete's, CCM leaders embraced a new form of 'politicized accumulation', building factional alliances within CCM based on ties to private business interests. These same leaders then struggled—and largely failed—to ensure CCM's institutional integrity as factional interests undermined both the party bureaucracy and parliamentary nomination process.

4.2.3 Presidential Succession and Its Discontents

While acknowledging CCM's institutional decline, it is nevertheless important to remember that this decline was relative to its past strength. Moreover, the legacy of this former institutional strength endured, shaping contemporary party politics in important ways. Perhaps the most striking indicator of this lasting strength is CCM's '*adaptability*', i.e. its routine leadership succession. Since 1985 up through the 2015 elections, the party oversaw a presidential succession every ten years in accordance with a constitutional two-term limit. Since 1990, newly elected presidents have also assumed the party chairmanship.

To make sense of CCM's succession politics is to grapple with the implications of *competing trends* in the party, both new and old. On the one hand, the presidential nomination emerged as the ultimate prize sought by rival patronage networks. On the other hand, factional tensions were at least partly kept in check due to CCM's *enduring institutional constraints*. This institutional legacy had *three, inter-related effects:*[95] one, it *delayed* the consolidation of factional patronage networks, which built up gradually through existing party structures; two, it heightened the *fragility* of these networks because of their dependence on the formal structures around which they were built; and three, it *discourages defections* due to this same dependence on formal structures. In what follows, I use the example of Edward Lowassa's drive to become

---

[95] As recalled earlier, these effects are consistent with Pierson's (2000) concept of 'increasing returns', which influence actors' behaviour so as to reproduce existing institutions, including through 'coordination effects' (e.g. being compelled to organize through CCM formal structures), 'learning effects' (e.g. learning to navigate those structures), and 'adaptive expectations' (e.g. anticipating organizing through CCM as the main route to success).

president to show both the growth of factional networks and how CCM's institutional inheritance helped limit their destabilizing potential. Lowassa's bid for the presidency in 2015 led to a striking mass defection from CCM; however, his painstakingly assembled patron–client network was later *systematically destroyed*, rooted out of the ruling party upon whose structures it had depended.

First, Lowassa and his factional allies are emblematic of Tanzania's new political economy and, specifically, the close relations between ruling party factions and the country's *nouveau riche*. Lowassa joined CCM as a paid district-level official immediately after graduating from university in 1977. He later came to personify a new breed of ambitious young politician within CCM. He amassed a considerable personal fortune, prompting Nyerere to raise doubts about its origins ('this guy, where does he get all that money?').[96] He also cultivated an extensive network of business 'friends'. Among them was his long-time ally, Rostam Aziz. Like Lowassa but on a still grander scale, Aziz was a beneficiary of the post-Nyerere forms of 'politicized accumulation' in Tanzania. Of Iranian descent, he hails from one of Tanzania's leading business families, was the country's first billionaire, and for a period, its wealthiest man. He was the first Tanzanian of Asian origin to win a parliamentary seat in 1992, telling a friend at the time that 'political leverage is good for business'.[97] His fortune came from investments in mining, the Dar es Salaam Port, real estate, and his holdings in Tanzania's largest telecoms company, which he partly sold off in 2014 for $240m.[98] As mentioned previously, he also briefly served as CCM Treasurer under Kikwete after aiding with the latter's 2005 presidential campaign.

Lowassa and Aziz used their financial muscle to build their factional base within the party, organizing from local to national level. Regarding district and regional organizing, Lowassa was first elected MP for Monduli constituency in 1995 after winning an impressive 87.3 per cent of the vote.[99] He went on to serve for another 20 years, always running either unopposed or winning by a landslide. Through a combination of generous development initiatives and a tightly controlled personal intelligence network, he 'put the constituency at

---

[96] Mtatiro, Julius, 'Edward Lowassa: Mbunge wa Monduli', *Mwananchi*, 11 May 2015.

[97] Interview with long-time CCM member, businessman, and family friend of Aziz, Dar es Salaam, April 2016.

[98] Nsehe, Mfonobong. 'Tanzania's Richest Man Concludes Sale of Vodacom Stakes'. *Forbes*, 2 May 2014. Accessed 26 June 2017: https://www.forbes.com/sites/mfonobongnsehe/2014/05/02/tanzanias-richest-man-concludes-sale-of-vodacom-stake/#23ebe30f6d83. Accessed 26 June 2017: http://www.azaniapost.com/agenda/rostam-is-among-the-longest-serving-board-member-of-vodacom-h1652.html.

[99] He was previously appointed as an MP in 1990.

his fingertips.[100] He also extended his reach through the local CCM structures to become the dominant political patron in Arusha region. In 2015,
both the Arusha CCM Regional Chairman and the Regional Publicity Secretary had started their political careers in Monduli and owed their success
to Lowassa.[101] Meanwhile, at the national level, Lowassa and Aziz built up a
support base through a series of painstaking interventions. They contributed
to the campaigns of parliamentary candidates. They also bought the loyalty of
members in CCM's key national structures, including the NEC, the Central
Committee, and the party youth wing, UVCCM.[102] As one long-time party
insider and family friend to Aziz commented, '[Party officials] were being
paid like they were employees. These chaps had money.'[103] Aziz also invested
in a media house, which was later used as an unofficial mouthpiece during
campaigns.[104]

The ultimate ambition of both Lowassa and Aziz was to secure the presidency, which proved a drawn-out saga. To win, aspirants had to clear several
hurdles in a process that—unlike parliamentary nominations—changed little
since 1995. First, they collect endorsements from a set number of party rank-
and-file. After submitting their nomination forms to the party headquarters,
they then wait for a stamp of approval from the party's ethics committee. Third,
the Central Committee, composed of top party cadres, selects five names
from the pool of eligible contenders. The NEC then selects three names from
the five, which are finally forwarded the National Conference, the supreme
decision-making body.[105]

Lowassa first entered the fray in 1995 alongside Kikwete, another of the
new breed of CCM politicians. The two campaigned together, adopting
an unprecedented and costly style of collecting their public endorsements
through mass mobilization. While Nyerere blocked the suspiciously wealthy
Lowassa from progressing through the vetting stage, Kikwete only narrowly
missed out to Mkapa in the final round of voting.[106] He then went on to serve
for 10 years as Mkapa's foreign minister. Lowassa also received a ministerial
portfolio.

[100] Interview with CHADEMA MP elected in 2015 after defecting from CCM, Dodoma, February
2016.
[101] Ibid.
[102] Interview with researcher and CCM activist, Dar es Salaam, August 2015.
[103] Ibid.
[104] Interview, journalist and businessman, Dar es Salaam, April 2016. Interview with a journalist,
Dodoma, January 2016.
[105] See CCM, 2010.
[106] Interview, journalist and businessman, Dar es Salaam, April 2016.

During this period, Lowassa continued to organize for another presidential bid. However, together with Aziz, he opted to support Kikwete's candidacy ahead of the 2005 elections, allegedly because he was himself still marked by 'Nyerere's fatwa'.[107] Already from 2003, Lowassa and Aziz set about building Kikwete's reputation; they attacked his rivals, mobilized support, and ultimately, organized large crowds to rally at the CCM headquarters in Dodoma.[108] By 2005, it appeared a foregone conclusion that Kikwete would be selected as CCM's presidential candidate. Yet 'Kikwete's momentum was not Kikwete's doing' but rather that of his *mtandao* (network), masterminded by Lowassa and Aziz.[109] Moreover, his candidacy was by no means uncontroversial. The party ethics committee recommended that he be eliminated from the race due to excessive campaign spending, but President Mkapa shelved the dossiers. As one long-time CCM cadre reported, 'Even the Intelligence people told Mkapa that Kikwete is like a whirlwind and the resources he has marshalled through Lowassa and Aziz, there is no way you can beat him with your own candidate.' The interviewee then concluded, 'So the rich and the wealthy had an open door into CCM.'

Kikwete eventually won the nomination, although the party was left divided.[110] His subsequent campaign and landslide electoral victory helped temporarily subdue these tensions,[111] but the honeymoon period did not last long. Relations between Kikwete and Lowassa, now appointed Prime Minister, soon soured with some alleging that Lowassa was angling to replace Kikwete in 2010 after only one term.[112] In February 2008, Lowassa resigned the premiership over a corruption scandal, which he maintained was a set-up.[113] But he was not long deterred and soon renewed his efforts to extent his network within the party hierarchy, seemingly in preparation for a future presidential bid.[114]

While he did not challenge Kikwete in 2010, the incumbent President's margin of victory shrank by nearly 20 percentage points, in part because he

---

[107] Ibid. Interview, former CCM MP, Dar es Salaam, August 2015.
[108] Ibid. Accessed 21 February 2017: http://www.theeastafrican.co.ke/news/-/2558/246228/-/item/ 1/-/hjywck/-/index.html.
[109] Multiple interviews with MPs, journalists, and other close political observers.
[110] Interview, journalist, Dodoma, January 2016. Accessed 21 February 2017: http://www. theeastafrican.co.ke/magazine/-/434746/245642/-/13yknf6/-/index.html.
[111] Mwikalo, Rama. 'The Kikwete Mystique', *The Guardian*, 7 October 2005, p. 8.
[112] Interview, CCM MP, June 2015. Interview, journalist, June 2015. Interview, CCM activist, August 2015; Interview with long-time CCM cadre, Dar es Salaam, April 2016.
[113] See Chapters 1 and 5 for more discussion of the scandal and Lowassa's resignation.
[114] Interview with a businessman and family friend to Aziz, Dar es Salaam, April 2016.

no longer had the support of the 2005 *mtandao*.[115] Meanwhile, a battle was brewing ahead of 2015. Besides the above-mentioned changes to the parliamentary nomination procedure, Kikwete attempted to use another rule change to diminish Lowassa's influence within CCM. In 2012, the party widened the range of people who could become members of NEC, one of the party organs responsible for selecting a presidential nominee. This was ostensibly a democratizing move. However, Lowassa had bankrolled the candidacies of numerous previously elected NEC members, and as such, the strategy behind the 2012 rule change was 'to dilute [the NEC] by bringing more people in who do not support Lowassa'.[116] The reform did little to limit intra-party competition, though. Reflecting on the state of CCM internal politics in the lead-up to the 2015 election, one former CCM member turned opposition MP confided, 'The divisions [within the party] started from top to bottom, even village, house-hold level.' He emphasized, 'All groups had unseen commanding officers', clarifying, 'They were made for targeting the presidency.'[117]

Come time for CCM to make its nomination for the 2015 race, an unprecedented 42 presidential hopefuls circled the country to collect endorsements. Lowassa had by far the most expensive and elaborate campaign. He launched his bid in late May at a rally that attracted thousands and was broadcast live on several TV channels. He went on to collect 850,000 endorsements from party members, far exceeding the required 450. He was not the only candidate to mobilize in this way, but he stood out from the pack. Among the other contenders was Bernard Membe, then Minister of Foreign Affairs and rumoured to be Kikwete's favourite.

In the end, Lowassa's mobilization efforts were for naught as Kikwete ensured that his name was eliminated from among the eligible aspirants by the CCM ethics committee. This move provoked an uproar in the NEC. Lowassa supporters retaliated by voting out two of Kikwete's known favourites, including Membe. Of the three remaining, the National Conference chose John Magufuli, a relatively low-profile underdog. The story did not end there, though. Only a few weeks later, the opposition coalition UKAWA announced Lowassa as its presidential candidate. His defection prompting a mini exodus from the ruling party, especially in his home region of Arusha where many

---

[115] Interview, journalist and businessman, Dar es Salaam, April 2016. Interview, former CCM MP, Dar es Salaam, August 2015; Interview, CCM activist, Dar es Salaam, August 2015.
[116] Interview, CCM MP, Dar es Salaam, July 2015. Interview, journalist, Dodoma, January 2016; Interview, CCM activist, Dar es Salaam, August 2015.
[117] Interview with the former chair of UVCCM for Arusha Region and now CHADEMA MP, Dodoma, January 2016.

CCM politicians and party officials remained loyal to Lowassa personally.[118] Yet other erstwhile Lowassa supporters—notably CCM parliamentarians— denounced his defection and pledged allegiance to Magufuli, presumably doubting Lowassa's calculation and fearing for their own political prospects. This reflex was consistent with what observers have referred to as CCM's 'political tradition of consensual politics' or, where consensus is lacking, a tendency to fall into line once a decision has been reached.[119]

Lowassa ended up winning an unprecedented 40 per cent of the vote for the opposition but was unable to live up to the pre-election hype of an historic CCM defeat. What's more, his remaining supporters within CCM had to contend with a post-election hunt for party 'traitors'. This search culminated in early 2017 when a reported 1519 rank-and-file members were expelled while a further 12 top cadres were ejected from the Party shortly thereafter.[120] Expulsions on this scale had never occurred and speak to the disruption CCM experienced as an organization in 2015. Yet, they also demonstrate the *vulnerability of informal patronage organizations* that are enmeshed within and therefore dependent on a formal party structure. Further indications of this vulnerability included the routine harassment of newly defected CHADEMA supporters in Monduli, Lowassa's old constituency, a process that spread countrywide.[121]

Finally, Lowassa's business backers were 'in a state of shock' with some moving their operations to neighbouring Zambia and Mozambique 'for fear that they would be treated badly'.[122] For instance, many were in the transport and logistics sectors and depended heavily on government contracts for their business. Unsurprisingly, the new Monduli MP lamented that Lowassa's erstwhile 'friends' were no longer interested in supporting constituency development.[123] Rostam Aziz, for his part, did not condone Lowassa's defection and left Tanzania for a period after the elections. Severed from its moorings within the ruling

---

[118] 'Mtikisiko mwingine CCM, M/kiti Arusha atimka', *Mwananchi*, 10 August 2015. Accessed 21 February 2017: http://www.mwananchi.co.tz/habari/Mtikisiko-mwingine-CCM—M-kiti-Arusha-atimka/-/1597578/2826492/-/qdb1sqz/-/index.html. Interview, CHADEMA MP previously in CCM, February 2016.

[119] Kelsall, 2003: 62. Interview, journalist, Dodoma, January 2016. Fear of potential consequences, including financial, should they defect and the opposition prove unsuccessful likely also played a role. See below discussion.

[120] 'Shock as CCM expels ex-minister, 11 strong cadres', *The Citizen*, 12 March 2017. Accessed 17 December 2023: https://www.thecitizen.co.tz/tanzania/news/shock-as-ccm-expels-ex-minister-11-strong-cadres-2582866.

[121] Interview, CHADEMA MP previously in CCM, February 2016.

[122] Interview, CCM MP, January 2016; Interview, journalist, January 2016.

[123] Interview, CHADEMA MP previously in CCM, February 2016.

party structures and cut off from its financial backers, Lowassa's painstakingly assembled patronage network quickly evaporated.

The Lowassa case shows that succession politics were a major focus of factional struggle, encouraged by Tanzania's changed dynamics of 'politicized accumulation'. Yet his long hunt for the presidency also attests to the enduring legacy of CCM as an 'institutionalized coalition'. Lowassa and Aziz had to coordinate their political offensive from within the party's formal structures, *gradually* building up their network, and their investment ultimately proved *fragile*, unable to survive Lowassa's defection. For contrast, we can revisit the fate of Kenya's erstwhile authoritarian party, KANU, identified in Chapter 3 as a 'bargained coalition' without strong institutional structures. Political heavyweights of Lowassa's stature within KANU defected immediately after Kenya's return to multiparty politics. Unlike Lowassa, though, they effectively mobilized their own informal patronage organizations outside the ruling party, reducing President Moi's share of the vote to a mere 36 per cent in the 1992 elections. They then drove KANU from power in 2002 when Moi attempted to hand over to a successor.[124] Thus, whereas Lowassa patronage base was slow to consolidate and could not survive outside of CCM, Kenya's political barons and their allied patronage networks asserted themselves quickly and forcefully, all but wiping KANU from the electoral map.

In sum, from the 1980s up through the 2015 elections, CCM experienced a process of institutional decay amidst dramatic changes to Tanzania's political economy. The autonomy of the party *bureaucracy* as well as the *complexity* and *coherence* of its formal structures all suffered due to increased factional contestation. Yet institutional checks endured and, despite factional disruptions, helped ensure a routine presidential succession process, evidence of its institutional *adaptability*.

4.2.4 Evaluating the Role of Opposition Pressures

I have argued that Tanzania's changing political economy accounts for CCM's partial institutional erosion. There nevertheless remains the alternative hypothesis whereby the transition to multiparty politics and resultant inter-party competition drove CCM's institutional changes, and in particular, party leaders' decision to adopt a more inclusive candidate selection

---

[124] Ajulu, 1999; Anderson, 2003.

procedure. This alternative hypothesis—while not irrelevant—appears of secondary significance relative to the main argument put forward here.

First, the multiparty transition itself resulted from a top-down decision by CCM leaders. Somewhat paradoxically, the motivations had more to do with *strengthening CCM*, i.e. responding to changes already occurring *within* the ruling party, than with accommodating opposition pressure. Throughout the late 1980s, Nyerere expressed concerns that CCM had become too bureaucratic and 'detached from the people'.[125] After handing over the party chairmanship to Mwinyi in 1990, he began to advocate a multiparty transition. While his position surprised many in CCM,[126] there was a clear logic behind it; this was in keeping with Hirschman's classic argument whereby an 'exit' option can push a flagging organization to address its weaknesses.[127] Just before CCM reinstated multi-party politics, Nyerere shared his views with a party delegation sent to consult at his home in Butiama District. As a member of that delegation recalled, 'One of the issues that arose at the Butiama meeting was this return to multipartyism is very healthy for Tanzanians... You need now competition in order for this CCM to renew and revitalize itself. [Nyerere] called it a "dead party".[128] Nyerere later played an instrumental role in pushing for multiparty reform during a National Conference convened in February 1992.[129]

So how significant then were the effects of this transition on CCM? The answer, to begin with at least, is not very. The institutional changes documented above—and specifically the moves towards more inclusive parliamentary nominations—came well before opposition parties started to pose any serious electoral threat. CCM's share of parliamentary votes actually *increased* as the first changes to the Party's primary procedure were introduced in 2000 and 2005 (Figure 4.4).

Admittedly, ahead of the 2010 polls, CCM's electoral support declined and the Party then moved towards a more radically inclusive nominations procedure. However, CCM's 2010 vote share was still healthy, especially as the 60 per cent of votes translated into 74 per cent of parliamentary seats. Moreover, as noted earlier, interviewees reported that the primary reason for the 2010 rule change was concern about factional tensions within the ruling

---

[125] Interview with Nyerere's former PA and long-serving CCM cadre, Dar es Salaam, March 2016. See also: Nyerere, *Kujitawala na Kujitegemea*, February 1987; Othman, 1994; Tripp, 1997: 84.

[126] Interview, CCM cadre, March 2016; Interview, journalist, 2016; Chachage, 2003: 28.

[127] Hirschman, 1970.

[128] Interview with family friend of Nyerere's and CCM cadre, Dar es Salaam, April 2016.

[129] Interview, CCM cadre, March 2016. Nyerere also argued that Tanzania must adapt to a changed geo-politics amidst the 'third wave' of democratization. Chachage, 2003.

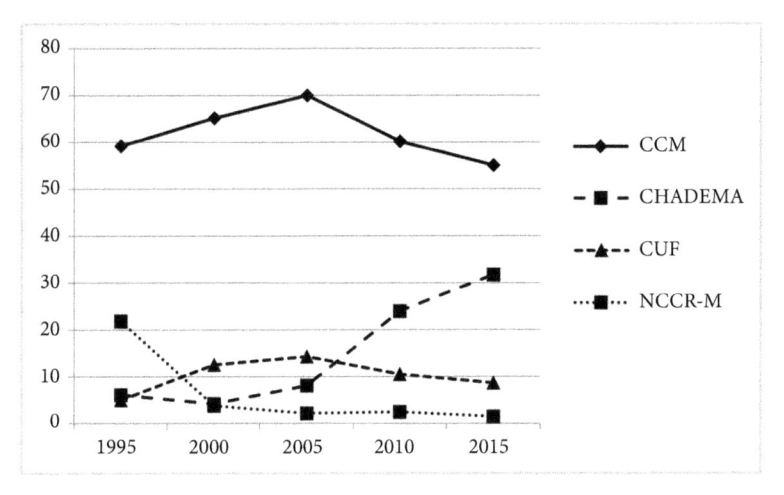

Figure 4.4 Tanzania—percentage of parliamentary vote by party

party itself. Come 2015, the CCM leaderships' decision to forego vetoing any winners of party primaries was at least partly out of fear that vetoed candidates would defect to the opposition. Yet even that fear cannot be understood without appreciating how *intra*-party tensions contributed to Lowassa's defection.

In sum, the opposition pressure thesis does not sufficiently explain why CCM kept altering its nomination procedures up through 2010. While inter-party competition had some belated influence, especially during the 2015 race, this emphasis offers at best a partial explanation of institutional changes within the party. These had much more to do with Tanzania's changed political economy and the rising factionalism within CCM.

4.3 The National Resistance Movement, a Weak Party with Ambitions

Having analysed the dynamics of continuity and change within an 'institutionalized coalition', and with a brief allusion to KANU for contrast, I now analyse the NRM's trajectory as a 'bargained coalition'. Unlike an institutionalized coalition whose strength may erode with time, a bargained coalition is unlikely to break from its path-dependent trajectory. This is because it would be difficult—and likely destabilizing—for party leaders to recentralize wealth accumulation, yet this is a necessary precondition for any successful party-building efforts. In keeping with this argument, I first show how NRM leaders maintained their preferred strategy of 'politicized accumulation' up through the 2016 elections, allowing for private sector expansion albeit policing the loyalty of Uganda's private accumulators. Next, I indicate how party leaders' parallel attempts to strengthen party discipline through formal institutional reforms failed, and this due to the continued proliferation of rival factions. As in the CCM case, I evaluate the NRM's institutional strength with reference to its *bureaucratic autonomy* as well as the *coherence* and *complexity* of its parliamentary candidate selection procedure. I also discuss the party's institutional 'adaptability', or in this case, lack thereof; indeed, President Museveni has personalized both the presidency and party chairmanship, reinforcing his grip on the leadership through a mix of economic tools and politically expedient manipulation of formal party rules, among other interventions. Finally, I evaluate whether inter-party competition influenced the institutional make-up of the NRM, concluding its effects were marginal.

4.3.1 Policing the Rich

The previous chapter outlined how NRM leaders—and principally President Museveni—cultivated a pro-regime business constituency, one that could accumulate relatively freely yet was still partly dependent on the leadership. I here elaborate both on how this constituency was maintained and on how, where individuals challenged top leaders, they were subject to ad hoc forms of *economic discipline.*

From the 1990s onward, NRM leaders continued to favour a politically marginal economic elite of Asian Ugandans and foreign investors, although a selection of African entrepreneurs also rose to the fore alongside a politico-cum-economic elite within Museveni's innermost circle.[130] This approach featured highly personalized ties between the President, key allies, and private entrepreneurs.[131] One businessman emphasized this point when interviewed.[132] A Kenyan Asian, he came to Uganda in the late 1990s and became involved in mineral exports, forex, and real estate. He stressed that, rather than working through formal associations, investor engagement in Uganda was 'like an informal sector', adding, 'I have my problem, I speak to the minister, and I'm done; I don't worry about the policy.' Several additional examples are

---

[130] Mwenda, 2008; Tangri and Mwenda, 2013, 2019.
[131] Bukenya and Hickey, 2017.
[132] Interview, businessman, Kampala, December 2014.

emblematic of the broader NRM tendency to award preferential treatment to particular entrepreneurs. As mentioned in Chapter 3, an Asian investor, Sudhir Ruparelia, was one such example. Known by his first name, Sudhir quickly emerged as Uganda's wealthiest man under the NRM, benefiting from various favours, for instance, Museveni intervening to block the Uganda Revenue Authority (URA) from recovering tax arrears.[133] Another one-time Museveni favourite was Hassan Basajjabalaba, the former chairman of the NRM entrepreneurs league and long-time backer of Museveni. He was repeated awarded loans and tax wavers by the Bank of Uganda (BoU) and URA, all at Museveni's behest.[134] Other apparent favourites included the real estate mogul Hamis Kiggundu, among the younger successful businessmen,[135] and Sudanese-Ugandan businessman, Mohammed Hamid. Although Hamid was known to have close ties with the President, he still shocked many when he personally contacted Museveni over an attempt by the State Minister of Labour to solicit a bribe, leading to the minister's arrest.[136] Finally, at the very top perched the NRM 'aristocracy', an overlapping mix of long-time ministers, family relations and military officers whose business interests and personal fortunes benefited most from their proximity to the President.[137]

The flip side of this emphasis on personalized contacts and favours is a weak private sector lobby with few notable business associations.[138] The Private Sector Foundation Uganda (PSFU) did assume a more prominent role after the 2016 elections, but this was not over a policy matter but rather to coordinate the demands of individual businessmen for an eye-watering Shs1.3tr ($389m) bailout from government.[139] PSFU chairman, Patrick Bitature, reportedly Uganda's second wealthiest man and one of the would-be beneficiaries,[140]

---

[133] Tangri and Mwenda, 2013: 111.

[134] Tangri and Mwenda, 2013: 113.

[135] Serunkuma, Yusuf. 'As Kenyan academician said: "you're a theif if you're richin this country', *The Observer*, 12 April 2017. Accessed 25 July 2017: http://observer.ug/viewpoint/52250-as-kenyan-academician-said-you-re-a-thief-if-you-re-rich-in-this-country.html.

[136] Kiggundu, Edris. 'AYA boss Hamid: Unveiling the man who fixed a minister', *The Observer*, 14 April 2017. Accessed 25 July 2017: http://observer.ug/news/headlines/52324-aya-boss-hamid-unveiling-the-man-who-fixed-a-minister.html.

[137] Izama, Angelo. 'Family Therapy: Dynasty and change in Utanda', *African Arguments*, 29 June 2015. Accessed 14 December 2021: https://africanarguments.org/2015/06/family-therapy-dynasty-and-change-in-uganda-by-angelo-izama/. See also: Vlassenroot et al, 2012; Tangri and Mwenda, 2013: 58, 112–113, 191; Khisa, 2016: 740–741; Chapter 6, this volume.

[138] Tangri and Mwenda, 2019.

[139] 'FULL LIST: 65 loan-stressed firms line up for Sh1 trillion taxpayer bailout', *Monitor*, 21 July 2016. Accessed 25 July 2017: http://www.monitor.co.ug/Business/65-loan-stressed-firms-line-up-for-Shs1-trillion-tax/688322-3305166-d6h193/index.html.

[140] 'Uganda's five richest men names', *Monitor*, 9 November 2012. Accessed 25 July 2017: http://www.monitor.co.ug/News/National/Uganda-s-five-richest-men-named/688334-1616168-qsmyxcz/index.html.

helped spearhead the initiative. Museveni proved initially receptive after receiving campaign contributions from many of the concerned entrepreneurs, including Bitature.[141] While the bailout plan was eventually dropped amidst heavy criticism from BoU and URA technocrats and the wider public,[142] funds were still allegedly delivered to select recipients as part of an informal bailout.[143] This push for a bailout aside, Museveni has not historically welcomed efforts by business leaders to organize, be it to support each other with loans or to form lobbying groups. An example is the Kwagalana group, which comprised roughly 40 mostly African entrepreneurs who, in addition to a range of business interests, also invested heavily in Kampala real estate.[144] Museveni proved loath to meet with Kwagalana collectively and, as of 2017, was openly deriding its members, having fallen out with several of the more high-profile representatives.[145]

This brings us to the topic of what, in fact, has happened to investors with whom Museveni is no longer on good terms. Just as the President has rewarded his allies economically, he has punished his adversaries. Sometimes it is a question of the President demanding proof of loyalty where not yet confirmed. New entrepreneurs, buoyed by Uganda's recent economic growth and private sector expansion, have been 'bound' by patronage or, at the very least, compelled to show political allegiance through campaign contributions.[146] Other investors have had a range of disciplinary tools used against them, including the denial of procurement contracts, aggressive crackdowns on tax evasion, suspension of informal capital subsidies, application of previously disregarded regulatory strictures, denial of business licences, and the like. The widely acknowledged use of the intelligence services to keep tabs on private

---

[141] Khisa, 2016: 741. 'Bail out is a hoax – Bitature', *New Vision*, 27 July 2016. Accessed 25 July 2017: http://www.newvision.co.ug/new_vision/news/1430945/bail-hoax-bitature. Gitta, Alex. 'Uganda bailout', *DW*, 28 July 2016. Accessed 25 July 2017: http://www.dw.com/en/uganda-company-bailouts-politically-motivated-critics-allege/a-19432023

[142] 'Uganda: Proposed govt bailout comes under attack', *The East African*, 20 August 2016. Accessed 25 July 2017: http://www.theeastafrican.co.ke/business/Uganda-Proposed-govt-bailout-comes-under-attack-/2560-3351556-72mwp9/index.html. Matsiko, Haggai. 'Fight over Museveni's business bailout money', *The Independent*, 19 July 2016. Accessed 25 July 2017: https://www.independent.co.ug/fight-musevenis-business-bailout-money/.

[143] 'Govt domestic arrears hit Shs2.7 trillion', *The Observer*, 21 May 2017. Accessed 25 July 2017: http://observer.ug/news/headlines/52972-govt-domestic-arrears-hit-shs-2-7-trillion.html.

[144] Tangri, 2015. 'Kwagalana Group Members Appraisal Raises Fear', *ChimpReports*, 5 December 2012. Accessed 25 July 2017: http://www.chimpreports.com/7244-kwagalana-group-members-appraisal-raises-fear/. Kabaani, Michael, and Ssebidde Kiryowa. 'The deepest pockets', *New Vision*, 6 January 2012. Accessed 25 July 2017: http://www.newvision.co.ug/new_vision/news/1298775/deepest-pockets.

[145] 'Uganda: What Museveni said at Ssebaana's vigil', *Monitor*, 13 July 2017. Accessed 25 July 2017: http://allafrica.com/stories/201707140082.html.

[146] Tangri and Mwenda, 2019.

entrepreneurs' activities, both economic and political, has further constrained investors room for manoeuvre.[147]

Most obviously, these tools of economic discipline act as a strong deterrent for would-be opposition politicians and political financiers.[148] A former Treasurer of the opposition party, Forum for Democratic Change (FDC), emphasized the pervasive fear within the business community when donating to the opposition. He noted, 'A businessman could not give you money. He would go secretly. [...] They would tell you, "Please, don't reveal where you've got money from". [...] The State would deny you contracts if they hear you are helping the opposition.'[149] The above-cited Kenyan-Asian businessman was even more blunt in his assessment, stating, 'No investor will go to support opposition. Investors will look at their own security, their own investment. I don't think any investor will take interest in politics as such.' This disinterest had its limits, though, as he later claimed to 'have' 50 MPs, implying they were indebted to him most likely due to campaign contributions.

The opposition aside, NRM politicians and their financiers have also proved vulnerable. This is true both of relatively low-ranking parliamentary backbenchers and of top-level NRM elite, should their relations with Museveni deteriorate. For instance, one interviewee, an NRM MP-cum-businessman, was branded a critic by the NRM leadership. He listed a range of ways his businesses were then 'sabotaged'.[150] 'They used URA', he explained, adding, 'They got all the accounts and squeezed the capital out of the business.'

More high-profile cases involved the above-mentioned businessman, Basajjabalaba, who after Museveni started to doubt his loyalty, was formally charged with alleged tax evasion in 2013.[151] More high-profile still was the case involving former Prime Minister, Amama Mbabazi. Like Basajjabalaba, Mbabazi was long considered one of the NRM 'untouchables', amassing a considerable fortune over the course of his nearly thirty years in government. He nevertheless encountered difficulties once rumours spread that he was vying for the presidency in 2016. One early indication that relations had soured between Mbabazi and Museveni came when the National Bank of Commerce (NBC), a bank in which Mbabazi had a large stake, was taken into receivership by BoU.[152] The case for taking over the bank appeared

[147] Interviews, NRM MP, November 2015; Interview, FDC MP, Kampala, January 2015.
[148] Khisa, 2016: 742.
[149] Interview, FDC MP, Kampala, January 2015.
[150] Interview, NRM MP and businessman, Kampala, August 2016.
[151] Tangri, 2015.
[152] Conversation with journalists, Kampala, July 2016.

sound.[153] Still, given that regulatory requirements were apparently overlooked in other cases, the general perception was that the take-over of NBC was 'about politics'.[154] It was, moreover, not the first time that a bank collapsed under such circumstances. A precedent was set in the late 1990s when, after initially supporting Greenland Bank, Museveni let it collapse amidst concerns that its managing director supported the opposition and intended to run for president.[155]

In a truly dramatic follow-up to the NBC saga, BoU also took over Crane Bank in October 2016. Established in 1995, Crane Bank grew to be Uganda's third largest commercial bank and was understood to be partially owned by the above-mentioned Sudhir, although it was later revealed that Sudhir in fact fully owned the bank. In 2012, BoU made the controversial decision to transfer NBC's assets to Crane Bank, seemingly punishing one regime insider while rewarding another. But again, with rumours spreading of a disagreement between Sudhir and Museveni,[156] Crane Bank's fortunes reversed, and it was taken over for failing to meet minimum liquidity requirements.[157] In June 2017, BoU took the additional step of suing Sudhir after an investigation suggested that the beleaguered businessman had embezzled over Shs400b ($112m) with the assistance of his business associates, including the Chairman of the by then much-maligned Kwagalana group, Godfrey Kirumira.[158] While BoU adopted a hard line in this instance, observers were quick to query its institutional integrity in making these decisions. It had previously bailed out Crane Bank in 2005 and then continued to sign off on Crane Bank's accounts despite years of malpractice.[159] BoU's inconsistency again suggests the fundamentally political nature of both Crane Bank's precipitous rise and its subsequent fall.

---

[153] Rupiny, David. ' BoU: National Bank of Commerce was in financial mess', *URN*, 28 September 2012. Accessed 28 April 2017: https://ugandaradionetwork.com/story/bou-national-bank-of-commerce-was-in-financial-mess.

[154] Conversation with journalists, Kampala, July 2016.

[155] Ibid. See also Mwenda, 2008; Tangri and Mwenda, 2019.

[156] Nsehe, Mfonobong. 'Former billionaire Sudhir Ruparelia loses lucrative forex bureaus in Uganda', *Forbes*, 19 May 2017. Accessed 26 July 2017: https://www.forbes.com/sites/mfonobongnsehe/2017/05/19/former-billionaire-sudhir-ruparelia-loses-lucrative-forex-bureaus-in-uganda/#7c6e903e243c. Email exchange with an academic and journalist, October 2016. Discussion with Uganda expert, February 2018.

[157] Mbanga, Jeff, and Alon Mwesigwa. 'How Crane bank got into trouble', *The Observer*, 21 October 2016. Accessed 31 October 2016: http://www.observer.ug/news-headlines/47112-how-crane-bank-got-to-trouble.

[158] 'Sudhir, Bank of Uganda case kicks off', *New Vision*, 13 September 2017. Accessed 17 December 2023:https://www.newvision.co.ug/news/1461514/sudhir-bank-uganda-kicks. Kiggundu, Edris. '2003: How term limits got not Ssempebwa report', *The Observer*, 19 July 2017. Accessed 17 December 2023: http://observer.ug/news/headlines/53923-2003-how-term-limits-got-into-ssempebwa-report.html.

[159] Ssemogerere, Karoli. 'Uganda: The Crane Bank Affairs Enter Murky Third Phase', *Monitor*, 13 July 2017. Accessed 17 December 2023: http://allafrica.com/stories/201707130144.html. 'Uganda:

The above discussion outlines how the NRM regime—with President Museveni at the helm—cultivated personal ties with particular entrepreneurs. By the same token, the President used a range of tools to impose economic discipline where political loyalties were suspect. Despite tolerating private wealth accumulation, any political threats from an empowered business community were thus kept in check. That said, even if direct challenges to President Museveni were not tolerated, factional contestation did persist, and as discussed below, routinely frustrated the NRM top leadership.

4.3.2 Party-Building, or Not

As was true during the initial period of NRM regime consolidation, private wealth accumulation continued to fuel factional rivalries heading into the 2000s. These rivalries—and the absence of a centralized source of party finance—then helped ensure the NRM's enduring institutional weakness. In particular, they presented a major obstacle to belated party-building efforts. The below analysis first highlights party leaders' repeated attempts at party strengthening. It then shows how these efforts failed, undercut by patronage pressures. Where the party leaders imposed discipline, it was achieved not by enforcing formal party rules but by using economic tools, among other means.

A major top-down initiative to strengthen the NRM came ahead of Uganda's 2005 multiparty transition. Somewhat paradoxically, and not dissimilar to the CCM case, NRM leaders saw multiparty politics as an opportunity to *strengthen ruling party* institutions, to make it 'the CCM of Uganda'. The idea was to develop formal mechanisms for enforcing party discipline, mechanisms that could 'silence [...] opposition groups *within* as well as outside the Movement'.[160] In December 2001, following a fractious election under the 'no party' system,[161] the NRM National Executive Committee (NEC) established an ad hoc committee to consider lifting the ban on opposition parties. While the committee report ultimately discouraged a multiparty transition, a minority report presented in January 2003 at State House was in favour. President Museveni sided with the pro-transition camp, making a return to multiparty politics 'more or less a concluded matter'.[162] During a speech

BoU let down Uganda on defunct Crane Bank', *Monitor*, 12 July 2017. Accessed 23 December 2023: http://allafrica.com/stories/201707120087.html.
    [160] Makara et al., 2009: 193–194 (emphasis added).
    [161] See Chapter 3.
    [162] Ssemujju, Ibrahim. 'NEC might agree to parties and then grant a third term', *The Daily Monitor*, 26 March 2003, pp. 16–17.

held at a NEC meeting the following March, Museveni justified this position, emphasizing concerns about the *internal* politics of the Movement.[163] He highlighted 'the tendency to clique formation', lamenting, 'These people are pulling this way and others are pulling the other way and they do it in public'. He also stressed that the Movement needed a 'smooth way of identifying candidates and funding them' to avoid the disorder that characterized the 2001 campaigns.

The Movement NEC and National Conference followed the President's steer and endorsed a return to multiparty politics. In 2005, Parliament passed a constitutional amendment to that effect while also lifting presidential term limits, discussed further below. The multiparty transition did not, however, have the disciplining effect Museveni and other leaders had anticipated. If anything, factional tensions intensified, prompting three formal investigations into the party's internal organization.

Immediately after the first multi-party elections in 2006, a committee chaired by long-time NRM National Vice Chairman, Al-Hajji Moses Kigongo, was commissioned to assess the NRM's election operations, and particularly the party's botched parliamentary nominations.[164] Despite raising serious concerns, the committee's report was never tabled for discussion within the party.[165] In 2009, a more thoroughgoing internal party probe was launched after two speeches by Chairman Museveni and Secretary General Mbabazi prompted the party NEC to establish the NEC Ad Hoc Issues Committee (NAIC).[166] The NAIC's Terms of Reference called for it to address Museveni's concerns about low party discipline, especially within the NRM parliamentary caucus. They also covered Mbabazi's more comprehensive list of organizational failings, such as: the lack of party activity between elections; vacant positions within the NRM structures; the insufficient facilitation and factional entanglements of Secretariat staff; the lack of a clear fundraising strategy and accountability; the lack of regular party meetings; and the absence of an accurate members' register.[167]

The NAIC consulted members of Cabinet, the parliamentary caucus and party leaders from across Uganda's four regions. Its final report revealed a

---

[163] Ssemujju, Ibrahim. 'President Museveni has a new vision for Uganda', *The Daily Monitor*, 28 March 2003, pp. 8–9.
[164] Mentioned in, 'Final Report of the NRM Parliamentary Caucus Select Committee on NRM Primary Elections' (Caucus report), July 2014.
[165] Ibid.
[166] See: 'Report of the NRM National Executive Committee Ad Hoc Issues Committee (NAIC)' (NAIC report), December 2009. Accessed in the Parliamentary Library, Parliament of Uganda.
[167] NAIC report, 2009: 17, 24–30.

high level of dissatisfaction over the party's organization and management. Yet once again, its recommendations were ignored ahead of the 2011 elections.[168] A third and final investigation, this time initiated by the NRM Parliamentary Caucus, delved into the renewed controversy surrounding the NRM's 2010 parliamentary nominations.[169] This report was only compiled after MPs, frustrated by the Secretariat's failure to probe irregularities in the party primaries, insisted that President Museveni allow them to investigate for themselves. The resultant report did see some of its recommendations implemented but, as discussed below, only those that could be instrumentalized to serve factional ends.

The failure of the successive investigations to remedy the NRM's organizational shortcomings is evident, first, in the continued weakness of the party bureaucracy. Mbabazi's concern that NRM structures did not operate between elections—or never materialized at all—was repeatedly raised in both the NAIC and Caucus reports as well as in interviews with NRM MPs. The NAIC report was particularly scathing. Local officials testified that regional and district party offices were 'not operational due to accumulated arrears'. NRM cadres from northern Uganda observed that, in their area, there were 'poor communication channels, no transport, no office imprest, no operational party work plan' and irregular or no meetings.[170] Respondents from central region added that there should be a clearer hierarchy within the NRM '[beginning] from the top leadership'.[171] Officials from eastern region warned that 'NRM structures are infiltrated by opposition members while other members within the structures have died, migrated or changed to other parties'.[172] Officials from western region, the home of many NRM top leaders and the party's principal vote bank, chided that party structures 'are in a slumber, which is a very bad political mistake for the NRM'.[173] Compiled five years later, the report produced by the NRM parliamentary caucus select committee was no more reassuring, observing, 'Party structures fall largely redundant during pre- and post-election periods, wasting vital human resource and compounding expenditure.'

In highlighting these various weaknesses, both the NAIC and parliamentary caucus reports direct their criticism at the NRM Secretariat. Between

---

[168] Caucus report, 2014.
[169] Ibid. Interview with the former Chairperson of the Select Committee, Kampala, February 2015. Interview, NRM MP, November 2014.
[170] NAIC report, 2009: 31.
[171] Ibid., 41.
[172] Ibid., 49.
[173] Ibid., 60.

elections, the Secretariat proved 'too disorganized' and under-resourced to run the party.[174] It lacked 'formal and functional communication linkages with party branches',[175] plus recruitment, pay, and retention of party cadres were all poor.[176] The reports note that party activities picked up during election campaigns but raise concerns about the impartiality of the Secretariat and NRM Electoral Commission. The NAIC report emphasizes the need to 'ensure that the NRM Secretariat offices are not used to de-campaign other NRM candidates'.[177] Meanwhile, the parliamentary caucus report observes, 'The NRM Electoral Commission is supposed to be responsible to the Central Executive Committee yet has been operating under the Secretariat, raising questions of authority, independence and credibility'.[178]

As already noted, the weaknesses of the NRM bureaucracy were tied to issues of party funding. Amidst repeated calls for the party to 'prepare annual budgets',[179] there was still no established revenue stream throughout the period under study. This led to a de facto 'reliance on the Chairman of the Party'.[180] Museveni was the NRM's principal funder, although he in turn relied on the diversion of public funds and donations from the carefully cultivated pro-regime business constituency.[181] Even these funds remained insufficient, though, and were frequently embezzled.[182] The parliamentary caucus report notes that during the 2010 NRM primaries, the party operated with a budget of only Shs4b despite a planned expenditure of Shs18b, or roughly $1.8m instead of $8m.[183] As a result, there were 'meagre resources supporting grassroots party officials', which left them 'vulnerable [. . .] to bribery by candidates'.[184] This bribery, plus the fact that the primaries were still 'highly monetized', was due to competing patron–client networks mobilizing their own private

---

[174] NAIC, 2009: 55; Caucus report, 2014.
[175] Caucus report, 2014.
[176] NAIC report, 2009: 53.
[177] Ibid., 28.
[178] Caucus report, 2014.
[179] NAIC report, 2009: 55; Caucus report, 2014.
[180] NAIC report, 2009: iv–v.
[181] Kiiza et al., 2008; Tangri and Mwenda, 2013: 116; ACFIM, 2016.
[182] Tangri and Mwenda, 2013: 115; ACFIM, 2016; Mugerwa, Yasiin, and Solomon Arinaitwe. 'Uganda: NRM Probes Party Officials Over Stolen Campaign Cash, to Be Prosecuted', *Monitor*, 22 March 2016. Accessed 25 November 2016: http://www.monitor.co.ug/News/National/NRM-probes-party-officials-over-stolen-campaign/-/688334/3127560/-/8wlk2hz/-/index.html.'NRM and campaign money, Kazibwe's AU bid', *New Vision*, 6 July 2016. Accessed 25 Nov 2016: http://www.newvision.co.ug/new_vision/news/1428752/todays-vision-nrm-campaign-money-kazibwes-au-bid. Baleke, Trevor. 'NRM officials miss salaries for 3 months', *The Observer*, 11 July 2016. Accessed 25 Nov 2016: http://www.observer.ug/news-headlines/45280-nrm-officials-miss-salaries-for-3-months.
[183] Caucus report, 2014.
[184] Ibid.

political finance, which dwarfed official party spending.[185] The factional rivalries were sometimes localized, for example, centred around a parliamentary candidate.[186] Yet, local factional battles often stretched up to the national level, involving NRM political bigwigs and their financiers.[187] The NAIC report is excoriating on this point. 'The rate at which intrigue, malice, and sabotage are taking roots in the Party is too much at all levels', it reads, then specifies, '[T]he prevailing conflicts originate nationally and descend locally'.[188] The report goes on to decry 'Godfathering',[189] insisting that 'senior party members from Kampala carrying money and distributing to candidates should be discouraged'.[190]

Turning from a discussion of the NRM's bureaucracy, this 'Godfathering' and candidate selection more generally put the party's fragile organization to the most severe test. As intimated earlier, chaotic primaries were the chief motivation behind *all three* of the NRM's formal investigations, which then also all agreed that factional tensions were primarily responsible for undermining formal party procedures. For example, the NAIC report observes that 'Independent candidates get support from NRM leaders' rather than the NRM party flagbearers.[191] The Caucus report adds that discipline is 'deteriorating', noting, 'senior party leaders facilitate particular aspirants during primaries and independents or even opposition candidates during the general election against party flag bearers'.[192]

Given these accounts, it is no surprise that reforming candidate selection procedure became a major focus of NRM leaders as they tried to strengthen party discipline. Yet factional jockeying continued while reform efforts failed. After the multiparty transition, the NRM first instituted what would later prove a relatively *complex* procedure for selecting parliamentary candidates through an electoral college.[193] Members of the sub-county and parish party conferences were tasked with selecting constituency candidates while members of the district and sub-county conferences selected district women candidates.[194] This procedure was immediately criticized, though, due to widespread

---

[185] Collord, 2016; Wilkins, 2016.
[186] Vokes, 2016; Wilkins, 2016, 2019, 2021.
[187] Kjaer and Katusiimeh, 2021.
[188] NAIC report, 2009: 36.
[189] For a definition, see Cheeseman, Bertrand, and Husaini, 2019.
[190] NAIC report, 2009: 52.
[191] NAIC, 2009: 40.
[192] Caucus report, 2014.
[193] This procedure was complex relative to what would come later. Yet if contrasted with CCM's candidate selection procedures, the NRM's approach was less complex, e.g. there was no formal vetting procedure or top-down veto power.
[194] 'Constitution of the NRM', as adopted 22 May 2003.

allegations of bribery and rigging. NRM-aligned aspirants used this alleged malpractice to justify running as Independents in the 2006 elections. Many later won their parliamentary seats, effectively defeating the purpose of the formal NRM nominations.

After these turbulent first primaries, NRM leaders altered the candidate selection procedure, adopting a far *simpler*—and more inclusive—approach. The idea was that all NRM members could participate in primaries. Yet in 2010, without a reliable register of NRM members to go on, *all voters in a constituency* could effectively participate. The logic motivating the switch to this *maximally inclusive* candidate selection procedure was near identical to the thinking behind CCM's institutional reforms, introduced around the same time. As one former NRM Minister explained, 'Few people can be bribed and swayed but you can't do this to the majority.'[195] As in, while a local party conference would be vulnerable to influence-peddling, no one candidate or allied faction could bribe an entire constituency electorate.

Again, as was true for CCM, this attempt to address factional rivalries through a procedural quick fix failed. The primaries in 2010 were, if anything, more controversial than in 2005, prompting the party to institute tribunals to handle over 600 petitions.[196] These came from disgruntled candidates who pointed to vote rigging, violence, and intimidation as reasons to contest the official primary results. Despite these irregularities, party leaders initially maintained their hard line against primary losers contesting as Independents. In October 2010, the NRM's National Vice Chairman, Kigongo, warned that the party would bar anyone who ran as an Independent for 20 years. He went on to denounce Independents, accusing, 'Some of you are self-seekers. You are just fighting for yourselves instead of fighting for the party. You will kill the party.'[197]

NRM-leaning Independents were, however, undeterred by these threats. Secretary General Mbabazi issued them with an ultimatum to stand down for the official NRM flag-bearers,[198] but a group of 80 Independents insisted that they would instead form their own district-level task forces to *mobilize*

[195] Karugaba, Mary, and Catherine Bekunda. 'NRM leaders back constitution review', *New Vision*, 25 May 2009. Accessed 25 November 2016: http://www.newvision.co.ug/new_vision/news/1243431/nrm-leaders-constitution-review.

[196] Among, Barbara. 'NRM lists winners, institutes tribunals to handle petitions', *New Vision*, 23 September 2010. Accessed 21 February 2016: http://www.newvision.co.ug/new_vision/news/1282194/nrm-lists-winners-institutes-tribunals-handle-petitions.

[197] Nambogga, Jackie. 'NRM vows to eliminate independents', *New Vision*, 3 October 2010. Accessed 15 June 2016: http://www.newvision.co.ug/new_vision/news/1281546/nrm-vows-eliminate-independents.

[198] Mugisa, Anne. 'NRM rebels given two weeks to quit', *New Vision*, 2 December 2010. Accessed 15 June 2016: http://www.newvision.co.ug/new_vision/news/1277849/nrm-rebels-weeks-quit.

jointly. They followed this up with a letter to President Museveni, calling on him as Chairman to intervene on their behalf. They also affirmed their love for the party and support for the President.[199] Museveni eventually acquiesced and talk of excluding Independents fizzled. This non-solution, though, only set the stage for a repeat of the same chaotic primary experience come 2015. Again, accusations and counteraccusations about the integrity of the primary process led to many NRM-leaning Independents.[200] Again, the Secretary General—now former Government Chief Whip, Justine Kasule Lumumba—threatened disciplinary action. Again, the party ultimately allowed defeated parliamentary aspirants to campaign as Independents without any sanction.[201] This occurred even as President Museveni criticised how the party primaries resembled a 'massive General Election'.[202] Informal patronage spending and factionalism thus subverted formal NRM nomination procedures.

Given this factional dynamic, the cumulative cost of parliamentary primary and election campaigns was a considerable burden, and one that only seemed to grow heavier. The 'commercialization' of politics dated back to the early 1990s and, as one MP bemoaned, 'is a cobweb we have found ourselves entangled in'.[203] Although estimates of average campaign expenditure varied,[204] MPs interviewed suggested it came to roughly Shs400m ($110k) per candidate. But where did the money come from? In keeping with the above analysis, the NRM Secretariat offered negligeable financial assistance, and this *only after the primaries* when an aspirant became the official NRM flagbearer.[205] Many

[199] Karugaba, Mary. 'NRM Independents warn party', *New Vision*, 8 December 2010. Accessed 15 June 2016: http://www.newvision.co.ug/new_vision/news/1277519/nrm-independents-warn-party.

[200] Competition in the 2016 general elections was fiercest between the official NRM flagbearers and NRM-leaning Independents who lost the primaries. There were 909 Independents contesting the parliamentary elections versus only 262 candidates fielded by Uganda's largest opposition party, the Forum for Democratic Change, and this for a total of 402 directly elected parliamentary seats. The Electoral Commission, 'List of Nominated Candidates for 2016 General Elections', accessed 25 November 2016: http://www.ec.or.ug/?q=info/list-nominated-candidates.

[201] Misege, Lawrence. 'Museveni now backs NRM independents', *The Observer*, 2 December 2015. Accessed 15 June 2016: http://www.observer.ug./new-headlines/41369-museveni-now-backs-nrm-independents.

[202] 'Dishonesty affected NRM primaries', *Monitor*, 18 November 2015. Accessed 21 February 2016: http://www.monitor.co.ug/OpEd/Commentary/Dishonesty-affected-NRM-primaries/-/689364/2961912/-/ykejjpz/-/index.html.

[203] NRM MPs speaking at a training workshop for committee chairpersons, Kampala, August 2012. Interview, former MP and Constituent Assembly member, Kampala, April 2013. See also Chapter 3.

[204] A survey of MPs of newly elected MPs found that, for the 113 willing to provide an answer out of 185 surveyed, the average declared spending per MP in 2016 was Ush219m or about $61,000. The range stretched from USh10m to USh1b or $280,000, a huge amount in a country where the GNI per capita is $670. See ACFIM survey. On GNI per capita, see site accessed 28 November 2016: http://data.worldbank.org/country/uganda.

[205] In 2016, the Secretariat allocated Ush25m per candidate, a sum that MPs dismissed as 'peanuts', 'paltry', 'nothing'. Interviews with NRM MPs, Kampala, July 2016.

candidates instead relied on 'personal resources',[206] drawing on a mix of savings, including from business investments, the mortgage or sale of personal property, and increasingly predatory bank loans.[207] Yet MPs also relied on local 'friends' as well as, in some cases, the NRM 'Godfathers'. In line with the various NRM reports, party leaders and Cabinet Ministers—some among the wealthiest individuals in Uganda—either supported candidates to oust rivals in neighbouring constituencies or else accused each other of fronting candidates in their own constituencies to orchestrate their electoral defeat.[208] Secretary General Mbabazi was no exception, which was another reason for the widespread distrust of the Secretariat as a neutral overseer of the 2005 and 2010 primaries.[209]

Museveni also frequently championed his favoured candidates while 'de-campaigning' NRM MPs with whom he had fallen out. While this strategy was first used under the Movement system,[210] and little changed in the post-2005 multiparty era. Up through 2016, Museveni continued to back select candidates, including by pitting rival contenders against troublesome incumbents, and this *within* the ruling party. One NRM MP, interviewed in 2016 following a gruelling but successful re-election campaign, reflected on how this informal disciplinary 'system' operates.[211] He noted that there was allegedly a list of 78 NRM MPs—all critical of government—who 'were not meant to come back', although 10 still won re-election. My interviewee claimed to have offended one of the 'untouchables', a minister with close family ties to Museveni. He scraped through in the primary, but in the general election, 'they' gave Ush900m to an Independent candidate to derail his campaign. He was then forced to take out additional bank loans and seek credit from business partners, endangering

---

[206] ACFIM survey of MPs conducted shortly after the 2016 elections.

[207] See: Vokes, 2016; Wilkins, 2016, 2018. Regarding loans, banks also began targeting newly elected MPs to offer special credit lines, the expectation being that the legislators' generous salaries would enable them to pay back the loans. This was a common theme in interviews.

'Legislators take Shs900m loans as swearing-in enters day two', *Monitor*, 17 May 2016. Accessed 21 February 2016: http://www.monitor.co.ug/News/National/Legislators-loans-as-swearing-in-enters-/-/688334/3207688/-/qsyn1xz/-/index.html.

[208] Tangri and Mwenda, 2013, especially chapter 8; Kjaer and Katusiimeh, 2021.

Namubiru, Lydia. 'Kutesa, Ssekikubo divide Sembabule', *New Vision*, 19 December 2009. Accessed 25 November 2016: http://www.newvision.co.ug/new_vision/news/1230439/kutesa-ssekikubo-divide-sembabule.Ssekika, Edward. 'Kadaga: Mbabazi is targeting me', *The Observer*, 28 September 2015. Accessed 25 November 2016: http://www.observer.ug/special-editions/40127-kadaga-mbabazi-is-targeting-me.

[209] Interviews with MPs and journalists. In addition to constituency MPs, Mbabazi was also rumoured to have backed a group of District Women representatives, dubbed 'Mbabazi's girls'.

[210] Carbone, 2008: 141–142. See also Chapter 3.

[211] Interview, NRM MP, August 2016.

the future of his own commercial interests. His business was further jeopardized by the government's efforts to couple political pressure with economic discipline, in this case, an inopportune audit by the URA.

To recap, since the 2005 multiparty transition, the NRM leadership has repeatedly committed to strengthening ruling party institutions. Yet, the party bureaucracy has remained weak, and the candidate selection process forever mired in controversy. Up through 2016, the reasons for this enduring party weakness lay with the factional tensions within the NRM, themselves a by-product of Uganda's more decentralized wealth accumulation. Low-profile parliamentary candidates leveraged their properties and personal businesses. Others benefited from the support of an elite class of accumulators whose networks extended from Kampala countrywide. As for politicians who fell out with the leadership, they met with a very particular kind of discipline, not formal but informal and often incorporating an element of 'economic discipline'. Although inefficient and costly, hence the repeated calls for party strengthening, this informal manoeuvring remained the status quo. As one interviewee noted, 'Anybody challenging the leadership should be disadvantaged and if money can do that, why not?'[212]

4.3.3 Party Politics and the Presidency for Life

While factional manoeuvring occurs at all levels within the NRM, direct challenges to Museveni have generated the most dramatic conflicts. The party's failure to transition to a new leader—its lack of 'adaptability'—is also the most obvious sign of its institutional weakness, not to mention a threat to Uganda's future political stability, as many increasingly fear.[213] Museveni's tenure has been maintained through a mix of patronage pressure, manipulation of formal party structures, constitutional changes, notably the scrapping of presidential term limits in 2005,[214] as well as violent repression.[215] The 2016 elections offers an insight into Museveni's overall approach, and this after the former Prime Minister and NRM Secretary General Amama Mbabazi opted to campaign against him for the presidency. Mbabazi was only the second high-profile

---

[212] Interview, NRM MP, November 2014.
[213] Khisa, 2023; Mutyaba, 2023.
[214] For more on this reform, see Chapters 5 and 6.
[215] This book explores in-depth one set of mechanisms to explain the institutional make-up of the NRM and Ugandan legislature, only touching incidentally on some of these other tools of authoritarian regime maintenance. For further discussion, see among others: Rubongoya, 2007; Tripp, 2010; Perrot et al., 2014; Wilkins and Vokes, 2016; Tapscott, 2021; Wilkins and Vokes, 2023.

NRM figure to challenge the party leader after Kizza Besigye first broke ranks in 2001.[216]

As noted earlier, Mbabazi long served as one of Museveni's closest allies and duly amassed the personal wealth to accompany his status. During the civil war of the 1980s, Mbabazi was based in Nairobi, directing the effort to mobilize resources to support the NRA insurgency. After the victory in 1986, he assumed a range of top ministerial positions, serving as Attorney General, Defence Minister, and from 2011, Prime Minister. In 2005, he was also elected NRM Secretary General. Over the course of his lengthy stay in government, he was repeatedly listed in high profile corruption scandals but always benefited from Museveni's political cover.[217] Many believed he was the President's heir apparent. Prior to their falling out, Mbabazi shared some of Museveni's political aura. As one journalist put it, '[Mbabazi] was powerful no matter where he went', adding, 'It was not about the institution [of Prime Minister] but rather the man.'[218]

Tensions between Museveni and Mbabazi emerged gradually. As discussed above, the 2012 takeover of a bank partially owned by Mbabazi was an early sign. The 2014 Parliamentary Caucus report further strained relations, and this just as rumours spread concerning a potential Mbabazi bid for the presidency. The Caucus report portrayed the then NRM Secretary General and his daughter, Nina, as heading a secretive operation within the Secretariat. This included compiling a new party member register, which could ostensibly be used to rig internal elections and candidate nominations, something many believed already occurred in 2010.[219] Under pressure, Mbabazi refused to avail the Caucus select committee responsible for drafting the report with a copy of the register, which he allegedly kept 'at his private office'. Nina, meanwhile, was faulted for refusing to answer questions regarding her role in heading a team of volunteers tasked with drawing up the new register. While the report's tacit criticism of the party Secretary General appeared legitimate, it is also worth noting that among the eight MPs sitting on the select committee, at least two were well-known for their long-standing rivalry with Mbabazi. In this sense, there is a degree to which the committee report, and certainly its implementation, suggests a more personalized settling of scores.

---

[216] In the 2021 elections, Museveni faced his first ever challenger who did not originate from within the NRM, namely Robert Kyagulanyi, better known as Bobi Wine. For more on how Bobi Wine has contributed to altering the political map in Uganda, see Wilkins and Vokes, 2023.

[217] Tangri and Mwenda, 2013: 107, 191.

[218] Conversation with journalist, Kampala, August 2016.

[219] Caucus report, 2014.

While most of the committee recommendations went unimplemented, those directly affecting Mbabazi and his position within the NRM were vigorously enforced. For instance, Museveni embraced the report's call for an amendment to the NRM constitution requiring the Secretary General to work as a full-time employee of the party. After stripping Mbabazi of the premiership in September 2014, Museveni called an extraordinary meeting of the NRM National Delegates Conference in December of the same year. Amidst a heavy military deployment and with the media largely barred from the meeting, roughly 10,000 carefully vetted delegates voted to change the party constitution, transforming the office of Secretary General into an appointed, full-time position and thereby stripping Mbabazi of that role too.[220]

Ultimately, it was not surprising when Mbabazi's presidential challenge ended in a flop. The former Prime Minister garnering a paltry 1.69 per cent of the official vote tally. During the campaign period, Museveni did not shy away from further bending NRM party rules to his advantage. In December 2015, he agreed to allow roughly 60 incumbent NRM MPs who lost their primaries to campaign as Independents without fear of a formal party sanction.[221] This decision came after the group of MPs threatened to support Mbabazi should Museveni reject their candidacies.[222] Museveni appears to have used his usual economic tools as well. After many parliamentary candidates flocked to Mbabazi, anticipating he would provide funds from his supposed campaign war chest, their would-be champion failed to deliver. It was later rumoured that he was prevented from accessing many of his assets, including in construction as well as the emerging oil and gas sector, leaving him short of cash during what ultimately proved an underwhelming presidential campaign.[223]

Mbabazi's path from the heights of the NRM to political humiliation indicates the extent to which the NRM machinery is shaped according to the whims of the party Chairman. Rules are enforced when they suit Museveni

---

[220] Matsiko, Haggai. 'Museveni worries about NRM Namboole conference', *The Independent*, 8 December 2014. Accessed 21 February 2017: https://www.independent.co.ug/cover-story/9551-museveni-worries-about-nrm-namboole-conference. 'Mbabazi "falls" as NRM changes constitution', *Monitor*, 15 December 2014. Accessed 21 February 2017: http://www.monitor.co.ug/News/National/Mbabazi—falls—as-NRM-changes-constitution/-/688334/2557632/-/item/1/-/5f14df/-/index.html.

[221] 'Stand as independents, Museveni tells NRM losers', *The Observer*, 1 December 2015. Accessed 15 June 2016: http://www.observer.ug/news-headlines/41343-stand-as-independents-museveni-tells-nrm-losers.

[222] Misege, Lawrence. 'NRM MPs threaten to join Mbabazi', *The Observer*, 27 November 2015. Accessed 15 June 2016: http://www.observer.ug/news-headlines/41283-nrm-mps-threaten-to-join-mbabazi.

[223] Matsiko, Haggai. 'What happened to Mbabazi's money?', *The Independent*, 1 February 2016. Accessed 28 July 2017: https://www.independent.co.ug/happened-mbabazis-money/. Khisa, 2016: 738.

and passed over when they do not. Mbabazi's case also exemplifies how strategies of politicized accumulation inform the balance of power amongst NRM elite. The former Prime Minister was from the NRM 'aristocracy'. As such, he benefited from the general patterns of wealth accumulation within the party, which enabled him to cultivate his own extensive patronage network. These operated semi-autonomously for a time, contributing to the internal tensions within the NRM. Yet once he broke with Museveni, his economic vulnerability became clear.

4.3.4 Evaluating the Role of Opposition Pressures

The above analysis shows how NRM party institutions remained weak due to the fragmented patronage networks within the party. But this leaves the question, does inter-party competition have any residual influence?

There is little reason to believe that weak NRM institutions—and in particular, the party's move towards a highly inclusive and largely uncontrolled primary system—was the result of opposition pressure. Indeed, the percentage of opposition MPs in parliament has declined since the first multiparty election in 2006 (Figure 4.5). Following the 2016 polls, the number of Independents elected—most of them NRM-aligned—actually exceeded that of

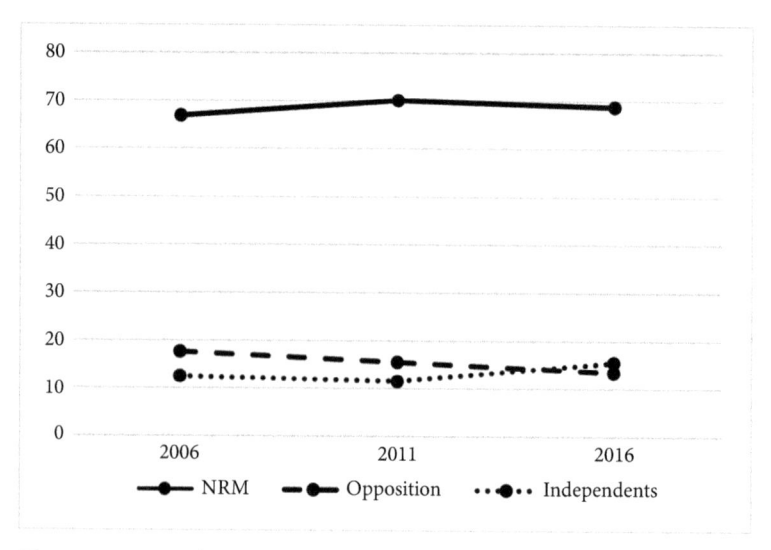

Figure 4.5 Uganda—percentage share of parliamentary seats

opposition MPs.[224] This pattern helps confirm that, rather than inter-party competition, it was factional tensions within the NRM that prompted the move towards more inclusive primaries and, more generally, account for the party's ongoing institutional weakness.

4.4 Conclusion

This chapter examined the conditions for institutional continuity and change within authoritarian parties, highlighting both the economic and institutional determinants.

For an 'institutionalized coalition' like CCM, the party's formal structures begin to erode where wealth accumulation becomes more decentralized and patronage networks fragment. But this institutional decline is relative, as the party still retains aspects of its past strength. In Tanzania, even as rival factions mobilized to capture the presidency in 2015, they were compelled to do so gradually and from within the ruling party as opposed to simply breaking away and taking their personalized patronage machines with them. Moreover, in the case of Lowassa's failed presidential bid, a carefully cultivated patronage network proved remarkably fragile. Cut off from its anchor within the formal structures of CCM, it dissolved.

Regarding a 'bargained coalition' like Uganda's NRM, the party trajectory is more straightforward. With the more decentralized pattern of wealth accumulation unlikely to change, patronage networks remain fragmented and party institutions weak, and this irrespective of leaders' party-building efforts. In the absence of effective formal structures and rules to govern intra-party politics, strategies of economic discipline and informal patronage pressures become an important means of managing the distribution of power amongst regime elites.

Finally, concerning the alternative hypothesis whereby inter-party competition drives the institutional transformation of incumbent parties, an analysis of the extent and timing of an opposition challenge indicates that inter-party competition did not drive institutional change within the NRM and only had a negligible and belated effect on CCM.

It is worth recalling here that an 'institutionalized coalition' or 'bargained coalition' remains an ideal type, and as such, something that a real-world party only approximates. By the same token, there is also variation amongst parties that broadly fit within one of these two categories. Here, for instance, we

---

[224] 'Elections in Uganda', *African Elections Database*. Accessed 21 February 2017: http://africanelections.tripod.com/ug.html.

can see a difference between KANU and the NRM; in particular, the development of relatively autonomous political financiers and local patrons arguably reached a more advanced stage in KANU than it has within the NRM. This, in turn, would help explain why factions were able to break away from the ruling party and challenge the incumbent, Daniel arap Moi, more successfully following Kenya's multiparty transition while would-be challengers to Museveni and the NRM in Uganda are more easily undermined, including economically.[225]

The previous chapter explained how contrasting authoritarian party types consolidate. This chapter then accounted for their divergent trajectories. The next chapter now considers how these differing patterns of authoritarian party politics affects another political institution, the legislature.

---

[225] Ajulu, 1999 and 2021.

5

Legislative Institutional Strength

From Party to Parliament

> [Speaker Sitta] was trying to arm Parliament with teeth strong enough
> to bite the CCM Government!
> —Pius Msekwa, Speaker of the Tanzanian Parliament
> (1994–2005)[1]

> The reactions and powers of the Speaker should always be much
> more vocal and clear when the person of a Member of Parliament is
> threatened, or its rules are challenged.
> —Rebecca Kadaga, Speaker of the Ugandan Parliament
> (2011–2021)[2]

The extent of ruling party dominance over the legislature varies across countries and over time. One indicator of this variation is the shifting attitude and
political power of the Speaker, effectively the leader of parliament.

In Tanzania, former Speaker Pius Msekwa continually affirmed the need
for party discipline in Parliament. He therefore saw the actions of his more
independent-minded successor, Samuel Sitta, as an aberration. More than a
difference in attitude or personal ambition, though, the contrast between the
two Speakers also reflected a deeper, structural change in Tanzania's politics. As factional tensions increasingly divided CCM, the legislature went from
marginal to a prized institutional resource, a means through which competing
groups could gain the upper hand.

In neighbouring Uganda, meanwhile, Speaker Rebecca Kadaga was more
focused on *preserving* parliament's institutional strength, as inherited from
an earlier period of Movement politics. The above-cited statement followed
an unprecedented effort by ruling party leaders to impose discipline in the

---

[1] Msekwa, 2012: 123.
[2] 'How Kadaga decided MPs' fate'. *Monitor*, 2 May 2013. Accessed 11 December 2017: http://www.
monitor.co.ug/News/National/How-Kadaga-decided-MPs--fate/688334-1839980-by7rwaz/index.
html.

Wealth, Power, and Authoritarian Institutions. Michaela Collord, Oxford University Press. © Michaela Collord (2024).
DOI: 10.1093/9780191945335.003.0005

House. They insisted that 'rebel' NRM MPs, once stripped of their party membership, must also forfeit their seats in parliament. This attempted expulsion failed, however, undermined by enduring factional tensions within the NRM as well as MPs' strong incentives to defend hard-fought legislative advantages.

The below discussion first expounds on the theoretical argument relevant to this chapter before presenting an empirical analysis, first of the Tanzanian and then the Ugandan case.

5.1 Argument and Methods

Whereas previous chapters examined differences across authoritarian parties, this chapter connects the dots, linking the analysis of politico-economic and party change to an understanding of legislative institutional trajectories. The key claim is that variation in patterns of accumulation—especially the extent of and control over private accumulation—affects *not only* the degree of cohesion and institutional strength within the ruling party; it also affects whether elite contestation *spills over from the ruling party into the legislature*, where it can help drive an institutional strengthening process.

Thus, where the ruling party resembles a 'bargained coalition', the legislature is likely to undergo a process of institutionalization. By contrast, where the ruling party is an 'institutionalized coalition', the legislature will remain institutionally weak. However, if an 'institutionalized coalition' begins to erode, losing some of its organizational strength and cohesion, the legislature will gain in prominence and institutional strength. This process is gradual, however, and the legislature is unlikely to acquire the same degree of autonomy as it otherwise might under a 'bargained coalition'.

In detailing this argument, I first briefly revisit my definition of legislative strength and, second, identify the mechanisms underpinning legislative institutionalization. I then clarify both how my argument differs from alternative explanations and, finally, what method I adopt to study institutional variation.

5.1.1 Legislative Strength, What Is It?

Legislative strength can be understood on two levels. This chapter considers parliament's *institutional strength* and the next chapter, its actual *performance*. Institutional strength refers to features of the legislature's institutional make-up that affect the *potential* for legislative actors to challenge the executive. This institutional make-up matters because—in keeping with a tradition of historical institutionalist analysis—it *reflects and magnifies* the distribution of power within the ruling elite; as in, legislative institutional change provides elite factions with new tools with which to challenge rivals in the executive, amplifying whatever informal pressures these factions could otherwise exert.

In assessing legislative institutional strength, I use three dimensions, namely the 'complexity', 'boundedness', and 'coherence' of parliament's structures and procedures.[3] *Complexity* refers to the multiplication and differentiation of organizational subunits, which I associate with the number of committees and the powers awarded them; a strong committee system allows for more efficient and focused work on key issues of interest to legislators.

Institutional *boundedness* I define as the legislature's organizational separation from external entities; this separation ensures that legislators are more accountable to their voters, factional backers, and each other rather than dependent on the executive and party leaders. I track four related elements of boundedness: (a) the mode of selecting MPs, namely the percentage of directly versus indirectly elected or appointed MPs; (b) whether Independent candidates are allowed to run in elections; (c) the mode of selecting parliamentary leaders—the Speaker and committee chairs—and whether this selection is by legislators, party officials, or the President; and (d) control over the legislative budget, including remuneration of MPs and administrative staff.

Finally, institutional *coherence* varies depending on whether formal legislative institutions reflect actual practice or are instead subverted by powerful actors, notably the President. As discussed more below, where appropriate, I supplement a general assessment of legislative complexity, boundedness, and coherence with in-depth studies of significant legislative reforms, notably concerning parliament's budgetary oversight powers.

5.1.2 How Legislative Institutions Strengthen

Several mechanisms explain the relationship between party and legislative institutional strength. The proximate drivers of legislative strengthening are endogenous to parliament itself; they stem from the actions of individual legislators and parliamentary leaders. However, to understand legislators' actions within parliament, we need to understand the *extra-parliamentary* political

---

[3] Huntington, 1968; Polsby, 1968; see Chapter 2 for further discussion.

context—i.e. we must link the *structural analysis* of accumulation and patronage politics to a micro-level analysis of the *individual actors* directly involved in legislative reform, namely MPs and their factional backers. This means examining the incentive structures they face as well as the more *contingent* ways the organization of patronage networks impacts their behaviour.

In the case of an 'institutionalized coalition', namely, where accumulation and patronage are centralized plus the ruling party is strong and cohesive, *individual legislators* have little opportunity to cultivate factional ties or a local patronage base. Instead, legislators must appeal to party leaders and, therefore, have little reason to risk offending them by supporting a legislative reform agenda. Similarly, ambitious politicians will not be able to use parliamentary leadership positions, for instance the Speakership, to develop a personal profile or to challenge the executive. They instead advance their careers through party and administrative ranks. The ruling party thus dominates as an institutional channel for elite advancement, easily asserting its power over a docile legislature.

By contrast, in a 'bargained coalition' or in an 'institutionalized coalition' in decline, more expansive private accumulation and factional contestation undermine party discipline such that MPs may adopt a more assertive stance in parliament. This is because stronger ties to patron–client factions outside the legislature give legislators both the political power and incentive to push for institutional reform within parliament, particularly where this *amplifies* their own material advantages and political influence.[4] Legislators can, for instance, use improved budgetary oversight powers either to satisfy constituency demands or to cater to the interests of their private political financiers.[5]

Rank-and-file MPs aside, legislative leaders—notably the Speaker and committee chairs—have similar incentives to strengthen parliament, again using it to help advance their political careers. On this point, it is important to stress that the translation of underlying structural conditions into actual factional organizing and institutional change is not automatic; rather, the power of patron–client factions depends notably on 'the capacity of their *leadership* to mobilize and enthuse'.[6] Skilled and ambitious leaders thus play an important role both in determining whether and when powerful patron–client factions organize as well as how they affect institutional change. In the case of the legislature, key leaders include the Speaker of Parliament

---

[4] On the material advantages MPs gain from office: Koter, 2017; Demarest, 2021; Opalo, 2022.
[5] Samuels, 2002.
[6] Khan, 2018: 5.

and committee chairs but, also, particularly enterprising political financiers, ministers, and the President.[7]

5.1.3 Alternative Explanations

The above-outlined argument does not explain all variation across legislatures in single or dominant party regimes, but rather aims to distil one important dynamic. There are also alternative arguments to consider, which I address in more depth in Chapter 2. Of these alternatives, some I challenge while others I seek to caveat.

To recap briefly, I contest the rational choice literature's functionalist argument that strong legislatures are the result of a rulers' strategic 'choice'. Instead, I argue that these institutions are the focus of ongoing struggle. Where a legislature strengthens, this signals that rival elites have to some extent *escaped the dictator's control* and are moulding the legislature to better advance their interests. I also challenge the Africanist claim that 'neo-patrimonial' politics 'retards the development and performance of the legislature'.[8] Instead, I show how fractions patron–client politics tend to *propel legislative strengthening.*

A third argument, namely that a multiparty transition results in legislative institutionalization, I do not reject but rather amend. I argue that, while not insignificant, a transition to multiparty politics alone does not lead to legislative institutionalization, particularly where an incumbent ruling party remains dominant.[9] Opposition parties can help galvanize legislative institutionalization but *only where low ruling party discipline is already conducive to legislative reform.* Moreover, opposition party influence requires that a few reformist MPs—who may also come from the ruling party—provide the *ideas* to direct institutional change, which after all, is an intellectual as well as a political project.[10]

Finally, while there is a materialist emphasis in my analysis of what structures shape MPs' incentives, the claim is *not* that MPs' motivations are reducible to material ones alone, without alternative normative aspirations. Rather, the point is to highlight how material conditions help shape broad patterns of elite contestation and institutional change. I explore when and why a

---

[7] On the institution-building influence of an ambitious Speaker benefiting from propitious extra-parliamentary political conditions, see Sheingate, 2009.

[8] Bratton and van de Walle, 1997; Barkan, 2009: 6, 16–17; Barkan, 2013.

[9] In the conclusion, I revisit the Kenyan case to consider the implications of more competitive inter-party politics on legislative institutionalization.

[10] On institutional change and ideas, see Blyth, 2002.

majority of more 'opportunist' MPs might unite with 'reformists',[11] who themselves have a variety of motivations, some material, some normative. There are also individuals who make considerable personal sacrifices, whether in relative isolation or with the passive support of opportunist colleagues. Again, my attention to the ways legislative activity reflects and magnifies external power struggles is not meant to diminish these individual efforts, but to set them in context.

5.1.4 Comparing Tanzania and Uganda

This chapter again combines within-case and cross-case comparison. I first show how Tanzania's legislature weakened in the late 1960s and through the 1970s amidst the consolidation of TANU—later CCM—as a strong 'institutionalized coalition' (Figure 5.1). It was only in the 1990s amidst profound economic changes and growing factionalism within CCM that the legislature began to strengthen. Even then, the process only gained momentum once the right constellation of factional rivalries emerged in the mid-2000s. Moreover, as discussed further in the conclusion, this legislative strengthening remains fragile. For instance, after assuming the presidency in 2015, Magufuli introduced new barriers to private accumulation and political finance. This intervention helped suppress rival factions within CCM, at least temporarily restoring party discipline and reversing prior legislative institutional gains.[12]

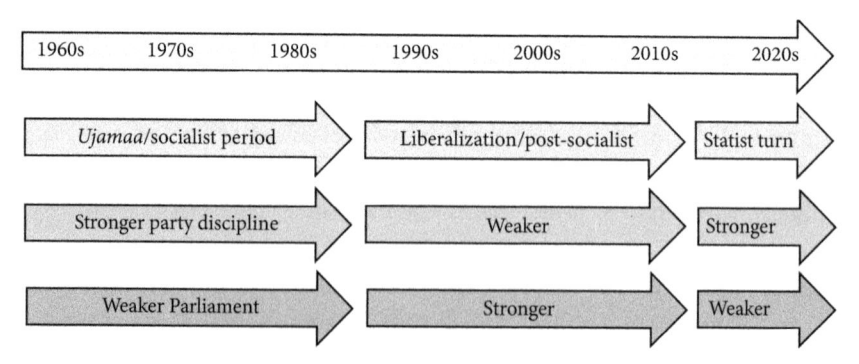

Figure 5.1 Periodization of legislative change in Tanzania

---

[11] See Barkan 2009 on legislative 'coalitions for change'.

[12] 'Temporarily' because, as also briefly discussed in the conclusion, President Samia's succession to the Presidency following Magufuli's death in 2021 has helped restore a status quo ante, returning CCM politics to something closer to the Kikwete era norm after the Magufuli rupture.

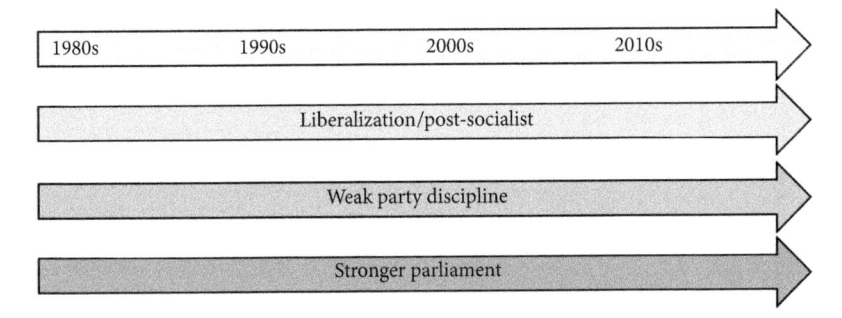

Figure 5.2 Periodization of legislative change in Uganda

Following the analysis of changes in Tanzania's legislature, I contrast it with a study of the Ugandan parliament's more consistent trajectory (Figure 5.2). After the NRM took power in 1986, factional contestation within this 'bargained coalition' drove early legislative institutionalization. The legislature's institutional strength then remained stable or increased up to the 2016 elections, and this despite repeated efforts by the executive to assert greater control.

Before I go on with the analysis, a brief methodological note is in order. First, when assessing legislative institutional strength, there are advantages to a more parsimonious, quantitative approach. Indeed, Figures 5.3 and 5.4 help illustrate the above-summarized legislative trajectories as reflected through measures of institutional *complexity* (number of committees) and *boundedness* (percentage of directly elected MPs). Regarding Tanzania's legislature, the two graphs help capture parliament's institutional decline until the 1980s followed by its gradual strengthening. They also point to the more stable pattern of institutional strengthening in Uganda. Meanwhile, Table 5.1 offers further evidence indicating the Ugandan legislature's relative boundedness, the one exception being a 2005 change in the procedure for selecting committee chairs.

This quantitative assessment of legislative strength, nevertheless, has its limitations. For instance, the data does not reflect Tanzania's additional legislative strengthening under President Kikwete (2005–2015). If anything, it points to an institutional decline during his presidency. The percentage of directly elected MPs reached a maximum in 1995, after which point it decreased.[13] The *number* of committees also fell, although this does not show how the formal powers of these committees continued to vary.

---

[13] This is due to the adoption of new constitutional provision for 'special seats' women MPs, which as discussed below, was contrived to strengthen CCM and its leadership.

These limitations suggest the need to go beyond quantitative measures. Explaining institutional variation—and its significance—requires a *contextually sensitive* study that can grasp how and why particular actors

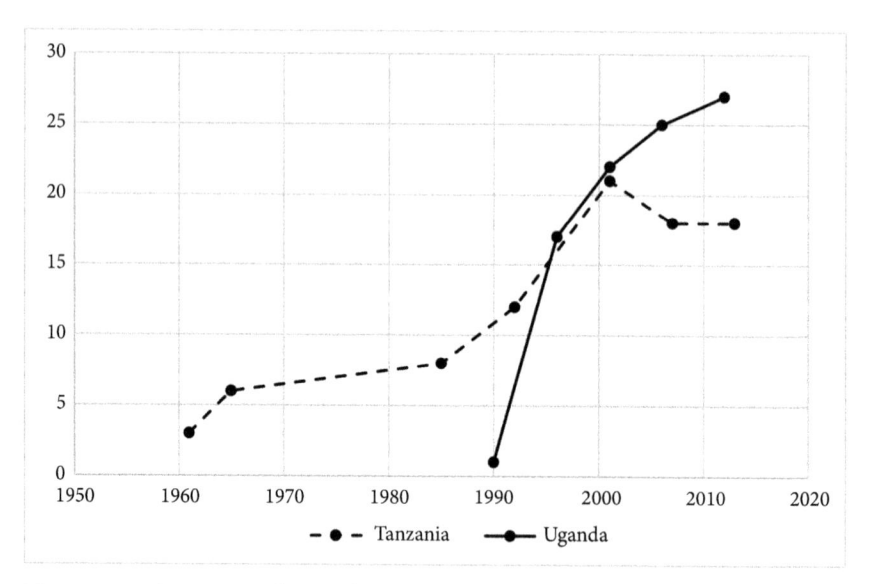

Figure 5.3 Tanzania and Uganda—number of parliamentary committees

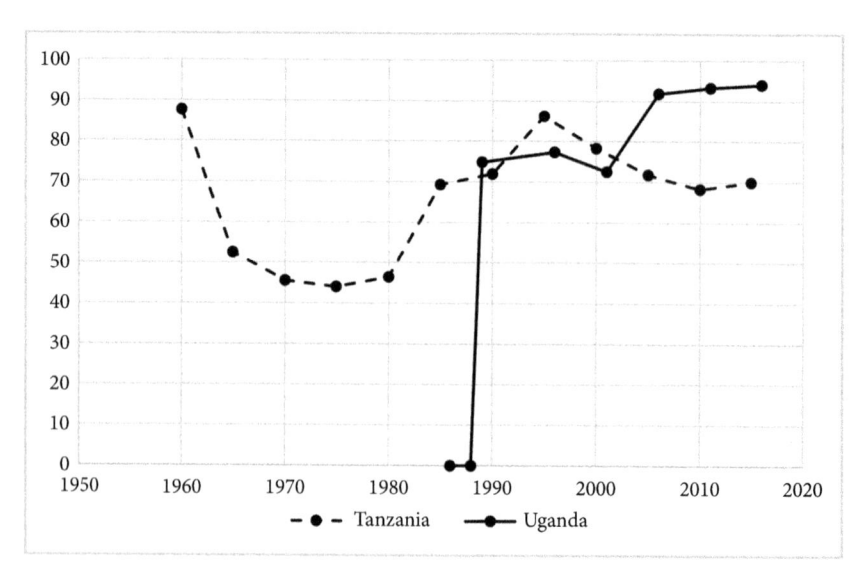

Figure 5.4 Tanzania and Uganda—percentage of directly elected MPs

Table 5.1 Legislative institutional boundedness

	Tanzania	Uganda
Percentage of directly elected MPs	See Figure 5.4	See Figure 5.4
Independents in Parliament	Illegal since 1965, despite court challenges after the 1992 multiparty transition.	Legal
MPs expelled from their party lose their parliamentary seat	Yes	No
Selection of Parliamentary Leaders	*Speaker*—Ruling party MPs vote to nominate their preferred candidate after initial vetting procedure by top party organs; ruling party nominee inevitably elected Speaker by whole House. *Committee Chairs*—Elected by all committee members.	*Speaker*—Ruling party MPs vote to nominate their preferred candidate, who put themselves forward without vetting by top party organs; ruling party nominee inevitably elected Speaker by whole House. *Committee Chairs*—Elected by all committee members until the 2005 multiparty transition when the Government Chief Whip was empowered to select Chairs for all except the four accountability committees.
Parliament administers its own budget	Yes, as if 2008 following the passage of the National Assembly Administration Act.	Yes, as of 1997 following the passage of the Administration of Parliament Act

push for reform, and what determines whether they are successful.[14] To meet these analytical demands, I draw on a legislative studies tradition of 'thick description',[15] which also accords with my process-tracing methodology. This analysis involves uncovering how changes in economic structure affected the organization of patron–client factions, the ambitions of actors embedded within those factions, and ultimately, prospects for successful legislative institutional reform.

---

[14] Cooper and Brady, 1981.
[15] On 'thick description' and its value in legislative studies, see: Shepsle, 2002: 389–390; Arter, 2006. There are trade-offs in pursuing this more granular analysis. It is one of the reasons I focus on a select few markers of legislative institutional strength. For instance, my analysis of causal mechanisms would become exceedingly cluttered if I traced what drives variation across the 32 indicators in Fish and Kroenig's influential Parliamentary Powers Index (PPI). That is not to dismiss the PPI, though it has its shortcomings (Chernykh et al., 2017). Rather, the key point is that my chosen indicators capture important aspects of legislative institutional strength while also allowing for a coherent and focused causal narrative.

5.2 Tanzania's *Bunge*

The below discussion traces the link between changes in Tanzania's economy, the make-up of its ruling party and a parallel process of legislative (de)institutionalization. It divides into three parts: a first on the legislature's institutional weakening in the 1960s and 1970s; a second on its gradual and halting institutional reversal beginning in the 1980s; and a third providing an in-depth analysis of the politics surrounding the institutionalizing reform drive of the mid-2000s to 2010s. There is also passing mention of the legislature's actual performance, although only where necessary to clarify the politics surrounding relevant institutional reforms. The issue of parliament's performance is then revisited in the next chapter.[16]

5.2.1 A Party Strengthens, a Parliament Declines

The future of Tanzania's parliament—or *Bunge*, in Swahili—was no more certain at Independence than was the country's economic trajectory or the fate of its ruling party. As observed in Chapter 3, TANU's consolidation as an 'institutionalized coalition' in the 1960s came only after an initial period of debate and experimentation. The status of *Bunge* within the new political system was similarly contested. It was only after Nyerere's 1967 Arusha Declaration that the future trajectories of both party and parliament took a more definite turn. As private wealth accumulation was restricted, factionalism suppressed, and ruling party institutions strengthened, *Bunge* grew increasingly marginal. In this section, I first trace the ups and downs of parliament through the mid-1960s before analysing its post-1967 institutional decline.

The legislature was anything but marginal during TANU's nationalist struggle pre-Independence. Rather, it was the 'gateway to the political kingdom',[17] an important channel for asserting TANU's strength and legitimacy. In line with British colonial practice, the Governor of what was then Tanganyika established a Legislative Council, or LEGCO, in 1926.[18] However, the first meaningful African representation only came after elections held in 1958. TANU won a 'devastating victory', taking 13 out of 15 seats.[19] Nyerere interpreted this as an important turning point, effusing, 'The atmosphere has been

---

[16] Elements of this section also appear in Collord, 2022.

[17] Kjekshus, 1974: 60.

[18] Tambila, 2004: 46; Barkan, 2009: 9.

[19] Iliffe, 1979: 555–556, 561–562. The party did not contest the two seats not won by TANU. See also: Mwakyembe, 1986: 21–22.

suddenly revolutionized.'[20] Certainly, the result foreshortened the time horizon for Tanganyika's Independence. By 1959, TANU had pressured the British
administration to allow for 'responsible government', and after further changes
to the legislature, an 81-member council formed in 1960. It had 10 nominated members and 71 elected representatives, all but one of whom won on
a TANU ticket.[21] The following year, this Assembly became Tanganyika's first
independent parliament.

Despite its early prominence, the legislature's position within Tanganyika's
post-Independence political order remained uncertain. Due to a series of
reforms introduced through the mid-1960s, parliament's *de jure* institutional
power declined; however, its *de facto* influence initially endured, or even
increased. The 1962 Republican Constitution, which introduced an executive
presidency, was a first step towards the legislature's *formal* marginalization.[22]
However, Tanganyika was not the only former British colony to abandon the
Westminster system, and the effects of this change on legislative activity were
hardly uniform. For instance, a similar constitutional reform in Kenya did little
to quell executive–legislative tensions; rather, rival factions within KANU—
representing different regions, economic interests, and financial backers—
continued to clash over questions of land reform, nationalization, and other
interventions central to the post-colonial restructuring of Kenya's economy.[23]

Meanwhile in Tanganyika, the next major *de jure* change came with the
introduction of a one-party state, although the implications for Parliament
were again ambiguous.[24] Nyerere claimed in a 1963 speech that one-party
rule would encourage 'democratic debate' in the legislature as there would
be no 'party line to follow'.[25] That said, the ensuing reforms did seem to
reduce the institutional strength of the legislature. The presidential commission tasked with reviewing the constitution argued that the TANU National
Executive Committee (NEC) should determine the 'basic assumptions of government policy' while Parliament would only implement them by drafting
'appropriate legislative measures and financial provisions'.[26] The Commission also recommended that NEC members receive the same emoluments
as MPs and that the NEC have the same powers as Parliament to summon

---

[20] Iliffe, 1979: 562. Citing Nyerere, 26 September 1958.
[21] The one independent candidate elected was a former TANU member who lost during the party
primaries. He later re-joined TANU post-election. Mwakyembe, 1986: 22.
[22] Ibid., 28–29.
[23] Gertzel, 1970.
[24] Cliffe, 1967a.
[25] Nyerere, 1963: 5.
[26] Report cited in Msekwa, 2012: 23–24.

witnesses and request information from government. Both recommenda-tions were later implemented.[27] The 1965 Interim Constitution, as it was known, also increased the number of appointed or nominated legislators. These included Regional Commissioners as ex officio members and, in the wake of Tanganyika's 1964 Union with Zanzibar, the addition of 32 unelected Zanzibari members.[28]

The changes to parliament's composition reduced the institutional *bound-edness* of the legislature as did the duplication of roles shared between the legislature and the TANU NEC. This duplication also encroached on the inter-nal *complexity* of parliament by threatening to make legislative committees redundant. Of the standing committees provided for in the 1961 parliamen-tary Standing Orders, only the Public Accounts Committee was active after 1965 while government continued to discourage parliament from forming select committees even though the legislature had the power to do so.[29]

The one-party transition nevertheless was *not* the decisive turning point for *Bunge* as its de jure and de facto powers continued to diverge. Indeed, if anything, parliament was more assertive after the 1965 one-party elections.[30] During the next year, increased challenges to the executive were evident through a quadrupling of oral questions to government and an increase in private member's motions.[31] Meanwhile, some left-leaning TANU MPs chal-lenged what were then the growth-oriented policies endorsed by Cabinet, faulting them for not aligning with the party's stated socialist objectives. These criticisms, far from empty rhetoric, contributed to the defeat of several government proposals.[32] The NEC, for its part, was not especially active in 1965–1966. It failed, for instance, to make use of its new powers to summon and interrogate government officials.[33]

The legislative–executive skirmishes of 1966 were nevertheless fairly mild. The real clash came after the January 1967 Arusha Declaration. The fact that the Declaration was first delivered to and subsequently endorsed by the NEC elevated the status of that institution relative to the legislature.[34] With Nyerere's later affirmation that 'to build socialism you must have socialists', the stage was set for a confrontation over the extent of TANU's disciplinary powers and,

---

[27] Mwakyembe, 1986: 41; Van Cranenburgh, 1990: 73–74.
[28] Kjekshus, 1974: 21.
[29] Ibid., 22, 29. *Standing Orders of the* National Assembly of Tanganyika, 1961 edition, Clauses 73–74, 83. Accessed, *Bunge* library.
[30] Cliffe, 1967a; Kjekshus, 1974; Tordoff, 1977.
[31] Cliffe, 1967a: 340–342.
[32] Ibid.; Hartmann, 1983: 109. See also Chapter 3 for more background.
[33] Martin, 1988: 80.
[34] Mwakyembe, 1986: 42; Msekwa, 2012: 29.

fundamentally, the independence of the legislature.[35] *By studying the ensuing stand-off opposing activist legislators and the executive-cum-party leadership, we gain a better understanding of what motivated each side and what determined their relative power.* I first detail the nature of the executive-legislative clash itself plus the outcome in terms of declining legislative strength. I then offer an explanation, stressing how the centralization of accumulation and patronage plus the effort to empower party and state officials relative to individual legislators contributed to parliament's marginalization.

What some observers referred to as the 'great supremacy debate' ran from 1967 through 1968.[36] This 'debate' featured legislators criticizing provisions in the Arusha Declaration as well as Tanzania's apparent authoritarian drift. The partly leadership and government responded by limiting the powers of elected MPs and of parliament as a whole. The debate kicked off in June 1967 when Hon. Ndobho (MP) requested that the Prime Minister clarify 'who is supreme', the National Assembly or the TANU NEC.[37] The following year, Parliament passed its first private member's motion opposing a decision to award various administrative and government officials gratuities equal to 25 per cent of their annual salaries.[38] Other concerns raised by MPs included the lack of democracy in Zanzibar and the excessive powers awarded to Regional Commissioners.[39] Picking up on Ndobho's earlier concern, the firebrand MP, Hon. Chogga, argued that the President should act only on the advice of Parliament, which was 'supreme'.[40]

Government and Party officials responded to MPs' calls by emphasizing the subordination of legislators and of parliament to the ruling party.[41] A junior minister insisted, 'The party picked you in nomination and the party has the right to discipline you and dictate your tasks', adding, 'It is high time the MPs should know where they come from, and it is above any doubt that *this parliament belongs to TANU*'.[42] In keeping with the sentiment of this statement, the Party National Conference amended the TANU constitution in October 1967, awarding the NEC new powers to expel party members.[43] The following October, after a stormy budget session, NEC put these powers to use. It

---

[35] Kjekshus, 1974: 28, 31.
[36] Msekwa, 2012: 31–40. See also: Saul, 1972; Van Velzen and Sterkenburg, 1972a & 1972b; Martin, 1988, especially chapter 5.
[37] Msekwa, 2012: 31.
[38] For an in-depth discussion of the motion, see Velzen and Sterkenburg, 1972a.
[39] Velzen and Sterkenburg, 1972b.
[40] Mwakyembe, 1986: 42.
[41] Ibid., 42; Kjekshus, 1974: 31.
[42] Mwakyembe, 1986: 42–43.
[43] Kjekshus, 1974: 30; Msekwa, 2012: 29.

expelled nine members, including seven MPs who then automatically lost their parliamentary seats. These expulsions undermined parliament's institutional *boundedness*, sending a clear message that 'the political elite were under the absolute control of the party'.[44] What's more, during the same meeting that ruled to expel the MPs, the NEC also decided that it should first receive and approve all major policy documents, including the second five-year development plan, before sending them to parliament. This move further confirmed the legislature's 'subordinate and purely technical role'.[45]

But while the above discussion details how party leaders ultimately won out over the legislature, it does not explain *why* they succeeded. For this, we need to revisit the analysis of how TANU increased its top down control after the Arusha Declaration, plus clarify how this process related to the legislature. Chapter 3 showed how TANU's consolidation relied on formal institutional changes. Crucially, this party strengthening process also depended on centralizing control over wealth accumulation and patronage, which included *curbing the wealth and patronage roles of elected MPs*. Building on this, if we revisit the 'great supremacy debate', *contestation over legislators' material status*—notably relative to party-cum-state officials—featured prominently.

First, regarding personal wealth, MPs' questions challenging the enforcement of the Leadership Code pertained overwhelmingly to its effects on their welfare and investments.[46] Meanwhile, party leaders' opposition to Chogga—one of the seven expelled MPs—was partly due to his success in spearheading the parliamentary campaign against some restrictions in the Code.[47] Nyerere, as the pre-eminent TANU leader and architect of the Arusha Declaration, was not only irked by this legislative challenge; he also took a dim view of MPs whom he saw as among the TANU leaders becoming 'entrenched in the accumulation of personal property'.[48] In that vein, another expelled MP, Mwakitwange, was notable for having considerable business interests,[49] and indeed, reappeared in Chapter 4 as one of the prominent businessmen who attempted to contest the 1990 elections only for Nyerere—yet again—to thwart his efforts.

---

[44] Velzen and Sterkenburg, 1972b: 263; Kjekshus, 1974: 31.
[45] Msekwa, 2012: 34.
[46] Hartmann, 1983: 205–206.
[47] Resnick, 1981: 101.
[48] Cited in Pratt, 1976: 236. See also Chapter 3.
[49] Hyden and Leys, 1972; Kiondo, 1994: 82–83. Mwakitwange was likely the only truly wealthy MP of the seven expelled. Chogga and Kibura, another of the seven, were nevertheless 'village entrepreneurs' and critical of the Arusha Declaration for limiting their ability to hire farm labour. Source: James Giblin, personal correspondence, September 2017. On Mwakitwange, including his business interests from the 1950s through to the 1980s, see also: Chachage, 2018: 248–253.

Leaving aside the issue of private wealth accumulation, elected MPs' patronage roles—particularly relative to party and state officials—were another key theme throughout 1967–1968. Legislators were particularly concerned about their status vis-à-vis Regional Commissioners, who rivalled them both as local power brokers and in parliament as ex officio MPs. Their concern was oņe factor motivating the above-referenced private member's motion passed in 1968, which opposed gratuities awarded to government officials, *including* Regional Commissioners. Relatedly, Chogga again angered TANU leaders by criticizing a party directive stipulating that MPs' finances be vetted but exempting Regional Commissioners. He framed this differential treatment as part of a campaign to undermine parliament's independence relative to the executive.[50] Finally, as outlined in Chapter 3, two more of the expelled MPs lost their seats because they challenged a Regional Commissioner over villagization programmes in their area, the cash crop-producing West Lake region. In taking their stand, the MPs were also representing local landed interests.[51] Their expulsion thus signalled the subordination both of elected legislators and private economic actors to party and state officials.

In brief, an important part of the 'great supremacy debate' was about the wealth and patronage power of MPs, and ultimately, what this meant for the strength of the legislature relative to party and executive leaders. By the next election in 1970, with the party exercising strict top-down management of nominations and campaigns,[52] there was little room left for MPs to resist the new policy direction, or its implications for private accumulation. As one ex-parliamentarian recalled some 20 years after the Arusha Declaration, 'It was like someone holding a sharp knife to one's side in such a way that it could not be pulled away without getting hurt.'[53]

Parliament continued to lose ground to the party and executive throughout the 1970s, and this because of both formal changes and the further centralization of accumulation and patronage distribution. In 1975, parliament unanimously passed a constitutional amendment entrenching *de jure* party supremacy.[54] The reform came with a reduction in to the number of directly elected constituency MPs, which fell from 107 to 88, less than half the total number of legislators.[55] When justifying the measure, then Prime Minister

---

[50] James Giblin, personal correspondence, September 2017.
[51] Hyden, 1977.
[52] This included control of 'unofficial' campaigns and private campaign finance. See Chapter 3.
[53] Cited in Tripp, 1997: 174.
[54] Mlimuka and Kabudi, 1986: 64; Branson, 2015.
[55] By way of comparison, all MPs in neighbouring Kenya were directly elected during this period. Hyden and Leys, 1972; Tambila, 2004: 63.

Kawawa denied any attempt to 'diminish the power of parliament or of parliamentarians'.[56] Rather, he claimed that the aim was to align constituency and administrative boundaries such that MPs could work alongside the TANU District Chairman and the District Secretary, who doubled as District Commissioner. In addition, Kawawa alleged that factional disputes between MPs within the same district would no longer disrupt service provision by government.[57] These seemingly reasonable justifications aside, there was arguably a further political rationale. Indeed, the reforms still cut the number of constituency MPs, who were by far the most active of Tanzania's legislators.[58] Moreover, the decision to have elected MPs work with TANU district chairmen and secretaries ensured that they would be the junior partners in a troika dominated by party-cum-state bureaucrats. As such, the 1975 reforms meant that MPs further relinquished their role as influential local patrons.[59]

The Tanzania Parliament finally hit its 'nadir' in 1977.[60] The merger of TANU and Zanzibar's *Afro-Shirazi Party* to form CCM plus the simultaneous adoption of a new 'permanent' constitution led to parliament being officially designated as a 'committee' of the ruling party.[61] At this stage, it was thoroughly dominated by CCM's NEC and Central Committee. Within their constituencies, MPs were also closely shadowed by party and state officials. This decline in the profile of both Parliament and individual parliamentarians occurred against the backdrop of further ruling party institutional strengthening and centralized control over wealth accumulation and patronage resources.[62] Even if MPs had wanted to reach out to private political financiers, for instance, to cultivate a stronger patronage base in their local area, they were hard pressed to find any either able or willing.

5.2.2 Parliament Begins, Slowly, to Strengthen

The downward trajectory of *Bunge* began to reverse in the 1980s. However, the significance of this reversal should not be exaggerated, particularly as reforms contributing to legislative strengthening were accompanied by other reforms that, if anything, weakened parliament. What explains this slow and

---

[56] Kawawa, 1975. My translation.
[57] Ibid.
[58] Kjekshus, 1974.
[59] On MPs' constituency work, see Okumu and Holmquist, 1984.
[60] Tambila, 2004: 63.
[61] Mwakyembe, 1986: 46–47.
[62] See Chapter 3.

uncertain reform process? Given the theory propounded in this book, we might expect more rapid change. Indeed, from the 1980s and especially during the 1990s, the expansion of private accumulation and proliferation of patron–client rivalries meant CCM grew more factional,[63] and these divisions did then surface in parliament. Yet, as noted earlier in this chapter, the mere presence of *enabling structural conditions* does not guarantee institutional change. Rather, this change also depends on more *contingent factors*, namely whether there is the organization and leadership to take advantage of new structural possibilities. Until the mid-2000s, the specific configuration of rival factions in CCM did not align behind a concerted reform agenda, and crucially, there was not the necessary parliamentary leadership 'to mobilize and enthuse'.

First, the economic crisis of the early 1980s prompted some degree of self-critique within CCM, including calls for more democracy and an amplified role for *Bunge* relative to the party.[64] Constitutional reforms introduced in 1984 increased the proportion of directly elected MPs, which neared 70 per cent of all members.[65] New parliamentary powers and privileges were also introduced and later entrenched in a 1988 law.[66] Yet, while these changes enhanced the legislature's institutional *boundedness*, parliament retained its constitutional designation as a 'special committee of the National Conference of the party'.[67] Policy continued to be discussed in closed meetings of the CCM Central Committee and NEC.[68] The party also remained the primary avenue for elite advancement, with a career in CCM offering a privileged route to a position in government.[69]

The 1992 multiparty transition triggered the next set of legislative reforms. It should be recalled, though, that the transition was engineered by the CCM leadership partly to *strengthen* CCM while marginalizing opposition parties.[70] It follows that the ensuing legislative reforms did not reflect some new political dynamism but were rather an automatic consequence of unpicking the *de jure* one-party state. For instance, the composition of parliament had to be amended. Regional Commissioners lost their *ex officio* membership, seats for MPs elected through CCM's affiliated mass organizations, such as the youth

---

[63] See Chapter 4.
[64] Van Donge and Liviga, 1986: 230; Van Cranenburgh, 1990: 83, 117.
[65] Tambila, 2004: 66.
[66] See the *Parliamentary Immunities, Powers and Privileges Act, 1988*. Tambila, 2004: 66–67.
[67] Ibid., 67.
[68] Mlimuka and Kabudi, 1986: 81–82; Martin, 1988.
[69] Van Donge and Liviga, 1986: 234; Killian, 2004: 187–188.
[70] See Chapter 4.

league, were scrapped, and presidential powers to appoint 15 MPs were eliminated. The main consequence was an increase in the proportion of directly elected MPs, which again enhanced *Bunge's boundedness*. At the same time, the multiparty transition ended CCM's formal party 'supremacy'. This change may partly explain why CCM leaders scrapped the party's oversight committees, which previously shadowed government ministries. Yet, as noted in Chapter 4, then party Chairman, Ali Hassan Mwinyi, was already moving to de-emphasize formal party structures all while building fresh alliances with Tanzania's expanding business elite. Either way, the change in CCM left room for *Bunge's* committee system to develop, thereby enhancing its *complexity*. Before, the only parliamentary standing committee with a clearly defined role was the Public Accounts Committee (PAC). By contrast, the 1994 Standing Orders list 13 committees, each shadowing one or more government ministries.[71] The 2001 Standing Orders then list an additional eight sectoral committee, formally tasked with reviewing ministries annual budget estimates.[72]

These reforms nevertheless remained flawed. For instance, the changes to parliamentary committees were far from transformative. The number of committees and their jurisdiction remained largely at the discretion of the parliamentary Speaker, as Chairman of the Standing Orders Committee. The eight sectoral committees tasked with parsing through ministerial budgets were still overburdened, each being responsible for several ministries. More generally, committees lacked funding and basic infrastructure, were allocated insufficient time to complete their work, and were at a permanent disadvantage relative to government due to their poor access to information and expertise.[73] Some committees were permitted by the Speaker to conduct more extensive investigations, including hearings with witnesses summoned to Parliament, but this was rare.[74]

These limitations aside, CCM leaders also pushed through more overtly regressive legislative changes. In this vein, they sought to counterbalance some of the legislative reforms that were automatically triggered by the multiparty transition. For instance, CCM lost many of its indirectly elected or appointed MPs. It then also used the 1992 constitutional reforms to create 'special seats' for women MPs, but these were *contrived to strengthen CCM and its leadership*.

---

[71] *Kanuni za Bunge* (Parliamentary Standing orders), 1994 edition, Clause 89. Wang, 2005b: 187; Msekwa, 2006: 177.
[72] *Kanuni za Bunge* (Parliamentary Standing orders), 2001 edition, sections 9 and 10; Msekwa, 2002.
[73] Chaligha, 2004: 152; Wang, 2005a: 11.
[74] Ibid.

Fifteen per cent of parliamentary seats were now reserved for women, but they were to be distributed across parties based on the proportion of constituency seats each party won. In practice, this increased CCM's already overwhelming legislative majority.[75] Moreover, the mechanism for selecting women MPs within CCM remained 'practically undemocratic', concentrating power with the National Executive Committee while compelling women MPs to promote the party position.[76]

Another way CCM leaders compensated for the multiparty-party transition, or even took advantage of it, was through the new CCM Parliamentary Caucus rules. These ensured considerable institutional overlap between the Caucus, on the one hand, and formal government and party structures, on the other.[77] The Prime Minister chaired the Caucus while any CCM MPs who also served on the party's Central Committee were automatically appointed to the Caucus leadership committee. The rules also detailed strict disciplinary measures, including the application of a three-line whip. In theory, this disciplinary procedure was to be invoked only 'where opposition from CCM MPs could lead to the fall of the government'; in practice, though, its use was commonplace after 1995.[78] To ensure its efficacy, President Benjamin Mkapa (1995–2005) warned CCM MPs that they would be barred from running for re-election should they fail to support key government initiatives.[79] This threat carried additional weight due to CCM's insistence that the ban on Independent candidates be retained post-transition,[80] meaning that short of joining the as yet weak and marginalized opposition,[81] de-selected CCM MPs would face a political dead-end.

New constitutional reforms introduced after the multiparty transition further weakened the legislature. During his first term, Mkapa initiated a constitutional review, appointing a special commission to conduct consultations. He was, however, dissatisfied with the commission's recommendations so sent its report first to the CCM Central Committee, NEC, and finally the Cabinet for revision. Parliament was then left to provide a belated rubber stamp. The amendments thus imposed included a provision restoring presidential powers to appoint 10 MPs. This change freed the President's hand when appointing

---

[75] Yoon, 2008: 64–65.

[76] Killian, 1996: 29; Yoon, 2008: 61.

[77] CCM, *Kanuni za Kamati ya Wabunge Wote wa Chama Cha Mapinduzi*, 16 October 1993, Dodoma.

[78] Ibid.; Mmuya, 1998: 100; Baregu, 2004; Killian, 2004; Tambila, 2004; Wang, 2005b: 194–195.

[79] Wang, 2005b: 194–195.

[80] Makulilo, 2012.

[81] On the opposition, see especially: Mmuya and Chaligha, 1994: 93–98; Hyden, 1999; Nyirabu, 2002: 104–105.

ministers, first to parliament then to Cabinet.[82] The proportion of 'special seat' MPs was also increased from 15 to 20 per cent ahead of the 2000 elections and then again to 30 per cent ahead of the 2005 elections, but with no change to the problematic selection mechanism.[83]

Having documented the limited nature of legislative reforms up through the early 2000s, we can return to the question posed at the start of this section, namely, what explains the slow pace of change? Given their small number, opposition MPs post-transition could have little impact. Meanwhile, within CCM, there was neither the right factional alignment nor the necessary leadership to channel intra-party tensions into a reformist agenda. Throughout his tenure, President Mkapa used his considerable political skill to keep mounting political pressure from becoming an impetus for legislative action. A key tool was his judicious use of ministerial appointments. For instance, following the fraught 1995 presidential nomination process, Mkapa appointed his main rival, Jakaya Kikwete, Minister of Foreign Affairs. Another failed presidential aspirant and notable Kikwete supporter, Edward Lowassa, received a ministerial portfolio as well. Mkapa also yielded to pressure and allowed an 'old guard' back into Cabinet,[84] including ministers whom Nyerere cited as part of the reason why Tanzania 'stinks of corruption'.[85] Although they had never before served in ministerial roles, Kikwete and Lowassa were also viewed with suspicion, notably due to their reliance on private finance from Tanzania's *nouveau riche* when campaigning for the 1995 presidential nomination.[86] Despite these latent factional tensions, Mkapa continued his successful appeasement strategy. He was later himself implicated in corruption scandals, but he still managed factional disputes largely within the party and behind closed doors.[87]

Mkapa's efforts to enforce party discipline in *Bunge* were greatly aided by the Speaker of Parliament, Pius Msekwa. Msekwa did oversee committee reforms, although these were generally tied to donor priorities and funding.[88] Overall, he acted more as a party representative monitoring MPs' actions than as a parliamentary leader safeguarding the legislature's autonomy and power. This attitude was consistent with his background as a veteran CCM cadre, much more the old-style apparatchik than the new breed of political entrepreneur.

---

[82] Nyirabu, 2002: 106–108.
[83] The mode of allocating special seats across parties was marginally improved, though; it was now determined based each party's share of votes rather than seats. Yoon, 2008: 63, 67.
[84] Mmuya, 1998: 79.
[85] Ibid.; Kelsall, 2002: 106.
[86] See Chapter 4.
[87] Gray, 2015. This point about Mkapa's leadership skill came up repeatedly in interviews with MPs from the Eighth Parliament (2000–2005).
[88] Msekwa, 2002.

Msekwa began his career as the first African clerk to the post-Independence legislature but, after the Arusha Declaration, was transferred to the party secretariat, a move that signalled parliament's then declining prominence. He later held numerous high-level party positions before returning to parliament as an MP in 1990. He was soon elected Deputy Speaker and then Speaker, serving throughout Mkapa's presidency.[89] As the first Speaker of Tanzania's newly multiparty parliament, Msekwa insisted, 'It is a *moral obligation* for [ruling party MPs] to support the government of their party on the floor of the House.'[90] He routinely attended CCM parliamentary caucus and NEC meetings,[91] making it no surprise that ruling party MPs characterized him as 'soft', easily influenced by party leaders.[92] In 2003, one opposition MP went so far as to lament, 'Msekwa is the number one agent for killing democracy in this country.' The MP was not, however, complaining about Msekwa's treatment of the opposition. Rather, the legislator declared, '[The Speaker] utilizes parliamentary rules of procedure to violate the constitution by silencing *CCM members* of the House.'[93]

In sum, Tanzania's *Bunge* began slowly to strengthen from the 1980s through the early 2000s. The legitimacy crisis confronting CCM in the 1980s and the de jure multiparty transition triggered some of these changes. Tanzania's evolving political economy—particularly the expansion of patron–client factions within CCM—had the potential to motivate more far-reaching reforms; however, mounting factional tensions were largely contained within the party, and this notably due to the skilful leadership of Mkapa and Msekwa. By contrast, developments in parliament after 2005 confirm how intra-party tensions—once unleashed—can bring about profound legislative institutional change.

5.2.3 '*Bunge Lenye Meno*', a Parliament with Teeth

Following the 2005 general election, an unprecedented reformist drive took hold in *Bunge*. This momentum lasted throughout Jakaya Kikwete's presidency, spanning the Ninth Parliament (2005–2010) and into the Tenth (2010–2015). Although the results were somewhat mixed, the overall effect was to greatly enhance *Bunge*'s institutional *complexity* and *boundedness*. Three key

---

[89] Msekwa, 2012: 48.
[90] Msekwa, 2002: 76. Emphasis added.
[91] Interview with an opposition MP, Dar es Salaam, April 2016. See also Wang, 2005b: 187–8.
[92] Interview with former CCM MP, Dar es Salaam, April 2016.
[93] Opposition MP cited in Baregu, 2004: 35. Emphasis added.

factors combined to drive this institutional strengthening. These included: (1) a fortuitous alignment of factional rivalries and individual ambitions; (2) MPs' growing desire—and need—to act as local patrons plus to reward financial backers; and (3) CCM leaders' inability to impose discipline due to their own factional entanglements. I deal with each of these in turn. I also incorporate details that indicate how all three are emblematic of Tanzania's post-socialist political economy, and more specifically, the expansion of private accumulation. Rather than simple personality politics, the contestation between different factional networks and their leaders was made possible by their access to private resources, by the leaders' ability to combine public office with lucrative private sector activity, and by the tendency for political conflicts to turn into proxy battles for Tanzania's leading domestic capitalists.

Regarding the first driver of legislative institutional strengthening, i.e. a fortuitous alignment of factional divisions, President Kikwete came to power on the back of an influential *mtandao*, or network, whose masterminds were Kikwete's long-time ally, Edward Lowassa, and the then billionaire, Rostam Aziz. As discussed in Chapter 4, Aziz was among the first Tanzanian businessmen of Asian origin to enter Parliament in 1992, at the time explaining to a friend, 'Political leverage is good for business.'[94] Lowassa, meanwhile, was part of a younger generation of CCM politicians who combined politics with business. Another notable member of the Kikwete faction was Samuel Sitta. A veteran CCM MP and former Minister, Sitta left parliament in 1995. He then assumed an influential perch as director of the Tanzania Investment Centre, notable for granting politically motivated tax exemption,[95] before in 2005, returning to parliament.

This *mtandao* leveraged its political and business ties to take over CCM's formal structures well ahead of the 2005 presidential nominations, building up a seemingly unstoppable momentum behind Kikwete's candidacy[96]. Trouble *within* the pro-Kikwete faction quickly surfaced, however, when it came time to distribute post-election rewards. Sitta was reportedly promised the role of Prime Minister, but Lowassa and Aziz wanted the premiership for Lowassa.[97] They therefore suggested that Sitta become Speak of Parliament. Never before had the Speakership been a sought-after position. Sitta's immediate predecessor, Msekwa, remained Speaker for 11 years after taking over from the ailing Chief Adam Sapi Mkwawa, who had served as Speaker since Independence.[98]

---

[94] Interview, businessman, Dar, April 2016.
[95] Therkildsen, 2012.
[96] See Chapter 4 for an in-depth discussion.
[97] The following paragraphs draw on interviews with CCM MPs, CCM activists, opposition MPs, and journalists.
[98] Msekwa, 2012: 48.

The game changed in 2005, though. That year, an unprecedented six aspirants, with Msekwa among them, competed for the CCM Speaker nomination.[99] After both Sitta and Msekwa survived the initial cull by the CCM Central Committee, it was up to ruling party MPs to elect their preferred nominee. Although Msekwa started as the bookies' favourite,[100] the *mtandao's* support for Sitta meant that he ultimately trounced the incumbent, taking over 80 per-cent of the vote.[101] As ever with the *mtandao*, the campaign for Sitta allegedly involved 'a significant sum of money', spent on parliamentarians to ensure their support.[102] The victory did not put an end to the discord, though, as Sitta still resented Lowassa for taking the premiership. One close ally claimed that he 'heard it from Sitta himself that he was tricked'.[103]

Although frustrated, Sitta continued to cultivate ambitions of higher office, his eye ultimately set on the presidency.[104] He used the Speakership to pur-sue this personal agenda, in part, through a legislative reform effort. As one CCM politician phrased it, 'Sitta succeeded very much in giving teeth to Par-liament',[105] adding, 'But [...] he expected to be rewarded. Because he was leader of one pillar [of government], he could easily switch to another pillar.' An oppo-sition MP made a similar comment while further emphasizing Sitta's growing rivalry with Lowassa. As he observed, 'Once Parliament is powerful, the head of Parliament becomes powerful as well', emphasising, 'There was also a very powerful Prime Minister, Prime Minister Lowassa, and Sitta wanted to match Parliament with that.'[106]

It is worth noting, Sitta may have had additional principled reasons to back legislative reforms, although this is contested.[107] In any case, he did work with several reformist MPs—both opposition and CCM—plus government offi-cials and advocacy organizations, who were important intellectual architects of the reforms.[108] Yet even so, *factional rivalries*—reinforced by private financial contributions—remained essential to the reform drive.

Sitta began his effort by appointing a committee of senior MPs to review the Standing Orders, a process that led to the revised 2007 edition and helped Sitta score his first political victories. Although the proposed changes fuelled tensions with the executive and particularly with Lowassa, they were adopted

[99] Mgaya Kingoba, "Dodoma yarindima", Mtanzania, 27 December 2005, pp 1 & 4.
[100] Nkolimwa, Dominic, "Msekwa eyes Speaker's seat again", The Guardian, 20 December 2005, p 1.
[101] Mgaya Kingoba, "Sitta Spika Mpya", Mtanzania, 29 December 2005, pp 1.
[102] Ibid; Interview with a CCM cadre and friend of Aziz, Dar es Salaam.
[103] Interview with a former MP, Dar es Salaam, August 2015.
[104] Sitta ultimately contested the CCM presidential nomination in 2015 but lost.
[105] Interview, CCM MP, Dar, July 2015.
[106] Interview, opposition MP, Dar, April 2016.
[107] For instance, Sitta's controversial chairing of debates in the 2014 Constituent Assembly led many to doubt his reformist bona fides.
[108] See, for instance, the advocacy informing the introduction of the Public Organisation Accounts Committee: Utouh, 2018.

and soon bore fruit. For instance, by facilitating the formation of select committees,[109] the new rules helped Sitta convene a committee tasked with probing the so-called Richmond scandal. The committee's investigation culminated in Lowassa's resignation as PM. Another innovation of the 2007 Standing Orders was the introduction of a powerful new oversight committee, the Public Organizations Accounts Committee (POAC). POAC was mandated to oversee parastatal enterprise and thereby to take over some of the workload of the Public Accounts Committee (PAC). The activities of both the PAC and POAC, challenging the executive, soon added to the impression that *Bunge* had growth 'teeth'.[110]

The revised Standing Orders also helped further advance the legislative strengthening process itself. A new provision in the Standing Orders enabled parliamentary committees to table their own legislation, and this provision was key to the enactment of the National Assembly Administration Act (NAAA). The Act started as a committee bill, which the government only 'took up on its own' after '[caving] to pressure'.[111] The NAAA helped secure the legislature's institutional *boundedness*. Among other things, it shifted control over the parliamentary budget, including salaries and allowances, from the Office of the Prime Minister, headed by Lowassa, to Parliament itself.

The merits of the NAAA aside, it was an especially strategic reform for Sitta; it appealed directly to the personal interests of parliamentarians, enabling the Speaker to extend his 'alliance' in the legislature. As one CCM MP recalled, 'Samuel Sitta was relatively powerful in the parliament because of the reforms he implemented, especially the pay package to the MPs'.[112]

Beyond the factional tensions fuelling Sitta's reformist ambitions, his success was also due to the changing ambitions of parliamentarians themselves, the *second major reform driver*. The increasing significance of money in politics—and the pressures this placed on individual MPs—incentivized them to support the legislative strengthening process, especially where it improved their access to both public and *private* patronage resources. For instance, in praising the NAAA during a House debate, MPs stressed how the new allowances would help them address constituency demands.[113] Meanwhile, legislative strengthening also made MPs more 'marketable' to would-be financiers, as in, better able to exchange political favours for private support.[114] Improvements

---

[109] Sitta et al., 2008: 34.
[110] Utouh, 2018.
[111] Interview, parliamentary officer in the Planning Department, Dodoma, July 2015.
[112] Interview, CCM MP, Dodoma, June 2015.
[113] Ibid.
[114] Interview, CCM MP, Dodoma, May 2015; Interview, CCM MP, Dodoma, June 2015; Interview, Opposition MP, Dar, April 2016.

to committee oversight, in particular, meant MPs could more effectively pressure ministers on issues of interest to their financial backers.

The third ingredient contributing to reform success was CCM leaders' own inability to discipline party members and their private sector allies. Informal patronage networks—reinforced by business rivalries-turned-political fights—split CCM at the highest levels, thereby undermining formal disciplinary mechanisms. The dividing lines first crystallized within Parliament, primarily due to the Sitta–Lowassa feud. Following Lowassa's 2008 resignation, a group of pro-Sitta MPs began referring to themselves as 'anti-corruption crusaders'; they were CCM-*safi* (clean) challenging Lowassa's camp, labelled CCM-*mafisadi* (corrupt).[115] The two groups soon began mobilizing outside of *Bunge* as well, focusing notably on MPs' constituencies.

For CCM-*safi*, the goal was to support each other to ensure re-election.[116] The group also attracted attention and money by leveraging rival private sector interests. As one member recalled, 'We got support [in our constituencies] from even businessmen.'[117] This affirmation was confirmed in the press. An article in *The Guardian* reported that the paper's owner and one of Tanzania's richest men, Reginald Mengi, was financing CCM-*safi* MPs.[118] Mengi was then at loggerheads with fellow businessman and Lowassa-backer, Rostram Aziz.[119] Aziz responded in kind, spending liberally on the CCM-*mafisadi* camp and, allegedly, backing rival CCM candidates to unseat the CCM-*safi* MPs.[120]

This informal jockeying affected party disciplinary measures at several levels. First, it undermined the CCM parliamentary caucus, which according to one former CCM MP, had become 'almost dysfunctional'.[121] More high-level efforts to discipline CCM MPs, including Sitta himself, also failed. During a NEC meeting in August 2009, there was a bruising debate over whether to strip Sitta of his CCM membership and thus his Speakership. It is unclear exactly who was behind this move. The Lowassa faction was reportedly 'pulling strings through the party leaders'.[122] Many veteran CCM cadres who valued the Party's tradition of discipline were also highly critical of Sitta.[123] There is some indication that Kikwete turned on him too because of Sitta's efforts to investigate

---

[115] Interviews with CCM and opposition MPs; Msekwa, 2012: 121.
[116] Interview, ex-CCM MP, Dar, August 2015.
[117] Ibid.
[118] *The Guardian*, 'Battle line for 2010 drawn—Lembeli', 9 August 2009. Mengi emerged as a prominent African capitalist in the 1980s, a leader in the new wave of indigenous accumulators, themselves integrated within transnational capitalist networks. See: Chachage, 2018: 349–364; Mengi, 2018.
[119] Interview, former CCM cadre and businessman, Dar, April 2016. On the Mengi-Rostam feud and its roots in deeper tensions linked to Tanzania's capitalist transition, see: Chachage, 2018: 374–375.
[120] *The Guardian*, 9 August 2009.
[121] Interview, former MP and high-level CCM cadre, Dar es Salaam, March 2016.
[122] Interview, CCM MP, Dodoma, June 2015.
[123] Msekwa, 2012: 123; Interview, CCM cadre, Dar es Salaam, March 2016.

the fraudulent diversion of funds from a Bank of Tanzania account allegedly to reward Kikwete's private business backers during the 2005 presidential campaign.[124] Ultimately, though, the case was deemed too volatile to manage through a formal disciplinary procedure. Instead of expulsion, the NEC tasked three CCM 'Elders' with 'reconciling the "warring" factions'.[125]

Many of the same dynamics driving legislative reform in the Ninth Parliament (2005–2010) continued into the Tenth (2010–2015), albeit with more mixed results. Despite Sitta surviving the initial attempted ouster, internal party tensions frustrated his efforts to return as Speaker after the 2010 elections, an initial blow to the reform agenda. To avoid a damaging split, the party's Central Committee declared it was time for a woman to lead Parliament, resulting in veteran politician Anne Makinda becoming Tanzania's first female Speaker.[126] This outcome was a successful 'balancing' effort,[127] eliminating the most immediate factional threat and, many hoped, the impulse 'to arm Parliament with teeth strong enough to bite the CCM Government'.[128] Yet the round-about effort to exclude Sitta also spoke to CCM's continued vulnerability, heralding further divisions to come.

Indeed, the first major legislative reforms of the Tenth Parliament saw MPs again leverage their informal, even cross-party networks to challenge the executive. Changes to the Standing Orders introduced in 2013 combined some top-down and largely regressive measures concerning Parliament's oversight committees with major reforms strengthening its budgetary review powers.

Regarding oversight committees, the new rules eliminated the POAC, first introduced under Sitta as noted earlier. The change came after corruption allegations made by POAC in 2012 led to the removal or 'firing' of several ministers and nearly toppled the Prime Minister. This attempt to subdue *Bunge's* oversight committees was only partially successful, though, at least in the Tenth Parliament. Against all expectations, the powerful former Chair and Vice Chair of POAC—from the opposition and from CCM, respectively—managed to get themselves reinstated as Chairs of the remaining Public Accounts Committee, which they promptly divided into two sub-committees, one of which took on the old POAC mandate.[129] Although 'nobody expected' this outcome, the duo succeeded by lobbying the Deputy Speaker and Speaker,

---

[124] *The Guardian*, 'Revealed: JK's role in Richmond deal', August 2009; Interview, former CCM MP, Dar es Salaam, August 2015.

[125] Msekwa, 2012: 123; *Mtanzania*, 'CCM yapeleka maumivu kwa wabunge', 19 August 2009.

[126] Interview, CCM activist, Dar, August 2015. While political factors helped her secure the speakership, Anne Makinda was also eminently qualified for the role. She had served as an MP since 1975 and as Deputy Speaker under Sitta from 2005 to 2010.

[127] Interview, CCM MP, Dar, July 2015.

[128] Msekwa, 2012: 123.

[129] Interview, former POAC/PAC Vice-Chair, May 2015, Dodoma; Interview, former POAC/PAC Chair, Dar, April 2016.

the Government Chief Whip, who chairs the CCM caucus, and various sympathetic CCM MPs. In other words, they were able to leverage factional divisions within CCM coupled with their own personal networks. Their influence also attests to the growing strength of parliament, and especially of its most 'marketable' committees. As the former POAC Chair explained, Ministers and CCM MPs supported his efforts because '[it] was like an *investment* for them that maybe when they have some problems, they could get help'.

This informal manoeuvring to save POAC was nevertheless a temporary fix, leaving parliament's formal institutional strength diminished.[130] By contrast, the changes to the budgetary review process, introduced through the 2013 Standing Orders and entrenched in the 2015 Budget Act, were an unambiguous win. Multiple factors drove this reform. The idea originated in the Ninth Parliament and was thus part of the momentum generated under Sitta.[131] Makinda then took over championing the changes, encouraged by rank-and-file MPs tired of 'being bulldozed by government'.[132] They complained that the budget review calendar left them little time to amend executive proposals while, after the budget was passed, government did not follow the approved budget.[133] MPs' enthusiasm for reform meant they were yet again willing to ignore pressure from the CCM government. As Makinda recalled, she had to meet with the President 'more times than ever before in my life', which was 'a headache!'[134]

As with the NAAA, parliament used the provision introduced in the 2007 Standing Orders to prepare the Budget Bill as a committee bill. Again, as with the NAAA, Government responded by quickly preparing its own legislation. This was, however, a watered-down version, prompting MPs to threaten that they would 'amend the whole thing in the House'.[135] The Budget Committee then worked with the Ministry of Finance to come up with a compromise, which culminated in the passage of the 2015 Budget Act. This 'compromise' incorporated '90 per cent' of parliament's initial reform agenda.[136]

What legislators did next with the Budget Committee helps confirm some of the career-advancing motivations behind their reformist zeal,[137] as well as

---

[130] The Chair and Vice-Chair also had to split the budget of a single committee to do the work of two.

[131] Interview, former Chair of the Budget Committee, Dar, July 2015.

[132] Interview, former chair of the budget committee; Interview with two Clerks of the Budget Committee, Dodoma, June 2015; Interview, Anne Makinda, Dar, March 2016.

[133] Interviews with multiple CCM and opposition MPs.

[134] Interview, Makinda.

[135] Ibid.

[136] Interview, Clerk to Parliament, Dodoma, June 2015; Interview, Hakielimu activist; Interview, Makinda; Interview, former chair of the budget committee.

[137] As stressed elsewhere, these motivations and their importance in shaping reform outcomes do not preclude some legislators embracing reforms for more normative reasons. Makinda, for instance, spoke emphatically about the evolving needs of a 'modern' parliament: 'We had to change because

the importance of the broader political economic context in which the reforms took place. MPs used the Committee to champion improved service delivery to constituents but also altered government tax legislation, and this following lobbying by various 'business interests'.[138] As one former government minister claimed, 'It is not professional lobbying of just making a case. It has another picture.'[139] A backbench CCM MP clarified, 'Businessmen in particular learned that the most powerful people are the MPs, and therefore they started to come [to Parliament] to corrupt them.'[140]

In sum, the Tenth Parliament (2010–2015), despite its shortcomings, continued the unprecedented institutional strengthening process initiated during the Ninth. Over the full 10-year period, the legislature's institutional *complexity* increased with powerful new committees like the Budget Committee plus the subdivision of the POAC and PAC mandates, even if that effort was in part lost to the executive. Its institutional *boundedness* also improved with the introduction of additional barriers to outside influence, for instance, through the new control over its own budget powers thanks to the NAAA. What explains these changes? Among the key drivers were, yes, some more normatively motivated MPs but aided by a heady mix of factional organization and personal ambition, here channelled into effective parliamentary leadership. Yet this new form of factional organizing was only possible due to structural change in Tanzania's political economy, namely the expansion of private accumulation in post-socialist Tanzania, which directly fed competition among politicians and domestic capitalists alike.

The discussion presented in this section demonstrates how the institutional strength of the Tanzanian Parliament has evolved in line with changes in the ruling party and—more fundamentally—changing patterns of 'politicized accumulation' and patronage distribution. When CCM consolidated as a strong 'institutionalized coalition' following the Arusha Declaration, *Bunge* declined to the point of becoming a mere 'sub-committee' of the party. Amidst the economic reforms of the 1980s and 1990s, however, the tides turned. Party discipline weakened as rival patronage networks began to consolidate and to compete for control. This process created the space for some incremental reforms to Bunge. However, it was not until the mid-2000s that the alignment

---

modern parliaments have to participate in the budgetary process of the government budget. The old system was not participatory per se. In real terms, the parliament had only five days to debate the budget and they even vote before they start talking. So, five days, the Ministry of Finance presents the budget second week of June, debate it five days, you vote it. You vote it!' Interview, Makinda.

[138] Interview, Makinda.

[139] Interview, former Deputy Minister of Finance, Dodoma, July 2015.

[140] Interview, CCM MP, Dodoma, January 2016. See Opalo (2022: 10) for further discussion of how legislators may prioritize work on committees that have 'important distributive implications for economic elites' and thus enable MPs to participate in an 'intra-elite distributive contest'.

of factional tensions within CCM spurred a major advance in legislative institutionalization. Even so, the relative decline of a party like CCM—and its consequent impact on legislative reform—still leaves room for reversals, as discussed further in the conclusion to this book.

5.3 Uganda's Parliament

Whereas the legislature is likely to remain weak under an 'institutionalized coalition', only strengthening when the cohesion and institutional coherence of the ruling party begins to erode, the conditions for legislative strengthening are more propitious under a 'bargained coalition'. The Ugandan Parliament under the NRM is a case in point.

To understand parliament's institutional trajectory, it is worth noting that NRM leaders' early quest for legitimacy led them to promise more progressive constitutional reform. This promise led to the 1995 Constitution, which awarded more powers to the legislature. While we should not disregard the significance of these early constitutional gains, they are far from the whole story. Since the NRM took power in 1986, the individual aspirations of MPs—notably to build their *local patronage base*—alongside more wide-ranging *factional rivalries* have directly contributed to parliament's institutional strengthening and assertiveness. *Ambitious legislative leaders*, especially the Speaker, have also played an important role. While opposition and seemingly more principled, reform-minded legislators have contributed as well, their actions succeeded *where they aligned with the patronage and factional manoeuvring of the NRM legislative majority*. Finally, the executive's failure to enforce formal party discipline—discussed in depth in Chapter 4—has also undermined its efforts to reliably subdue the legislature. This is not to say that the Ugandan Parliament is in any way an ideal model of a strong legislature; it remains vulnerable to executive pressure, and its strength is *relative* to that of its neighbours. Yet, even as President Museveni has undone some legislative gains, he has repeatedly failed to roll-back others, and instead, remained stuck in a protracted 'war' with his MPs.[141]

I examine the institutional trajectory of parliament under the NRM in four parts. First, I explain the NRM leadership's early tolerance of a stronger legislature, although even at this stage, factional politics were also driving legislative change. Second, I consider how MPs in the Sixth Parliament (1996–2001) further strengthened the legislature. Third, I consider the repeated efforts by the executive to tame parliament, particularly around the 2005 multiparty

---

[141] For more on the nature of authoritarian legislative strength, and its significance in Uganda, see Chapters 1 and 2, especially page (15).

transition. Finally, I indicate how and why MPs in the Eighth and Ninth Parliaments (2006–2016) continued to bargain with the President, sometimes ceding but often resisting executive efforts to limit parliament's institutional strength.

5.3.1 Parliament and the Promise of 'Fundamental Change'

The NRM remained in a precarious political position after seizing power in 1986.[142] To help broaden their support, NRM leaders denounced the abuses of past regimes, promising a more democratic institutional order. This commitment is among the reasons the legislature was granted more powers in the 1995 Constitution. Factional contestation was, however, also shaping legislative politics and institutional reforms even before the new constitution came into force.

Pre-1986, the history of Uganda's parliament reflected the fractious nature of post-Independence ruling coalitions, and their collapse into violent and autocratic rule.[143] As such, the legislature was at the heart of the 1966 constitutional crisis. Having lost the support of opposition parties as well as most of his own party, the then Prime Minister Milton Obote faced a near unanimous legislative rebellion. All but one MP voted in favour of a motion to suspend Colonel Idi Amin on suspicion of smuggling gold,[144] a motion that also implicated Obote. In response, he arrested five Cabinet ministers, declared himself Executive President, promoted Amin to Army Commander, and suspended the 1962 Constitution. Later in April, he introduced a new constitution and, in May, placed Amin in charge of the 'battle of Buganda', which saw the Kabaka—the King—flee into exile. In 1967, Obote introduced another constitution, which granted extensive presidential powers.[145] In 1971, Amin orchestrated a coup against Obote, having fallen out with his erstwhile ally. He then abolished the legislature altogether.

Invoking this turbulent history, Museveni promised 'fundamental change' during his 1986 swearing-in speech as President of Uganda. With Legal Notice No. 1, the newly formed NRM government immediately suspended parts of the 1967 constitution, including sections providing for the composition and powers of Parliament.[146] It also instituted the 'Movement' or no-party system, which involved a ban on all party activities, as part of a 'transitional'

---

[142] See Chapter 3.
[143] Jorgensen, 1981; Low, 1988; Mutibwa, 1992.
[144] Young, 1966; Mutibwa, 1992: 33–34.
[145] Low, 1988: 42–43; Mutibwa, 1992: 37–41, 58–61.
[146] Mukholi, 1995: 25.

arrangement.[147] This was pending the adoption of a new constitution, the formal preparation for which began with the creation of a constitutional commission in 1988.[148]

While the constitution-making process was to prove relatively inclusive and progressive, the NRM leadership used the intervening years to consolidate its hold on power, including by retaining control over what served as an interim legislature. Following Legal Notice No. 1, the National Resistance Council (NRC) became Uganda's legislative body.[149] Created in 1981 to organize civilian committees during the bush war, the NRC was in 1986 composed of between 22 and 38 former guerrilla commanders. Museveni himself served as Chairman, the equivalent of the Speaker.[150] The following year, the NRC grew to 80–98 members and, in 1989, expanded again following indirect elections.[151] While relatively free, these elections were nevertheless designed to make it difficult for either UPC or DP-leaning candidates to perform well.[152] An NRM-sympathizing majority was thus retained within the NRC, further reinforced by the still large proportion of 'historicals' (i.e. former rebels) and presidential nominees.[153]

This is not to say the NRC was an insignificant institution, a mere rubber stamp. Already at this early stage, and despite Museveni presiding as Chairman-cum-Speaker, the post-1989 NRC both reflected and magnified factional tensions then emerging within the NRM. It provided a space for 'groups and individuals to propagate their competing hidden political agendas, for political bargaining, for access to political and material rewards and for the advancement of particularistic interests'.[154] In some instances, these particularistic interests also fuelled contestation over more fundamental issues, notably relating to Uganda's post-conflict economic restructuring. NRC members challenged Museveni's preferred strategy of 'politicized accumulation', at least where it conflicted with their own material aims.[155] In 1993, for instance, the NRC forced a pause in the ongoing privatization process on grounds that government was unfairly favouring foreign investors over indigenous entrepreneurs. Beyond directly contesting material issues of concern to them, NRC members also fashioned their own legislative reform agenda, working to strengthen the NRC as a tool to challenge the executive. They thus introduced

---

[147] See Chapter 4 for further discussion.
[148] Kasfir, 1995: 15.
[149] Mukholi, 1995: 25.
[150] Museveni, 1997: 135–137; Carbone, 2008: 157.
[151] Carbone, 2008: 157.
[152] See Chapter 3.
[153] Kasfir, 1991; Mudoola, 1991.
[154] Mudoola, 1991: 236.
[155] See Chapter 3.

the first legislative institutional innovations, including the creation of new committees, increasing parliament's *complexity*.[156]

Yet while the NRC was no rubber stamp, it was still viewed by many as a 'discredited' legislative body, and certainly not one with the requisite legitimacy to debate and approve Uganda's new constitution.[157] As such, legislation was passed in 1993 to allow for the creation of a directly elected Constituent Assembly. Elections were held the next year. Having by then carefully prepared the political terrain, the NRM could be sure of a majority. After Movement-supporting candidates captured over two-thirds of seats, Museveni notoriously celebrated having 'won' the election, and this despite there being no recognized party competition.

The Constituent Assembly convened later in 1994 and spent 18 months debating and approving the draft Constitution, which had been prepared by the Constitutional Commission following nation-wide consultations. As noted earlier, the framing narrative was that the new constitution should correct for previous authoritarian transgressions, notably by creating a strong legislature.[158] The Chairman of the Constitutional Commission later asserted, 'It is now generally accepted that the 1995 Constitution was made to correct the mistakes of the past, to redefine Uganda, and to restore constitutional rule based on democracy and respect for human rights.'[159] He then added, 'We have therefore sought to strengthen the powers of Parliament as the supreme legislative body [...]'. During the proceedings of the Constituent Assembly, NRM leaders seemed broadly on board with this agenda, so long as the ban on political parties was preserved.[160]

The Movement system was enshrined in the 1995 Constitution, which critics denounced as a move towards a one-party state.[161] At the same time, though, the Constitution greatly expanded the powers of the legislature, which included the ability to vet ministers prior to their appointment and to censure them in case of malpractice.[162] It also catered for the institutional make-up of Parliament, stipulating that the Speaker would be elected by all MPs, that committee chairpersons would be elected by the committee members, and that legislators themselves would be voted in the basis of universal adult suffrage,

---

[156] Tukahebwa, 1998: 65. See also: Kasfir and Twebaze, 2009; Twebaze, 2014; The Interim Rules of Procedure for the NRC of Uganda.

[157] *Hansard*, 20 April 1993; Mukholi, 1995: 35–36. The creation of a newly elected Constituent Assembly was also in keeping with the recommendations of the Constitutional Commission (Wapakhabulo, 2001: 118).

[158] See, for example: Njuba, 1991; Odoki, 2005.

[159] Odoki, 1997. Paper delivered at a seminar for parliamentarians.

[160] Interview, former member of the Constituent Assembly committee tasked with reviewing provisions relating to the powers of the executive, legislature and judiciary, Kampala, December 2014.

[161] Oloka-Onyango, 2000.

[162] See Chapter VI of the 1995 Constitution.

except for those representing special interest groups.[163] Parliament was also given powers to determine important aspects of its budget, including the pay of MPs. Together these provisions helped ensure the *boundedness* of the legislature, safeguarding against executive incursions. The Constitution also catered for parliament's institutional *complexity* by providing for standing and select committees and specifying their powers, including the power to summon witnesses and demand information from government.

In sum, while the NRM was still working to ensure its legitimacy, Museveni and his inner circle allowed for a constitutionally empowered legislature to emerge. Even before this, however, the make-shift legislative body that was the NRC showed how legislative assertiveness and institutional innovation could result from the NRM's elite factionalism.[164]

5.3.2 Parliament Asserts Itself

The first Parliament to convene after the adoption of the 1995 Constitution pushed through additional institutional changes, which on balance further strengthened the legislature. A select few reformist MPs played a galvanizing role, but their efforts succeeded notably because MPs were organizing informally to pursue their ambitious as local patrons. More elite-level factional disputes also fuelled legislative oversight activity. In both instances, the lack of formal party discipline outside the legislatures at this time—as documented in Chapters 3—meant NRM leaders were similarly unable to reliably discipline MPs within parliament.

The first major institutional change in the Sixth Parliament (1996–2001) was a step back for the legislature. Shortly after Parliament was sworn in, President Museveni sought approval to increase the number of ministers from the maximum of 21 set in the Constitution. Despite a public outcry, MPs had a personal interest in the proposal and passed it 'without any serious debate'.[165] Museveni later used the allocation of ministerial portfolios to silence vocal MPs and to encourage others to follow the government line in hopes of entering Cabinet.[166] As such, this change was a score for the executive, supplying Museveni with a new tool for subduing the legislature. MPs' acceptance of

---

[163] These special interest groups included a woman MP per district, 10 military MPs, and MPs for workers, youth, and people with disabilities. These representatives were elected by electoral colleges. Given the close ties between these colleges and the Movement, some Constituent Assembly delegates feared they would be biased in favour of the NRM.

[164] See also Chapter 3 on debates over land and land tenure in the Constituent Assembly, which demonstrate that body's relevance to ongoing elite contestation over the terms of post-conflict 'politicized accumulation'.

[165] Waliggo, 2001: 65.

[166] Carbone, 2008; Kasfir and Twebaze, 2009; Interviews with MPs and parliamentary staff.

the proposal showed how their efforts to bargain with the executive could strengthen or weaken parliament, so long as their interests were served.

During the Sixth Parliament, though, institutional changes mostly strengthened the legislature. The Administration of Parliament Act (APA) (1997) and the Budget Act (2001) were especially key. These two pieces of legislation came more than a decade before Tanzania's National Assembly Administration Act (2008) and Budget Act (2015), for which they in fact served as models.[167] Uganda's APA instituted the Parliamentary Commission responsible for the institutional development of the legislature. It also catered for parliament's fiscal autonomy, which crucially gave MPs more control over their own salaries and emoluments.[168] Finally, it created the parliamentary service, which meant staff recruitment and salaries were determined separately from the rest of the civil service. Altogether, the APA enhanced parliament's institutional *boundedness*. In particular, the legislature's newfound financial autonomy meant it could no longer be described as 'an administrative department of the government'.[169] The Budget Act (2001), meanwhile, established the Budget Office and the Budget Committee, which among other tasks, reviewed and synthesized proposed budgetary amendments from select committees, thereby easing their passage in the House.[170] The Act also required government to share information about the budget in a timelier manner. Finally, it stipulated that any supplementary budgets whose value exceeded three per cent of the total budget would require prior parliamentary approval.[171] Ultimately, the Budget Act increased parliament's *complexity* while also enhancing key oversight powers, particularly through the Budget Committee.[172]

As suggested above, these reforms came about notably due to a lack of formal party discipline as well as MPs' patronage ambitious. It is worth stressing, these political dynamics diverged sharply from the status quo prevailing in Tanzania for much of its post-Independence history. Both the APA and Budget Act started as private member's bills, fronted by reform-minded MPs.[173] By contrast, recall that in Tanzania's *Bunge*, with its history of strong party discipline, no private member's bill has ever been passed; only in the mid-2000s did MPs first challenge government with committee bills, which were later taken over as government legislation. In Uganda, the APA and Budget Act also won

---

[167] Interview, former chair of the budget committee, Dar es Salaam, July 2015; Interview, staff member of the Tanzanian Parliament, Dodoma, July 2015.

[168] Nakamura and Johnson, 2003: 9; Administration of Parliament Act, 2005.

[169] Nakamura and Jonson (2003: 10) citing Ogalo, the MP responsible for tabling the Administration of parliament bill.

[170] The Budget Act (2001).

[171] Budget act (2001); Kasfir and Twebaze, 2009: 81–83.

[172] Kasfir and Twebaze, 2009. Interview, staff from the Parliamentary Budget Office, Kampala, February 2015.

[173] Nakamura and Johnson, 2003; Carbone, 2008; Kasfir and Twebaze, 2009.

the enthusiastic backing of a cross-section of MPs who hoped to further their personal and political ambitions, and in the process, were willing to ignore government directives. Indeed, shortly after the APA was enacted, parliamentarians increased their salaries despite ministerial objections.[174] Meanwhile, the two principal backers of the Budget Act both felt that its popularity was due to the 'opportunity [it] provided for all MPs to influence the budget for the benefit of their own constituencies'.[175]

Beyond MPs' individual motivations, their *informal organizing*—which began with a shared interest in addressing local patronage concerns—also contributed to institutional reform efforts, as well as other legislative challenges to the executive. This informal organizing centred on the creation of rival 'caucuses'. Among the earliest and most prominent of these groupings was the Young Parliamentary Association (YPA), formed in 1997. It brought together a cross-section of Movement-leaning and pro-multiparty MPs, whose initial aim was to support each other's constituency development efforts.[176] As one former member recalled, the YPA's first actions involved members agreeing, 'Let's go for a fundraising [*sic*]',[177] something akin to the Kenyan practice of *Harmabee*; MPs could both perform their patronage roles while also inviting political allies and the wider community to contribute to a constituency development project. The popularity of this collective initiative led to over 100 MPs joining the group.[178] 'There were very many members', another former YPA adherent stressed, 'and every weekend all of them would be in one constituency mobilizing people.'[179] In this same vein, the YPA Constitution included among its objective 'liaising in matters of mutual concern especially development' while the group's 'Development Coordinator' was responsible for initiating projects and advising on potential sponsors, including private financiers.[180] YPA also helped MPs organize for the next elections, forming a joint saving scheme to help fund the 2001 race.[181]

As intimated earlier, the YPA later escalated its aims, pursuing a legislative strengthening agenda alongside other, often controversial legislative activities.[182] For instance, the mover of the private member's bill that became the

[174] Nakamura and Johnson, 2003: 11–12.
[175] Kasfir and Twebaze, 2009: 82.
[176] See: 'The Constitution of Young Parliamentary Association', 1997; Carbone, 2008; Kasfir and Twebaze, 2009.
[177] Interview, former Constituent Assembly member, Kampala, January 2015.
[178] Interview, former Constituent Assembly member, Kampala, January 2015. The YPA Constitution lists 86.
[179] Interview, former Constituent Assembly member, Kampala, December 2014.
[180] 'The Constitution of Young Parliamentary Association', 1997.
[181] Ibid.; Kasfir and Twebaze, 2009: 102.
[182] Carbone, 2008; Kasfir and Twebaze, 2009; Interview, former Constituent Assembly member, Kampala, January 2015.

APA was a YPA member and used his connections in the caucus to mobilize support.[183] The YPA's organizational infrastructure also enabled a then unprecedented mobilization to censure government ministers on suspicion of corruption.[184] However, as discussed further in the next chapter, factional rivalries between senior ministers belonging to the NRM's wealthy 'aristocracy' also invigorated the censure effort, thereby indicating the disruptive potential of factionalism for executive–legislative relations.

To reiterate, institutional changes in the Sixth Parliament—most of which served to strengthen the legislature—largely depended on MPs' informal organizing and fundraising efforts, which escalated from a focus on local patronage interests to more ambitious legislative concerns. More generally, MPs' patronage roles, their need to self-finance and mobilize 'sponsors', the scope for informal organizing, and the factional tensions dividing rival elites are all bound up with the nature of the NRM as a 'bargained coalition'; its patronage structure and (lack of) formal party-building outside parliament, both documented in previous chapters, were then reflected—indeed, amplified—within the legislature.

5.3.3 The Executive Backlash

The executive's irritation when confronted with this unexpectedly unruly legislature soon became apparent. Shortly after the Sixth Parliament (1996–2001) convened, President Museveni insisted that he must be allowed to implement his 'contract' with the electorate, which he warned 'some groups' were trying to 'frustrate'.[185] The former rebel leader then queried, 'How many wars shall I fight?', lamenting that he was now 'fighting' MPs.[186] Museveni and his Ministers soon reversed their initial, more permissive stance vis-à-vis parliament. They began by trying to use informal pressures to enforce de facto party discipline. They then sought to introduce more formal disciplinary checks. This effort culminated in the 2005 multiparty transition, aimed at instituting formal discipline both outside parliament—as documented in the last chapter—and within.

Museveni's *informal* attempts to control his parliamentary majority involved, first, creating the Movement Caucus, which emerged in response

---

[183] Interview, former Constituent Assembly member, Kampala, December 2014.
[184] Interview, former Constituent Assembly member, Kampala, January 2015. See also: Tamale, 1999; Carbone, 2008; Kasfir and Twebaze, 2009.
[185] Citing a 1999 Monitor article, Carbone, 2005: 9.
[186] Ibid.

to the YPA. As one former member of both groupings recalled, the YPA was the more formal of the two as it had its own executive committee and constitution.[187] What the Movement Caucus lacked in formality, it made up for through other means. There were widespread rumours of bribes being distributed so that MPs would support controversial government positions. The President also intervened in the selection of caucus leaders and later appointed several ministers, simultaneously cementing their loyalty and raising their status.[188] Some YPA members were similarly co-opted, joining the rapidly growing Cabinet.[189] The use of informal pressures, both financial and coercive, then escalated ahead of the 2001 elections. NRM leaders consolidated an approach to campaigns that would become emblematic of their ad hoc factional politicking.[190] Due to aggressive 'de-campaigning' efforts, fewer oppositional MPs returned to the Seventh Parliament (2001–2006). Those remaining did try to reinstate the YPA but were 'fought' by the NRM leadership. As one former member recalled, 'When we were holding elections for the [YPA] executive, [a group of Museveni supporters] swarmed the room and elected themselves. [...] They took positions, put the people they wanted and destroyed us.'[191]

Dissatisfied with these informal efforts to discipline MPs, which were both costly and unreliable, NRM leaders soon began to advocate more formal party discipline. As one Minister asserted, 'The absence of a whip means you can't count on an MP's vote.'[192] Museveni himself quickly identified the problem and abandoned his commitments to the Movement system in all but name. Thus in 1999, he affirmed that 'all MPs were elected either on a pro-Movement platform or a Multiparty-ist one', adding, 'Even if there are no parties in Uganda in the strict sense of the word, those MPs who came through the Movement ticket must remember that their primary loyalty is to the Movement and parliament is secondary.'[193] After the 2001 elections, NRM leaders went a step further and backed a formal return to multiparty politics. Chapter 4 documents how Museveni hoped to use formal party discipline to address factional tensions outside parliament, notably when it came to candidate selection and elections.[194] Even before this electoral focus, though, Museveni's experience

---

[187] Interview, former Constituent Assembly member, Kampala, December 2014.
[188] Kasfir and Twebaze, 2009: 95.
[189] Interview, former Constituent Assembly member, Kampala, January 2015.
[190] See Chapter 2.
[191] Interview, former Constituent Assembly member, Kampala, January 2015.
[192] Cited in Kasfir and Twebaze, 2009: 95; see also Carbone, 2008.
[193] Cited in Kasfir and Twebaze, 2009: 95.
[194] Ssemujju, Ibrahim. 'President Museveni has a new vision for Uganda', *The Daily Monitor*, 28 March 2003, pp. 8–9.

during the Sixth Parliament convinced him that he needed to *strengthen his hold over the legislature*, including through formal party discipline.

Besides advocating a return to multiparty politics, NRM leaders hoped to manipulate the constitutional reform process to further weaken parliament in other ways.[195] Museveni appointed a new Constitutional Review Commission (CRC) in 2001,[196] but when the CRC's submitted its report, Cabinet responded by issuing its own contradictory set of proposals in a White Paper.[197] Unlike the original report, the White Paper recommended that the President be granted powers to dissolve Parliament. It also recommended lifting presidential term limits, which promised to further centralize power in Museveni's hands.

In sum, the NRM leadership—frustrated the shortcomings of its largely informal efforts to discipline an unexpectedly assertive parliament—tried to change its strategy. However, the attempts to introduce more formal executive and party checks on legislative autonomy proved only partially successful, notably because of the ongoing factional contestation within the NRM.

5.3.4 The Tug-of-War Continues

The package of reforms accompanying the 2005 multiparty transition did weaken the legislature, yet the overriding impression is one of continuity rather than change. Parliament lost some of its institutional advantages, but the fractious internal politics of the NRM meant that it preserved or even gained others. In the following discussion, I first review how legislators—up through the end of the Ninth Parliament (2011–2016)—gave in to some executive efforts to weaken legislative institution; however, on key issues, they resisted this pressure, or indeed, further strengthened legislative institutions. I then, in a second section, explain *why* this resistance has endured. In short, informal patronage networks continued to fuel elite rivalries, undermining party discipline and exacerbating executive–legislative tensions.

5.3.4.1 Institutional Continuity
First, the executive used Uganda's multiparty reforms to chip away at the legislature's institutional defences. MPs ultimately gave in to Museveni's demands

---

[195] 'The Report of the Commission of Inquiry (Constitutional Review): Findings and Recommendations', 10 December 2003. See, in particular, the Terms of Reference.

[196] 'Cabinet to veto Ssempebwa Report', *The Daily Monitor*, 22 August 2003.

[197] Ibid; 'Government White Paper on: (1) The Report of the Commission of Inquiry (Constitutional Review); (2) Government Proposals not addressed by the report of the Commission of Inquiry (Constitutional Review)', 2004.

that they remove presidential term limits. Each pocketed a Shs5m ($2.9k) reward in exchange, and this just as election campaigns were heating up. NRM leaders also engineered the constitutional review process to ensure parallel changes to the Administration of Parliament Act and the parliamentary Rules of Procedure.[198] While these were aimed at accommodating political parties—including opposition parties—in parliament, they also empowered NRM leaders to intervene more directly in legislative affairs. For instance, party whips were made responsible for selecting the membership of parliamentary committees, and the Government Chief Whip—a presidential appointee who sits in Cabinet—chose committee chairs.[199] This top-down selection was a radical departure from the previous norm, which let MPs choose their committees on a first-come-first-serve basis. Meanwhile, committee members had elected their own chairpersons.[200] By giving more powers to party whips, and particularly the Government Chief Whip, the new parliamentary rules weakened the legislature's institutional *boundedness*, creating new opportunities for the ruling party and executive to intervene.

However, not all attempts to use the multiparty transition as a pretext for strengthening the executive succeeded. MPs voted down the government proposal granting the president the power to dissolve parliament.[201] They also proved resistant to formal party discipline, much to the chagrin of Museveni and his Ministers.[202] In a statement sent to members of the NRM parliamentary caucus in July 2006, Museveni declared, 'If you are a Movement MP or a pro-Movement independent, you should not engage in altercations with ministers in Parliament.'[203] He clarified, 'You should instead raise the concerned issues in the Movement Caucus which must always be attended by all ministers.' This message was not well received by NRM MPs, many of whom 'had assumed that [contradicting ministers during debates] was precisely why they were in Parliament'.[204]

This early disagreement heralded more trouble to come. Indeed, efforts to enforce formal discipline remained contested throughout the Eighth

---

[198] Interview, former Leader of the Opposition, Kampala, December 2014.

[199] 'Rules of Procedure of the Parliament of Uganda', 14 June 2006. The only exception being the chairs of oversight committees, who come from the opposition.

[200] 'Rules of Procedure of the Parliament of Uganda', Sixth and Seventh Parliaments.

[201] Ssemujju, Ibrahim. 'NEC proposes 3rd term for Museveni—delegates confused over parties' fate', *The Daily Monitor*, 29 March 2003; Kasfir and Twebaze, 2009: 95.

[202] 'Don't criticise the government in House, Museveni warns Movt MPs', *The Daily Monitor*, 20 July 2006. 'Mwesigye warns undisciplined NRM leaders', *The Daily Monitor*, 2 August 2006.

[203] 'Don't criticise the government in House, Museveni warns Movt MPs', *The Daily Monitor*, 20 July 2006.

[204] 'Clarify MPs' roles under multiparty', *The Daily Monitor*, 28 July 2006.

Parliament (2006–2011). As one veteran MP recalled, he was summoned to the appear before the NRM Disciplinary Committee for tabling a private member's bill without the consent of the NRM Caucus. When he refused to go and appealed to the Constitutional Court, arguing that he was within his constitutional rights as an MP, the NRM leadership dropped the matter.[205] Many legislators and critical observers still worried that party leaders were using the NRM parliamentary caucus to silence MPs.[206] But the disciplinary strategies used by the executive, largely *informal and patronage-based*, were neither so different from nor significantly more effective than those deployed pre-2005.

NRM leaders' difficulty enforcing party discipline only grew more acute in the Ninth Parliament (2011–2016). A new crop of MPs, nicknamed 'young Turks' in the media, challenged the NRM Whip. They were aided by a seemingly more independent Speaker, Rebecca Kadaga.[207] Shortly after Parliament convened, NRM legislators criticized Museveni's appointment of a new Chief Whip, John Nasasira, taking aim at his plans for a new 'Code of Conduct' to ensure party discipline.[208] Despite executive efforts to head off a simmering rebellion, the Ninth Parliament only grew more assertive, prompting many to compare it to the oft-celebrated Sixth (1996–2001).[209] Executive-legislative tensions culminated in an unprecedented move by the NRM leadership to expel four 'rebel' MPs from the party. Yet even this disciplinary attempt was partially undermined when the Speaker Kadaga refused to eject the four MPs from the House, as demanded by other NRM leaders. The expelled MPs went on to fight a legal battle against the NRM, which they ultimately won. In a further ironic twist, President Museveni starting to court them, trying to win their support ahead of the 2016 elections. With an overall rate of legislative turnover exceeding 60 per cent, it is telling that all four MPs made it back to the Tenth Parliament (2016–2021), and two of them *on an NRM ticket*. What is more, they very quickly reverted to making trouble for the President.[210] The whole episode highlighted NRM leaders' failure to extend party discipline to

---

[205] Interview, NRM MP, Kampala, February 2015.

[206] Statements to this effect, and particularly denunciations of the NRM Caucus retreats at the Kyankwanzi National Leadership Institute, were common in interviews with both NRM and opposition MPs as well as with journalists and other observers.

[207] Sserunjogi, Eriasa, 'Power slipping away from Museveni in the NRM', *The Independent*, 20 July to 4 August 2011, 10–13.

Lumu, David. 'MPs to Museveni: You are one of Uganda's problems', *The Observer*, 18–21 August 2011, 3. Imaka, Isaac. 'MPs prove heavy for Museveni to swing', *The Sunday Monitor*, 28 August 2011, 9. 16–17.

[208] Sserunjogi, 2011.

[209] These executive-legislative clashes are discussed in the next chapter.

[210] Kaaya, Sadab Kitatta. 'Bullish anti-age limit MPs "will not be intimidated"', *The Observer*, 14 September 2017. Accessed 15 December 2017: http://observer.ug/news/headlines/54950-bullish-anti-age-limit-mps-will-not-be-intimidated.html.

the legislature, or even to delineate clearly between who was and was not a party member.

Besides successfully evading formal disciplinary measures, MPs have also secured several institutional gains since the 2005 transition. In the 2006 elections, women district representatives—who constituted a growing proportion of legislators due to the multiplication of districts—were for the first time directly elected through universal adult suffrage instead of Movement-based electoral colleges.[211] This change increased the *boundedness* of the legislature. Other gains have included the introduction of new committees, improving scrutiny of government, and enhancing the *complexity* of the legislature. In the Eighth Parliament (2006–2011), for instance, the committee with the unenviable task of covering health, education, sport, gender, labour, and social development was split in two, thereby easing the workload.[212] In the Ninth Parliament, MPs again pushed to divide the Social Services Committee, forming a committee for health and another for education and sports.[213]

The Ninth Parliament also saw another executive challenge, this time to its budgetary review powers, a challenge that MPs largely blocked. In 2012, government tabled the Public Finance Bill (PFB). While ostensibly designed to improve fiscal policymaking, macroeconomic management, and accountability,[214] the Bill met with a wave of criticism. Parliamentarians were especially concerned that the PFB would repeal and replace the Budget Act (2001), which many credited with enabling the legislature to effectively oversee government spending. The PFB also did not safeguard the Parliamentary Budget Office or the Budget Committee, both essential innovations of the Budget Act.

Legislative push-back ultimately transformed the PFB as initially tabled by government. Speaker Kadaga led the charge. She warned, 'Government wants to remove [the Budget Act] so that we do not know what they are bringing in the final budget', thereby returning Parliament to its former status as a 'rubber stamp'.[215] Legislators quickly rallied behind her, and the government began to give ground.[216] In May 2013, the Finance Minister addressed a letter to the

[211] Wang and Yoon, 2018: 301, 321.

[212] 'Rules of Procedure of the Parliament of Uganda', 2006.

[213] 'Rules of Procedure of the Parliament of Uganda', 2012. Interview, former Chairperson of the Education Committee, Kampala, February 2015.

[214] For a more complete account of the bills aims, see Public Finance Bill (2012).

[215] 'Kadaga mobilises MPs against plan shutting House on budget', *Monitor*, 26 September 2012. Article accessed 4 November 2017: http://www.monitor.co.ug/News/National/Kadaga-mobilises-MPs-against-plan-shutting-House-on-budget/688334-1518446-a7tq37/index.html.
Article accessed 4 November 2017: http://www.monitor.co.ug/Magazines/PeoplePower/Changing-Budget-Act-would-mean---/689844-1721636-t4eeog/index.html.

[216] Article accessed 4 November 2017: http://www.monitor.co.ug/News/National/MPs-support-Kadaga-in-bid-to-reject-Bill/688334-1636610-iptea/index.html. The bill was reviewed by a tri-partite committee composed of the Finance, Budget and Natural Resources Committees.

Chairperson of the Committee on Finance detailing a total of 55 amendments to the PFB, rechristened the Public Finance Management Bill (PFMB), 2012.[217] MPs were not satisfied, though, and the Chairperson of the Budget Committee threatening to withhold his support unless the Finance Minister showed 'line by line' that the Budget Act was fully preserved in the new legislation.[218] The final committee report on the PFMB affirmed that 'Parliament should be the appropriate locus of overall financial accountability', adding, 'Its role should be to approve actions rather than to rubber-stamp decisions already taken.'[219]

When Parliament finally passed the PFMB in November 2014, it had largely won the battle with government and even enhanced its own powers. Reflecting on the PRMB review process, one long-time parliamentary staffer working with the Budget Office remarked, 'There is no other law that has received more vigorous scrutiny than that in the 12 years I have been in Parliament. Eighty per cent of the original bill was changed.' He added, 'We did some work, and our efforts I think paid off as the Budget Act, which is at the heart of Parliament, was not repealed.'[220] In effect, the legislature had succeeded—with help from several advocacy organization—in making the PFMB arguably 'one of the best pieces of legislation enacted by the Ninth Parliament'.[221]

That was not, however, the end of the story. The PFMB is an example both of Parliament's strength and its vulnerability. Less than six months after the President assented to the new legislation, a Public Finance Management (Amendment) Bill was tabled, seeking to ease many of the checks placed on government borrowing and expenditure. After the Finance Committee initially resisted the changes,[222] Parliament eventually passed the amended legislation in November 2015, crucially, shortly before an election and at the end of the 'parliamentary business cycle', as theorized in Chapter 6. The legislature acquiesced to several provisions that it had previously resisted.[223] Even so, it held out on others, and the budgeting process laid out in the Budget Act

---

[217] 'Amendments to the Public Finance Bill, 2012', 21 May 2013. Letter from Minister of Finance, Maria Kiwanuka, to the Chairperson of the Sectoral Committee on Finance, Parliament of Uganda.

[218] 'Drama as MPs fight over Finance Bill', *Monitor*, 19 November 2013. Article accessed 4 November 2017: http://www.monitor.co.ug/News/National/Drama-as-MPs-fight-over-Finance-Bill/688334-2079822-15et15u/index.html.

[219] Report, 12–13.

[220] Interview, member of Parliament staff, Kampala, January 2015. By 'not repealed', he meant that its key provisions were preserved within the PFMB.

[221] Wamajji, Reagan. 'A commendable job by Parliament's Finance Committee on the Public Finance Management (Amendment) Bill', *Parliament Watch*.

[222] Ibid.

[223] Wamajji, Reagan. 'Five things we learnt from the passing of the Public Finance (Amendment) Bill, 2015', *Parliament Watch*.

was largely preserved.[224] Both the Budget Committee and the Parliamentary Budget Office also stayed as before.

In sum, although Parliament lost some of its erstwhile institutional strength post-2005, NRM MPs still resisted formal party disciplinary measures while successfully—if inconsistently—challenging executive attempts to further erode legislative strength. The question then is, why?

5.3.4.2 Explaining Parliament's Enduring Institutional Strength

Parliament's institutional staying power stems from the Movement legacy as a 'bargained coalition', which has endured despite NRM leaders' best efforts. This legacy manifests in several ways, including: (a) individual NRM MPs' enduring expectations regarding party discipline, or rather its absence; (b) the intensity of factional tensions within the NRM, riven by competing patron–client networks and associated financial interests; and relatedly, (c) the desire of both MPs' and parliamentary leaders to use parliament as a platform to achieve their personal political ambitions. I address each of these in turn.

First, NRM stalwarts were resistant to the very idea of a multi-party transition.[225] Responding to sceptical NRM cadres, Museveni sent a series of mixed messages when advocating reform. He called for more discipline while claiming that the NRM would remain 'multi-ideological'.[226] The decision to register the Movement as the NRM-Organization (NRM-O), rather than NRM Party, was a further mark of this compromise, or fudge.[227] Post-2005, many NRM MPs still expressed nostalgia for the no-party system, lamenting the new restrictions on open debate. They consequently justified instances of legislative opposition to the executive by using the old language of a 'multi-ideological' movement organization committed to the principle of 'individual merit' and legislative 'independence'.[228]

Beyond entrenched expectations,[229] though, the continued relevance of the 'individual merit' concept—and MPs' associated commitment to parliamentary autonomy—itself reflected continuities in the ruling party's

---

[224] Mugoya, Musa. 'Public Finance Management Act (PFMA) simplified the work of the tax man', *Parliament Watch*.

[225] Ssemujju, Ibrahim. 'NEC proposes 3rd term for Museveni—delegates confused over parties' fate', *The Daily Monitor*, 29 March 2003.

[226] Ssemujju, Ibrahim. 'President Museveni has a new vision for Uganda', *The Daily Monitor*, 28 March 2003.

[227] Kiiza et al., 2008.

[228] Interviews with NRM MPs.

[229] Note that these can be likened to Pierson's (2000) theorization of institutional continuity through 'increasing returns' and, specifically, 'learning effects' and 'adaptive expectations'.

internal organization. Of particular relevance was its failure either to centralize political finance or to manage bruising party primaries, as discussed
in Chapters 3–4. A party official working in the Office of the Government
Chief Whip made explicit the link between campaign finance and a Movement
legacy in a statement that is worth citing in full:

> *People still have a hang-over of individual merit* where they could offer them-
> selves as individuals, come to parliament and talk as they want, debate as they
> want and arrive at whatever position they want as individuals. So, disciplin-
> ing them to toe the party line is a serious problem. *One of the reasons is that it
> is a little bit expensive for someone to finance himself or herself to come to par-
> liament* to the tune of about Shs400m ($120,000), but the party contributes
> between Shs20m and Shs25m, less than 10% of what this person is spending
> to come to parliament. So, when this person comes to parliament, *owning
> him or her becomes difficult*, so therefore disciplining him or her is difficult,
> much as he is carrying the party flag.[230]

A report compiled by an NRM parliamentary caucus committee on the
troubled 2010 primaries, discussed more in Chapter 4, reached a similar conclusion. In the absence of reliable financial support from the party, 'Candidates
are subject to the vagaries of personally funding campaigns, *which dilutes party
control over members.*'[231]

While the self-financing of rank-and-file MPs has proved politically problematic for the NRM, more concerning still is how this self-financing is
bound up with more entrenched rivalries between competing patron–client
factions. For instance, factional manipulation within the Movement was a
major reason why the old system of voting for women district representatives through electoral colleges—which were widely viewed as corrupt—was
replaced by universal adult suffrage ahead of the 2006 polls. As noted earlier, this change increased the proportion of directly elected MPs and thereby
improving parliament's *boundedness*.[232]

Factional tensions surfacing within parliament itself also directly motivated
the push for legislative institutional strengthening. This dynamic, while apparent from the NRC and Ninth Parliament onwards, was particularly notable
in the Ninth Parliament (2011–2016). Speaker Kadaga and Prime Minister

---

[230] Interview with official in the Office of the Government Chief Whip (OGCW), Kampala, January 2015. Emphasis added.
[231] 'Final Report of the NRM Parliamentary Caucus Select Committee on NRM Primary Elections', July 2014.
[232] Interviews with several NRM Women District MPs.

Mbabazi had a longstanding feud, with Kadaga accusing Mbabazi of fronting rival candidates in her constituency.[233] Both also drew on accumulated personal wealth to back their allies and challenge their rivals. Chapter 4 addresses Mbabazi's economic interest and factional manoeuvring—particularly as NRM Secretary General—in more depth. Kadaga, although not on Mbabazi's level, reportedly amassed considerable economic interests while serving as a top party leader. Her assets included a tract of land with one of Uganda's largest pine plantations.[234] In 2014, she also invited Museveni to inaugurate a hotel that she had built for a stated three billion Uganda Shillings, or approximately $1,700,000.[235] Kadaga used a portion of this wealth to cement her position as a Kingmaker within her home district, Kamuli, feeding directly into the hotly contested and even violent NRM primaries in the area.[236]

As for other key players in the Ninth Parliament, they were also tied into the same factional feuds. Muhammad Nsereko, one of the 'rebel' NRM MPs whom Mbabazi played an instrumental role in expelling from the NRM, also had reason to oppose the Prime Minister, having previously clashed over election campaign finances and ministerial positions.[237] Similarly, Theodore Ssekikubo, also an NRM 'rebel', was at loggerheads with another Cabinet Minister, Sam Kutesa, Museveni's brother-in-law and reportedly one of Uganda's wealthiest individuals.[238] Kutesa had repeatedly backed Ssekikubo's rivals while allegedly trying to rig him out of the NRM primaries.[239]

Over the course of the Ninth Parliament, these elite-level tensions repeatedly formal party discipline, and this in ways that helped legislators mobilize to protect parliament's institutional strength. The battle over the fate of NRM 'rebels' offers a particularly clear illustration of this point. As noted previously, Speaker Kadaga played a key role in ensuring that the four expelled MPs could

---

[233] Ssekika, Edward. 'Kadaga: Mbabazi is targeting me', *The Observer*, 28 September 2015. Accessed 25 Nov 2016: http://www.observer.ug/special-editions/40127-kadaga-mbabazi-is-targeting-me.

[234] Okello, Dickens. 'Kadaga, IGG Mulyagonja Parade Wealth', *ChimpReports*, 3 March 2015. Accessed 24 December 2021: https://chimpreports.com/kadaga-igg-mulyagonja-parade-wealth/.

[235] 'Kadaga's Shs3bn Hotel Opened', *ChimpReports*, 17 June 2014. Accessed 18 December 2023: https://chimpreports.com/21008-kadagas-shs3bn-hotel-opened/

Kadaga was later forced to defend a decision to convene a meeting of the Inter-parliamentary Union executive council at this same hotel. 'Kadaga defends decision to host IPU meet at own hotel', *The Observer*, 18 September 2016. Accessed 18 December 2023: https://observer.ug/news-headlines/46499-kadaga-defends-decision-to-host-ipu-meet-at-own-hotel

[236] Kjaer and Katusiimeh, 2021.

[237] Sserunjogi, 2011.

[238] Interview, NRM MP, Kampala, July 2012.

[239] Ibid. See also: Kjaer and Katusiimeh, 2021. Namubiru, Lydia. 'Kutesa, Ssekikubo divide Sembabule', *New Vision*, 19 December 2009. Accessed 25 Nov 2016: http://www.newvision.co.ug/new_vision/news/1230439/kutesa-ssekikubo-divide-sembabule.

retain their seats in Parliament, thereby helping to set a new legal precedent.[240] While principled, this decision was nevertheless also a direct challenge to her political rival, Mbabazi. It offered a way for Kadaga to regain the upper hand after previous clashes with the Prime Minister and President left her on the defensive.[241] In the words of one observer, 'Kadaga's stature has been enhanced by the last ruling. [...] While outside Parliament, the President and Prime Minister may rule, the Speaker has for now stated that inside the walls of Parliament, her word is law.'[242] Kadaga's decision was celebrated by the rebels themselves as well as other dissident NRM MPs, one of whom reportedly led chants of 'God bless you! God bless you!' when she read out her verdict.[243] Ultimately, the support base she gained through this decision helped her efforts to retain the Speakership following the 2016 elections. She was fiercely opposed by her former Deputy, who was backed by a taskforce within the NRM that initially considered Sam Kutesa as a potential contender.[244] But the rebel MPs, some opposition members and a number of other backbenchers within the ruling party rallied behind her.[245]

Finally, when it comes to explaining why MPs fought to amend the PFMB and preserve their budgetary oversight powers, Kadaga's interest in safeguarding Parliament's strength and consolidating her own political position were again important factors. However, the personal interests of backbench MPs were also significant. These included their preoccupation with providing services to their constituencies and thereby building their political base. As discussed further in the next chapter, MPs achieved this aim partly by influencing government spending.[246] '[T]he budget is about taking bread to your people', observed a former Leader of the Opposition (LoP), adding, 'So

---

[240] 'How Kadaga decided MPs' fate', *Monitor*, 2 May 2012. Accessed 11 December 2017: http://www.monitor.co.ug/News/National/How-Kadaga-decided-MPs--fate/688334-1839980-by7rwaz/index.html.

[241] Interviews with several NRM and opposition MPs.

[242] Ssemogerere, Karoli. 'House Speaker Kadaga uses pulpit to score big', *Monitor*, 9 May 2013. Accessed 11 December 2017: http://www.monitor.co.ug/OpEd/columnists/KaroliSsemogerere/House-Speaker-Kadaga-uses-pulpit-to-score-big/878682-1846308-224klh/index.html.

[243] 'Expelled rebel MPs retain their seats', *Monitor*, 2 May 2013. Accessed 11 December 2017: http://www.monitor.co.ug/News/National/Expelled-NRM-MPs-retain-their-seats/688334-1799668-sn3yn/index.html.

[244] Misege, Lawrence. 'How NRM plans to oust Kadaga', *The Observer*, 22 April 2016. Accessed 11 December 2017: http://www.observer.ug/news-headlines/43818-how-nrm-plans-to-oust-kadaga.

[245] Misege, Lawrence. 'MPs ready to "die" for Kadaga to be speaker', *The Observer*, 21 March 2016. Accessed 11 December 2017: http://www.observer.ug/news-headlines/43194-mps-ready-to-die-for-kadaga-to-be-speaker. Two of the rebel MPs interviewed after Kadaga's decision were enthusiastic in their support for the Speaker. Kadaga was eventually ousted as Speaker in 2021 after another battle. See Khisa, 2023.

[246] Interviews with several opposition and NRM MPs.

there was always commonality [among MPs mobilizing against the PFMB].'[247] Beyond their constituency concerns, MPs could also trade on their 'marketability' to potential financiers, another theme discussed more in the next chapter. Whichever the motivation, though, MPs had ample reason to try and defend their budgetary oversight powers.

In sum, the Ugandan legislature's ability to preserve its institutional strength post-2005 is due to a combination of an individual merit 'hang over', weak formal party discipline, and MPs' shared interest in using Parliament's institutional strength—particularly regarding budgetary oversight—to fulfil personal political aims. Underlying all three factors is the continued fragmentation of patronage networks within the NRM. The resultant intra-party rivalries and personalization of politics undermine the NRM's own institutional coherence both outside the legislature and within.

5.4 Conclusion

In an authoritarian context, variation in legislative institutional strength is closely—if inversely—related to the institutional strength and cohesion of the ruling party. Where party institutions are strong, buttressed by a more centralized accumulation and patronage distribution, the legislature is likely to be marginalized and institutionally weak. By contrast, where ruling party institutions are themselves fragile, undermined by a fragmented patronage network, the result is more legislative strengthening. As such, the institutional strength of the Tanzanian *Bunge* first declined during the 1960s and 1970s, when the ruling party consolidated as an 'institutionalized coalition'. This downward trajectory only reversed amidst the economic crisis and liberalization of the 1980s when the institutional strength and cohesion of the ruling party itself began to erode. Even so, it was not until the mid-2000s, when factional alignments fuelled executive-legislative tensions, that the legislative reform process took off. As for the Ugandan Parliament, it has followed a more consistent path, undergoing a process of legislative strengthening, which NRM leaders have struggled to reverse. This institutional outcome is largely a consequence of the NRM's own fractious internal politics.

The core idea throughout is that, where MPs enjoy a patronage base of their own and where factional rivalries proliferate, elite contestation spills into the legislature. Legislators' efforts to then strengthen parliament come from

---

[247] Interview, former Leader of the Opposition, Kampala, December 2014.

a desire to arm themselves with new institutional tools that both *reflect—and crucially—magnify their power*. This analysis challenges several core assumptions from the comparative politics and Africanist literature.

First, it contradicts the notion that a 'ruler', acting rationally, moulds institutions to suit his own political calculus. Instead, this chapter argues that the success of authoritarian leaders in engineering institutional outcomes depends on the underlying distribution of power. For instance, Museveni has repeatedly tried to introduce formal measures to enforce ruling party discipline in parliament, only to find them subverted by informal factional pressures. The chapter also challenges the Africanist 'neo-patrimonial' view whereby patronage politics undermines legislative institutional strength, which must be cultivated to suppress neo-patrimonial tendencies. The chapter argues, by contrast, that variation in the structure of patronage networks, rather than their presence or absence, is what explains differences in parliamentary strength. The chapter also counters the idea that a multi-party transition is a key turning point. Rather, it shows how the influence of multiparty transition and of opposition MPs within parliament, while not insignificant, depend on the internal politics of the incumbent dominant party. Finally, it is worth reiterating that MPs' have diverse motivations, material and normative. However, the aim in focusing on material conditions is to help account for broad patterns of elite contestation and how they shape institutional change.

Still, explaining variation in legislative institutions is only part of the story. To get a better sense of the substantive implications of this variation, as well as the precise nature of intra-elite bargaining within the legislature, we need to study parliaments' actual performance.

6

Legislative Influence

Magnifying Elite Contestation

> These tax measures will be debated in parliament in its next sitting, but in the meantime, they have to be paid by everyone.
>
> —President Nyerere, announcing new tax measures during his New Year's address, 1 January 1982[1]

> We shall pass all the amendments in Parliament that we want. The period of beseeching is over.[2]
>
> —President Museveni, anticipating a more docile Parliament after the 2005 multiparty transition

In 1982, the legal requirement that Tanzania's Parliament approve all government fiscal plans seemed an afterthought for President Nyerere, as his above-quoted statement indicates. Yet when he voiced this disregard for *Bunge*, the power balance in CCM was already shifting. Over the ensuing decades, as economic crisis and liberalization invigorated patron–client factions within the party, *Bunge* changed too. It became a forum for elite contestation where, rather than an afterthought, distributive issues like government tax policy at times took centre stage.

While Tanzania's parliament started marginal and then only gradually became more assertive, the Ugandan legislature began to assert itself soon after the NRM took power. Top regime leaders thus found themselves periodically 'beseeching' a recalcitrant legislature. President Museveni hoped that the 2005 multiparty transition and reintroduction of formal party discipline would quell legislative dissent. But this expected outcome did not materialize. Instead, the enduring fragmentation of patronage networks within the NRM fuelled continued legislative activism.

In both cases, the legislature's influence—its ability to disrupt an executive agenda—reflected the wider distribution of power within the regime, a point

---

[1] Cited in Tambila, 2004: 64.
[2] Cited in Carbone, 2005: 9.

Wealth, Power, and Authoritarian Institutions. Michaela Collord, Oxford University Press. © Michaela Collord (2024). DOI: 10.1093/9780191945335.003.0006

which I now seek to explore further. More specifically, I aim to address two questions. What *explains* variation in legislative influence? And what is the nature and *significance* of this influence, as in, whose interests does a more assertive legislature serve? In what follows, I outline a theory of legislative assertiveness and its significance as well as the data and methods used to evaluate my theory. I then, in the next sections, analyse the Tanzanian and Ugandan legislatures in turn.

6.1 Argument and Methods

6.1.1 Explaining Legislative Performance and Its Significance

Previous chapters showed how, within an authoritarian regime, differing patterns of accumulation and patronage distribution affect ruling party discipline and legislative institutional strength. This chapter now examines how *ruling party factionalism* plus parliament's own *institutional strength* jointly influence *legislative assertiveness*. In seeking to explain this assertiveness, the claim is not that authoritarian legislatures are 'strong' by some standard conventionally applied to parliaments in more democratic settings;[3] rather, the aim is to understand whether and how these institutions magnify political contestation, creating uncertainty in executive–legislative relations, and compelling authoritarian leaders to accommodate legislative challenges, at least some of the time.

The argument goes as follows (Figure 6.1). Where the distribution of power within a ruling party leads to more elite contestation, as in where private accumulation is more expansive and rival patron–client factions proliferate, the legislature is more likely to become an arena for intra-elite bargaining. Thus, elite contestation directly animates legislative activity (Path A). This same contestation also—as observed in Chapter 5—informs efforts to strengthen legislative institutions (Path B), which then further reinforce legislative activism (Path C). In other words, while a legislative–executive clash may occur even where a parliament is institutionally weak, elites will find the legislature a more potent tool for challenging the executive where it has undergone an institutional reform process.

This explanation suggests when the legislature is more likely to alter an executive agenda. It nevertheless leaves open the question, what is the broader

---

[3] A classic legislative studies literature also queries this 'democratic' standard: Blondel, 1970; King, 1976.

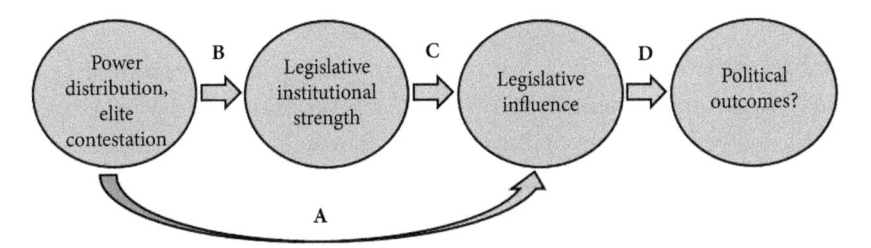

Figure 6.1 Explaining legislative influence

significance of heightened legislative influence? Whose interests does a more assertive legislature serve, and what salient political outcomes does it affect (Path D)?

The literature on authoritarian institutions and democratization presents various hypotheses about the legislature's effect on, for instance, regime survival, economic growth, and democratic accountability.[4] I explore a related but nevertheless distinct theme, namely how a stronger parliament may influence *distributive outcomes*, as in, 'who gets what, when and how'.[5] My theory of parliament as an arena for elite contestation, as *reflecting and magnifying* an elite power distribution, directly informs my analysis of its distributive consequences. Contra much of the literature, I propose an alternative mechanism to explain why legislative interventions—be they budgetary amendments, oversight of executive spending, or changes to government tax legislation—are often *regressive*; they favour a wealthy elite rather than redistributing to poorer voters.

First, to summarize, studies of both authoritarian and democratic legislatures suggest that parliaments have a *progressive* distributive influence. Regarding authoritarian regimes, the comparative literature claims that legislatures facilitate power-sharing arrangements, which then encourage policy compromises favouring, for instance, higher social spending.[6] Meanwhile, the literature on more democratic contexts, including an Africanist literature, maintains that democratic institutions like competitive elections and legislatures encourage greater responsiveness by individual legislators to *median voter interests*, which similarly favours progressive redistribution.[7]

---

[4] See Chapter 2, which this section builds on.
[5] Laswell, 1936.
[6] See Gandhi, 2008.
[7] For a review, see Golden and Min, 2013. For an Africanist literature, see: Van de Walle, 2009; Lindberg, 2010; Weghorst and Lindberg, 2013; Grossman and Michelitch, 2018; Ofosu, 2019. There is also a more executive-centred literature, which suggests that electoral competition can lead to more social spending. See: Stasavage, 2005; Harding and Stasavage, 2014.

Despite the widespread claim that stronger parliaments encourage progressive redistribution, both the underlying *theory and evidence* are disputed. Regarding evidence, the Africanist scholars evaluating whether electoral incentives influence politicians' behaviour find that, beyond increased constituency service, there is no discernible effect on policy-making.[8] Other scholars directly challenge the supposedly positive relationship between progressive spending and incumbent success.[9] Research examining the aggregate distributive effects of democratization shows that democracies tend to benefit *middle- and upper-income groups* rather than the poor or median voter.[10] In keeping with these findings, research examining Brazilian legislators' allocative decisions shows they cater to their political financiers rather than directly to their voters.[11] Some recent Africanist scholarship points in a similar direction.[12]

Regarding theory, scholars have challenged the preoccupation, at least in the democratization literature, with supposed *median voter* influence; instead, they emphasize the impact of *organized interests*. Khan argues that the 'distribution of organizational abilities affects the identification of preferences' and that, in developing country democracies, these abilities are concentrated not in the hands of the median voter but in powerful patron–client factions.[13] The influence of these factions, in turn, helps to 'explain why electoral competition does not in general result in government preferences being set by the poor even though they constitute huge majorities'.[14] In a similar vein, the political sociologists Hacker and Pierson argue that scholars should look beyond the 'politics of *electoral spectacle*' to instead analyse the 'politics of *organized combat*', i.e. 'the role of organized interests in shaping large-scale public policies that mediate distributional outcomes'.[15]

These studies of politics as 'organized combat' emphasize the elite-dominated nature of policymaking in *democracies*;[16] we can safely assume that this elitist quality would be still more pronounced in authoritarian contexts where elections are more obviously flawed and the legislature weaker. My argument nevertheless emphasizes that, even where would-be democratic

---

[8] Humphreys and Weinstein, 2012; Grossman and Michelitch, 2018; Ofosu, 2019.
[9] De Kadt and Liebermann, 2020.
[10] Nel, 2005; Ross, 2006.
[11] Samuels, 2002.
[12] Collord, 2021; Demarest, 2021; Opalo, 2022.
[13] Khan, 2005: 707. For authors raising similar concerns, see: Nel, 2005; Rodan and Jayasuriya, 2012; Ansell and Samuels, 2014; Gray and Whitfield, 2014; Pepinsky, 2014; Whitfield et al., 2015; Behuria et al., 2017.
[14] Khan, 2005: 707.
[15] Hacker and Pierson, 2010: 154.
[16] Ibid. See also: Domhoff, 2007; Winters and Page, 2009; Gilens and Page, 2014; Hacker and Pierson, 2010; Weaver and Prowse, 2020.

institutions strengthen, this does not necessarily signal more popular account-ability or median-voter influence. Rather, as noted above, I argue that a stronger, more assertive parliament reflects an intensification of elite contes-tation, notably driven by greater private accumulation and more factionalism. Returning to the theme of *distributive outcomes*, it follows that legislative inter-ventions often have *regressive* distributive implications; i.e. they are shaped by politicians' efforts to direct material rewards towards themselves and their factional allies, including their political financiers.

But then does legislative activity *never* results in more 'pro-poor' policy? Clearly they do, but I argue that progressive redistributive outcomes are likely the exception to the rule. Explaining this exception can, however, deepen our understanding of how the politics of 'organized combat' channels through par-liament. For normative reasons, it is also worth analysing when and why this redistributive outcome might occur.

Here I have a two-part argument, which expands the focus beyond elite patron–client factions to consider the (admittedly weaker) influence of unions, cooperatives, farmers associations, and the like. First, I argue that pressure from these 'mass-based' interest groups, as I refer to them, can *galvanize more redistributive legislative interventions*. However, their influence on MPs also depends on the structure of elite power, and in particular, the organizational strength and cohesion of the ruling party. My second argument, therefore, is that mass-based groups are more successful where *elite factional divisions are more acute*. Finally, the politics of 'organized combat' is never static, and chal-lenges from one group lead to countermeasures from another. As such, a caveat is in order. Even where mass-based groups ally with a legislative faction capa-ble of driving through pro-poor policy, an executive backlash to this initial success will likely prevent sustained legislative action.

The above discussion summarizes my core arguments about, one, what drives legislative assertiveness, two, why legislative interventions have largely regressive redistributive implications, and three, the political conditions underlying (admittedly more rare) progressive distributive outcomes. This leaves me with *four clarifying points*.

The first relates to timing. Just as studies of 'political business cycles' reveal electorally timed fiscal and monetary interventions by the executive,[17] I identify a 'parliamentary business cycle'. Put simply, the legislature is more likely to challenge the executive on substantive distributive issues earlier in

[17] Block, 2002.

a parliamentary term; by contrast, it will more likely rubber stamp executive initiatives as elections loom. To the extent that legislators collectively pressure the executive late in a parliamentary term, their demands more likely centre on their own emoluments, the aim being to maximize their material advantage going into campaigns.

The second clarification is about the role of the opposition. As emphasized in Chapter 4, I argue that opposition parties in a competitive authoritarian regime can help spur legislative action, but the success of this action depends on the cohesion of the ruling party. Moreover, opposition politicians may themselves be enmeshed in patron–client factions such that their motivations may not be qualitatively different from those of their ruling party colleagues. I develop this point further in the conclusion to this book.

Third, a strong legislature may mediate distributive politics and thus influences *some* distributive outcomes; however, even where parliament is relatively assertive, we can safely assume that most elite bargaining occurs outside legislative channels.[18] Yet, to the extent that the legislature does influence an executive agenda, it is worth understanding how and why, plus what this influence says about the balance of elite power in a regime. As such, this chapter centres the *political processes* whereby elites—and in some instances, more mass-based groups—pursue their interests through the legislature.

Finally, as noted elsewhere in this book, my aim is to theorize mechanisms that, in this instance, can help explain important tendencies in legislative activity, not to explain all such activity. Rather, the complex causality and multiplicity of actors in play—domestic and foreign, e.g., donors and investors—invites ongoing theorization and further refinement. Also, despite my materialist focus, I still do not overlook more normatively motivated MPs. These legislators play an important role, not least as allies supporting progressive lobbying efforts.

6.1.2 Assessing Legislative Influence

My focus on unpacking political process—on understanding the *mechanisms* underpinning legislative action—also informs the methodological approach adopted in this chapter. In what follows, I first review some of the quantitative measures for capturing the *magnitude* of legislative influence over the executive. I then explain my emphasis on a 'process-oriented' approach, which has its own strengths and weaknesses.

---

[18] See Pepinsky, 2014.

Quantitative analyses of legislative performance endeavour to answer Mezey's classic question, 'how much' policy power do parliaments exert? How much legislation do they enact?[19] There are a variety of relevant indicators. One is 'box scores', or the percentage of executive-initiated legislation enacted by parliament.[20] Tables 6.1 and 6.2 offer a quick comparison of overall legislative output and box scores for the Tanzanian and Ugandan parliaments in recent decades, although a lack of data complicates this effort.[21] What—if anything—can we conclude? First, there is notable variation in box scores *between parliamentary sessions* in both Tanzania and Uganda. There is no clear *cross-country* contrast, though, as the difference between the mean legislative output and mean box scores is not statistically distinguishable from zero.[22]

If we go on to contrast Uganda and Tanzania's legislative output with results from elsewhere, they appear relatively low. Whereas the average president—albeit from middle- to high-income democracies—initiates 109 bills each year,[23] that figure exceeds the average number of executive-initiated bills in

Table 6.1 Tanzanian parliament—legislative output

Parliament	Bills Initiated	Bills Passed	Box Score
Ninth (2005–2010)	102	101	99
Tenth (2010–2015)	65	59	91
Average	84	80	95

Table 6.2 Ugandan parliament—legislative output

Parliament	Bills Initiated	Bills Passed	Box Score
Sixth (1996–2001)	96	80	83
Seventh (2001–2006)	100	100	100
Eighth (2006–2011)	96	91	94
Ninth (2011–2016)	101	93	92
Average	98	91	92

[19] Mezey, 1979; Arter, 2006.

[20] Saiegh, 2014: 490. See also: Opalo, 2019.

[21] For Uganda, Kasfir and Twebaze, 2016. For the Tanzanian Parliament, there is no official record keeping but a member of parliamentary staff, who kept count of the number of bills introduced and passed since he began work at Parliament, kindly provided me with the data in Table 6.1.

[22] As in, t-tests indicate we cannot reject the null hypothesis that there is no difference between the mean legislative output or and mean box scores for the two countries.

[23] Saiegh, 2014: 494. This average is pulled from a sample of 50 countries from across Europe (19), Latin America (14), Asia and the Middle East (11), Oceania (3), Africa (2), and North America (1). They are all categorized as democracies and almost all are middle- or high-income.

Uganda and Tanzania *over an entire five-year parliamentary term.* Arguably, though, these findings say more about the executive than the legislature in the two countries. Regarding box scores, parliaments from the same, above-cited country sample approve three-quarters of executive-initiated legislation on average, although there is considerable variation cross- and within-country.[24] While Uganda's and Tanzania's box scores are far higher than this three-fourths average, they compare more favourably with the mean legislative passage rates in parliamentary regimes featuring single-party majority governments (88 per cent).[25] Ultimately, though, this analysis does not yield very concrete findings, except perhaps that neither the Ugandan nor Tanzanian Parliament seems very assertive and that there is no marked difference between the two. *Would a different measure complicate this story?*

A comparison of the proportion of private member's bills initiated in each Parliament does point to more contrasting results. Whereas only one private member's bill has ever been debated in Tanzania and none passed,[26] roughly 10 per cent of bills initiated in Uganda since 1996 were introduced by private members.[27] Most were introduced by Movement-sympathizing or NRM MPs, with the numbers *increasing* significantly after the 2005 multiparty transition. Most of these private member's bills also passed. These results suggest at least one way that the independence of Uganda's Parliament under the NRM has endured and has exceeded that of its Tanzanian counterpart.

However, an analysis of legislative performance cannot rest on private members' bills alone. Moreover, the weak conclusions emerging from the study of legislative output and box scores suggest the need to explore alternatives ways of assessing performance. This could be through *more elaborate quantitative measures,* for instance, drawing on Blondel's seminal work advocating a measure of legislative 'viscosity' and, for instance, incorporating the number of legislative amendments.[28] Some Africanist and authoritarian institutions scholarship has developed more refined quantitative data, and this remains an important avenue for future research.[29] But Blondel's analysis also underscores the complex and often subtle ways in which legislative influence is exerted at all stages of the legislative process. This emphasis suggests a second major, *process-oriented approach* to studying legislative influence.

---

[24] Ibid., 490.
[25] Ibid., 491.
[26] Msekwa, 2012. Interview with parliamentary clerk.
[27] Kasfir and Twebaze, 2016.
[28] Blondel, 1970: 80.
[29] See: Opalo, 2019, 2021; Demarest, 2021. On legislative amendments in authoritarian parliaments, see Krol, 2021.

This approach has two potential advantages. First, it can capture *otherwise overlooked* aspects of legislative influence. In this vein, Arter advocates an 'anatomy of legislative influence approach', which begins 'with 'thick description' in the form of a nuanced cartography of the multiple and multi-faceted patterns of legislative participation in the policy process'.[30] The second advantage of a process-oriented study of legislative influence is that it aligns well with the *process-tracing* approach used for theory-testing throughout this book. This chapter now adopts the same approach to analyse legislative assertiveness. I examine the constellation of organized interests, be they patron–client factions or more 'mass-based' groups; I then examine a series of legislative interventions to assess whether and how these interests influence MPs' motivations, their behaviour, and ultimately, legislative decision-making and distributive outcomes.

There are admittedly downsides to the process-oriented study of legislative influence; the analysis tests the theorised mechanisms of what *drives* legislative action but reveals less about the overall magnitude of legislative influence. Even so, this chapter outlines important trends in legislative activity, using both within- and cross-case comparisons. At the same time, it explores in-depth the mix of elite contestation and more bottom-up pressures shaping legislative action.

6.2 The Fall and Rise of Tanzania's Parliament

In this section, I first outline variation in legislative performance over time in Tanzania, indicating how *Bunge* was marginalized from the late 1960s until the early 1990s, when it began to reassert itself. I focus, in a second instance, on the more recent period of legislative activism. I indicate how heightened elite contestation, buttressed by previous rounds of legislative institutional strengthening, led to more assertive legislative interventions, albeit with seemingly regressive distributive implications.

6.2.1 An Historical Overview of Legislative Performance

Bunge's assertiveness has varied along with contestation among rival economic interests and associated patron–client factions within CCM. Legislative activism first declined after the Arusha Declaration and only began to increase

---

[30] Arter, 2006: 479.

again following economic liberalization in the 1980s. It nevertheless continued to fluctuate up to 2015, sometimes higher, sometimes lower. This more contingent variation reflected ad hoc political manoeuvring among CCM elites and the shifting configuration of patron–client networks.

As discussed in Chapter 5 with reference to *Bunge*'s institutional strength, it was not obvious at Independence the legislature would be sidelined, at least not to the extent that it was. Parliament was initially relatively assertive, particularly after the 1965 elections when it challenged the government on the status of Zanzibar, government fiscal policy, and its own 'supremacy'.[31] The key turning point came only after the Arusha Declaration led to tighter controls over private accumulation, political finance, and MPs' efforts to cultivate a local patronage base.[32] It also inaugurated a parallel tightening of party discipline, which included the 1968 expulsion of seven CCM MPs from the party and, hence, from *Bunge*.[33] Amidst the general push to strengthen the ruling party, legislative challenges became 'rare' or 'incidental'.[34] The exception that helped prove the rule was parliament's 1973 rejection of an Income Tax Bill. The legislation would have increased the tax burden of those who, like MPs, earned more than average income.[35] In response to the legislative rejection, then President Nyerere threatened to dissolve parliament, resulting in the unanimous enactment of the previously rejected bill.[36] By the late 1970s, *Bunge*'s lacklustre performance prompted one observer to conclude that it continued to exist 'by default'.[37] Its marginal status was perhaps best exemplified by President Nyerere's notorious 1982 New Year's message, quoted at the start of this chapter, in which he ignored the legal requirement that parliament approve new tax measures.[38]

However, around the time of Nyerere's message, the balance of power began to shift in parliament's favour. This change occurred as economic instability and liberalization gave way to heightened elite contestation.[39] At first, the CCM National Executive Committee managed the fallout, for instance, by censuring ministers for corruption.[40] *Bunge*, although more prominent as a 'critical

---

[31] Cliffe, 1967a: 339–342; Van Velzen and Sterkenurg, 1972a; Tordoff, 1977; Hartmann, 1983: 109; Martin, 1988.
[32] See Chapter 5.
[33] See Chapter 5. Velzen et al, 1972b; Kjekshus, 1974b; Tordoff, 1977; Martin, 1988; Tambila, 2004.
[34] Kjekshus, 1974b: 73–75; Tordoff, 1977: 238.
[35] Tordoff, 1977: 237.
[36] Tambila, 2004: 62.
[37] Tordoff, 1977: 241.
[38] Tambila, 2004: 64.
[39] See Chapter 4.
[40] Mwakyembe, 1986; Tambila, 2004: 65.

platform', remained 'of minor importance as a legislative body'.[41] But by the 1990–1995 session, and leading up to the first multiparty elections, parliament began to surprise many with its newfound assertiveness.[42]

At this stage, legislative challenges were more explicitly ideological in tenor, and reflected some legislators' concern with Tanzania's new political and economic direction. These MPs—including long-time party members sympathetic to *Ujamaa* principles—sought to scrutinize an emergent, seemingly exploitative accumulating class.[43] An informal caucus coalesced, known as the group of 55 or G55, and helped push through three controversial private motions in parliament.[44] The first of these, and the one that brought the group together, raised concerns about the privatization of Tanzania's 'national patrimony'.[45] One former G55 member recalled that the government was 'treating our natural resources like they belonged to no-one, like they could be disposed of, given to X, Y and Z [...]'.[46] The motion ultimately led to the sacking of the Tourism Minister. This came after a parliamentary select committee linked him to a scandal regarding the leasing of hunting blocks to the Deputy Minister for Defence of the United Arab Emirates.[47] The G55 then pushed another motion demanding that party and government officials declare their assets, the aim being to curb corruption and to salvage something of the old Leadership Code, abolished in 1990 as President Mwinyi took over as CCM Chairman and welcomed Tanzania's expanding business elite into the party.[48] The enduring fear of G55 members was that scrapping the Code 'meant [the removal of] all the hindrances that were there in terms of amassing wealth, some of it illicitly, and not declaring anything'.[49]

While the legislature during the 1990–1995 session was at the centre of elite contestation within CCM, notably linked to Tanzania's changing political economy, it again grew more muted during President Mkapa's tenure (1995–2005).[50] The official opposition was weak; the G55 dissolved;[51] and as detailed in Chapter 5, Mkapa more effectively managed factional divisions,

[41] Van Donge and Liviga, 1986.
[42] Killian, 2004.
[43] Killian, 2004; Interview with member of the G55 parliamentary group, *Dar es Salaam*, April 2016.
[44] Interview with G55 member, April 2016.
[45] Ibid.
[46] Ibid. The G55 also challenged top party leaders, including Nyerere, over the status of Zanzibar in the Union. See Shivji et al., 2020: 375–376.
[47] Wang, 2005a: 186.
[48] See Chapter 4.
[49] Interview with G55 member, April 2016.
[50] Kelsall, 2003; Killian, 2004; Tambila, 2004; Wang, 2005.
[51] Its members mostly stayed in CCM, though, evidence that the G55 did not emerge in anticipation of the multiparty transition. Interview with former G55 member, Dar es Salaam, April 2016.

largely keeping them from spilling into parliament. There were still executive–legislative clashes, though, and where these occurred, they were largely *fuelled by MPs' personal material concerns, competing economic interests, and associated patron–client factions.* For instance, among the first backbench rebellions of the multi-party era saw *Bunge* reject the Pension Bill (1998), partly because it did not cater for MPs' own benefits.[52] Parliament also forced the resignation of then Minister of Finance, Simon Mbilinyi, over a tax exemption scandal. While this move was initially celebrated as an example of *Bunge* holding the executive to account, it later emerged that Mbilinyi—whom many saw as a committed reformer—had been 'fitted up' by CCM heavyweights left out of Mkapa's first Cabinet.[53] The factional in-fighting continued in 2001 when Parliament played a key role in pushing the Minister of Trade and Industries, Iddi Simba, to resign. Many MPs were critical of Simba's seat in Cabinet, attributing it to his close family ties to Mkapa and his financial contributions to CCM, Simba being a wealthy businessman and high-profile advocate for Tanzania's emerging indigenous entrepreneurs.[54] Calls for his ouster, though, were an immediate response to his Ministry's controversial handling of sugar import licences.[55] He was, moreover, also among the key actors behind Mbilinyi's earlier resignation. It was MPs from Mbilinyi's home region, forming the so-called 'Southern bloc', who took the lead in demanding his removal.[56]

While elite contestation occasionally surfaced in parliament under Mkapa, the intensity of legislative pressure during Kikwete's presidency (2005–2015) was of a different order. This came as a new constellation of patron–client factions within CCM undermined the President's control over intra-party wrangles, which then moved into the legislative arena.[57] The consequences were multiple, including more aggressive parliamentary review of the government budget and repeated legislative challenges, including attempts to pass controversial private member's bills.[58] Perhaps most widely noted, though, was how often parliament forced ministers to resign. Prime Minister Lowassa's

[52] Killian, 2004: 198.

[53] Mmuya, 1998: 75–77; Kelsall, 2002: 606; Chaligha, 2004: 151–152.

[54] For more background on Simba and the indigenization debates, see Chachage (2018), especially Chapter 5, 'Liberalization and the Indigenization of Business (c. 1980–2005)'. Chachage identifies Simba as amongst a cohort of African capitalists who 'disengaged with the creed of Ujamaa in the early 1980s and played an instrumental role in starting networks to push for an increasing role for the private sector' (35).

[55] Kelsall, 2002: 607.

[56] Kelsall, 2003: 65; Chaligha, 2004.

[57] See Chapter 5.

[58] See Chapter 5.

2008 resignation even triggered the fall of his government. President Kikwete ultimately reshuffled his Cabinet seven times removing over 60 ministers
due to parliamentary pressure.[59] This degree of legislative activism would be
remarkable in any advanced democracy, let alone in Tanzania where *Bunge*
was long marginalized.

In sum, this brief review indicates how legislative performance in Tanzania
has varied along with changes in the wider distribution of power within CCM.
Under Kikwete (2005–2015), these changes led to an unprecedented assertion
of *Bunge*'s powers, a development which I now explore in more depth. I first
analyse how elite contestation and, with it, legislative activism varies over a
'parliamentary business cycle'. I then examine a series of legislative interventions through more in-depth case studies. I do not, for the Tanzania case,
explore the influence of 'mass-based' pressures, saving that for the Ugandan
parliament.

6.2.2 Tanzania's 'Parliamentary Business Cycle'

Overall, *Bunge* appeared more assertive under Kikwete, but activism waxed
and waned in a cyclical manner. As noted at the start of this chapter, the idea
is that this 'parliamentary business cycle' tracks the election cycle; in particular, MPs are likely *less assertive* as new campaigns approach, *except* when
defending their own pecuniary interests. In keeping with this anticipated pattern, CCM MPs during Kiwete's presidency readily acquiesced to controversial
executive initiatives pre-election yet became *more* assertive when demanding
financial rewards for themselves.

Both of Kikwete's two terms ended with the government tabling controversial legislation under a 'certificate of urgency', which limits the scope for parliamentary scrutiny.[60] Kikwete's government first used this procedure in 2010 to
push through the Mining Act (2010). In 2015, it tabled not one but three highly
significant bills: the Petroleum Bill (2015), the Oil and Gas Revenue Management Bill (2015), and the Tanzania Extractive Industry (Transparency and
Accountability) Bill (2015). At least in the case of the Mining Act, government
had been preparing the legislation for some time and, arguably, simply wanted

---

[59] For further discussion, see: Collord, Michaela. 'As corruption spreads under President Kikwete, Parliament quietly gains strength'. Presidential Power, 13 February 2015. Accessed at https://
presidential-power.net/?p=2759.
[60] Kjekshus, 1974a: 22.

to ensure its enactment.[61] The same could not be said about the petroleum-related legislation in 2015, which one CCM MP claimed were a copy-paste of legislation from Uganda.[62] Advocacy groups, legislators, and relevant stakeholders all voiced concerns about the bills' apparent weaknesses,[63] yet MPs ultimately passed all three, despite their being 'something fishy'.[64] The legislation was tabled just before President Kikwete was schedule to dissolve *Bunge* ahead of the 2015 elections, and many CCM MPs were already absent from the House, preferring to focus on their constituency campaigns. The Opposition came out against, but the Speaker responded by suspending disruptive opposition MPs such that, by the time the bills were finally passed, barely any were present to vote.[65] CCM MPs, seemingly more susceptible to disciplinary pressures,[66] then sided with the government to present a common front against opposition criticism.

Even pre-elections, though, CCM MPs were still willing to run a hard bargain when their own material interests were on the line.[67] They repeatedly demanded, for instance, tax exemptions on the 'gratuity' payments they received at the end of a five-year term.[68] They also contested the overall value of these gratuities. For instance, in 2015, just days after rubber stamping the controversial petroleum legislation, CCM legislators engaged in a remarkable brinksmanship exercise over the gratuity issue. They raised the alarm after the treasury disbursed 'only' Sh160m ($75k) into their accounts instead of the expected Sh230m ($107k).[69] Either way, the pay-out far exceeded the Sh43m ($26k) MPs received in 2010.[70] Yet CCM legislators reacted by refusing to debate a final piece of legislation. This was the Teachers' Service Commission Bill (2015), which incidentally focused on ensuring suitable pay not for MPs

[61] Interview, former Commissioner for Minerals, *Dodoma*, July 2015.

[62] Interview, CCM MP, *Dodoma*, July 2015.

[63] 'Extractive industries related bills: The Tanzania CSO extractive industries working group position'. *Policy Forum*, 26 June 2015. Accessed 18 December 2023: https://www.policyforum-tz.org/news/2015-06-26/extractive-industries-related-bills-tanzania-cso-extractive-industries-working.

[64] Interview, CCM MP, *Dodoma*, July 2015.

[65] 'Bill passed with only two opposition MPs in House', *The Citizen*, 6 July 2015. Accessed 7 April 2018: http://www.thecitizen.co.tz/News/Bill-passed-with-only-two-opposition-MPs-in-House/-/1840340/2776768/-/item/1/-/lb1xpg/-/index.html.

[66] Interviews, CCM and Opposition MPs, *Dodoma*, July 2015. Interviews, several CCM MPs, *Dodoma*, July 2015.

[67] For evidence of a more general 'political business cycle' in Kikwete's Tanzania, see Therkildsen, 2012.

[68] Ibid.

[69] 'MPs anxious about send-off package ahead of JK speech'. *The Citizen*, 9 July 2015. Accessed 7 April 2018: http://www.thecitizen.co.tz/News/MPs-anxious-about-send-off-package/1840340-2780778-grql72z/index.html.

[70] 'MPs poised to pocket Sh160m send-off pay'. *The Citizen*, 30 January 2014. Accessed 7 April 2018: http://www.thecitizen.co.tz/News/MPs-poised-to-pocket-Sh160m-sendoff-pay/-/1840392/2165628/-/swkclfz/-/index.html.

but for Tanzania's educators. After refusing to debate the bill, MPs next threat-ened to block Kikwete from delivering his closing speech in *Bunge* unless they received their full payment. The money duly appeared in their accounts.

Further research is needed to confirm the extent of cyclical changes in legislators' behaviour under Kikwete, and whether the same pattern holds across different administrations. The idea of a 'parliamentary business cycle' nevertheless provides a useful heuristic to capture the changing pre-election dynamics of elite contestation as channelled through executive–legislative relations. This then leaves us with the question, what explains the nature and extent of legislative activism outside of campaign season?

6.2.3 Elite Contestation, Legislative Activism, and Distributive Politics

Competing economic interests and factional rivalries directly contributed to *Bunge's* more assertive stance during Kikwete's presidency (2005–2015). Meanwhile, legislative reforms helped *magnify* this trend, providing new insti-tutional tools for elite actors to pursue their agenda through parliament. To demonstrate this argument, as well as the regressive distributive implications of this legislative activism, I first review how political financiers and their allies mobilized through parliament. I then examine several case studies regarding, first, legislative oversight of the executive and, second, budgetary review.

6.2.3.1 Elite Bargaining and Legislative Activity

In Tanzania, there are at least three ways that competing economic interests and allied factions have channelled their political activity through the legis-lature. Private sector financiers: one, contest for parliamentary seats directly; two, fund MPs' campaigns and, thereby, build up networks of supporters; and three, lobby in a more ad hoc, issue-based manner.

First, from the 1990s when Nyerere handed over the CCM Chairmanship to Mwinyi, members of Tanzania's expanding business class began vying for parliamentary seats. As outlined in Chapter 4, the prominent Lowassa sup-porter, Rostam Aziz, became an MP in 1992, the first Tanzanian of Asian origin to do so. From one of Tanzania's leading business families, Aziz told a friend that he decided to enter Parliament because 'political leverage is good for business'.[71] Following Aziz, the number of politicians-cum-businessmen

---

[71] Interview, family friend of Aziz, Dar es Salaam, April 2016.

entering *Bunge* rose throughout the 1990s and 2000s.[72] The above-mentioned Iddi Simba was a notable example, but unlike the very vocal Simba, many chose to keep a low profile. For instance, during the Ninth Parliament (2005–2010), some of Tanzania's wealthiest businessmen-MPs ranked among the least active contributors to formal debates in the House. With zero contributions, Aziz ranked last of 267 backbench CCM MPs. Another prominent businessman and at the time Tanzania's only other billionaire, Mohammed Dewji, fared little better, ranking 254 with a total of 10 contributions.[73] Some businessmen-MPs did intervene in debates; others found numerous, more subtle ways of using committees or informal networks to promote their business interests.[74] Indeed, there are numerous ways to exercise 'political leverage' without personally intervening in legislative politics.[75]

Taking a more indirect route, private sector actors—whether MPs themselves or not—have sought to amass political influence in Parliament by financing networks of legislators, whom they then rely on to do their political work.[76] Chapter 4 details how, starting in the 1980s, factional rivalries between competing CCM aspirants involved a mix of locally and nationally prominent financial backers whose economic interests ranged from agriculture to trading to mining and more. In interviews, MPs elaborated further on their efforts to recruit corporate sponsors, including by setting up political offices in Dar es Salaam, Tanzania's commercial capital.[77] Contributions from private sector financiers came with 'expectations', though.[78] As one MP affirmed, '[Financiers] can be businessmen who want, through you, to be helped to win tenders in the councils, in the government', adding, 'There are businessmen who expect through you to be protected in terms of their illegal business contracts and some tax evasions and malpractices of the sort.'[79] Explaining who these financiers are, the MP indicated, 'Mostly they are big businessmen in the country. For instance, they are tycoons in Dar es Salaam who sponsor a big number of MPs, each with Sh5m. They try to make a team in parliament to protect them when something wrong comes here to be discussed about their business.' While these 'networks' form around elections, driven notably

---

[72] Chaligha, 2004; Languille, 2015.
[73] Twaweza, 2010.
[74] Languille, 2015: 92–93.
[75] Interview, former Vice Chairman of the PAC, Dodoma, May 2015.
[76] See Chapter 5 for further examples.
[77] Interviews with CCM and Opposition MPs as well as their personal assistants. Many MPs do not develop such extensive networks, preferring instead to rely on family, friends, and local, smaller-scale business interests.
[78] Interviews, opposition MP, Dodoma, January 2016.
[79] Interview CCM MP, Dodoma, June 2015.

by competition within CCM, interviewees were clear that they continue to exist 'even after elections'.[80]

The attempts of political financiers to assemble 'a team' in *Bunge* are complimented by more ad hoc yet intense lobbying efforts. Former Speaker Anne Makinda (2010–2015) stressed that 'there are interested parties' lobbying 'because of some personal reasons'.[81] She clarified that, 'Even the budget time, [business interests] come to lobby about taxes'.[82] A businessman and CCM grandee observed that 'parliament has been subjected to corrupt transactions' where 'you grease the members and you soften their voices or even keep their voices shut over certain happenings'.[83] This 'greasing' practice was especially common under Kikwete. As one CCM MP noted, 'The general public, and the businessmen in particular, learned that the most powerful people are the MPs and therefore they started to come [to Parliament] to corrupt MPs'.[84] Meanwhile, being a vocal MP was seemingly its own currency. An opposition legislator affirmed, 'my experience is that if you become a vocal MP in the House, then government listens to you and they bargain with you'.[85] Other interviewees suggested not only government, but private sector actors listened as well.

In sum, private sector and broader factional interests mobilize through the legislature through a range of means, including seeking direct election, building factional 'teams' in parliament through campaign finance contributions, and lobbying on a more ad hoc basis. The following case studies detail how this elite manoeuvring through the legislature fuelled parliamentary activity during Kikwete's presidency.

6.2.3.2 Executive Oversight Cases

Bunge's activism during the Kikwete years was perhaps most pronounced—and certainly most eye-catching—when it involved scrutinizing executive corruption scandals. As mentioned earlier, this scrutiny prompted an unprecedented number of cabinet reshuffles. Commenting on parliament's role, the then Vice Chair of the Public Accounts Committee (PAC) quipped, 'President Kikwete only hires [ministers]. He doesn't fire. We have been firing for him.'[86] In the following three case studies, I demonstrate how rival economic

---

[80] Interview, CCM and opposition MPs.
[81] Interview, Makinda, Dar es Salaam, March 2016. Chaligha (2004) describes similar, if less widespread, lobbying practices under President Mkapa.
[82] Ibid.
[83] Interview, Dar es Salaam, April 2016.
[84] Interview, CCM MP, Dodoma, January 2016.
[85] Interview, opposition MP, Dodoma, June 2015.
[86] Interview, former PAC vice chair, Dodoma, May 2015.

interests and allied factions within CCM, making use of newly empowered parliamentary oversight committees, helped drive this intensified legislative scrutiny. While in some instances this oversight did help uncover corruption, doubtless an important goal for certain legislators, it largely failed to secure meaningful action in response. This failure helps confirm the key political factors motivating legislative interventions; i.e. many MPs were seemingly more focused on settling factional scores by ousting ministers than they were on demanding follow-up to ensure more genuine accountability.

The first case study relates to the Richmond scandal.[87] The scandal arose following the 2006 government decision to award the Richmond Development Company a \$123.2m tender to generate gas-fired electricity, the aim being to address nation-wide shortage due to drought and a fall in the hydro-electric supply.[88] After major delays in commissioning the new Richmond plant, Speaker of Parliament, Samuel Sitta, convened a parliamentary select committee in 2007 to investigate. The committee later found that Richmond was a shell company, which was taken over in 2006 by Dowans Holdings, based in the United Arab Emirates.[89] The committee chair, Dr Harrison Mwakyembe (CCM), called on Prime Minister Lowassa to resign as he was held responsible for awarding Richmond the controversial tender.[90] The select committee's report further claimed that Richmond was jointly owned by Prime Minister Lowassa and prominent businessman-cum-political financier, Rostam Aziz, who allegedly also had ties to Dowans.[91] The committee's investigations, and the resultant furore in Parliament, prompted Prime Minister Lowassa to resign in February 2008. He was followed shortly thereafter by the then Minister of Energy, Nazir Karamagi, himself a rich businessman with shares in Tanzania-based multinationals. Nine ministers ultimately lost their jobs after Lowassa's resignation as premier prompted the dissolution of Cabinet.[92] Aziz meanwhile, had already lost his position as CCM Treasurer and, in 2011, resigned his position on the CCM Central Committee and his parliamentary seat, citing the ruling party's 'gutter politics'.[93]

Besides a few CCM heavyweights losing their positions, though, what came of *Bunge*'s Richmond investigations? The answer is not much, at least

---

[87] See Chapter 5 for more detail on the factional tensions relating to Richmond. See also Gray, 2015.
[88] Cooksey, 2017.
[89] Ibid.
[90] 'Report on Richmond Scandal'. *Tanzanian Affairs*, 1 May 2008. Accessed 15 April 2018: https://www.tzaffairs.org/2008/05/report-on-richmond-scandal/.
[91] Ibid. See also endnotes 10 and 11 in Cooksey, 2017.
[92] 'Cleaning the stables', *Africa Confidential*, 15 February 2008.
[93] Mosoba, Tom. 'Tanzania: Rostam Quits Politics'. *The Citizen*, 13 July 2011. Accessed 15 April 2018: http://allafrica.com/stories/201107140303.html.

under Kikwete. During the debates about the scandal, MPs passionately declared, 'We have to protect the welfare of millions of Tanzanians who are dying simply because of problems caused by these dubious contracts.'[94] Yet following the 2008 Cabinet reshuffle, neither Parliament nor the Government conducted meaningful follow-up investigations and there were no prosecutions. Instead, Tanzania continued to pay dearly for the Richmond tendering debacle, including a multi-million-dollar monthly flat fee owed to Dowans even when it produced no electricity.[95] Given this lack of follow-up, there is reason to believe ousting CCM heavyweights *was itself* a principal motivating factor behind *Bunge's* Richmond investigations. As discussed in Chapter 5, Speaker Sitta was looking for ways to get at his political rival, Lowassa. Lowassa, for his part, rejected the allegations against him, including his supposed partial-ownership of the Richmond company.[96] He instead pointed a finger at President Kikwete, suggesting that if there was anyone who had something to answer for, it was him.[97] Ultimately, those most instrumental in pushing Parliament's (short-lived) activism over Richmond, including Sitta and Mwakyembe, went on to assume ministerial posts of their own during the Tenth Parliament, at which point they became markedly less vocal on corruption issues.

Parliament's oversight activism nevertheless continued, extending into the next parliamentary session. The first major executive-legislative clash in the Tenth Parliament came in 2012, following pressure from *Bunge's* Public Organisations Accounts Committee (POAC). It should be remembered that the POAC was created in the Ninth Parliament following the adoption of the 2007 Standing Orders, championed by then Speaker Sitta.[98] The committee began to assert itself in Tenth Parliament, though, with the prominent opposition MP serving as Chair and the fast-rising CCM MP as Vice Chair. In April 2012, the duo responded to a damning report from the Controller and Auditor General (CAG) by recommending the removal of ministers who had failed to reign in alleged corruption and financial laxity in their ministries.[99] The recommendation caused another furore in Parliament, and notably within CCM. During a raucous CCM parliamentary caucus meeting, Prime Minister Mizengo Pinda—the caucus Chair—barely succeeded in dissuading MPs from calling for *his own* removal, which would have led to the second Cabinet

---

[94] *Tanzanian Affairs*, 2008.
[95] Cooksey, 2017.
[96] *Tanzanian Affairs*, 2008.
[97] Cooksey, 2017.
[98] See Chapter 5.
[99] 'Corrupt but open', *Africa Confidential*, 22 April 2012.

dissolution in less than five years.[100] President Kikwete and the CCM party leadership ended up ceding to the parliamentary caucus, with the CCM Central Committee agreeing that Kikwete should sack eight ministers named by Parliament.[101]

The removal of the ministers, including the Minister of Finance, was certainly a dramatic outcome. But, again, what did this round of legislative pressure accomplish? It is unclear how firing the ministers, described in the press as a 'burden' on government finances, would on its own address the breach of accountability rules, fraud, and embezzlement identified in the CAG report.[102] There were also allegations that the targeting of certain ministers was not done in good faith. One of the former ministers ousted in 2012 claimed, for instance, that his efforts to enforce government policy had alienated a group of businessmen, who then 'syndicated money', bribing MPs to demand his resignation.[103] While the concerned former ministers acknowledged that there was a 'smell of corrupt conduct' in his actions, he insisted that 'those who were leading were the ones who'd been corrupted'. The former minister would, of course, have every reason to make these counteraccusations, shifting blame to his challengers. It is nevertheless worth noting that there was no further action taken against him, and he stayed on in Parliament as a backbench MP. However culpable he may have been, this result alone raises questions about the substantive impact of Parliament's oversight efforts.

A final legislative-executive clash, one of the biggest during Kikwete's presidency, concerned the so-called Escrow scandal. Yet again the subject was corruption in Tanzania's energy sector. In 2007, Tanesco, the state-owned electric supply company, dragged a private company with which it had a contract, Independent Power Tanzania Ltd (IPTL), into international arbitration.[104] The dispute was over the allegedly inflated monthly fee IPTL was demanding in capacity charges. For the next seven years, while the case was ongoing, the disputed charges owed by Tanesco to IPTL were paid into an escrow account. In February 2014, the international court of arbitration finally upheld Tanesco's claims, thereby clearing the way for it to reclaim money from the escrow account. However, over half the deposited funds—or $122m—had already been fraudulently paid out to IPTL's new owner, Pan African Power

---

[100] 'Mawaziri wa JK walivyosulubiwa', *Nipashe*, 22 April 2012, pp. 1, 4; 'Pinda kuwaumbua mawaziri kesho', *Nipashe*, 22 April 2012, pp. 1, 4. Interview, CCM MP, May 2015, Dodoma.

[101] 'Kamati Kuu CCM yabariki mawaziri nane kung'oka', *Nipashe*, 28 April 2012, pp. 1, 4.

[102] 'Corrupt but open', *Africa Confidential*, 22 April 2012. 'Pinda kuwaumbua mawaziri kesho', *Nipashe*, 22 April 2012, pp. 1, 4.

[103] Interview, former minister, Dodoma, July 2015.

[104] For background, see Cooksey, 2017.

Solutions (PAP), which to top it off, appeared to have acquired IPTL illegally. The scandal was revealed in a series of articles by *The Citizen* newspaper and picked up by *Bunge*'s Public Accounts Committee (PAC), which tasked the CAG to investigate.[105] PAC's intervention occurred, again, under the leadership of the same duo of opposition and CCM MPs who, after POAC was eliminated in 2013, managed to return as Chairs of PAC and sub-divide the committee's activities to cover both the mandate of the former POAC and PAC.[106] This manoeuvre proved essential in enabling the escrow investigations and the drafting of PAC's damning report, which detailed a financial saga whose origins lay in the early 1990s and whose many threads crisscrossed from Malaysia to Hong Kong to the British Virgin Islands to Kenya and back to Tanzania.[107]

Given Parliament's central role in uncovering the escrow scandal, was it any more effective in securing follow-up? Again, the answer is no. The combined pressure from CCM and Opposition legislators compelled still more ministers to resign;[108] observers, however, deemed these resignations 'symbolic' while noting the lack of major prosecutions.[109] Even those ministers who did resign were not necessarily directly implicated in the escrow scandal. The case of then Minister of Energy and Minerals, Sospeter Muhongo, was particularly concerning, seemingly constituting a mini corruption scandal of its own. Indeed, there were widespread rumours that MPs demanded Muhongo's resignation not because of the escrow scandal, with which he had no obvious link, but because of pressure from business interests frustrated with the Minister's intransigence over licensing, among other issues.[110] One interviewee offered a particularly dramatic account, alleging that during the escrow scandal, 'there were two groups [of MPs] who were fighting, both being bribed'.[111] He clarified that one group was 'being paid by those people who wanted Muhongo out'. Meanwhile, the Minister, 'after learning that there are people who have come

[105] Interview, former POAC/PAC Chair, Dar es Salaam, April 2016; Cooksey, 2017.

[106] See Chapter 5.

[107] 'Facts on IPT deal ahead of the tabling of escrow scam report'. *The Citizen*, 24 November 2014. Accessed 15 April 2018: http://www.thecitizen.co.tz/News/Facts-on-IPTL-deal-ahead-of-the-tabling-of-escrow-scam-report/-/1840392/2532948/-/item/1/-/n85pjsz/-/index.html.

[108] 'MPs uproar over runaway corruption in government'. *The Citizen*, 31 January 2015. Accessed 15 April 2018: http://www.thecitizen.co.tz/News/MPs-uproar-over-runaway-corruption-in-government/-/1840392/2608238/-/o6n4pbz/-/index.html.

[109] Cooksey, 2017. The IPTL and PAP owners were finally arrested in 2017, almost two years after President Magufuli succeeded Kikwete and amidst a much-altered political environment, discussed further in the conclusion to this book.

[110] Interviews with MPs.

[111] Interview, CCM MP, Dodoma, June 2015. The detail of such allegations must be taken with a grain of salt. However, as similar rumours were repeated by multiple interviewees, not to mention in the press, they point to a genuine concern.

with money to lobby MPs for [him] to be sacked', went on to 'solicit' money from the 'escrow beneficiaries' to ensure that he was 'defended'. Muhongo was later cleared of any corrupt involvement in escrow, and he was duly reappointed as Minister of Energy by Kikwete's successor, President Magufuli.[112] More generally, the PAC Chair and Vice-Chair—who as noted above, helped bring the escrow scandal to light, on its own an unambiguously positive step—acknowledged the lack of follow-up in implementing parliament's resolutions. 'Even in PAC', the former Chair noted, 'we are not very good with follow-up'. He then explained, 'It is out of the political will of the chairperson and the committee members.'[113]

In sum, during the Kikwete years, heightened parliamentary scrutiny appeared to signal a more assertive legislature demanding accountability from the executive. Yet *Bunge's* oversight zeal was at least partly a product of competing elite interests. What explains their power to influence legislative activity? One, this elite contestation—fuelled by competing patron–client factions and private interest lobbies—was emblematic of Tanzania's post-*Ujamaa* political economy. Two, elite factions were better able to use parliament as a *tool* to achieve their aims because of prior legislative institutionalization, in particular, efforts to strengthen *Bunge's* oversight committees.

6.2.3.3 Budgetary Review and Fiscal Policy

A similar story can be told about *Bunge's* engagement with fiscal policy issues under Kikwete. Here I focus on Parliament's interventions following the introduction of the new Budget Committee in 2013.[114] Prior to this reform, *Bunge* did occasionally attempt to influence the budget on substantive issue, but these interventions lacked coordination, making the legislature a 'rubber stamp' on fiscal matters.[115] By contrast, with the advent of the Budget Committee, Parliament gained a direct 'avenue' to the Minister of Finance.[116] It could intervene earlier during the budget drafting phase and, during the approval phase, could coordinate across sector committees. Where need be, it could also pressure the Ministry of Finance to agree an increase in the overall budget ceiling and thereby accommodate increased spending in various sectors.[117] I discuss the politics driving these reforms in Chapter 5. Once instituted, they encouraged

---

[112] Admittedly, he did not last long. Accessed 15 April 2018: http://www.thecitizen.co.tz/News/The-rise-and-fall-of-Prof-Muhongo-/1840340-3940022-c6d94qz/index.html.
[113] Interview, former POAC/PAC chair, Dar es Salaam, April 2016.
[114] See Chapter 5.
[115] Interview, parliamentary clerk (1), Dodoma, June 2015.
[116] Interview, parliamentary clerk (2), Dodoma, June 2015.
[117] Ibid; interview, clerk (1); interview, former Budget Committee Chair, Dar es Salaam, July 2015. See Chapter 5 for more detail on reforms relating to the Budget Committee.

more ambitious budgetary review during the Tenth Parliament. However, lobbying by business interests helped ensure that *Bunge*'s interventions—at least those that were more effective in achieving their goals—had largely *regressive* distributive implications.

The Budget Committee started out by helping sector committees push for more spending in popular areas, and particularly when there was outside lobbying by various advocacy groups. These 'civil society organizations' (CSOs) began to engage in more parliamentary lobbying in the mid-2000s, relying less on direct political pressure—as we shall see is more common in Uganda—but rather on the supply of 'evidence' to help 'convince' MPs.[118] It was through the efforts of CSOs and the coordinating work of the Budget Committee that, in 2013, MPs rallied behind several amendments aimed at increasing expenditure in key 'pro-poor' sectors. An additional Tsh184b ($116m), for instance, was allocated to the Ministry of Water to improve access countrywide.[119] In 2014, parliament again pushed for several amendments, raising the budget ceiling for the Ministry of Health by approximately five per cent.[120]

These interventions did not, however, have the desired effect. This was because the executive consistently overestimated revenue collection such that actual spending fell far short of planned expenditure. Implementation of the budget for financial year 2013/2014 was so poor that, when it came to the water sector, 'It didn't even get the amount originally allocated before the Tsh184b increase.'[121] This weak budget implementation prompted the Budget Committee, and consequently Parliament, to shift strategies. The committee, supported by CSOs and various donors, began to recommend areas where government should *reduce* 'unnecessary' expenditure, thereby demanding greater fiscal discipline. There was also a growing consensus that Parliament should reorient its budgetary review away from a focus on expenditure towards an emphasis on revenue collection. The stated rationale was that *Bunge* could help identify new sources of revenue to then support government expenditure, including on priority social services.[122]

The Tenth Parliament did end up intervening on tax issues. Contrary to legislators' rhetorical commitments, though, *Bunge*'s actual impact was not especially 'pro-poor'. Its handling of the Value Added Tax (VAT) Act (2015)

---

[118] Interviews with staff at leading CSOs involved in budget advocacy, including Policy Forum, Hakielimu, and Sikika.
[119] Interview, clerk (2).
[120] Interview, staff at Sikika, Dodoma, May 2015.
[121] Interview, clerk (2).
[122] This point came up repeatedly in interviews, including with parliamentary clerks, the former chair of the Budget Committee, Speaker of Parliament Anne Makinda, and the Vice Chair of the PAC.

is a case in point, indicating the far more ambivalent role Parliament played in safeguarding elite interests. The new legislation was introduced to repeal and replace the original VAT Act of 1997, which although initially celebrated as a 'best model', was later amended to incorporate a growing number of exemptions.[123] The older legislation also made it relatively easy for the Minister of Finance or the Tanzania Investment Centre (TIC) to award fresh exemptions to investors on a discretionary basis, a practice which created a 'vampire tax collecting regime'.[124] Tanzania ranked among the countries with the lowest VAT productivity in southern and eastern Africa while, between 2001 and 2011, the value of tax exemptions averaged 24.5 per cent of total tax collection, spiking to as high as 38.6 around elections.[125]

Following the 2010 election, though, both Parliament and Government took steps towards fiscal reform. Speaker Makinda convened a special parliamentary committee, referred to simply as the Speaker's Committee, and tasked it with recommending changes to Tanzania's tax regime, including to decrease the number of exemptions.[126] Prompted in part by Parliament's efforts, Government later established its own technical reform team, which led to the tabling of the VAT Bill (2014).[127] The proposed legislation abolished all but a few exemptions, eliminated special reliefs for named bodies, and removed the discretionary powers of the Minister of Finance to grant fresh exemptions. Many of these changes were in line with recommendations made by *Bunge's* own Speaker's Committee.[128] And yet Parliament proceeded to amend the VAT Bill, rolling back many of the key changes. Exemptions abolished through the Bill were reinstated; there was no clarity on what should happen to exemptions granted by the TIC, which in 2011/12, amounted to 13 per cent of the total; and the discretionary powers of the Minister of Finance were reduced but not removed.[129] As the former Deputy Minister of Finance declared, the proposed reforms were substantially 'diluted'.[130]

But why did MPs, after first presenting a 'common stand in favour of reducing exemptions',[131] reverse their position? This outcome was the result

---

[123] Policy Forum Budget Working Group, 2013; Fjeldstad et al., 2015.
[124] Fjeldstad et al., 2015; Interview, Tanzanian businessman and long-time CCM cadre, Dar es Salaam, April 2016.
[125] This pattern points to an important feature of Tanzania's 'political business cycle'. See: Therkildsen, 2012; Fjeldstad et al., 2015.
[126] Interview, Makinda, Dar es Salaam, March 2016.
[127] Interview, clerk (2); Fjeldstad et al., 2015.
[128] Interview, former Deputy Minister of Finance and former member of the Speaker's Committee, Dodoma, July 2015.
[129] Ibid; Interview, clerk (2); Fjeldstad et al., 2015.
[130] Interview, former Deputy Minister of Finance.
[131] Ibid.

of extensive lobbying, targeting notably members of the Budget Committee. Some of this advocacy was open. For instance, the Tanzania Private Sector Foundation engaged PricewaterhouseCoopers to make its case to MPs. The Ministers of Agriculture and of Tourism also came out in opposition to the Bill, demanding that exemptions for their sectors be preserved.[132] Aside these more visible interventions, though, many alleged that a different kind of influence-peddling was going on behind the scenes. The Deputy Minister of Finance, for instance, insisted, 'It is not even professional lobbying of just making a case. It has another picture.'[133] This underhand dealing, he argued, led MPs and Ministers alike to start 'changing the goal posts'. Regarding the actions of some of his ministerial colleagues, he remarked, 'It was amazing that a minister who passed a bill in Cabinet could later go to the Budget Committee and say, "No, it is not right."'[134] Like her Deputy, the Minister of Finance 'wasn't happy at all'.[135] As one parliamentary clerk recalled, 'She said, even in Parliament, the aim of the government is to reduce exemptions, but it seems MPs do not keep their word.'[136]

In sum, Parliament engaged government more actively on fiscal policy following the 2013 introduction of the Budget Committee. As was true of its other oversight activities, *Bunge*'s fiscal interventions were affected by heightened elite contestation and, consequently, had *regressive* distributive implications.

This analysis supports my broader argument, namely that variation in Tanzania's legislative performance mirrored changes in the composition and strength of patron–client factions within CCM. As such, *Bunge* remained marginalized during the *Ujamaa* period but began to reassert itself following economic liberalization and, with it, the expansion of competing private interests and patronage networks. Under President Kikwete (2005–2015), this legislative activity appeared to follow a 'parliamentary business cycle', shaped by MPs' changing incentives ahead of expensive re-election campaigns. This cyclical dynamic aside, though, legislative activism reached unprecedented levels. Indeed, the Kikwete years were a high-water mark as the combination of legislative institutional strengthening and acute factional rivalries encouraged parliamentary challenges to the executive.

---

[132] Fjeldstad et al., 2015. Interview, clerk (2).
[133] Interview, former Deputy Minister of Finance. As others have documented, this 'other picture' of lobbying is not at all unusual when it comes to Tanzania's fiscal policy. See: Therkildsen, 2012.
[134] Interview, former Deputy Minister of Finance.
[135] Interview, clerk (2).
[136] Ibid.

6.3 The Continued Assertiveness of Uganda's Parliament

While *Bunge* began weak and grew more assertive, at least through to the end of Kikwete's presidency, Uganda's Parliament under the NRM has proved a relatively consistent thorn in the executive's side, and this despite expectations that the 2005 multiparty transition would herald a new era of legislative subservience. Factionalism within the NRM—both pre- and post-2005—has meant that elite tensions continue to spill over into the legislature; NRM MPs pursue personal and factional interests, often going against the party line. Meanwhile, prior rounds of legislative reform also provide the institutional tools to help magnify legislators' efforts.

In this section, I briefly review the performance of Uganda's Parliament under the NRM before examining *why* legislative-executive tensions have endured. I explore, first, how elite bargaining plays out over a 'parliamentary business cycle'. I then show, through a series of fiscal and legislative case studies, how elite contestation continues to drive executive-legislative clashes. This elite focus aside, I examine how more mass-based organizing can fuel legislative activism, particularly where these groups are able to leverage existing elite divisions. This activism may engender more *progressive* distributive outcomes, going against the generally *regressive* trend. But it also elicits an executive backlash directed both at parliament itself and at external, organized groups. As such, these more pro-poor legislative interventions remain rare, and their long-term success elusive.

6.3.1 An Overview of Legislative Performance

The performance of Uganda's parliament, while fluctuating, did not register any marked decline up through 2016, i.e., the period under study. In the pre-transition period, NRM leaders could blame legislative activism on the lack of formal party discipline and the clear examples of factional contestation within the broad 'Movement' church. There was, however, no obvious decline in legislative performance after the 2005 transition and the introduction of an NRM party whip. This outcome suggests that informal intra-party pressures continue to override formal party and parliamentary institutional constraints.

Even before the ratification of the 1995 Constitution, elite contestation led to tensions between the legislature, then the National Resistance Council, and the executive.[137] The Constituent Assembly (1994) itself was an important arena of

---

[137] See Chapter 5.

contestation, particularly over issues relating to land and its distributive implications.[138] It was the activities of the Sixth Parliament (1996–2001), though,
that began to attract serious attention.[139] MPs enacted a series of important
private member's bills,[140] challenged the government over corruption allegations, and moved to censure ministers. These efforts, while in part borne out
of a principled desire to hold government to account, also became a focus for
factional jostling. For instance, the *Daily Monitor* newspaper reported in 1999
on a controversial letter written by a presidential advisor and addressed to a
select group of MPs.[141] The letter allegedly raised concerns that 'senior Cabinet
ministers and NRM historicals had failed to mobilize parliament for Museveni
and were instead using the legislature to settle personal scores and censure
their colleagues', thereby 'causing political insecurity in the Movement'. The
President's move to sack some ministers only further fuelled the flames, with
ousted Minister of Energy, Sir Richard Kaijuka, vowing to speak even louder
than anti-corruption leader, Winnie Byanyima, 'since I am no longer a minister.'[142] More generally, the outcome of the Sixth Parliament's oversight activities
resembled the results of *Bunge*'s more recent efforts; there were no prosecutions while Museveni only dropping a few ministers, many of whom he later
reinstated.[143] As such, we can question the Sixth Parliament's efficacy in overseeing the executive, but there is no doubt that it was used to air factional
differences.

Taken aback by the Sixth Parliament's assertiveness, President Museveni
moved to suppress it. He replaced the independent-minded Speaker, instituted
the Movement Parliamentary Caucus, and more aggressively monitored MPs'
behaviour.[144] The partial muzzling of the Sixth Parliament, and the apparent
further weakening of its successor,[145] fits with an overall impression of gradual
authoritarian retrenchment under the NRM. Public esteem for the legislature perhaps reached its nadir in 2005 when MPs amended the constitution
to remove presidential term limits, and this after most legislators received a
USh5m bribe. Observers also forecast that the introduction of a party whip

[138] See Chapter 3, section 3.3.1.1.
[139] Tamale, 1999; Carbone, 2008; Kasfir and Twebaze, 2009.
[140] See Chapter 5.
[141] 'Mutale sparks off new row among MPs', *The Daily Monitor*, 10 April 1999.
[142] 'Kaijuka joins Byanyima crusade—Mushega consoles Otafiire, Kaijuka', *The Daily Monitor*, 7 April 1999.
[143] Tangri and Mwenda, 2013, especially chapter 10.
[144] See Chapter 5.
[145] Carbone, 2008; Kasfir and Twebaze, 2009.

following the multiparty transition would lead to a more disciplined NRM majority in Parliament.[146]

However, a review of Parliament's performance pre- and post-transition upsets any easy narrative of uninterrupted legislative decline. Even during the supposedly more subservient Seventh Parliament (2001–2006), legislators used the institutional gains brought about during the Sixth, notably the introduction of the Budget Committee and the strengthened sectoral committees, to exercise greater fiscal oversight.[147] They also continued these, and other activities, largely unabated into the multiparty Eighth and Ninth parliamentary sessions.

Available quantitative data helps confirm the consistency of Parliament's overall performance.[148] For instance, throughout the NRM period, MPs have played an active role tabling private members' bills. The number actually *increased* post-2005, going from six bills tabled in the Sixth Parliament to 18 in the Ninth (2011–2016), of which seven were enacted.[149] Most of this legislation was introduced by NRM or NRM-sympathizing MPs.

Regarding Parliament's review of government bills, there is again no straightforward pattern of rising or falling engagement. There was a higher average number of committee proposals on government legislation introduced in the Seventh and Ninth Parliaments while the total number of amendments to government legislation was roughly the same in the no-party and multi-party periods.[150]

Finally, Parliament's accountability committees have consistently struggled to produce reports in a timely manner and, even once completed, reports are often never debated.[151] Parliament has occasionally come into the limelight after moving to censure ministers, including in the Eighth and Ninth Parliaments. There have been no high-profile prosecutions, though, and the concerned ministers tend to return to Cabinet in short order.[152] These interventions are nevertheless significant as a means of settling factional scores and as a focal point for influence-peddling by various business interests.[153]

---

[146] Ibid.; Rubongoya, 2007.

[147] Kasfir and Twebaze, 2009; interviews with staff in the Parliamentary Budget Office, *Kampala*, February 2015. A review of the *Daily Monitor*'s coverage of the Seventh Parliament's budget sessions also indicates routine legislative challenges of executive spending priorities.

[148] I did not include this quantitative data in my comparative analysis at the start of this chapter as I lack similarly detailed information for Tanzania's *Bunge*.

[149] Kasfir and Twebaze, 2015.

[150] Ibid.

[151] Centre for Policy Analysis, 'Strengthening the oversight function of Parliament of Uganda: An assessment of accountability committees', September 2014.

[152] Tangri and Mwenda, 2013.

[153] Ibid., 35–36. Vlassenroot et al., 2012: 15.

That said, ministers suspected of corruption and pursued through legislative channels are, it seems, only genuinely sidelined if they fall out with Museveni himself.[154]

This brief review indicates that legislative activity in Uganda has remained largely stable, and this despite NRM leaders' efforts to impose more discipline both pre- and post-2005.[155] I now examine in more depth what factors underpin continued executive-legislative bargaining in the multiparty era.

6.3.2 Uganda's 'Parliamentary Business Cycle'

While factionalism within the NRM continued to drive legislative activity after the multiparty transition, this activity also showed a tendency to fluctuate over the course of a parliamentary term, following a similar pattern as Tanzania's *Bunge*. To the extent that the legislature challenged the executive, it was more likely to do so earlier in a parliamentary term. When a fresh election neared, MPs tended to rubber stamp government initiatives, demanding more personal and pecuniary rewards in exchange.

As noted in the previous chapter, legislators' responsibility for raising their own campaign funds reinforced an 'individual merit' hangover from the no-party era. The expense of financing a parliamentary campaign and the party's own meagre contributions meant that, when an NRM candidates won their parliament seat, '*owning* him or her [was] difficult, so therefore disciplining him or her [was] difficult'.[156] Perhaps the greatest irony was that it is MPs from the west of Uganda, the supposed NRM heartland, who faced the highest levels of intra-party competition and who, consequently, demonstrated some of the lowest levels of loyalty and discipline once they reached parliament.[157]

What at first made MPs more independent, however, later became a source of vulnerability and political passivity. Legislators' indebtedness was widespread, exacerbated by costly campaigns, constituency demands, and targeting by aggressive loan sharks.[158] President Museveni, meanwhile, often

---

[154] For the example of former Minister of Education Jim Muhwezi, see Tangri and Mwenda, 2013: 135–136.

[155] For further detail, in addition to the below discussion, see Chapter 5.

[156] Interview, NRM party official, Kampala, January 2015. See also: NRM Caucus report, 2014.

[157] ACFIM report; Interview, NRM party official, January 2015.

[158] Walusimbi, Deo. 'Heavy debt MPs named'. *The Observer*, 6 May 2015. Accessed 15 June 2016: http://www.observer.ug/news-headlines/37701-heavy-debt-mps-named.
'Legislators take Shs900m loans as swearing-in enteres day two'. *Monitor*, 17 May 2016. Accessed 25 Nov 2016: http://www.monitor.co.ug/News/National/Legislators-loans-as-swearing-in-enters-/-/688334/3207688/-/qsyn1xz/-/index.html. This issue was raised by several interviewees.

seemed to celebrate MPs' financial woes, observing that only 50 MPs in the Ninth Parliament had an independent source of income.[159] As one parliamentarian remarked, 'Museveni calls MPs 'internally displaced'', referring to the way some legislators elude creditors by hiding in their parliamentary offices, from which they cannot be arrested.[160]

This financial distress meant that Museveni could make a show of bailing out parliamentarians, trading favours for discipline.[161] The Office of the Government Chief Whip (OGCW) also used classified expenditure—primarily from Defence and State House—to provide extra, off-budget support to MPs.[162] As one NRM official working in the OGCW recounted, the use of classified expenditure enabled the Office to help individual MPs with 'personal problems'. The official added this support was 'very important' as it ensured MPs knew that they belonged to 'a party that cares'.[163] The Party's 'caring' attitude then helped address issues of NRM indiscipline, although it was also used to win over opposition MPs. Finally, beyond addressing 'personal problems', the OGCW linked MPs to Ministers. This practice was especially effective for quelling opposition to government budget proposals. As the official explained,

> There have been people who have come here and said, 'We have been trying to meet the Minister of Works about roads in our constituency, but we have not managed to meet him, so why should we support his ministerial policy statement?' [. . .] So when the Chief Whip calls them, listens to them, addresses such issues, then they get back to the fold.[164]

This statement highlights how MPs would bargain with party leaders, who could then exploit the legislators' financial stress to buy back their loyalty. The strategy involved individualized patronage, thereby discouraging collective legislative efforts to, for instance, challenge a ministerial budget.

MPs' willingness to accept a party line was especially notable around elections. A common theme in interviews with MPs was that any serious legislative business had to be achieved in the first two to three years of a five-year

---

[159] 'Broke MPs plead with Museveni'. *The Observer*, 13 March 2013. Accessed 15 June 2016: http://www.observer.ug/component/content/article?id=24180:president-says-only-50-mps-can-sustain-themselves. ACFIM survey of MPs on Campaign Finance; Interviews, NRM and Opposition MPs.

[160] Interview, NRM MP, Kampala, February 2015.

[161] Kaaya, Sadab Kitatta. 'State of emergency as MPs get bailed out'. *The Observer*, 10 August 2014. Accessed 15 June 2016: http://www.observer.ug/news-headlines/33244--state-of-emergency-as-mps-get-bailed-out.

[162] Interview, NRM party official, January 2015.

[163] Ibid.

[164] Ibid.

parliamentary session. As elections neared, legislators' attendance declined as did their willingness to challenge the executive, notably on fiscal matters. At the tail end of the Eighth Parliament (2006–2011), for instance, Museveni gave MPs Ush1m ($400) to retrospectively approve an unprecedented supplementary budget of $740m, money that had already been used to buy fighter jets and other military hardware from Russia.[165] It was later alleged that the cost of the jets was inflated, thus implying that money had been diverted to the NRM campaigns. While nothing as extravagant occurred ahead around the 2016 polls, there was nevertheless a spike in parliamentary approval of supplementary budgets, again likely freeing up extra cash for campaigns.[166]

Even pre-election, though, MPs are not always this passive. Indeed, as in Tanzania, Uganda's MPs tended to adopt a more assertive posture when their own financial interests were at stake. For instance, in 2005, just before the first multi-party elections, Parliament passed a bill establishing a pension scheme for legislators.[167] The bill stipulated that the scheme would cater for MPs serving since 2001, i.e. the very same MPs responsible for enacting it. The State Minister for Pensions was vehemently opposed to the legislation, notably criticizing an amendment compelling Government to contribute 30 per cent of each MP's salary to the scheme, triple what it pays for other public service pensions. This executive opposition notwithstanding, the Parliamentary Pensions Bill sailed through the House.

Another way MPs extracted benefits from government, especially pre-elections, was by increasing the parliamentary budget. The Administration of Parliament Act (1997) ensured this budget was set by the Parliamentary Commission, although the Ministry of Finance still had to approve the overall ceiling.[168] Figure 6.2 shows the increase in approved expenditure from the end of the Eighth Parliament (2006–2011) through to the end of the Ninth (2011–2016).[169] Overall during this period, the parliamentary purse grew by 231 per cent, with 52 per cent of that increase accruing in the *last two years* of the Ninth

---

[165] 'Uganda government takes Shs1.7 trillion for jet fighters.' *Monitor*, 26 March 2011. Accessed 19 April 2018: http://www.monitor.co.ug/News/National/688334-1133504-aohn4hz/index.html.
  Bariyo, Nicholas. 'Uganda buys fighter jets'. *WSJ*, 7 April 2011. Accessed 19 April 2018: https://www.wsj.com/articles/SB10001424052748704013604576248094099823846. Interview, public health activist, Kampala, March 2015.
[166] ACFIM report (2016), chapter 11.
[167] 'Members of Parliament to get Pension'. *Uganda Radio Network*, 6 January 2006. Accessed 19 April 2018: https://ugandaradionetwork.com/story/members-of-parliament-to-get-pension.
[168] See Chapter 5.
[169] Data sourced from Approved Budget Estimates for FY 2009/2010 through 2016/2017, available at: http://www.budget.go.ug/.

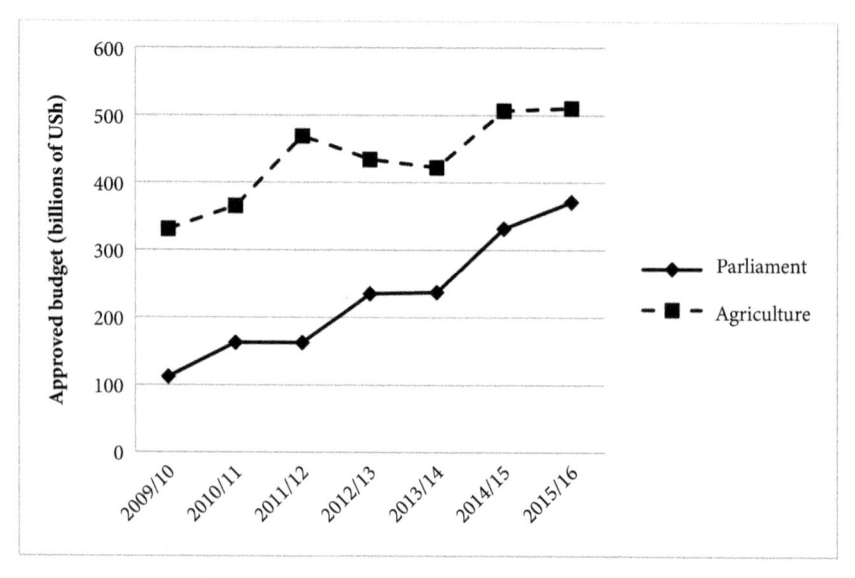

Figure 6.2 Uganda—parliament and agriculture sector budgets compared

Parliament.[170] By way of comparison, this growth in parliament's budget easily surpassed the already high 209 per cent increase in the total government budget during the same period.[171] Moreover, it far and away exceeded the 54 per cent increase in the agriculture budget, which in financial year 2015/16 was only 37 per cent higher than that of Parliament. The comparison with agriculture is particularly revealing as the agriculture sector employs roughly 70 per cent of Ugandans and contributes 26 per cent to GDP.[172]

In sum, the nature and extent of executive-legislative bargaining has varied considerably over the course of a parliamentary term. In the Eighth and Ninth Parliaments, MPs seemingly grew more subservient as political and financial pressures mounted pre-election. When legislators *did* challenge the executive, their aim was often to secure further financial benefits for themselves. As such, this elite bargaining dynamic had sharply regressive distributive implications. This cyclical trend aside, though, it remains to be seen what drove legislative

---

[170] An increasing portion of this budget goes towards MPs salaries and other emoluments. These are the fourth highest in Africa, where only South African, Nigerian, and Kenyan MPs are better remunerated.

Oluka, Benon Herbert. 'How Ugandan MPs' pay compares with counterparts' worldwide'. *The Observer*, 3 October 2016. Accessed 19 April 2018: http://observer.ug/news-headlines/46774-how-ugandan-mps-pay-compares-with-counterparts-worldwide.

[171] The total approved budget grew from Ush7.8tr in 2009/2010 to Ush24tr in 2015/2016.

[172] Deloitte, 'Uganda Economic Outlook 2016'.

activism earlier in a parliamentary session, and whether it could lead to more progressive distributive outcomes.

6.3.3   Case Studies—Elite Contestation Meets 'Mass-Based' Organizing

In what follows, I first elaborate on how elite contestation—coupled with non-elite pressures—motivated legislative activity in the post-transition period. I then use three case studies to analyse the influence of extra-parliamentary, 'mass-based' organizations, indicating how these groups benefit from elite divisions when pushing parliament to support more redistributive legislative and policy measures.[173]

6.3.3.1   Elite Contestation and Mass-Based Mobilization

Elite contestation, and occasionally non-elite organizing, have continued to shape legislative activity in several ways post-2005.

First, unlike in Tanzania, Uganda's top private sector elite—the Ruperalias, the Madhvanis, and others who did not accumulate their wealth while already in politics—have tended not to seek election to parliament. However, as documented in Chapter 4, business elites have invested in MPs' campaigns, with some purporting to 'have' legislators who will defend their interests in Parliament. These private sector financiers have also engaged in more ad hoc lobbying, including through bribes and other inducements. As in Tanzania, oversight committees have proved a prime target. While there were concerns pre-2005 about private sector bribery,[174] similar allegations have been repeated post-transition. These related notably to the Public Accounts Committee.[175] Rumours about other committees have also been common. One former committee chair recalled, 'There are business interests, many other interests who come and say, "Do this, say this", and many other things.'[176] These various

---

[173] Elements of this section draw on Collord, 2021. Also, unlike in other sections, I do not systematically retrace here the origins of the elite divisions discussed. For more information about their link to Uganda's prevailing patterns of accumulation and associated factional tensions within the NRM, please see Chapters 4 and 5, including details relating to key figures like Mbabazi, Kadaga, Kutesa, and others.

[174] Tangri and Mwenda, 2013: 93. Interview, former MP under Movement system, Oxford, June 2014.

[175] 'What happened to PAC?' *The Independent*, 17 April 2017. Accessed 19 April 2018: https://www.independent.co.ug/analysis-happened-pac/.
'Nadala denies bribe claims by UNRA probe'. *Monitor*, 28 May 2016. Accessed 19 April 2018: http://www.monitor.co.ug/News/National/Nandala-denies-bribe-claims-by--UNRA-probe/688334-3223066-elegc6/index.html.

[176] Interview, long-serving NRM MP and former committee chairperson, Kampala, February 2015.

interests 'compromise the chairpersons or the committee' to ensure Parliament does not exercise effective scrutiny.

Aside the interventions of private sector actors, a distinct class of accumulators—often long-time ministers close to Museveni—have used their political office to amass wealth,[177] and rivalries within this NRM elite have periodically surfaced in the legislatures. These personal animosities often go back decades, but they have been kept alive, notably re-animated during elections when rivals have accused each other of interfering in their campaigns.[178] In parliament, these same tensions have then resurfaced when, for instance, ministers have tried to marshal rank-and-file MPs to target other ministers. That said, another notable cleavage has emerged between backbench MPs and their more privileged frontbench colleagues.[179]

These various tensions have made Parliament a tinderbox ready to light. But elite differences could also provide leverage for more mass-based groups, be they unions, famers' associations, faith groups, or other advocacy organizations. In Uganda, these organizations have grown more sophisticated in their efforts to lobby Parliament. They have, notably, learned how to use political organizing and pressure to rally backbench MPs, prompting legislators to substitute their more individualized lobbying efforts for collective, legislative action.[180]

Through the below case studies, two involving budgetary review and one relating to controversial legislation, I show how these mass-based and advocacy groups have played a galvanizing role, encouraging MPs to support more *redistributive* policy. I also note how they have benefited from stronger legislative institutions, especially *stronger parliamentary committees*. Regarding legislators' response to outside pressure, I show how it has depended on prevailing factional tensions. While some MPs may have more consistent, principled motivations, the majority have championed a cause only when politically expedient, notably when seeking to outmanoeuvre rival factions within parliament. Finally, I underscore how successful legislative interventions have triggered an executive backlash, targeting both MPs and organizations outside parliament. This backlash has involved, among other things, using patronage

---

[177] See Chapters 3 and 4.
[178] See Chapter 4 for some details, although this is discussed more in the below case studies.
[179] Interviews with NRM MPs.
[180] I draw on interviews with MPs as well as NGO and union staff, including from: Uganda National Teachers' Union (UNATU), Uganda Medical Workers' Union (UMWU), Parliament Watch CSBAG, Advocates Coalition for Development and Environment (ACODE), NGO Forum, White Ribbon, Health Gap, Uganda National Health Consumers' Organisation, Action Group for Health, Revenue Watch Institute (RWI), Uganda Women's Network.

to divide mass-based organizations, thereby reasserting a hierarchical relation-ship between ruler and ruled, a common strategy in contexts where clientelist politics pervade.[181]

As discussed at the start of this chapter, there are alternative arguments—notably regarding electoral pressure—to explain why MPs' might support redistributive policy measures. Although research findings remain mixed, I do not discount this argument here. However, to understand when and why politicians pursue more pro-poor policy outcomes, we cannot focus only on the so-called politics of 'electoral spectacle' but must consider *the wider distri-bution of power across organized interests*, plus how this distribution shapes an ongoing politics of 'organized combat'.

6.3.3.2 The Health Budget

In September 2012, Parliament refused to pass the annual budget for the 2012/2013 financial year unless government agreed to allocate additional funds to the Ministry of Health. The threat of a government shutdown came after the Social Services Committee had for years flagged Uganda's critical shortage of health workers without making any strong demands of the exec-utive nor eliciting any government response. What changed in 2012? An extra-parliamentary campaign coalition ramped up pressure on legislators, prompting them to take a firmer stance opposing government policy. Simul-taneously, elite divisions within the NRM added fuel to the fire as MPs and ministers used the occasion to challenge one another, thereby intensifying the legislative–executive clash. The intervention resulted in a partial success for the legislature, although a subsequent executive backlash discouraged continued demands for increased health sector spending in later years.

At the start of the Ninth Parliament, a loose coalition of advocacy groups, unions and professional associations working in the health sector united around a key campaign goal: to increase recruitment and salaries for med-ical workers.[182] This goal was not merely about addressing the professional interests of health workers, but rather, was consistent with a broader effort to address the acute 'human resources for health' crisis undermining health services countrywide.[183] From the start, the coalition focused its attention on Parliament's Social Services Committee, which then became the key driver of an alternative health agenda in the legislature.

---

[181] See: Chubb, 1981: 81–82; Berman, 1998; Cooper, 2002, chapter 4.
[182] Where there is no added specification, the below narrative come from a mix of interviews MPs, parliamentary clerks, NRM party officials and health campaigners.
[183] On the HRH crisis and how it undermines poorer patients' access to health care: Afriyie et al., 2019.

The health activists were lucky in that the new Committee Chairman, Sam Lyomoki, was an ally. He was not sympathetic merely due to some personal proclivity, though; rather, he was himself embedded in the very organizations then seeking to lobby parliament, further indicating their significance. An NRM MP for 'workers', one of the 'special interest' groups represented in the Ugandan Parliament,[184] Lyomoki was a trained medical professional himself and oversaw the founding of the Uganda Medical Workers Union (UMWU) in the 1990s before serving as its secretary general.[185]

Although the activist coalition began mobilizing in 2011, it intensified its efforts in 2012. Its members took a hands-on approach to guiding the Social Services Committee, attending meetings and contributed directly to the Committee's report. The committee ultimately recommended that the Ministry of Finance reallocate Ush260b ($104m) from other sectors to health, specifying that the additional funds should be used both to recruit new medical workers and to improve their pay.[186]

When the report was brought to the House, it attracted strong, cross-party support and was soon adopted. Crucially, the report endorsed by MPs included a commitment *not to pass the annual budget* until the additional funds were provided to the health sector. Unlike previous parliamentary recommendations, this one had teeth.

Why this strong support? During the ensuing parliamentary debate, individual MPs did emphasize voter demands for improved health services.[187] However, electoral pressure is not sufficient to explain the 2012 legislative intervention; again, that intervention came after years of similar concerns being raised with no follow-up. It was *only once campaign organizations began to mobilize through the social services committee* that MPs took meaningful action.

The story does not end there, though. After the initial adoption by Parliament of the Social Services Committee recommendations, Parliament's powerful Budget Committee had to respond by reviewing government spending proposals and translating the recommendations into a concrete alternative expenditure proposal.[188] The Budget Committee identified Ush39.2b ($15.7m)

---

[184] Uganda's 1995 Constitution provides for representation of women, youth, workers, people with disabilities and the military.

[185] Interview, NRM MP, Kampala, February 2015.

[186] 'Report of the Parliamentary Committee on Health on the Ministerial Policy Statement for the Health Sector for the Financial year 2012/2013', August 2012, 35.

[187] The *Hansard* includes numerous MP statements highlighting the pressure they face from voters due to poor health services.

[188] The Budget Committee reviews all proposals from sector committees.

to re-allocate through a 30 per cent cut in non-wage spending across all sectors.[189] Campaigners as well as MPs on the Social Services Committee never expected their demands to be fully satisfied, so even though the Ush39.2b was only 15 per cent of the initial sum requested, they supported the Budget Committee's proposal.

Government nevertheless remained staunchly opposed. Given the intransigence of the NRM top brass, what kept the budget debate alive? On this point, the factional dynamics within the NRM played an important role. One notable divide emerged between backbench MPs who were quick to attack President Museveni's inner circle of Ministers for prioritizing their own privileges over the welfare of ordinary Ugandans, for instance, through their own state-sponsored trips to receive healthcare abroad.[190]

Accompanying these backbench-frontbench tensions were ad hoc, personal antagonisms, borne out of the acute patron–client factionalism characteristic of the NRM. The Prime Minister, Amama Mbabazi, was a principal target. As discussed elsewhere in this book, Mbabazi then served as NRM Secretary General and had alienated many NRM MPs during the chaotic party primaries that preceded Uganda's 2011 general election. He was chief among the 'senior party leaders' who MPs later accused of abusing their role to 'facilitate particular aspirants during the primaries and independents or even opposition candidates during the general election against party flag bearers'.[191]

While the hostility towards Mbabazi was widespread during the 2012 budget debates, a few specific rivalries proved especially important. A backbench NRM MP, Chris Baryomunsi,[192] from a constituency neighbouring Mbabazi's own in Kunungu district, used the occasion to individually shame the Prime Minister for his negligence as an MP, noting that 'I have six [constituents] from Kanungu in my house and two of them are from the Prime Minister's constituency because they cannot get service in Kanungu.'[193] Another personal rival of Mbabazi's, Speaker Rebecca Kadaga, had previously accused him of funding alternative candidates to oust her from her Kamuli constituency. She

---

[189] 'Report of the Budget Committee of Parliament on the harmonization of the budget figures before supply', September 2012, 5.

[190] *Hansard*, 18 September 2012.

[191] 'Final report of the NRM Parliamentary Caucus Select Committee on NRM Primary Elections', 2014.

[192] In an example of how these personal battles can play out within the NRM, Baryomunsi later served on the special NRM committee convened to investigate the 2010 primaries. The committee report implicated Mbabazi and contributed to his ouster, both from his party and government positions. Baryomunsi, meanwhile, went on to assume a ministerial position, becoming a notable defender of government policy.

[193] *Hansard*, NRM MP, September 2012.

then used her chairing of the budget debate to pile pressure on her opponent, letting the debate drag on and personally challenging Mbabazi's claim that there were no funds to reallocate to health.[194]

Although these elite divides within the NRM helped ensure that the health debate took off, the coalition of health organizations responsible for instigating the debate also kept the pressure up. Activist organizations used the media to encourage people to contact their MPs and insist they hold firm.[195] They also amplified the call-in campaign by contacting their members and health workers in MPs' constituencies. Legislators interviewed confirmed receiving numerous calls and text messages throughout the budget debate.

Finally, with the clock ticking down and the government in danger of running out of cash, Prime Minister Mbabazi arrived with an alternative proposal. He asserted that the government would provide, as a 'first step', approximately Ush49.5b ($19.8m) to recruit more health workers and to provide them with additional allowances. He indicated a small portion of these funds would come from reallocations while the remainder, he promised, would arrive as a supplementary budget later in the year.

Many feared this was an evasion strategy and that the government would never provide the additional funds. Even so, parliament accepted Mbabazi's offer and passed the budget. The Social Service Committee along with outside advocacy organizations then set about monitoring government to ensure it delivered on its promises. After the Committee threatened the Minister of Finance with a censure motion, the money was duly released.[196] The Ministry of Health then undertook the recruitment of a targeted 10,231 health workers, considerably more than the 6,172 the Ministry first estimated it could afford.[197]

This 'first step' also proved the last, however, frustrating both campaigners and legislators who had hoped for a sustained recruitment effort. Instead, government responded to the unprecedented level of legislative activism with a calculated counterattack. The targets included dissident NRM MPs. The Chairperson of the Social Services Committee, the 'workers' MP with a medical and unionist background, was moved to the committee on defence,

[194] *Hansard*, NRM MP, September 2012.
[195] Interview, former Executive Director of Uganda National Health Consumers' Organisation, February 2015.
[196] Interview, NRM MP, Kampala, February 2015.
[197] 'Remarks by the Hon. Minister of Finance, Planning and Economic Development on the Shs43b required as supplementary budget for the remuneration of health workers for FY 2012/13', February 2013.
'Progress report on the recruitment of health workers for HCIV & HCIII', Ministry of Health, February 2013. Both documents were submitted to the Social Services Committee.

about which be professed to 'know nothing.'[198] He was then replaced by a loyal ruling party cadre who was later appointed NRM Deputy Treasurer.

Largely because of this executive backlash, Parliament returned to making minor amendments and non-binding recommendations to the health sector budget. Even so, what the 2012 confrontation clearly demonstrated was the potential for outside pressure to mobilize MPs to push for increased public goods provision, and for tensions within the NRM to further enflame a heated House debate.

6.3.3.3 The Education Budget

The executive–legislative clash over the health budget was not a one-off occurrence. Similar tensions over education spending further indicate how extra-parliamentary mobilization can prompt legislative interventions. Throughout the Ninth Parliament (2011–2016), the Uganda National Teachers' Union (UNATU) led repeated calls for an increase in teachers' salaries. Far from a narrow interest group concern, increased salaries were considered critical to ensuring teacher recruitment and retention and thus to improving the quality of education services.[199] UNATU helped galvanize rank-and-file MPs to intervene over the education budget, an effort that also benefited from elite tensions within the NRM. This combination of outside pressure and internal divisions forced the executive to make important concessions, but this then gave way to a concerted backlash, targeting UNATU itself.

The Union's emergence as a political force was itself a considerable achievement. Labour organizing has long been repressed in Uganda, including under the NRM.[200] The NRM Government blocked the registration of a teachers' union until 2003, when it ceded in the face of sustained protest.[201] After overcoming this initial hurdle, UNATU slowly consolidated, expanding its membership until, ahead of the 2011 elections, its potential to pose a political threat was finally confirmed.

Aware of the Union's success in recruiting and organizing new members, President Museveni embarked in 2009 on a nationwide tour to meet with secondary school teachers. The tour was ostensibly aimed at advising on how to teach patriotism to students, although opposition politicians claimed teachers

---

[198] Interviews, NRM MP, Kampala, February 2015.
[199] On the importance for quality education of teacher retention, including through increased salaries: Kjaer and Muwanga, 2016.
[200] Barya, 2010.
[201] Interview, NRM MP, Kampala, February 2015; Interview, former Secretary General of UNATU, Kampala, January 2015.

were being forced to join the NRM.[202] Whatever the intention, UNATU remained unmoved by these presidential overtures. Throughout 2009 and 2010, the Union continued to denounce the poor performance of Universal Primary Education (UPE), the NRM's flagship programme, while pushing for an increase in teachers' pay.[203]

Shortly after the 2011 elections, UNATU redoubled its efforts, calling a strike in July with a demand that teachers receive a 100 per cent salary increment. The union's main target was initially government; however, Museveni evaded its demands while the Prime Minister and Minister of Education appeared actively hostile. UNATU therefore shifted its focus to parliament's Social Services Committee where, in the words of UNATU's then Vice National Chairperson, 'the debate picked [sic] with excitement.'[204] The Committee recommended an immediate 20 per cent increase in teachers' salaries, urging Government to phase in the full 100 per cent increment over three years.[205] A majority of MPs then endorsed these recommendations in the House and directed the Budget Committee to identify funds from other sectors to cover the increase in the education budget.

In making its overtures to Parliament, UNATU did appeal to the electoral concerns of backbench MPs.[206] As was true of Parliament's action on health, though, MPs' action did not emerge spontaneously from their shared concern for voter demands; rather, it was instigated and guided by UNATU, indicating the importance of interest group pressure. The Union's lobbying was, moreover, not limited to the Social Services Committee and the hallways of Parliament. Its branch structures reached nationwide, ensuring a presence in MPs' constituencies. It also encouraged legislators to join a 'Quality Education Forum' in Parliament, offering the carrot of a constituency visit and an endorsement to MPs who supported the Union's demands.[207]

Spurred on by UNATU's effective organizing, MPs continued supporting the teachers. However, it is likely they would have folded had it not been for the elite tensions that further strengthened legislators' resolve. Mbabazi, as Prime Minister, was again a lightning rod for MPs' grievances. As UNATU launched

---

[202] *Daily Monitor*, 29 March 2009. Accessed 9 June 2018: http://www.monitor.co.ug/Magazines/PeoplePower/-/689844/701754/-/4ljoqx/-/index.html.

[203] UNATU's criticisms of government appear in the Union's newsletter, Voice of the Teachers.

[204] James Tweheyo, *Voice of the Teachers*, June 2012, pp. 4–5.

[205] 'Report of the Committee on Social Services on the Ministerial Policy Statement and Budget Estimates for the Financial Year 2011/12', 7–8.

[206] Interview, former UNATU General Secretary, Kampala, January 2015; Interview, NRM MP, Kampala, February 2015.

[207] Interview, several NRM MPs and members of the 'Quality Education Forum', Kampala, February 2015; Interview, Tweheyo.

a second round of industrial action in early September 2011, Mbabazi declared striking teachers would be fired.[208] MPs responded by demanding the Prime Minister's resignation.[209]

Even with Parliament's support, though, the resolve of striking teachers was beginning to wane. Many were suffering at the hands of strike-breaking local officials. The Budget Committee then reported back to Parliament after holding a meeting at a luxury hotel paid for by Government. It rejected the proposed salary increment for teachers.[210] Soon thereafter, UNATU called off its strike.[211]

What at first looked like a defeat nevertheless proved to be a partial success. Soon after the strike ended, Mbabazi announced that Government would increase teachers' salaries by 50 per cent over three years in instalments of 15, 20 then 15 per cent. Keeping government to its word was the next challenge, and the effort devolved into a game of cat-and-mouse between Government and UNATU with Parliament in the middle.

In 2012, Government delivered the first 15 per cent increment as demanded by UNATU with Parliament's continued support. It however reneged on its promise of a 20 per cent pay raise in 2013, citing austerity conditions after a multi-million-dollar corruption scandal prompted donors to suspend aid.[212] UNATU responded by announcing further strikes. It also turned to Parliament for support and was again well received by the Education Committee, which had since split from Social Services.[213] The Committee backed teachers' demands, and Parliament voted to task the Budget Committee with finding the additional funds for the 20 per cent increment.[214] President Museveni was unflinching, though, threatening to halt infrastructure developments in dissident NRM MPs' constituencies while declaring that uncooperative teachers should be '[swept] aside' in favour of new recruits.[215] Ultimately, when the Budget Committee reported that no funds were available for teachers'

[208] *Monitor*, 5 September 2011. Accessed 9 June 2018: http://www.monitor.co.ug/News/National/-/688334/1230474/-/bjcqliz/-/index.html.

[209] 'MPs ask Mbabazi to resign over strike'. *Monitor*, 6 September 2011. Accessed 9 June 2018: http://www.monitor.co.ug/News/National/-/688334/1231134/-/bjc4q9z/-/index.html.

[210] 'Budget Committee Report on the Budget Estimates for FY 2011/12', 8.

[211] 'Why government failed to increase teachers' salary'. *Monitor*, 18 September 2011. Accessed 9 June 2018: http://www.monitor.co.ug/News/Education/-/688336/1238498/-/f1l9a7/-/index.html.

[212] 'Don't pass budget, teachers urge MPs'. *Monitor*, 28 June 2013. Accessed 9 June 2018: http://www.monitor.co.ug/News/National/Don-t-pass-Budget--teachers-urge-MPs/-/688334/1898028/-/u628sp/-/index.html.

[213] See Chapter 5 on improvements to the committee system, including the creation of the Social Services Committee followed by the further sub-division into the Health and Education Committees.

[214] 'Report of the Committee on Budget on the instruction from Parliament to find funds for a 20% salary increment for teachers from the budget estimates for FY 2013/14', 2013.

[215] 'Museveni: sack striking teachers', *The Observer*, 18 September 2013.

salaries,[216] the overwhelming majority of NRM MPs voted to accept this verdict. Soon thereafter, UNATU suspended its strike, although not without demanding some assurance from Government that it would allocate a fresh increment the following year.[217]

This it did in 2014,[218] marking another partial success, but come 2015, Government refused to provide the final salary increment.[219] This time, there was no resistance from Parliament. With the 2016 general election fast approaching, it was the wrong time in the 'parliamentary business cycle'; NRM MPs were focused on the upcoming and highly competitive party primaries. UNATU, meanwhile, was struggling against varied government attempts to undermine the organizational strength of the Union.[220] The Ministry of Education had started transferring teachers known to be active UNATU members. It was also trying to 'sabotage' the Union by circumventing the UNATU leadership when disbursing seed capital to teachers' Savings and Credit Cooperatives, thereby splitting the membership. The UNATU General Secretary was later co-opted, accepting a position as an advisor in State House.

In sum, the struggle over teachers' salaries in many ways exemplifies the fraught 'politics of organized combat' underlying legislative support for more pro-poor policy. By appealing directly to MPs and leveraging—if unwittingly—internal NRM divisions, UNATU was able to extract concessions from Government, making gains that both served teachers' interests and aligned with popular demands for quality education. Both legislators and UNATU itself nevertheless struggled to withstand the executive backlash, which mixed patronage and intimidations to undermine their organizational power and, thus, their campaign.

6.3.3.4 Uganda's Oil Economy and Legislative Review

The politics of health and education spending already reveal much about the factors shaping legislative activism, at least early in a parliamentary term. It is hard to understand the trajectory of Uganda's Ninth Parliament, though,

---

[216] 'Report of the Committee on Budget', 2013.

[217] 'Teachers' protest off as UNATU strikes deal with government'. *Monitor*, 25 September 2013. Accessed 9 June 2018: http://www.monitor.co.ug/News/National/Protest-off-as-Unatu-strikes-deal-with-government/-/688334/2007384/-/157ymr1/-/index.html

[218] 'Government allocates Shs215 billion for teachers'. *Monitor*, 13 June 2014. Accessed 9 June 2018: http://www.monitor.co.ug/News/National/Government-allocates-Shs215-billion-for/-/688334/2346558/-/b4gwlv/-/index.html.

[219] 'Government should swallow its pride and pay teachers'. *Monitor*, 31 May 2015. Accessed 9 June 2018: http://www.monitor.co.ug/Magazines/PeoplePower/Government-should--swallow-its-pride-and-pay--teachers/-/689844/2734474/-/5pvg9dz/-/index.html.

[220] Interview, former UNATU General Secretary, Kampala, January 2015; Interview, former UNATU Communication and Advocacy Officer, Kampala, January 2015.

without considering the executive-legislative maelstrom that arose out of the 2011–2012 petroleum debates. The 2006 discovery of oil in Uganda's western region fuelled excitement about the country's future wealth, but also fears of a resource curse. After several years delay, Parliament finally intervened. Pressure from outside advocacy organizations, media scrutiny, and broader popular mobilization helped motivate and guide this legislative action; however, factional tensions within the NRM—involving wealthy party heavyweights— was directly responsible for putting oil at the top of the parliamentary agenda. Ultimately, the legislature ensured the enactment of much improved—if still flawed—legislation regulating the petroleum sector. Even so, the executive backlash was fierce, limiting the potential for sustained legislative intervention.

Shortly after Uganda's oil discovery, which occurred during the Eighth Parliament, a range of national and international NGOs as well as donor agencies began advocating for stronger policy and legislation to regulate the new sector. Parliament was among the main targets of this advocacy, and the Parliamentary Forum on Oil and Gas (PFOG) was duly set up, headed by an ambitious backbench NRM MP, Henry Banyenzaki. The Forum was 'not very outspoken' at that stage, though, and Banyenzaki, after causing a mild stir, was appointed minister after the 2011 elections.[221] By then, little progress had been made as Government repeatedly delayed formulating petroleum legislation while early draft bills were widely criticized as deficient by advocacy groups.[222]

Parliament's lacklustre engagement changed entirely in October 2011 when MPs mobilized to recall the House for a special sitting.[223] The two-day session centred on a set of documents tabled by Independent MP Gerald Karuhanga.[224] The documents purportedly revealed that senior ministers had taken multimillion-dollar bribes from Anglo-Irish oil company, Tullow. The ministers named were Prime Minister, Amama Mbabazi, Foreign Affairs Minister, Sam Kutesa, and Internal Affairs Minister, Hilary Onek. MPs responded by passing a resolution calling on all three to resign. They also voted for a moratorium on new oil contracts pending the enactment of legislation to ensure accountability in the oil sector. More generally, the highly mediatized debate helped redirect the national conversation as, beforehand, 'Many MPs and the country [did not know] what oil meant for Uganda.'[225]

---

[221] Interview, former PFOG Secretary General, Kampala, January 2015.
[222] Accessed 21 April 2018: http://www.oilinuganda.org/categories/oil-timeline.
[223] Interview, former PROG Secretary General.
[224] 'Makerere professor criticises MPs as they seek oil sector role'. *Oil in Uganda*, July 2012. Accessed 21 April 2018: http://www.oilinuganda.org/features/law/makerere-professor-criticises-mps-as-they-seek-oil-sector-role.html.
[225] Interview, opposition MP, Kampala, April 2013.

Parliament was rewarded for its efforts when, in early February 2012, Government tabled two petroleum bills in the House.[226] While ministers insisted they had been preparing the legislation since 2008, MPs and transparency advocates credited the parliamentary uproar with pushing government to act. This promising initial outcome aside, though, new questions were being raised about the October 2011 debates. It had emerged that MP Karuhanga's documents were forged and were passed to him by the Justice Minister, Kahinda Otafiire.[227] Otafiire's alleged aim, shared by a supportive clique of NRM legislators, was to side-line long-time rivals. Prime Minister Mbabazi, among the targeted ministers, then retaliated by pressuring the Ugandan High Court to revisit its decision to clear Otafiire in a case relating to his commercial investments in sugar.[228]

This high-level power struggle was laid bare during a meeting of the NRM Central Executive Committee in early January 2012.[229] President Museveni used the occasion to announce he was investigating Otafiire over his alleged involvement in leaking the bribery documents. The President also attempted to address another set of tensions, this time between Prime Minister Mbabazi and Speaker Kadaga. His intervention only aggravated the situation, though, as Mbabazi reportedly accused Kadaga of letting the backbench 'prosecute' him during the October debate, adding that she denied him the opportunity to defend himself. Kadaga shot back, 'Why do you lie to yourself?'

Museveni's frustrations with this intra-party squabbling were made plain in a two-hour speech delivered to Parliament just days after the new petroleum legislation was tabled. The President lamented the political fragmentation within the NRM, demanding greater party 'discipline'.[230] Instead, a broad cross-section of MPs joined the now reanimated PFOG and, enticed partly by the luxury venues, began attending donor-funded and NGO-organized workshops.[231] When the Natural Resources Committee, tasked with reviewing the petroleum bills, finally tabled its report in September 2012, NRM MPs, opposition members, and various NGOs were united in their criticism. Of

---

[226] The Petroleum (Exploration, Development and Production) Bill and the Petroleum (Refining, Gas Processing and Conversion and Storage) Bill.

[227] Accessed 21 April 2018: http://www.monitor.co.ug/Magazines/PeoplePower/-/689844/1255796/-/13vloiyz/-/index.html. Interview, staff at the donor-funded Democratic Governance Facility, Kampala, February 2015.

[228] Ibid. 'Otafiire defies Museveni on sugar'. *Monitor*, 28 September 2011. Accessed 21 April 2018: http://www.monitor.co.ug/News/National/688334-1244752-a4rmgyz/index.html.

[229] 'Museveni probes Otafiire over oil bribe documents'. *Monitor*, 4 January 2012. Accessed 21 April 2018: http://www.monitor.co.ug/News/National/-/688334/1300296/-/b24o2sz/-/index.html.

[230] Museveni, Hansard, 10 February 2012.

[231] Interviews, DGF and ACODE staff as well as PFOG members.

particular concern was the committee's failure to address the controversial 'Clause 9', which gave the Minister of Energy far-reaching licensing powers. The creation of a 'super minister', many argued, went against basic account-ability requirements, and given his role as appointing authority, essentially left President Museveni to sign off on licences.[232]

A frenzied period of lobbying ensued. In late October, PFOG along with supportive NGOs invited all legislators to a 'harmonizing session' at Mun-yonyo Speke Resort where participants discussed alternatives to the recom-mendations in the Natural Resources Committee report.[233] Days later, the NRM leadership followed suit, calling a parliamentary caucus meeting.[234] The debate then kicked off in Parliament, and on 12 November, MPs voted to sub-stantially dilute Clause 9. This was 'our greatest day', declared the PFOG Chair, NRM MP Theodore Ssekikubo.[235]

The victory was short-lived. President Museveni, taken aback by the move, demanded that Clause 9 be re-incorporated in its original form. Speaker Kadaga agreed that the clause would be debated afresh on 27 November, with an emergency NRM caucus planned for the day before. On the morning of the scheduled debate, Parliament's gates were mobbed by people push-ing to watch from the gallery. This included residents of Bunyoro, in the heart of the oil region, who had travelled, in the words of one woman, 'because there is a very important law that is going to be passed, and I want to see [...] how am I going to benefit'.[236] MPs eventually intervened to ensure those jostling outside were allowed to enter Parliament, and this amidst accusations that the Bunyoro group had been 'facilitated' by Kampala-based NGOs.

<hr />

[232] Interview with former PFOG Secretary General.
'Oil bills: Lukyamuzi to table minority report in Parliament'. *Oil in Uganda*, 6 September 2012. Accessed 21 April 2018: http://www.oilinuganda.org/features/law/oil-bills-lukyamuzi-to-table-minority-report-in-parliament.html.
'Committee report leaves ministers powers inact'. *Oil in Uganda*, 6 September 2012. Accessed 21 April 2018: http://www.oilinuganda.org/features/law/committee-report-on-oil-leaves-ministers-powers-intact.html.
[233] 'Last minute scramble to salvage petroleum bills.' *Oil in Uganda*, 24 October 2012. Accessed 21 April 2018: http://www.oilinuganda.org/features/law/last-minute-scramble-to-salvage-petroleum-bills.html.
[234] Izama, Angelo. 'Uganda: battle over national oil company reveals strains of the sector'. *African Arguments*, 29 October 2012. Accessed 21 April 2018: http://africanarguments.org/2012/10/29/uganda-battle-over-national-oil-company-reveals-strains-of-the-sector-by-angelo-izama/.
[235] With roughly 50 MPs voting, the House was not quorate when the amendment was passed, an indication that the NRM leadership had taken their eye off the ball. Regarding the MPs, the PFOG Secretary General lamented, 'Most of the people in that legislature are so indifferent', adding, 'They only rush for workshops because there is a monetary inducement.'
[236] 'Bishops: MPs prise open parliament doors to public'. *Oil in Uganda*, 27 November 2012. Accessed 21 April 2018: http://www.oilinuganda.org/features/law/bishop-mps-prise-open-parliament-doors-to-public.html.

The debate itself proved riotous with some MPs calling for a vote, others singing the national anthem, and the NRM Chief Whip patrolling, trying to coral MPs into voting. Speaker Kadaga eventually slipped out through a back entrance, insisting she would not reconvene Parliament until the disruptive MPs were disciplined. This was a tall order as the Chairman of the parliamentary Rules, Privileges and Discipline Committee identified 239 MPs to be investigated.[237] On 5 December, legislators again refused to vote on the controversial Clause 9, demanding a compromise position be reached with Government.[238] While the Minister of Energy did negotiate a consensus with a group of PFOG MPs, this was overruled by Cabinet.[239] Museveni then set about calling MPs individually and, on 7 December, Parliament finally voted to re-introduce the original Clause 9. Only five NRM MPs voted against the reintroduction, but a further 100 stayed away from the House, a '*de facto* abstention'.[240] The debate was also overseen not by Kadaga but by her deputy, Jacob Oulanyah, who later accused his boss of letting him take the heat.

This unprecedented show of legislative independence did not go unpunished. On 13 December, President Museveni delivered a blistering address in Parliament. He called out by name three MPs along with the Executive Director of a prominent NGO and accused them of 'acting on behalf of foreign interests'. The Director was ultimately forced out of his position, interpreted by some as an effort to 'break' the NGO so it could '[serve] as an example to others'.[241] The named MPs were also targeted for further intimidation, with two of them taken to Museveni's personal ranch, where he allegedly threatened, 'I'm going to lock you up'.[242] Donors, meanwhile, distanced themselves from PFOG, taken aback by their designation as meddling 'foreign interests'.[243]

The story took a final, tragic turn. The sudden death of a vocal NRM MP only a day after Museveni's 13 December address left many accusing the NRM

---

[237] 'MPs revolt against creation of a super oil minister'. *Oil in Uganda*, 27 November 2012. Accessed 21 April 2018: http://www.oilinuganda.org/features/law/mps-revolt-against-creation-of-a-super-oil-minister.html.
'Speaker Kadaga demands disciplinary action over oil bill fracas'. *Oil in Uganda*, 30 November 2012. Accessed 21 April 2018: http://www.oilinuganda.org/features/law/speaker-kadaga-demands-disciplinary-action-over-oil-bill-fracas.html.
[238] 'Parliament adjourns to consider consensus on oil clause 9'. *Oil in Uganda*, 5 December 2012. Accessed 21 April 2018: http://www.oilinuganda.org/features/law/parliament-adjourns-to-consider-consensus-on-oil-clause-9.html.
[239] 'Museveni edges towards victory as oil fatigue sets in'. *Oil in Uganda*, 7 December 2012. Accessed 21 April 2018: http://www.oilinuganda.org/features/law/museveni-edges-towards-victory-as-oil-fatigue-sets-in.html. Interviews, former PFOG Secretary General and Chair.
[240] 'Oil bill: Executive finally prevails'. *Oil in Uganda*, 8 December 2012. Accessed 21 April 2018: http://www.oilinuganda.org/features/law/oil-bill-executive-power-finally-prevails.html.
[241] Interview, ACODE staff member, Kampala, January 2015.
[242] Interview, former PFOG Secretary General.
[243] Interview, DGF staff.

leadership of murder. MPs responded by again mobilizing to recall Parliament, this time demanding that the President appear before the special session for questioning. Museveni, in turn, threatened a 'coup' *against Parliament*, should it not abandon its recall plans and fall back in line.[244] While the details are murky, Speaker Kadaga was also widely rumoured to have been personally intimidated, the result being that the recall did not go ahead.[245] The unprecedented expulsion of four NRM MPs in early 2013, and the subsequent efforts to eject them from Parliament, offered a final warning to any other would-be 'rebel' parliamentarians.[246] Ultimately, the oil debates were a turning point in the Ninth Parliament, with the Speaker, the NRM caucus, and Parliament as a whole coming out of it much subdued, although by no means defeated.[247]

Whether through its fiscal oversight or its legislative interventions, the Ugandan Parliament has repeatedly intervened to alter the executive agenda, including to secure more progressive distributive outcomes. In the oil case, the debate was mainly framed in terms of 'fighting corruption', itself a progressive aim.[248] These interventions were, in part, borne out of factional tensions between NRM top brass, who double as both political and economic elites, as well as the frustrations of rank-and-file NRM MPs. As illustrated through the above three case studies, though, pressure form more mass-based, extra-parliamentary organizations helped direct these fractious party politics into productive forms of collective action. This legislative activity contrasts with the dominant trend whereby elite bargaining, when channelled through the legislature, points to distinctly *regressive* distributive outcomes.

6.4 Conclusion

This chapter argues that legislative performance in single and dominant party regimes varies along with the internal cohesion and institutional coherence of those parties. Where the distribution of power across economic elites and rival factions is more decentralized, as was true in Tanzania *after the 1980s* up to the 2015 elections and in Uganda under the NRM, this encourages a more assertive Parliament. The dynamics of elite contestation—and thus the nature of legislative activity—do then vary over the course of an electoral

---

[244] 'Coup Calls', *Africa Confidential*, 1 February 2013.
[245] Interviews, NRM and opposition MPs.
[246] See Chapter 5.
[247] See Chapter 5 for more examples of Speaker Kadaga and Parliament's oppositional stance.
[248] This was the dominant narrative in the media as well as one echoed by MPs.

term, following a 'parliamentary business cycle'; the overall trend nevertheless points towards more legislative challenges to the executive.

But why should we care about a legislature absorbed by ruling party factionalism and elite influence-peddling? What does this explanation of legislative activity say about its significance? Certainly, the implications are more normatively ambivalent than is often assumed in a literature that associates an assertive legislature with democratization. Moreover, when it comes to the distributive outcomes of legislative interventions, a common assumption is that individual legislators will respond to electoral pressures by favouring more progressive redistribution. By contrast, I theorize why the distributive implications of legislative activity are in many instances likely regressive, benefiting one elite group over another. This is *not* to say that pro-poor outcomes fail to materialize altogether, but they are seemingly the exception to a dominant trend. I nevertheless propose an explanation of how they are likely to occur, namely when extra-parliamentary organizations—including unions, professional associations, and advocacy groups—galvanize legislative action. I show how, in the Ugandan case, these groups redirected factional tensions towards more redistributive ends.

7

Conclusion

Wealth, Power, and the Struggle for Democracy

> At independence, democracy was not championed or challenged
> with respect to its content of rights, but was the mechanism
> through which political power would be gained or distributed,
> and with it, economic power and status.
> —Sam Nolutshungu, 1990

> The struggle for democracy and development is a complex process
> about which there are not reliable predictions as to the outcome.... The
> post-colonial state remains the terrain of contest, particularly between
> the various factions and fractions of the petty bourgeoisie.
> —Ibbo Mandaza, 1994

This book presents a fresh analysis of where authoritarian institutions come from and how they order power within a regime. It traces the trajectories of ruling parties and legislatures from an early period of regime consolidation through subsequent episodes of socio-economic and institutional change.

Like Ibbo Mandaza in the above-cited passage, the book understands the post-colonial state as a 'terrain of contest', one dominated by contending economic and political interests. It explores how political institutions—including authoritarian parties and parliaments—become a focus of this elite contestation, both reflecting and *magnifying* a given power distribution across rival factions. Digging a layer deeper, the book underscores how this power distribution itself partly depends on differing post-colonial trajectories of state-led capitalist development. I say 'partly' because, as noted at various points throughout, power has many sources, and politics is nothing if not messy, belying as Mandaza warns, 'reliable predictions'. The book nevertheless offers its analytical framework as one guide among others, sketching some of the material conditions that help structure broad patterns of elite contestation and institutional change.

Wealth, Power, and Authoritarian Institutions. Michaela Collord, Oxford University Press. © Michaela Collord (2024).
DOI: 10.1093/9780191945335.003.0007

To elaborate briefly, the argument breaks down into a three-part analysis encompassing a study of power, parties, and parliaments. First, even if one among multiple, material wealth is an important source of power. Patterns of wealth accumulation vary across authoritarian regimes and within regimes over time, subject notably to post-colonial leaders' contrasting strategies of 'politicized accumulation', themselves informed by varying ideological orientations, strategies of political control, and more. These varying patterns of accumulation then impact on the structure of patron–client factions, and consequently, both party and legislative institutional change.

Where wealth accumulation is more centralized, as in, more closely controlled by state and party leaders, competing elites are less able to finance rival patron–client factions, and authoritarian leaders are better able to discipline the ruling party. In the absence of notable elite contestation, the legislature remains a largely docile and marginal institution.

By contrast, where wealth accumulation is more diffuse, as in, where there is a semi-autonomous class of private accumulators, regime-aligned elites can bankroll rival patron–client networks, the ruling party is more fractious, and elite contestation surfaces within parliament, which thus emerges as an arena for intra-elite bargaining. In so far as legislators and their factional allies then see parliament as a valuable channel through which to pursue their competing interests,[1] they are better able to invest in strengthening it as an institution; they can change the procedure, structure, and material endowment that determine how useful a tool it is for challenging the executive. In this way, a stronger legislature is not only borne out of elite contestation but also helps amplify it, creating new institutional channels for elite actors to pursue their ends.

Understanding that strong legislatures are a product of—and help channel—intra-elite bargaining then helps explain through what mechanisms a strong parliament may impact, notably, distributive outcomes. Given that legislative assertiveness results largely from elite tensions, the influence of the legislature over government budgetary proposals often caters to elite interests. As such, the legislature may favour policies with fairly inegalitarian outcomes, although this is not always the case. The policies parliaments pursue depend on contingent patterns of political organization. Through analyses of specific

---

[1] As clarified at various points throughout the book, the claim is not that legislators are solely motivated by material considerations; some pursue normative aspirations, and sometimes at considerable personal costs. However, the focus on structures of patron–client networks aims to help make sense of broad patterns of elite contestation and institutional change, which constitutes important background context that more normatively motivated MPs must then navigate.

legislative interventions, the book explores when and why legislators do push for more redistributive fiscal policy goals. This occurs where two conditions pertain: one, where elite divisions motivate rival factions to leverage these policy struggles to their advantage; and two, where legislators respond to pressure from popular political organizations outside parliament, notably trade unions, farmers' associations, advocacy groups, and the like.

The study combines cross-case and within-case comparison through an analysis of Tanzania and Uganda with further reference to Kenya and Rwanda as shadow cases. The cross-case comparison helps demonstrate difference in trajectory. As in, where wealth accumulation is relatively centralized and the ruling party disciplined (Tanzania until the 1990s and Rwanda), the legislature remains more marginal. Conversely, where accumulation is more diffuse and the ruling party more fractious (Kenya and Uganda), the legislature gradually strengthens. Within-case comparison, meanwhile, helps confirm that the theorized causal steps linking wealth accumulation and party discipline, on the one hand, and legislative strength, on the other, are present in each case. This within-case analysis also helps explain change over time; as in, regime trajectories can alter and even begin to converge, particularly where—as my theory implies—the underlying economic conditions and patterns of accumulation in a country change. More specifically, economic liberalization in Tanzania from the 1980s gradually fed into greater factional divisions within the ruling party and the rise of a more assertive legislature up to the 2015 elections.

This conclusion now briefly engages with three additional areas of inquiry. First, it expands on the earlier discussion of *authoritarian discontinuities*, examining the significance of John Magufuli's presidency in Tanzania (2015–2021) and the political rupture it caused. Second, moving beyond the focus on dominant party regimes, it engages with the implications of *more competitive multiparty politics* for legislative strengthening. Finally, it reflects on the relationship between legislative strengthening and *democratization*. The analysis elaborated in this book speaks to all three themes while also suggesting avenues for further research. It clarifies how a combination of authoritarian institutional legacies along with changing strategies of 'politicized accumulation' shape the evolving trajectories of authoritarian regimes. It highlights the ongoing interplay between patronage politics and institutional change, including as it pertains to evolving multiparty systems. It also invites a reassessment of the relationship between development and democracy, pointing towards a more circumspect assessment of 'democratic' consolidation and its transformative potential.

7.1 The Political Economy of Authoritarian Discontinuities

As noted above, this book examines not just variation across authoritarian regimes but also how these regimes evolve over time, a point often overlooked in the recent literature on authoritarian parties.[2] Much of the book's discussion of within-case change focuses on Tanzania, whose ruling party many scholars identify as among the most institutionalized in Africa.[3] While this assessment is accurate when comparing cross-country, it again risks downplaying changes in Tanzania's institutional landscape over time, particularly the erosion of CCM's institutional strength after the country's economic liberalization in the 1980s. The ruling party then experienced another notable change in its political economy and institutional make-up after 2015, the cut off point for this study. The latest shift only further underscores the significance of authoritarian discontinuities, and the value of analytical tools that can help make sense of them.

The framework presented in this book provides some of these tools. As before, patterns of wealth accumulation and party structures continued to influence the degree of centralized control exercised by the new President, John Pombe Magufuli. His presidency also draws attention to the politics of succession and the prospects for new leaders to engineer a rupture, or more accurately, a reversal. In brief, he sought to recentralize power through both economic interventions and party reforms, in part aided by CCM's legacy as an 'institutionalized coalition'.

While a full discussion of Magufuli's presidency is beyond the scope of this conclusion, it is worth briefly contextualizing his strategies of regime consolidation within Tanzania's broader post-colonial history. To recap, the book details how Tanzania's founding leaders first centralized wealth accumulation. This then helped them centralize power through a relatively robust party-administrative apparatus while simultaneously ensuring the political marginalization of parliament. Yet economic decline and liberalizing reforms from the 1980s onward upset this balance, leading to more diffuse accumulation, heightened factional contestation, the erosion of CCM's institutional strength, and ultimately, a more assertive legislature. Even with these changes, the institutional legacy of a strong and cohesive ruling party did help delay and, to some extent, limit the process of party institutional decline. For instance, despite a general erosion in CCM's institutional strength after the 1980s, a

---

[2] See Chapter 2 for a discussion of this literature.
[3] Smith, 2005; Morse, 2019.

wealthy and ambitious politician like Edward Lowassa still had to painstakingly build his network through the party structures. Moreover, as detailed
in Chapter 4, he ultimately saw his presidential aspirations thwarted by President Kikwete, who could use party procedure as an alternative source of power
against Lowassa.

Magufuli was the surprise beneficiary of these intra-party tensions, winning
the CCM presidential nomination after Lowassa and Kikwete's rival factions
knocked each other out of the running.[4] Yet as nominee, Magufuli lacked
a strong *mtandao* or faction of his own. He faced a further challenge after
Lowassa defected to become the presidential candidate for an emboldened
opposition coalition, bringing political financiers and CCM members with
him. This was the biggest defection CCM had ever seen, prompting Magufuli's former rivals for the presidential nomination to lend their own support
and campaign infrastructure to a newly constituted election task force.

But what started as a challenge arguably became an opportunity for Magufuli once in office.[5] Although he still needed to build his own base, Lowassa's
departure undermined one of the most powerful informal networks for political coordination within CCM. Meanwhile, many of Lowassa's associates—still
in the party—were left fearful of being labelled *wasaliti*, or traitors. Magufuli
seized this opportunity to fill a vacuum, working to centralize power under his
control both as President and, from mid-2016, as CCM Chairman.

Key to this broader effort was a *new strategy of 'politicized accumulation'*,
which involved tighter control over private sector activity, targeted policing of
private sector elites, and greater investment by and through the State, thereby
shifting ownership and accumulation opportunities to centrally administered
state agencies and state- and military-owned firms. The overarching effect
of these interventions was to limit private accumulation, or at least to make
it more conditional on political loyalty and perhaps, as scholars like Anto-
nio Andreoni argue, economic discipline; at the same time, Magufuli's statist
emphasis redirected the flow of resources through public sector entities, of
whose managing directors he was himself the appointing authority. In so far as
this economic strategy served to *recentralize power*, it went hand-in-hand with
a parallel campaign to reform CCM. As party Chairman, Magufuli introduced
changes to party structures and procedures, for instance, reforming candidate
selection to make it more exclusive, tightening internal party controls over
campaign finance, slashing the frequency of party meetings, and reducing

[4] See Chapter 4 for details.
[5] This and the following paragraph draw on Collord, 2022.

the membership of key party organs. Observers saw these moves as aimed at marginalizing the established factional networks within these bodies. Magufuli and those close to him talked about creating a 'New CCM', albeit 'new' in the sense of renewing an older tradition of centrally controlled, 'institutionalized' ruling party structures insulated from the 'corrupting' influence of factional politics.[6] The pursuit of more centralized control and discipline also—in keeping with the theory of this book—included an effort to politically dominate the legislature as an important arena of elite contestation.[7]

Magufuli was effectively trying to turn back the clock, working to control private political finance and reinvesting in the institutional discipline of the ruling party. He used other tools to recentralize power as well, including overtly repressive manoeuvres targeting both actors within CCM and opposition parties.[8] His broader ideological orientation and development intentions—leaving aside the political steps he adopted to achieve them—were also complex and deserve further attention, particularly his brand of 'authoritarian populism' and 'state capitalism'.[9] Yet in saying he sought to 'turn back the clock', I here retain a narrower focus on his project to reorder power within CCM.

Crucially, this strategy further underscores the significance of the analytical framework presented in this book. His approach indicates both the importance of CCM's institutional legacies and the need for a complimentary politico-economic strategy to reinforce direct party strengthening efforts. Tanzania's recent history under Magufuli can also shed light on authoritarian discontinuities elsewhere, notably how intersecting economic and institutional dynamics can reorder power within a ruling coalition.[10]

---

[6] Some observers might liken Magufuli's institutional manipulation more to 'personalization' than 'institutionalization' in so far as a primary outcome was to centralize control under his leadership. Yet as Slater (2003: 82) helpfully underscores, 'personalization' and institutionalization' are 'not as antithetical in authoritarian regimes as in democracies', adding, 'Despotic power (the power to decide) can become highly personalized even as infrastructural power (the power to implement) remains highly institutionalized.' In this vein, CCM reforms under Magufuli arguably improved the ruling party's 'infrastructural power' even as they further consolidated Magufuli's 'despotic power'.

[7] It is worth noting that, while unresponsive and authoritarian in his treatment of many, especially elite actors, his administration was not entirely closed off to popular protest or organized interest group demands where these were addressed directly to the Party and Presidency and not via parliament or more diffuse elite networks. For instance, his unprecedented 'machinga ID' policy—which enabled street vendors, hawkers, and other informal workers to operate more freely in urban areas— was influenced by a combination of protests and advocacy by workers' associations and trade unions. Key informant interviews, Dar es Salaam, July and August 2023. Steiler and Nyirenda, 2021; George et al., 2023. See also below on Magufuli's 'populism'.

[8] Paget, 2017, 2021a.

[9] On Magufuli's 'populism' as well as Tanzania's evolving 'state capitalism', see: Jacob and Pedersen, 2018; Nyamsenda, 2018; Paget, 2020, 2021b; Dye et al., 2022; Shivji, 2021.

[10] See for instance the political rupture within Angola's MPLA following the transition from President Dos Santos to João Lourenço. Generoso de Almeida, 2018.

In addition, it invites further reflection on the relative importance of *authoritarian structures versus the agency of individual leaders,* who act from within but can also seek to reshape the structural constraints confronting them when they gain office.[11] Magufuli's predecessors in the post-socialist period—Presidents Mwinyi (1985–1995), Mkapa (1995–2005), and Kikwete (2005–2015)—all had their own strategies of 'politicized accumulation' and party control. However, these focused largely on reordering factional alliances without—after the initial period of structural adjustment reforms—radically altering Tanzania's broader politico-economic trajectory. Magufuli, by contrast, sought to break more fundamentally with this trajectory, in part, by targeting its very economic foundations. His ambition in this regard surprised many. It served as a reminder of the economic power of the state, even in a post-structural adjustment context.[12] It was also far riskier and more politically controversial, both at home and abroad, than the actions of his predecessors. He was, in effect, defying structural constraints. The challenges involved—along with Magufuli's unique political position and personal outlook—perhaps go some way towards explaining why more authoritarian leaders do not attempt something similar.

While Magufuli's presidency is an important case on which to reflect, we cannot know where his ambitions may have led. His death in 2021 and the succession of President Samia Suluhu Hassan—who is close to former President Kikwete and revived much of his economic orientation and political networks—curtailed what was ultimately a brief effort in politico-economic restructuring.[13]

7.2 Multiparty Competition and Parliament

In so far as this book discusses a multiparty transition, the analysis relates to contexts where an incumbent, dominant party retains power. The argument put forward stresses that, under these circumstances of dominant party rule, a multiparty transition is itself not necessarily a watershed moment, particularly where legislative autonomy is concerned. Rather, it is the configuration of patron–client networks within the ruling party that is most important in determining both its cohesion as well as the extent of legislative strengthening and assertiveness. Where there are pre-existing factional tensions within the ruling

---

[11] For more on Magufuli, succession politics, and the importance of structure versus agency in shaping authoritarian regimes trajectories, see Collord (2021b, 2022).

[12] Please see Chapter 3 for further discussion.

[13] On further changes in Tanzanian politics under Magufuli's successor, President Samia Suluhu Hassan, see Nyamsenda and Collord, *forthcoming.*

party, emerging opposition parties can help galvanize legislative activity, in part leveraging these tensions. But where ruling party cohesion and discipline remain strong, opposition parties will struggle. The performance of Tanzania's *Bunge* under President Magufuli helps confirm this point. Despite opposition parties winning a historically unprecedented number of legislative seats in the 2015 elections, they had minimal impact in the legislature. This was due to the direct repression they experienced but also to the *renewed discipline within CCM itself*.[14]

The above-outlined argument nevertheless leaves open the question, what happens when a ruling party starts to face a more serious opposition challenge? Or indeed, what happens when dominant party politics gives way to regular alternation between different parties in government? Again, the conclusion does not leave space to do these questions justice, but I will outline two ways in which the analytical framework in this book may inform further research.

First, regarding opposition parties themselves, there is reason to think that, as they gain more electoral appeal, their institutional strength and cohesion will depend on many of the same factors as shape authoritarian party organization. We should look especially at how patterns of accumulation and political finance affects the institutional make-up of opposition parties, notably whether they are more personalized and fractious entities or whether they show signs of greater institutional consolidation and unity. This emphasis harks back to an older Africanist literature more preoccupied with how party politics in the late colonial and post-Independence period reflected 'domestic struggle among classes competing for control', to quote from Jan Jalmert Jorgensen's excellent analysis of Uganda's party politics.[15] More recent work also re-engages with questions of private accumulation, economic structure, and inequality as they pertain to multiparty politics, albeit with somewhat divergent analytical approaches and findings.[16]

Questions of accumulation aside, the legacies of authoritarian parties themselves likely influence the conditions for opposition party development, with contrasting outcomes across countries. There is already a burgeoning literature on the authoritarian roots of opposition party organization.[17] What this book helps draw attention to, though, is the need to examine both the material base of opposition party organizing and the institutional context

---

[14] Collord, 2021, 2022.

[15] Jorgensen, 1981: 176. See also Hodgkin, 1971; Sklar, 1963; Sathyamurthy, 1975; Nolutshungu, 1990.

[16] Mmuya and Chaligha, 1994; Ajulu, 1999; Arriola, 2013; Boone et al., 2022.

[17] From the comparative Africanist literature, see for instance: Lebas, 2011; Riedl, 2014; Cheeseman and Larmer, 2015; Paget, 2019.

within which these parties operate, particularly how this context is shaped by an authoritarian inheritance. Tanzania's largest opposition parties, which were gaining ground until a renewed authoritarian crackdown after the 2015 elections, have tended to build up formal institutional structures that mirror the ruling party.[18] In Uganda, meanwhile, opposition parties have institutional structures that are less coherent and more clearly dominated by informal patronage networks, bearing some notable similarities to the NRM.[19] As for Kenya, the institutionally weak and fractious KANU fragmented after the 2002 elections, giving way to an array of personalized and often short-lived opposition parties.[20] In all three instances, the structure and prominence of rival patronage networks, combined with institutionalized patterns of political organization established under authoritarian rule, appear to have a direct influence on opposition party development.

There are, it should be stressed, other factors influencing party organization and electoral politics more generally. Perhaps most frequently discussed in the literature is ethnicity. Yet taking ethnicity as an example, future research could examine possible links between patterns of accumulation and patronage politics, party institutionalization, and the political salience of ethnicity. There is on older literature as well as important recent work exploring these relationships, suggesting it is an area ripe for continued research.[21] Beyond ethnicity, there is also growing interest in the ideological or policy orientation of parties. Ideational differences often appear to be lacking among elite-dominated parties,[22] or else are reducible to valence issues;[23] more recent scholarship complicates this view, though. Notably, it underscores how where these ideational differences do emerge, either across parties or 'persistent regional electoral blocs', they can be understood as 'the expression of territorial politics arising from regional economic differentiation'.[24]

This discussion of opposition parties aside, the analysis in this book can also shed light on how multiparty competition affects legislative politics. The difference between an authoritarian or dominant party parliament versus a multiparty parliament is likely one of degree rather than kind. As in, holding all else constant, the introduction of more multiparty representation in parliament will not change the fact that, one, elite contestation helps drive heightened legislative activity and, two, the intensity of this contestation

[18] Paget, 2019.
[19] Wilkins et al., 2021.
[20] Anderson, 2003.
[21] Koter, 2013; Boone and Nyeme, 2015; Boone et al., 2022; Pengl et al., 2022.
[22] Nathan, 2019.
[23] Bleck and van de Walle, 2018.
[24] Boone et al., 2022; 2. See also Resnick, 2014; Kim, 2020; Boone, 2024.

depends on the prevailing configuration of elite factions.[25] As implied in the previous section, this factional politics is not the unique preserve of authoritarian ruling parties; rather, there is a need to better understand: the factional composition of both ruling *and opposition* parties; where these intra-party tensions stem from, including underlying structures of accumulation; and ultimately, how they affect party discipline in parliament.[26]

The strength of ties *between parties*, notably when in coalition, is also significant.[27] In this vein, the Kenyan parliament after the 2002 elections was relatively assertive, and this because then President Mwai Kibaki exerted little influence over the parties that sponsored him in the election.[28] He also struggled to hold his coalition partners together, many of whom were established politicians with powerful patronage networks. By contrast, the Kenyan Parliament later grew more subservient, and this after President Uhuru Kenyatta worked to centralize control over his coalition, albeit temporarily, with efforts to turn it into a party.[29]

In sum, this book, although a study of authoritarian parties and legislatures, may also provide additional insights to guide an analysis of party organizing and legislative politics in a more multiparty context. Certainly, the significance of intra-party factions and elite bargaining in the legislature may not necessarily be much diminished where dominant parties lose their hegemonic hold.[30] This somewhat pessimistic assertion does, however, raise further questions about how we should understand democratization more broadly.

7.3 The Struggle for Democracy, the Struggle for Power

There is a substantial institutionalist literature that suggests legislative strengthening furthers democratic consolidation, particularly when accompanied by heightened multiparty competition.[31] An assertive legislature can, it

---

[25] On elite contestation, see Opalo, 2022.

[26] As discussed in Chapters 4 and 5, the wider legislative studies literature notes that intra- as well as inter-party politics influences legislative activity more widely, not just in a particular region or time periods.

[27] Chaisty et al., 2018.

[28] Opalo, 2014.

[29] Ibid.

[30] In addition to the above note on the wider legislative studies literature, there is also a political sociology literature on the 'power elite' and a varied political economy literature that draws out the dominance of elite networks within parties and legislative institutions, and this across a diversity of geographies and regimes types, be they conventionally labelled 'authoritarian' or 'democratic': Khan, 2005; Domhoff, 2007; Winters and Page, 2009; Hacker and Pierson, 2010; Rodan and Jayasuriya, 2012; Gilens and Page, 2014.

[31] See Chapter 2.

is argued, provide a check on the executive and ensure more popular representation; it is the forum within which parties, which otherwise serve as mere electoral vehicles, can work to address the interests of their voters.[32] The analysis in this book presents a more normatively ambivalent view. While a stronger parliament may entail greater political participation, a key feature of democratization,[33] those who dominate may still belong to a narrow socio-economic stratum. The book's approach thus diverges from an analysis that first ascribes a set of classic functions to the legislature and then derives conclusions about its democratizing potential.

There is, however, a historically rooted strand of the democratization literature with which this book is more closely aligned. This work acknowledges the internal contradictions and indeterminacy of what is essentially a piecemeal process, one that we may—largely in retrospect—label 'democratization'.[34] Capoccia and Ziblatt, for instance, reject the 'common and misleading assumption that the contemporary functions of particular political institutions can always explain their historical emergence'.[35] Rather, referencing the study of European democracies, they argue that scholars should '[bring] in the politics of institutional change' and, in so doing, reconstruct 'what actors were actually fighting about' when institutional reforms were first introduced.[36] Similarly, referring to the more recent history of southeast Asian regimes, Rodan and Jayasuriya stress that to truly understand an institutional reform agenda and its significance, '[I]t is paramount to understand who is actually supporting particular institutional reform projects, why and what conflicts and interests might be marginalized or privileged as a result.'[37]

What then, to return to the original question, does this say about legislative change and democratization, particularly in Africa? Again drawing on Capoccia and Ziblatt, one view could be that African parliaments *initially* strengthen because of elite contestation and serve elite interests, but they could over time become part of the 'complex institutional configuration of democracies', as has happened elsewhere.[38] As such, they could provide a stronger check on executive overreach and allow for a more genuinely inclusive politics.[39] This

---

[32] Fish, 2006: 12–13.
[33] See Dahl (1971) on the importance of participation and liberalization, or contestation, for democracy.
[34] Capoccia and Ziblatt, 2010; Rodan and Jayasuriya, 2012.
[35] Capoccia and Ziblatt, 2010: 939.
[36] Ibid., 940.
[37] Rodan and Jayasuriya, 2012: 187.
[38] Capoccia and Ziblatt, 2010: 940. See also Bermeo, 2010.
[39] There are already examples of some parliaments, e.g. blocking the removal of presidential term limits. In an argument that resonates with this book's emphasis on elite power struggles, Cheeseman

optimistic idea nevertheless leaves the question, what further changes would be needed to transform legislative politics in this way?

A set of 'big picture', political economy arguments point to a decidedly pessimistic answer, albeit one that resonates with the analysis in this book. In the advanced industrialized economies where democracy has taken root, the democratization process accompanied a range of profound socioeconomic changes, including the expansion of a bourgeois accumulating class.[40] Meanwhile, diverse social movements—including an organized working class— were essential in securing greater political inclusion and more egalitarian distributive outcomes across lines of race, class, gender, disability, and more.[41] Yet unique political and economic conditions enabled the above, still fragile transformations in Global North democracies—and often at Africa's expense.[42] Moreover, today's global political economy—not to mention unfolding ecological crisis—present the continent with serious challenges in its efforts to achieve similar socio-economic change, despite notable variation in outcomes across countries.[43]

This emphasis on the importance of structural transformation hardly resolves whether or how the legislature could become part of a 'complex institutional configuration of democracies'; instead, it opens a much broader discussion about the relationship between democracy and development. It is a discussion that critics of a western-backed 'democratization agenda' have raised since the 1990s, all while questioning an excessive focus on institutions. In this vein, Adebayo Olukoshi, Thandika Mkandawire, and others have observed how a preoccupation with elections, parties, and the like risked overlooking how the wider context of externally-imposed structural adjustment reforms was both denying citizens genuine 'choice' and eroding the capacity of would-be developmental states to satisfy popular expectations.[44] Issa Shivji has argued even more forcefully for a 'new democracy' rooted in 'popular livelihoods', 'popular power', and 'popular participation'.[45] More recently,

---

(2019: 311) identifies two key factors shaping whether term limits are preserved, 'namely the extent of organized opposition and the ability of the president to enforce unity within the ruling party'. He adds, 'Significantly, while these factors are shaped by the quality of democracy, they are not reducible to it.'

[40] On the importance of a rising bourgeoisie accumulating class, at least for the early stages of economic reform, see: Moore, 1966; Rodan and Jayasuriya, 2012; Ansell and Samuels, 2014.

[41] See for instance: Davis, 1983; Esping-Andersen, 1990; Taylor, 2016. More inclusive and egalitarian gains also remain imperfect and are in retreat in many established democracies, including due to changed economic circumstances and weakened popular mobilization: Hacker and Pierson, 2010; Palier and Thelen, 2010; Taylor, 2016.

[42] Rodney, 2018; Hickel et al., 2021.

[43] Arrighi, 2002; Mkandawire, 2017; Jha et al., 2021; Fox and Goodfellow; Goodfellow, 2022.

[44] Mkandawire and Olukoshi, 1995; Mkandawire, 2001, 2017.

[45] Shivji 2013.

amidst renewed concern about autocratization, Ken Opalo has commented, 'Making democracy work in the 2020s will require significant unlearning of the lessons of the 1990s.'[46] It will require moving beyond 'merely institution- alizing politics and routinizing electoral processes', which has left 'large shares of citizens [...] condemned to live precarious lives.' Instead, there needs to be 'developmentalist democracy'. Consistent with the emphasis in this book, such a democracy would involve 'cultivating and mobilizing voters' through their own, mass-based interest groups.

Returning to the legislature, a more modest set of considerations present themselves. Rather than speculate about a future, more democratic parlia- ment, we would do well to focus on 'what really matters to politics' now.[47] This book has argued that an institution like the legislature works as a tool to maintain, magnify, or contest power, shaping whose interests are served and whose repressed. It follows that, instead of focusing more narrowly on legisla- tive institutions and institutional change, more energy could be invested in understanding the intersection between these institutions and the underlying political organization that determines in whose interests they operate.

Of central importance, as argued in earlier chapters,[48] is the organization of otherwise marginalized groups—small farmers and traders, transport workers, wastepickers, residents of underserved informal settlements, and professionals providing key social services, like health workers and teachers, among oth- ers. When and how do these groups organize into associations, unions, or co-operatives? How do they seek to influence decision-making, and how—if at all—do they leverage formal legislative processes? As examples from Uganda,[49] Tanzania,[50] and Nigeria illustrate,[51] there are instances of creative organizing to study and learn from. Pursuing this inquiry further—including what it entails in terms of practical support and solidarity—is one fruitful direction for future research. This work can, for instance, develop a more fine-grained analysis of sectoral and sub-national variation in patterns of accumulation, organizing, and party accountability, thereby improving our understand of when and how organised interests are able to intervene in particular issue areas.[52]

[46] Opalo, 2023.
[47] Rodan and Jayasuriya, 2012: 187.
[48] See Chapter 6. See also: Collord, 2022.
[49] See Chapter 6.
[50] Collord, 2022.
[51] Okafor, 2009.
[52] There is a still a relatively small body of work exploring this area as it pertains to legislative accountability. More generally on the significance of sectoral and sub-national variation, see: Kjaer, 2015; Martiniello and Nyamsenda, 2018; Kim, 2020; Boone et al., 2022.

Ultimately, popular organizing will hardly overturn a prevailing elite bias in political decision-making. Reflecting on prospects for democratization in early 1990s Nigeria, Sam Noluthshungu wrote,

> It is difficult to see how Nigeria could be any nearer democracy without the political organisation of the vast majority of the population through structures over which they have some direct control. As in most of the continent, they are caught in a vicious circle: workers, artisans, small traders, and small farmers are not politically organised because there is no democracy, but there can be no democracy because the people are not organised.

I share both Nolutshungu's emphasis on the significance of popular organization and his concern about the obstacles limiting its scope. Yet in regimes where political elites dominate, be they authoritarian or democratic, elite tensions can still leave room for popular organizations to gain political leverage and to advance a more progressive redistributive agenda, including—on occasion—through the legislature.

Bibliography

Interviews

Tanzania (68)

CCM MP	19
CHADEMA MP	8
NCCR-Mageuzi MP	4
CUF MP	3
ACT-Wazalendo MP	1
MP Assistant	1
Parliamentary Staff	9
Civil Society Campaigner, Organiser	7
Party Officer/Activist	12
Journalist	2
Businessman	2

Uganda[1] (90)

NRM MP	20
FDC MP	9
DP MP	3
UPC MP	5
Conservative Party MP	1
Independent MP	3
Parliamentary Staff	10
Civil Society Campaigner, Organiser	20
Party Officer/Activist	7
Journalist	3
Businessman	3
Donors	7

[1] For MPs who served in either the Constituent Assembly or in the pre-2006 Movement parliament, I list them with the party they joined after the multiparty transition.

Newspapers and Other Contemporary Periodicals

The following newspapers and periodicals were consulted by means of keyword search, 'tip offs' in other primary and secondary sources, particularly interviews, or by focusing on selected dates of significance.

Africa Confidential (UK)
Azania Post (Tanzania)
Citizen (Tanzania)
Daily Monitor (Uganda)

Daily News (Tanzania)
East African (Kenya)
Independent (Uganda)
Indian Ocean Newsletter (France)
Majira (Tanzania)
Mawio (Tanzania)
Mtanzania (Tanzania)
Mwananchi (Tanzania)
New Vision (Uganda)
Nipashe (Tanzania)
Observer (Uganda)
Raia Mwema (Tanzania)
Tanzania Affairs (UK)
Tanzania Daima (Tanzania)
Voice of Teachers (Uganda)

Government, Party and Parliamentary Publications

Parliament of Tanzania

Bunge la Tanzania. 1995. 'Kanuni za Kudumu za Bunge, Toleo la 2007'. (Parliamentary Standing Orders, ed. 1995). Dodoma, Tanzania. Accessed, *Bunge* library.

Bunge la Tanzania. 2001. 'Kanuni za Kudumu za Bunge, Toleo la 2007'. Dodoma, Tanzania. Accessed, *Bunge* library.

Bunge la Tanzania. 2007. 'Kanuni za Kudumu za Bunge, Toleo la 2007'. Dodoma, Tanzania. Accessed, *Bunge* library.

Bunge la Tanzania. 2013. 'Kanuni za Kudumu za Bunge, Toleo la Aprili 2013'. Dodoma, Tanzania. Accessed, *Bunge* library.

National Assembly of Tanganyika. 1961. 'Standing Orders and Rules of the National Assembly of Tanganyika'. Dar es Salaam, Tanzania. Accessed, *Bunge* library.

Tanganyika African National Union/Chama Cha Mapinduzi

CCM. 2010. 'Katiba ya Chama cha Mapinduzi 1977, Toleo la 2010'. Dodoma, Tanzania: CCM.

CCM. 16 October 1993. 'Kanuni za Kamati ya Wabunge Wote wa Chama Cha Mapinduzi'. Dodoma, Tanzania: CCM. Accessed, *Bunge* Library.

Kikwete, Jakaya Mrisho. 23 July 2016. 'Hotuba ya Mhe. Jakaya Mrisho Kikwete, Mwenyekiti wa Chama Cha Mapinduzi, Wakati wa Mkutano Mkuu wa CCM'. Meeting of the CCM NEC, Dodoma, Tanzania: CCM. Accessed July 2016: ccm.or.tz

Magufuli, John Pombe. 23 July 2016. 'Hotuba ya Mhe. Dkt. John Pombe Magufuli, Rais wa Jamhuri ya Muungano wa Tanzania na Mwenyekiti wa Chama cha Mapinduzi Kwenye Mku-tano Mkuu wa Taifa wa CCM'. Meeting of the CCM NEC, Dodoma, Tanzania: CCM. Accessed July 2016: ccm.or.tz

Government of Uganda

Constitutional Review Commission. 2003. 'The Report of the Commission of Inquiry (Constitu-tional Review): Findings and Recommendations'. Kampala, Uganda: Government of Uganda. Accessed, Parliament library.

Government of Uganda. 2004. 'Government White Paper on: (1) The Report of the Commission of Inquiry (Constitutional Review); (2) Government Proposals not addressed by the report of the Commission of Inquiry (Constitutional Review)'. Kampala, Uganda: Governemnt of Uganda. Accessed 23 June 2018: https://www.cmi.no/pdf/?file=/uganda/doc/government-whitepaper.pdf

Government of Uganda. 2012. 'Public Finance Bill'. Kampala, Uganda: Government of Uganda. Accessed 18 December 2023: https://resourcegovernance.org/sites/default/files/documents/uganda_public_finance_bill_20121.pdf

Kiwanuka, Maria. 21 May 2013. Letter from Minister of Finance, Planning and Economic Development to the Chairperson of the Sectoral Committee on Finance, Planning and Economic Development, 'Re: Amendment to the Public Finance Bill, 2012'. Kampala, Uganda. Accessed, Parliament library.

Parliament of Uganda

NRC. Date unspecified. 'The Interim Rules of Procedure for the National Resistance Council of Uganda'. Kampala, Uganda. Accessed, Parliamentary library.

Parliament of Uganda. September 2011. 'Report of the Committee on Social Services on the Ministerial Policy Statement and Budget Estimates for the Financial Year 2011/12'. Kampala, Uganda. Accessed, Parliament library.

Parliament of Uganda. 8 September 2011. 'Budget Committee Report on the Budget Estimates for FY 2011/12'. Kampala, Uganda. Accessed, Parliament library.

Parliament of Uganda. August 2012. 'Report of the Parliamentary Committee on Health on the Ministerial Policy Statement for the Health Sector for the Financial year 2012/2013'. Kampala, Uganda. Accessed, Parliament library.

Parliament of Uganda. September 2012. 'Report of the Budget Committee of Parliament on the harmonisation of the budget figures before supply'. Kampala, Uganda. Accessed, Parliament library.

Parliament of Uganda. 18 September 2012. 'Report of the Committee on Budget on the instruction from Parliament to find funds for a 20% salary increment for teachers from the budget estimates for FY 2013/14'. Kampala, Uganda. Accessed, Parliament library.

Parliament of Uganda. Date unspecified. 'Rules of Procedure of the Parliament of Uganda', 6th Parliament (1996–2001). Kampala, Uganda. Accessed, Parliament library.

Parliament of Uganda. Date unspecified. 'Rules of Procedure of the Parliament of Uganda', 7th Parliament (2001–2006). Kampala, Uganda. Accessed, Parliament library.

Parliament of Uganda. 2006. 'Rules of Procedure of the Parliament of Uganda'. Kampala, Uganda. Accessed, Parliament library.

Parliament of Uganda. 2012. 'Rules of Procedure of the Parliament of Uganda'. Kampala, Uganda. Accessed, Parliament library.

YPA. Date unspecified. 'The Constitution of the Young Parliamentary Association'. Kampala, Uganda. Accessed, Parliament library.

National Resistance Movement

NRM. 2003. 'Constitution of the National Resistance Movement (ed. 2003)'. Kampala, Uganda: NRM. Accessed, Parliament library.

NRM National Executive Committee Ad Hoc Issues Committee. 2009. 'Report of the NRM National Executive Committee Ad Hoc Issues Committee (NAIC)'. Kampala, Uganda: NRM. Accessed, Parliamentary Library.

NRM Parliamentary Caucus Select Committee. 2014. 'Final Report of the NRM Parliamentary Caucus Select Committee on NRM Primary Elections'. Kampala, Uganda: NRM. Accessed, courtesy of journalist.

Kenya African National Union

KANU. 1970. 'Report by the KANU Re-Organization Committee'. Mombasa, Kenya: KANU. Accessed, Lionel Cliffe's personal archive.

KANU. 1971. 'Meeting of the KANU National Governing Council'. Mombasa, Kenya: KANU. Accessed, Lionel Cliffe's personal archive.

Published books and articles

Abidi, S. 1996. 'The return of Asians to Uganda'. *Africa Quarterly* 36 (3):45–58.

Abrahamsen, Rita, and Gerald Bareebe. 2016. 'Uganda's 2016 Elections: Not Even Faking it Anymore'. *African Affairs* 115 (461): 751–765.

ACFIM (Alliance for Campaign Finance). 2016. 'Extended Study on Campaign Financing for Presidential and Member of Parliament Races'. ACFIM.

Afriyie, Osie, Jennifer Nyoni, and Adam Ahmat. 2019. 'The State of strategic plans for the health workforce in Africa'. *BMJ Global Health* 4(9): 1–5.

Ajulu, Rok. 1999. 'Kenya: The survival of the old order'. In Daniel, R. Southall and M. Szeftel (eds), *Voting for Democracy: Watershed Elections in Contemporary Anglophone Africa*. Ashgate. 110–135.

Ajulu, Rok. 2021. *Post-colonial Kenya: The Rise of an Authoritarian and Predatory State*. Routledge.

Allen, Chris. 1995. 'Understanding African politics'. *Review of African Political Economy* 22(65): 301–320.

Aminzade, Ronald. 2013. *Race, Nation and Citizenship in Post-colonial Africa: The Case of Tanzania*. Cambridge University Press.

Anderson, David. 2003. 'Kenya's Elections 2002: The Dawning of a New Era?' *African Affairs* 102(407): 331–342.

Ansell, Ben, and David Samuels. 2014. *Inequality and Democratization: An Elite-Competition Approach*. Cambridge University Press.

Ansoms, An, and Donatella Rostagno. 2012. 'Rwanda's Vision 2020 Halfway Through: What the Eye Does Not See'. *Review of African Political Economy* 39 (133): 427–450.

Arrighi, Giovanni. 2002. 'The African Crisis: World Systemic and Regional Aspects'. *New Left Review* 15 (May–June): 5–35.

Arriola, Leonardo Rafael. 2013. *Multi-ethnic Coalitions in Africa: Business Financing of Opposition Election Campaigns*. Cambridge University Press.

Arter, David. 2006. 'Conclusion. Questioning the 'Mezey Question: An Interrogatory Framework for the Comparative Study of Legislatures'. *The Journal of Legislative Studies* 12 (3–4): 462–482.

Babeiya, Edwin. 2011. 'Electoral Corruption and the Politics of Elections Financing in Tanzania'. *Journal of Politics and Law* 4 (2): 91–103.

Balachandran, P.K. 1981. 'An Embattled Community: Asians in East Africa Today'. *African Affairs* 80 (320): 317–325.

Baregu, Mwesiga. 2004. 'Parliamentary Oversight of Defence and Security in Tanzania's Multiparty Parliament'. In L. R. Le Roux and M. Ngoma (eds), *Guarding the Guardians—Parliamentary Oversight and Civil–Military relations: The Challenges for SADC*. Institute for Security Studies. 33–43.

Barkan, Joel. 1979. 'Bringing Home the Pork: Legislator Behavior, Rural Development, and Political Change in East Africa'. In J. Smith and L. Musolf (eds), *Legislatures in Development*. Duke University Press. 265–288.

Barkan, Joel, ed. 2009. *Legislative Power in Emerging African Democracies*. Lynne Rienner Publishers.

Barkan, Joel. 2013. 'Emerging Legislatures'. In N. Cheeseman, D. Anderson. and A. Scheibler (eds), *Routledge Handbook of African Politics*. Routledge. 252–264.

Barker, Jonathan, and John Saul. 1974. 'The Tanzanian Elections in post-Arusha Perspective'. In C. K. C. D. e. S. E. S. Committee (ed.), *Socialism and Participation: Tanzania's 1970 National Elections*. Tanzania Publishing House. 9–43.

Barya, John-Jean. 2010. 'Trade Unions, Liberalisation and Politics in Uganda'. In B. Beckman, S. Buhlungu, and L. Sachikonye (eds), *Trade Unions and Party Politics: Labour Movements in Africa*. Human Sciences Research Council Press. 85–108.

Basedau, Matthias, and Alexander Stroh. 2008. 'Measuring Party Institutionalization in Developing Countries: A New Research Instrument Applied to 28 African Political Parties'. In G. I. o. G. a. A. Studies (ed.), *GIGA Working Papers*.

Bates, Robert H. 2014. 'The New Institutionalism'. In S. Galiani and I. Sened (eds). *Institutions, Economic Growth, and Propety Rights: The Legacy of Douglass North*. Cambridge University Press. 50–65.

Bavu, Immanuel. 1990. 'Ilala: The Politics of Ethnicity in a Cosmopolitan Setting'. In Haroub Othman, Immanuel Bavau, and Michael Okema (eds), *Tranzania: Democracy in Transition*. Dar es Salaam University Press, 88–102.

Baylies, Carolyn, and Morris Szeftel. 1984. 'The Rise of the Political Prominence of the Zambian Business Class'. In C. Gertzel, C. Baylies, and M. Szeftel (eds), *The Dynamics of the One-Party State in Zambia*. Manchester University Press. 58–78.

Baylies, Carolyn, and Morris Szeftel. 1992. 'The Fall and Rise of Multi-Party Politics in Zambia'. *Review of African Political Economy* 54 (2): 75–91.

Beach, Derek, and Rasmus Brun Pedersen. 2013. *Process-Tracing Methods*. University of Michigan Press.

Behuria, Pritish. 2016. 'Centralising Rents and Dispersing Power while Pursuing Development? Exploring the Strategic Uses of Military Firms in Rwanda'. *Review of African Political Economy* 43 (150): 630–647.

Behuria, Pritish, Lars Buur, and Hazel Gray. 2017. 'Studying Political Settlements in Africa'. *African Affairs* 116 (464): 508–525.

Behuria, Pritish, and Tom Goodfellow. 2016. 'The Political Settlement and "Deals Environment" in Rwanda: Unpacking Two Decades of Economic Growth'. In E. S. I.D. Centre (ed.), *Effective States and Inclusive Development Working Papers No. 57*. University of Manchester. 1–41.

Beinin, Joel. 2021. 'Introduction'. In Joel Beinin, Bassam Haddad, and Sherene Seikaly (eds), *A Critical Political Economy of the Middle East and North Africa*. Standford University Press: 1–21.

Berman, Bruce. 1998. 'Ethnicity, Patronage and the African State: The Politics of Uncivil Nationalism'. *African Affairs* 97: 305–341.

Bermeo, Nancy. 2010. 'Interests, Inequality and Illusion in the Choice for Fair Elections'. *Comparative Political Studies* 43 (8–9): 1119–1147.

Bienen, Henry. 1970. *Tanzania: Party Transformation and Economic Development*. Princeton University Press.

Bienen, Henry. 1974. *Tanzania: Party Transformation and Economic Development* (second edition). Princeton University Press.

Bleck, Jaimie, and Nicholas Van de Walle. 2018. *Electoral Politics in Africa since 1990: Continuity in Change*. Cambridge University Press.

Block, Steven. 2002. 'Political Business Cycles, Democratization and Economic Reform: The Case of Africa'. *Journal of Development Economics* 67: 205–228.

Blondel, Jean. 1970. 'Legislative Behaviour: Some Steps towards a Cross-national Measurement'. *Government and Opposition* 5 (1): 67–85.

Blondel, Jean. 1973. *Comparative Legislatures*. Prentice-Hall.

Blyth, Mark. 2002. *Great Transformations: Economic Ideas and Institutional Change in the Twentieth Century*. Cambridge University Press.

Boix, Carles, and Milan Svolik. 2013. 'The Foundations of Limited Authoritarian Government: Institutions, Commitment, and Power-Sharing in Dictatorships'. *The Journal of Politics* 75 (2): 300–316.

Boone, Catherine. 1990. 'The Making of a Rentier Class: Wealth Accumulation and Political Control in Senegal'. *The Journal of Development Studies* 26 (3): 425–449.

Boone, Catherine. 1992. *Merchant Capital and the Roots of State Power in Senegal, 1930–1985*. Cambridge University Press.

Boone, Catherine. 2003. *Political Topographies of the African state: Territorial Authority and Institutional Choice*. Cambridge University Press.

Boone, Catherine. 2007. 'Property and Constitutional Order: Land Tenure Reform and the Future of the African State'. *African Affairs* 106 (425): 557–586.

Boone, Catherine. 2014. *Property and Political Order in Africa: Land Rights and the Structure of Politics*. Cambridge University Press.

Boone, Catherine. 2024. *Inequality and political cleavage in Africa: Regionalism by design*. Cambridge University Press.

Boone, Catherine, and Lydia Nyeme. 2015. 'Land Institutions and Political Ethnicity in Africa: Evidence fromTanzania'. *Comparative Politics* 48 (1): 67–86.

Boone, Catherine, Michael Wahman, Stephan Kyburz, and Andrew Linke. 2022. 'Regional Cleavages in African Politics: Persistent Electoral Blocs and Territorial Oppositions'. *Political Geography* 99: 1–24.

Booth, David, and Frederick Golooba-Mutebi. 2012. 'Developmental Patrimonialism? The Case of Rwanda'. *African Affairs* 111 (444): 379–403.

Brady, David, and Epstein, David. 1997. 'Intraparty Preferences, Heterogeneity, and the Origins of the Modern Congress: Progressive Reformers in the House and Senate, 1890–1920'. *The Journal of Law, Economics and Organizations* 13 (1): 26–49.

Branson, Nick. 2015. 'Party Rules: Consolidating Power through Constitutional Reform in Tanzania'. Africa Research Institute.

Bratton, Michael, and Nicholas van de Walle. 1997. *Democratic Experiments in Africa*. Cambridge University Press.

Brierley, Sarah. 2012. 'Party Unity and Presidential Dominance: Parliamentary Development in the Fourth Republic of Ghana'. *Journal of Contemporary African Studies* 30 (3): 419–439.

Brownlee, Jason. 2007. *Authoritarianism in an Age of Democratization*. Cambridge University Press.

Bryceson, Deborah. 2002. 'The Scramble in Africa: Reorienting Rural Livelihoods'. *World Development* 30 (5): 725–739.

Bryceson, Deborah, Jesper Jonsson, Crispin Kinabo, and Mike Shand. 2012. 'Unearthing Treasure and Trouble: Mining as an Impetus to Urbanisation in Tanzania'. *Journal of Contemporary African Studies* 30 (4): 631–649.

Bukenya, Badru, and Sam Hickey. 2017. 'Dominance and Deals in Africa: How Politics Shapes Uganda's Transition from Growth to Transformation'. In Lant Pritchett, Kunal Sen, and Eric Werker (eds), *Deals and Development: The Political Dynamics of Growth Episodes*. Oxford University Press. 183–216.

Callaghy, Thomas. 1987. 'Absolutism, Bonapartism, and the Formation of Ruling Classes: Zaire in Comparative Perspective'. In L. Markovitz (ed.), *Studies in Power and Class in Africa*. Oxford University Press. 95–117.

Capoccia, Giovanni, and Daniel Kelemen. 2007. 'The Study of Critical Junctures: Theory, Narrative and Counterfactuals in Historical Institutionalism'. *World Politics* 59 (3): 341–369.

Capoccia, Giovanni, and Daniel Ziblatt. 2010. 'The Historical Turn in Democratization Studies: A New Research Agenda for Europe and Beyond'. *Comparative Political Studies* 43 (8–9): 931–968.

Carbone, Giovanni. 2005. 'Populism' Visits Africa: The Case of Yoweri Museveni and No-Party Democracy in Uganda'. In *Crisis States Programme*. LSE Development Studies Institute. 1–22.

Carbone, Giovanni. 2008. *No-Party Democracy? Ugandan Politics in Comparative Perspective*. Lynne Rienner.

Carey, John, and Matthew Shugart. 1995. 'Incentives to Cultivate a Personal Vote: A Rank Ordering of Electoral Formulas'. *Electoral Studies* 14 (4): 417–439.

Centre for Policy Analysis. 2014. *'Strengthening the Oversight Function of Parliament of Uganda: An Assessment of Accountability Committees'*. Centre for Policy Analysis.

Chachage, Chachage. 1995. 'The Meek Shall Inherit the Earth But Not the Mining Rights: The Mining Industry and Accumulation in Tanzania'. In P. Gibbon (ed.), *Liberalised Development in Tanzania: Studies on Accumulation Processes and Local Institutions*. Nordiska Afrika institutet. 37–108.

Chachage, Chachage. 2003. *Globalisation and Democratic Governance in Tanzania*. Development Policy Management Forum.

Chaisty, Paul, Nic Cheeseman, and Timothy Power. 2014. 'Rethinking the 'presidentialism debate': conceptualizing coalitional politics in cross-regional perspective'. *Democratization* 21(1): 72–94.

Chaisty, Paul, Nic Cheeseman, and Timothy Power. 2018. *Coalitional presidentialism in comparative perspective: Minority presidents in multiparty systems*. Oxford University Press.

Chaligha, Amon. 2004. 'Lobbying the Parliament in Tanzania: Structures and Processes'. In R. S. Mukandala, S. S. Mushi, and C. Rubagumya (eds), *People's Representatives: Theory and Practice of Parliamentary Democracy in Tanzania*. Fountain Publishers Ltd. 134–165.

Cheeseman, Nic (ed.). 2018. *Institutions and Democracy in Africa: How the Rules of the Game Shape Political Developments*. Cambridge University Press.

Cheeseman, Nic. 2019. 'Should I Stay or Should I Go? Term-Limits, Elections, and Political Change in Kenya, Uganda and Zambia'. In Alexander Baturo and Robert Elgie (eds), *The Politics of Presidential Term Limits*. Oxford University Press, 311–337.

Cheeseman, Nic, Eloise Bertrand, and Sa'eed Husaini. 2019. *A Dictionary of African Politics*. Oxford University Press.

Cheeseman, Nic, and Marja Hinfelaar. 2009. 'Parties, Platforms, and Political Mobilization: The Zambian Presidential Election of 2008'. *African Affairs* 109 (434): 51–76.

Cheeseman, Nic, and Miles Larmer. 2015. 'Ethnopopulism in Africa: Opposition Mobilisation in Diverse and Unequal Societies'. *Democratization* 22 (1): 22–50.

Chemouni, Benjamin. 2014. 'Explaining the Design of the Rwandan Decentralization: Elite Vulnerability and the Territorial Repartition of Power'. *Journal of Eastern African Studies* 8 (2): 246–262.

Chernykh, Svitlana, David Doyle, and Timothy Power. 2017. 'Measuring Legislative Power: An Expert Reweighting of the Fish-Kroenig Parliamentary Powers Index'. *Legislative Studies Quarterly* 42 (2): 295–320.

Chijoriga, Marcellina. 1999. 'Political Interventions and Bank Failure in Pre-liberalized Tanzania'. *The African Journal of Finance and Management* 9 (1): 14–30.

Chubb, Judith. 1981. 'The Social Bases of an Urban Political Machine: The Christian Democratic Party in Palermo'. In S. N. Eisenstadt and R. Lemarchand (eds), *Political Clientelism, Patronage and Development*. Sage Publications.

Cliffe, Lionel. 1967a. 'The Impact of the Elections'. In L. Cliffe (ed.), *One Party Democracy: The 1965 Tanzania General Elections*. East African Publishing House.

Cliffe, Lionel. 1967b. 'The Political System'. In *The 1965 Tanzania General Election: One Party Demoracy* ed. L. Cliffe. Nairobi: East African Publishing House. 1–20.

Cliffe, Lionel. 1972. 'Personal or Class Interest: Tanzania's Leadership Conditions'. In L. Cliffe and J. Saul (eds), *Socialism in Tanzania: An Interdisciplinary Reader*. East African Publishing House.

Cliffe, Lionel, and John Saul. 1972. 'Tanzania: Socialist Transformation and Party Development'. In L. Cliffe and J. Saul (eds), *Socialism in Tanzania*. East African Publishing House.

Coldham, Simon. 2000. 'Land Reform and Customary Rights: The Case of Uganda'. *Journal of African Law* 44: 65–77.

Collier, Ruth Berins, and David Collier. 1991. *Shaping the Political Arena: Critical Junctures, the Labor Movement and Regime Dynamics in Latin America*. Princeton University Press.

Collord, Michaela. 2016. 'From the Electoral Battleground to the Parliamentary Arena: Understanding Intra-elite Bargaining in Uganda's National Resistance Movement'. *Journal of Eastern African Studies* 10 (4): 639–659.

Collord, Michaela. 2018. 'The Legislature: Institutional Strengthening in Dominant-Party States'. In Nic Cheeseman (ed), *Institutions and Democracy in Africa: How the Rules of the Game Shape Political Developments*. Cambridge University Press.

Collord, Michaela. 2021. 'Pressuring MPs to Act: Parliament, Organized Interests and Policy-making in Uganda and Tanzania'. *Democratization* 28(4): 723–741.

Collord, Michaela. 2021b. 'Authoritarian Party (Dis)continuities: The Case of Tanzania's President Magufuli and the "New" Chama Cha Mapinduzi'. Unpublished manuscript available via Researchgate: http://dx.doi.org/10.13140/RG.2.2.21029.83687

Collord, Michaela. 2022. 'Wealth, Power and Institutional Change in Tanzania's Parliament'. *African Affairs* 121(482): 1–28.

Cooksey, Brian. 2012. 'Politics, Patronage and Projects: The Political Economy of Agricultural Policy in Tanzania'. In B. Ouma (ed.), *FAC Political Economy of Agricultural Policy in Africa*. Future Agricultural Consortium. 1–44.

Cooksey, Brian. 2017. 'IPTL, Richmond and "Escrow": The Price of Private Power Procurement in Tanzania'. In *Briefing Note*. Africa Research Institute.

Cooper, Frederick. 2002. *Africa since 1940: The Past of the Present*. Cambridge University Press.

Cooper, Frederick. 2014. *Africa in the World*. Harvard University Press.

Cooper, Ian. 2017. 'Dominant Party Cohesion in Comparative Perspective: Evidence from South Africa and Namibia'. *Democratization* 24 (1): 1–19.

Cooper, Joseph, and David W. Brady. 1981. 'Toward a Diachronic Analysis of Congress'. *The American Political Science Review* 75 (4): 988–1006.

Coulson, Andrew. 1982. *Tanzania: A Political Economy*. Clarendon Press.

Coulson, Andrew. 2013. *Tanzania: A Political Economy*. Oxford University Press.

Dahl, Robert. 1971. *Polyarchy: Participation and Opposition*. Yale University Press.

Davis, Angela. 1983. *Women, Race and Class*. Vintage.

De Kadt, Daniel, and Evans Lieberman. 2020. 'Nuanced Accountability: Voter Responses to Service Delivery in Southern Africa'. *British Journal of Political Science* 50(1): 185–215.

De Waal, Alex. 2015. *The Real Politics of the Horn of Africa: Money, War and the Business of Power*. Polity Press.

Deloitte. 2016. 'Uganda Economic Outlook 2016: The Story Behind the Numbers', Deloitte.

Demarest, Leila. 2021. 'Men of the People? Democracy and Prebendalism in Nigeria's Fourth Republic National Assembly'. *Democratization* 28 (4): 684–702

Diamond, Larry. 1999. *Developing Democracy: Toward Consolidation*. The Johns Hopkins University Press.

Domhoff, William. 2007. 'C. Wright Mills, Floyd Hunter, and 50 Years of Power Structure Research'. *Michigan Sociological Review* 21: 1–54.

Doornbos, Martin, and Federick Mwesigye. 1995. 'The New Politics of Kingmaking'. In H. B. Hansen and M. Twaddle (eds), *From Chaos to Order: The Politics of Constitution-Making in Uganda*. Fountain Publishers. 61–77.

Dye, Barnaby, Seth Schindler, and Deusdedit Rwehumbiza. 2022. 'The Political Rationality of State Capitalism in Tanzania: Territorial Transformation and the entrepreneurial individual'. *Area Development and Policy* 7(1): 42–61.

Edgell, Amanda, Valeriya Mechkova, David Altman, Michael Bernhard, and Staffan Lindberg. 2018. 'When and Where Do Elections Matter? A Global Test of the Democratization by Elections Hypothesis, 1900–2010'. *Democratization* 25 (3): 442–444.

Eggers, Andrew, and Jens Hainmueller. 2009. 'MPs for Sale? Returns to Office in Post-war British Politics'. *American Political Science Review* 103 (4): 513–533.

Ermakoff, Ivan. 2015. 'The Structure of Contingency'. *American Journal of Sociology* 121 (1): 64–125.

Ermakoff, Ivan. 2017. 'Shadow Plays: Theory's Perennial Challenges'. *Sociological Theory* 35 (2): 128–137.

Esping-Andersen, Gosta. 1990. *The Three Worlds of Welfare Capitalism*. Princeton University Press.

Fenno, Richard. 1986. 'Observation, Context, and Sequence in the Study of Politics'. *The American Political Science Review* 80 (1): 3–15.

Field, Bonnie, and Peter Siavelis. 2008. 'Candidate selection procedure in transitional polities'. *Party Politics* 14(5): 620–639.

Fish, M. Steven. 2006. 'Stronger Legislatures, Stronger Democracies'. *Journal of Democracy* 17 (1): 5–20.

Fish, M. Steven, and Matthew Kroenig. 2009. *The Handbook of National Legislatures: A Global Survey*. Cambridge University Press.

Fjeldstad, Odd-Helge, Lise Rakner, and Prosper Ngowi. 2015. 'Shaping the Tax Agenda: Public Engagement, Lobbying and Tax Reform in Tanzania'. In I. Hestad (ed.), *CMI Brief* 14(5). Chr. Michelsen Institute. 1–4.

Fox, Sean and Tom Goodfellow. 2022. 'On the Conditions of "Late Urbanisation"'. *Urban Studies* 59 (10): 1959–1980.

Gandhi, Jennifer. 2007. 'Authoritarian Institutions and the Survival of Autocrats'. *Comparative Political Studies* 40 (11): 1279–1301.

Gandhi, Jennifer. 2008. *Political Institutions under Dictatorship*. Cambridge University Press.

Gandhi, Jennifer, and Adam Przeworski. 2006. 'Cooperation, Cooptation, and Rebellion under Dictatorship'. *Economics & Politics* 18 (1): 1–26.

Gandhi, Jennifer, Ben Noble, and Milan Svolik. 2020. 'Legislatures and legislative politics without democracy'. *Comparative Political Studies* 53 (9): 1359–1379.

Gauthier, Bernard, and Ritva Reinikka. 2006. 'Shifting Tax Burdens through Examptions and Evasions: An Empirical Investigation of Uganda'. *Journal of African Economies* 15 (3): 373–398.

Geddes, Barbara. 1999. 'What Do We Know about Democratization after Twenty Years?' *Annual Review of Political Science* 2(1): 115–144.

Gehlbach, Scott, and Philip Keefer. 2011. 'Investment without Democracy: Ruling-Party Institutionalization and Credible Commitment in Autocracies'. *Journal of Comparative Economics* 39(2): 123–139.

Geist, Judith. 1995. 'Political Significance of the Constituent Assembly'. In H. B. Hansen and M. Twaddle (eds), *From Chaos to Order: The Politics of Constitution-Making in Uganda*. Fountain Publishers. 90–113.

Generoso de Almeida. 2018. 'The ruling party's "exemplary transition": The MPLA's winds of change and continuity'. Presidential Power. Accessed 18 December 2023: https://presidential-power.net/?p=8704.

George, Constantine, Coman Titus, and Hezron Makundi. 2023. 'Formalisation of Street Vending in Dar es Salaam: Implementation and Enforcement of the Wamachinga Identity Card Initiative'. *Forum for Development Studies* 50(2): 283–302.

Gerring, John. 2007. *Case Study Research: Principles and Practices*. Cambridge University Press.

Gertzel, Cherry J. 1970. *The Politics of independent Kenya, 1963–8*. East African Pub. House.

Getachew, Adom. 2019. *Worldmaking after Empire: The Rise and Fall of Self-Determinism*. Princeton University Press.

Ghai, Yash. 1965. 'Kenya's Socialism'. *Transition* 20: 20–23.

Gibbon, Peter. 1995. *Liberalised Development in Tanzania: Studies on Accumulation Processes and Local Institutions*. Nordiska Afrika institutet.

Gibbon, Peter. 2001. 'Cooperative Cotton Marketing, Liberalization and "Civil Society" in Tanzania'. *Journal of Agrarian Change* 1 (3): 389–439.

Gibbon, Peter ed. 1995. *Liberalised Development in Tanzania: Studies on Accumulation Processes and Local Institutions*. Nordiska Afrika institutet.

Gilens, Martin, and Benjamin Page. 2014. 'Testing Theories of American Politics: Elites, Interest Groups, and Average Citizens'. *Perspectives on Politics* 12 (3): 564–581.

Gokgur, Nilgun. 2011. *Formulating a broad-based private sector development strategy fo the Ministry of Trade and Industry, Rwanda – Inception Report*. Unpublished, cited in Ansoms and Rostagno (2012).

Gokgur, Nilgun. 2012. 'Rwanda's Ruling Party-Owned Enterprise: Do They Enhance or Impede Development?' Institute of Development Policy and Management.

Golden, Miriam, and Brian Min. 2013. 'Distributive Politics around the World'. *Annual Review of Political Science* 16: 73–99.

Golooba-Mutebi, Frederick, and David Booth. 2013. 'Bilateral cooperation and local power dynamics: The case of Rwanda'. Overseas Development Institute. 1–28.

Goodfellow, Tom. 2018. 'Seeing Political Settlements through the City: A Framework for Comparative Analysis of Urban Transformation'. *Development and Change* 49 (1): 199–222.

Goodfellow, Tom. 2022. *Politics and the Urban Frontier: Transformation and Divergence in Late Urbanizing East Africa*. Oxford University Press.

Gray, Hazel. 2015. 'The Political Economy of Grand Corruption in Tanzania'. *African Affairs* 114 (456): 382–403.

Gray, Hazel. 2018. *Turbulence and Order in Economic Development: Institutions and Economic Transformation in Tanzania and Vietnam*. Oxford University Press.

Green, Elliott. 2006. 'Ethnicity and the Politics of Land Tenure Reform in Central Uganda'. *Commonwealth & Comparative Politics* 44 (3): 370–388.

Green, Elliott. 2010. 'Patronage, District Creation and Reform in Uganda'. *Studies in Comparative International Development* 45 (1): 83–103.

Green, Elliott. 2011. 'The Political Economy of Nation Formation in Modern Tanzania: Explaining Stability in the Face of Diversity'. *Commonwealth & Comparative Politics* 49 (2): 223–244.

Greene, Kenneth. 2007. *Why Dominant Parties lose: Mexico's Democratization in Comparative Perspective*: Cambridge University Press.

Grossman, Guy, and Kristin Michelitch. 2018. 'Information Dissemination, Competitive Pressure, and Politician Performance between Elections: A Field Experiment in Uganda'. *American Political Science Review* 112 (2): 280–301.

Policy Forum Budget Working Group. 2013. 'Tanzania and the Problem of Tax Exemptions'. In *Policy Brief*. Policy Forum. 1–4.

Hacker, Jacob, and Paul Pierson. 2010. 'Winner-Take-All Politics and Political Science: A Response'. *Politics & Society* 38(2): 266–282.

Hall, Peter A., and Rosemary Taylor. 1996. 'Political Science and the Three New Institutionalisms'. *Political Studies* XLIV: 936–957.

Hansen, Holger Bernt. 2013. 'Uganda in the 1970s: A Decade of Paradoxes and Ambiguities'. *Journal of Eastern African Studies* 7 (1): 83–103.

Hansen, Holger Bernt, and Michael Twaddle. 1998. 'The Changing State of Uganda'. In *Developing Uganda*, ed. M. Twaddle and H. B. Hansen. Oxford: James Currey. 1–18.

Harding, Robin, and David Stasavage. 2014. 'What Democracy Does (and Doesn't Do) for Basic Services: School Fees, School Inputs, and African Elections'. *The Journal of Politics* 76 (1): 229–245.

Harris, Belle. 1967. 'The Electoral System'. In L. Cliffe (ed.), *One Party Democracy: The 1965 Tanzania General Elections*. East African Publishing House. 21–52.

Hibbing, John R. 1988. 'Legislative Institutionalization with Illustrations from the British House of Commons'. *American Journal of Political Science* 32 (3): 681–712.

Hickel, Jason, Dylan Sullivan, and Huzaifa Zoomkawala. 2021. 'Plunder in the Post-Colonial Era: Quantifying Drain from the Global South through Unequal Exchange, 1960–2018'. *New Political Economy*, 26 (6): 1030–1047.

Himbara, David. 1997. 'The 'Asian Question' in East Africa'. *African Studies* 56 (1): 1–18.

Hirschman, Albert O. 1970. *Exit, Voice, and Loyalty: Responses to Decline in Firms, Organizations, and States*. Harvard University Press.

Hodgkin, Thomas. 1971. *African political parties: An introductory guide*. Peter Smith.

Holmquist, Frank. 1984. 'Class Structure, Peasant Participation, and Rural Self-help'. In J. Barkan (ed.), *Politics and Public Policy in Kenya and Tanzania*. Praeger Publishers. 48–66.

Hont, Istvan. 2005. *Jealousy of trade: international competition and the nation-state in historical perspective*. Harvard University Press.

Hopkins, Raymond F. 1971. *Political Roles in a New State: Tanzania's First Decade*. Yale University Press.

Huntington, Samuel. 1968. *Political Order in Changing Societies*. Yale University Press.

Hyden, Goran. 1977. 'Political Engineering and Social Change: A Case Study of Bukoba District, Tanzania'. In Lionel Cliffe, J. S. Coleman, and M. R. Doornbos (eds), *Government and Rural Development in East Africa: Essays on Political Penetration*. Martinus Nijhoff. 183–200.

Hyden, Goran. 1999. 'Top-Down Democratization in Tanzania'. *Journal of Democracy* 10(4): 142–155.

Hyden, Goran, and Colin Leys. 1972. 'Elections and Politics in Single-Party Systems: the case of Kenya and Tanzania'. *British Journal of Political Science* 2 (4): 389–420.

Ibn Zackaria, Abraham, and Yaw Appiah-Marfo. 2022. 'Implications of Political Clientelism on the Effectiveness of Legislators in Ghana'. *The Journal of Legislative Studies* 28(1): 26–46.

Ichino, Nahomi, Nathan, and Noah. 2012. 'Primaries on Demand? Intra-Party Politics and Nominations in Ghana'. *British Journal of Political Science* 42 (4): 769–791.

Iliffe, John. 1979. *A modern history of Tanganyika*. Cambridge University Press.

Iliffe, John. 1983. *The Emergence of African Capitalism*. The Macmillan Press Ltd.

Jha, Praveen, Walter Chambati, and Lyn Ossome. 2021. *Labour Questions in the Global South*. Palgrave Macmillan.

Jones, Will. 2012. 'Between Pyongyang and Singapore: The Rwandan State, Its Rulers, and the Military'. In M. Campioni and P. Noack (eds), *Rwanda Fast Forward: Social, Economic, Military and Reconciliation Prospects*. Palgrave Macmillan. 228–248.

Jorgensen, Jan Jelmert. 1981. *Uganda: A Modern History*. Croom Helm.

Judge, David. 2003. 'Legislative Institutionalization: A Bent Analytical Arrow?' *Government and Opposition* 38 (4): 497–516.

Karas, David, and Pinar Donmez. 2023. 'Crises of Authoritarian Financialization: Monetary Policy in Hungary and Turkiye in the Polycrisis'. In Mustafa Yagci (ed.) *Central Banking in a Post-Pandemic World: Challenges, Opportunities, and Dilemmas*. Routledge. 186–220.

Kasfir, Nelson. 1991. 'The Ugandan Elections of 1989: Power, Populism and Democratization'. In M. Twaddle and H. B. Hansen (eds), *Changing Uganda: The Dilemmas of Structural Adjustment and Revolutionary Change*. Currey. 247–278.

Kasfir, Nelson. 1995. 'Ugandan Politics and the Constituent Assembly Elections'. In H. B. Hansen and M. Twaddle (eds), *From Chaos to Order: The Politics of Constitution-Making in Uganda*. Foutin Publishers.

Kasfir, Nelson. 2000. '"Movement" Democracy, Legitimacy, and Power in Uganda'. In J. Mugaju and J. Oloka-Onyango (eds), *No-Party Democracy in Uganda: Myths and Realities*. 60–78.

Kasfir, Nelson. 2005. 'Guerrillas and civilian participation: the National Resistance Army in Uganda, 1981–86'. *Journal of Modern African Studies* 43(2): 271–296.

Kasfir, Nelson, and Hippo Twebaze. 2016 'Performance and Effectiveness of Lawmaking and Oversight: The 6th–9th Ugandan Parliaments'.

Kasfir, Nelson, and Stephen Hippo Twebaze. 2009. 'The Rise and Ebb of Uganda's No-Party Parliament'. In J. Barkan (ed.), *Legislative Power in Emerging African Democracies*. Lynne Rienner. 73–108.

Kawawa, Rashidi M. 1975. 'Chama Kushika Hatamu: Hotuba ya Waziri Mkuu na Makamu wa Pili wa Rais Ndugu R.M. Kawawa akiwakilisha katika Bunge Muswada wa kubadili Katiba ya Muda tarehe 2 Juni, 1975'. Dar Es Salaam: Government Printers.

Kelsall, Tim. 2000. 'Governance, Local Politics and Districtization in Tanzania: The 1998 Arumeru Tax Revolt'. *African Affairs* 99: 533–551.

Kelsall, Tim. 2002. 'Shop Windows and Smoke-Filled Rooms: Governance and the Repoliticisation of Tanzania'. *The Journal of Modern African Studies* 40 (4): 597–619.

Kelsall, Tim. 2003. 'Governance, Democracy and Recent Political Struggles in Mainland Tanzania'. *Commonwealth & Comparative Politics* 41 (2): 55–82.

Kennedy, Paul. 1988. *African Capitalism: The Struggle for Ascendency* Cambridge University Press.

Kent, Frank. 1924. *The Great Game of Politics: An Effort to Present the Elementary Human Facts about Politics, Politicians, And Political Machines, Candidates and Their Ways*. Doubleday.

Khan, Mushtaq. 2005. 'Markets, States and Democracy: Patron–Client Networks and the Case for Democracy in Developing Countries'. *Democratization* 12 (5): 704–724.

Khan, Mushtaq. 2010. *Political Settlements and the Governance of Growth-Enhancing Institutions*. SOAS.

Khan, Mushtaq. 2018. 'Political Settlements and the Analysis of Institutions'. *African Affairs* 117 (469): 636–655.

Khisa, Moses. 2016. 'Managing elite defection in Museveni's Uganda: the 2016 elections in perspective'. *Journal of Eastern African Studies* 10(4): 729–748.

Khisa, Moses. 2020. 'Politicisation and Professionalisation: The Progress and Perils of Civil-Military Transformation in Museveni's Uganda'. *Civil Wars* 22(2–3): 289–312.

Khisa, Moses. 2023. 'Uganda's ruling coalition and the 2021 elections: change, continuity and contestation'. *Journal of Eastern African Studies* 17(1–2): 325–343.

Kiiza, Julius, Lars Svasand, and Robert Tabaro. 2008. 'Organising Parties for the 2006 Elections'. In J. Kiiza, S. Makara and L. Rakner (eds), *Electoral Democracy in Uganda: Understanding the Institutional Processes and Outcomes of the 2006 Multiparty Elections*. Fountain Publishers. 201–230.

Killian, Bernadeta. 1996. 'A Policy of Parliamentary "Special Seats" for Women in Tanzania: Its Effectiveness'. *Ufahamu: A Journal of African Studies* 24 (2–3): 21–31.

Killian, Bernadeta. 2004. 'Comparing Performance: The 1990–1995 Single-Party Parliament and the 1995–2000 Multi-Party Parliament'. In R. S. Mukandala, S. S. Mushi, and C. Rubagumya (eds), *People's Representatives: Theory and Practice of Parliamentary Democracy in Tanzania*. Fountain Publishers. 183–200.

Kim, Eun Kyung. 2020. 'Economic Signals of Ethnicity and Voting in Africa: Analysis of the Correlation between Agricultural Subsectors and Ethnicity in Kenya'. *The Journal of Modern African Studies* 58 (3): 361–395.

Kimei, Charles Stephen. 1987. *Tanzania's Financial Experience in the Post-war Period*. Uppsala University.

King, Anthony. 1976. 'Modes of Executive-Legislative Relations: Great Britain, France, and West Germany'. *Legislative Studies Quarterly* 1 (1): 11–36.

Kiondo, A. S. Z. 1994. 'Economic Power and Electoral Politics in Tanzania'. In R. S. Mukandala and H. Othman (eds), *Liberalization and Politics: The 1990 Election in Tanzania*. Dar es Salaam University Press. 67–89.

Kiwanuka, Maria. 2013. 'Amendments to the Public Finance Bill, 2012'. Kampala Ministry of Finance, Planning & Economic Development.

Kjaer, Anne Mette. 2015. 'Political Settlements and Productive Sector Policies: Understanding Sector Differences in Uganda'. *World Development* 68: 230–241.

Kjaer, Anne Mette, and Mesharch Katusiimeh. 2012. 'Growing but Not Transforming: Fragmented Ruling Coalitions and Economic Developments in Uganda'. DIIS Working Paper. Copenhagen, Denmark.

Kjaer, Anne Mette, and Mesharch Katusiimeh. 2021. 'Nomination Violence in Uganda's National Resistance Movement'. *African Affairs* 120 (479): 177–198.

Kjaer, Anne Mette and Nansozi Muwanga. 2016. 'Inclusion as Political Mobilisation: The Political Economy of Quality Education Initiatives in Uganda'. ESID working paper no. 65, University of Manchester.

Kjekshus, Helge. 1974a. 'Parliament in a One-Party State—The Bunge of Tanzania, 1965–1970'. *The Journal of Modern African Studies* 12 (1): 19–43.

Kjekshus, Helge. 1974b. 'Perspectives on the Second Parliament, 1965–1970'. In U. o. D. e. S. The Election Study Committee (ed.), *Socialism and Participation: Tanzania's 1970 National Elections*. Tanzania Publishing House Ltd. 60–92.

Koter, Dominika. 2013. 'King Makers: Local Leaders and Ethnic Politics in Africa'. *World Politics* 65 (2): 187–232.

Koter, Dominika. 2017. 'Costly Electoral Campaigns and the Changing Composition and Quality of Parliament: Evidence from Benin'. *African Affairs* 116 (465): 573–596.

Krol, Gerrit. 2021. 'Amending legislatures in authoritarian regimes: power sharing in post-Soviet Eurasia'. *Democratization* 28(3): 562–582.

Langston, Joy. 2006. 'The Changing Party of the Institutional Revolution: Electoral Competition and Decentralized Candidate Selection'. *Party Politics* 12 (3): 395–413.

Languille, Sonia. 2015. 'The Scramble for Textbooks in Tanzania'. *African Affairs* 115 (458): 73–96.

Laswell, Harold. 1936. *Politics: Who Gets What, When and How*. Whittlesey House.

LeBas, Adrienne. 2011. *From Protest to Parties: Party-building and Democratization in Africa*. Oxford University Press.

Lee, J. M. 1963. 'Parliament in Republican Ghana'. *Parliamentary Affairs* 16 (4): 376–395.

Lemarchand, Rene, and Keith Legg. 1972. 'Political Clientelism and Development: A Preliminary Analysis'. *Comparative Politics* 4 (2): 149–178.

Lentz, Carola. 2016. 'African Middle Classes: Lessons from Transnational Studies and a Research Agenda'. In H. Melber (ed.), *The Rise of Africa's Middle Class: Myths, Realities, and Critical Engagements*. Zed Books, 17–53.

Levi, Margaret 2009. 'Reconsiderations of Rational Choice in Comparative and Historical Analysis'. In M. I. Lichbach and A. Zuckerman (ed.), *Comparative Politics: Rationality, Culture, and Structure*. Cambridge University Press.

Levine, Katherine 1972. 'The TANU Ten-Cell System'. In L. Cliffe and J. Saul (eds), *Socialism in Tanzania: An Interdisciplinary Reader*. East African Publishing House. 329–336.

Levitsky, Steven, and Lucan Way. 2010. *Competitive Authoritarianism: Hybrid Regimes after the Cold War*. Cambridge University Press.

Levitsky, Steven, and Lucan Way. 2012. 'Beyond Patronage: Violent Struggle, Ruling Party Cohesion and Authoritarian Durability'. *Perspectives on Politics* 10 (4): 869–889.

Lewis, Peter. 2019. 'Responses to Economic Crisis in Africa'. In Nic Cheeseman (ed) *Oxford Research Encyclopedia of Politics*. Oxford University Press. https://doi.org/10.1093/acrefore/9780190228637.013.705

Leys, Colin. 1978. 'Capital Accumulation, Class Formation and Dependency: The Significance of the Kenyan Case'. *Socialist Register* 15 (15): 241–266.

Lindberg, Staffan. 2006. *Democracy and Elections in Africa*. The Johns Hopkins University Press.

Lindberg, Staffan. (ed.). 2009. *Democratization by Elections: A New Mode of Transition*. Johns Hopkins University Press.

Lindberg, Staffan. 2010. 'Some Evidence on the Demand Side of Private-Public Goods Provision by MPs'. In *African Power and Politics Programme*: Overseas Development Institute.

Lindberg, Staffan. 2010. 'What Accountability Pressures Do MPs in Africa Face and How Do They Respond? Evidence from Ghana'. *Journal of Modern African Studies* 48 (1): 117–142.

Lindemann, Stefan. 2011. 'Just Another Change of Guard? Broad-Based Politics and Civil War in Museveni's Uganda'. *African Affairs* 110 (440): 387–416.

Linz, Juan, and Alfred Stepan. 1996. 'Toward Consolidated Democracies'. *Journal of Democracy* 7 (2): 14–33.

Low, D. A. 1988. 'The Dislocated Polity'. In H. B. Hansen and M. Twaddle (eds), *Uganda Now: Between Development and Decay*. Currey. 36–53.

Lü, Xiaobo, Mingxing Liu, and Feiyue Li. 2020. 'Policy Coalition Building in an Authoritarian Legislature: Evidence from China's National Assemblies (1983–2007)'. *Comparative Political Studies* 53(9): 1380–1416.

Lubeck, Paul. 1987. *The African Bourgeoisie: Capitalist Development in Nigeria, Kenya and the Ivory Coast*. Lynne Rienner.

Lust-Okar, Ellen. 2006. 'Elections under Authoritarianism: Preliminary Lessons from Jordan'. *Democratization* 13 (3): 456–471.

Lynch, Gabrielle. 2006. 'Negotiating Ethnicity: Identity Politics in Contemporary Kenya'. *Review of African Political Economy* 33 (107): 49–65.

Mabikke, Samuel. 2011. 'Escalating Land Grabbing in Post-conflict Regions of Northern Uganda'. In *International Conference on Global Land Grabbing*. University of Sussex. 1–27.

Maddicott, John Robert. 2010. *The Origins of the English Parliament, 924–1327*. Oxford University Press.

Magaloni, Beatriz. 2006. *Voting for Autocracy: Hegemonic Party Survival and Its Demise in Mexico*. Cambridge University Press.

Magaloni, Beatriz. 2008. 'Credible Power-Sharing and the Longevity of Authoritarian Rule'. *Comparative Political Studies* 41 (4/5): 715–741.

Magaloni, Beatriz, and Ruth Kricheli. 2010. 'Political Order and One-Party Rule'. *Annual Review of Political Science* 13: 123–143.

Mahoney, James. 2000. 'Path Dependence in Historical Sociology'. *Theory and Society* 29 (4): 507–548.

Mahoney, James, and Kathleen Thelen. 2009. 'A Theory of Gradual Institutional Change'. In J. Mahoney and T. Kathleen (eds), *Explaining Institutional Change: Ambiguity, Agency and Power*. Cambridge University Press. 1–37.

Mahoney, James, and Richard Snyder. 1999. 'Rethinking Agency and Structure in the Study of Regime Change'. *Studies in Comparative International Development* 34 (2): 3–32.

Makara, Sabiti, Lise Rakner, and Lars Svasand. 2009. 'Turnaround: The National Resistance Movement and the Reintroduction of a Multiparty System in Uganda'. *International Political Science Review* 30 (2): 185–204.

Makoba, Wagona. 1998. *Government Policy and Public Enterprise Performance in Sub-Saharan Africa: The Case Studies of Tanzania and Zambia, 1964–1984*. Edwin Mellen Press.

Makulilo, Alexander B. 2008. *TANZANIA: A De Facto One Party State?* Saarbrücken: VDM Verlag.

Makulilo, Alexander B. 2012. 'The Fallacy of de facto Independent Candidacy in Tanzania: A Rejoinder'. *Central European University Political Science* 6 (1): 111–137.

Malik, Adeel, and Bassem Awadallah. 2013. 'The Economics of the Arab Spring'. *World Development* 45: 296–313.

Mamdani, Mahmood. 1988. 'Uganda in Transition: Two Years of the NRA/NRM'. *Third World Quarterly* 10 (3): 1155–1181.

Mamdani, Mahmood. 1995. *And Fire Does Not Always Beget Ash: Critical Reflections on the NRM*. Monitor.

Mandaza, Ibbo. 1994. 'The State and Democracy in Southern Africa: Towards a Conceptual Framework'. In E. Osaghae (ed.), *Between State and Civil Society in Africa*, CODESRIA, 249–271.

Mann, Laura, and Marie Berry. 2016. 'Understanding the Political Motivations that Shape Rwanda's Emergent Developmental State'. *New Political Economy* 21 (1): 119–144.

Manning, Carrie. 2005. 'Assessing African Party Systems after the Third Wave'. *Party Politics* 11 (6): 707–727.

Marquardt, Mark, and Abby Sebina-Zziwa. 1998. 'Land Reform in the Making'. In H. B. Hansen and M. Twaddle (eds), *Developing Uganda*, James Currey. 176–184.

Martin, Denis-Constant. 1988. *Tanzanie: l'Invention d'une culture politique*. Karthala Editions.

Martiniello, Giuliano, and Sabatho Nyamsenda. 2018. 'Agrarian Movements in the Neoliberal Era: The Case of MVIWATA in Tanzania'. *Agrarian South: Journal of Political Economy* 7 (2): 145–172.

Martz, John. 2013. 'Political Parties and Candidate Selection in Venezuela and Colombia'. *Political Science Quarterly* 114 (4): 639–659.

Masha, F. Lwanyantika. 2011. 'The Story of the Arusha Delcration (1967)'. Accessed, Lionel Cliffe's personal archive.

Matotay, Edmund. 2014. 'Inequalities and Structural Transformation in Tanzania'. *Development* 57 (3–4): 591–600.

Mayhew, David R. 1974. *Congress: The Electoral Connection*. Yale University Press.

Mayhew, David R. 1986. *Placing Parties in American Politics: Organization, Electoral Settings, and Government Activity in the Twentieth Century*. Princeton University Press.

McHenry, Dean. 1983. 'A Measure of Harmony/Disharmony in a One-Party State: Low-Level Party Leaders' Choices for Members of Parliament Compared with Those of Both High-Level Party Officials and People in Tanzania, 1965–1975'. *The Journal of Developing Areas* 17 (3): 337–348.

Meng, Anne. 2020. *Constraining Dictatorship: From Personalized Rule to Institutionalized Regimes*. Cambridge University Press.

Meng, Anne. 2021. 'Ruling Parties in Authoritarian Regimes: Rethinking Institutional Strength'. *British Journal of Political Science* 51(2): 526–540.

Mengi, Reginald. 2018. *I Can, I Must, I Will: The Spirit of Success*. Independently Published.

Mezey, Michael. 1979. *Comparative Legislatures*. Duke University Press.

Michels, Robert. 2001. *Political Parties*: Botoche Books.

Mkandawire, Thandika. 2001. 'Thinking about Developmental States in Africa'. *Cambridge Journal of Economics* 25: 289–313.

Mkandawire, Thandika. 2017. 'State Capacity, History, Structure, and Political Contestation in Africa'. In D. Mistree, M. Centeno, A. Kohli, and D. Yashar (eds), *States in the Developing World*. Cambridge University Press, 184–216.

Mkandawire, Thandika and Adebayo Olukoshi. 1995. *Between Liberalisation and Oppression: The Politics of Structural Adjustment in Africa*. CODESRIA.

Mlimuka, A. K. L. J., and P. J. A. M. Kabudi. 1986. 'The State and the Party'. In I. Shivji (ed.), *The State and the Working People in Tanzania*. CODESRIA. 58–86.

Mmuya, Maximilian. 1998. *Tanzania: Political Reform in Eclipse: Crisis and Cleavage in Political Parties*. Friedrich Ebert Stiftung.

Mmuya, Maximilian. 1994. 'Floods and Elections in Mtwara'. In Rwekaza Mukandala and Haroub Othman (eds), *Liberalization and Politics: The 1990 Election in Tanzania*. Dar es Salaam University Press, 233–257.

Mmuya, Max, and Amon Chaligha. 1994. *Political Parties and Democracy in Tanzania*. Dar es Salaam University Press.

Moore, Barrington. 1966. *Social Origins of Dictatorship and Democracy: Lord and Peasant in the Making of the Modern World*. Beacon Press.

Morgenbesser, Lee, and Thomas Pepinsky. 2019. 'Elections as Causes of Democratization: Southeat Asia in Comparative Perspective'. *Comparative Political Studies* 52(1): 3–35.

Morgenstern, Scott, and Benito Nacif. 2002. *Legislative Politics in Latin America*. Cambridge University Press.

Morse, Yonatan. 2019. *How Autocrats Compete: Parties, Patrons, and Unfair Elections in Africa*. Cambridge University Press.

Mozaffar, Shaheen, and James Scarritt. 2005. 'The Puzzle of African Party Systems'. *Party Politics* 11 (4): 399–421.

Mpangala, G. P. 1994. 'The Organization and Management of the 1990 Parliamentary Elections'. In R. S. Mukandala and H. Othman (eds), *Liberalization and Politics: The 1990 Election in Tanzania*. Dar es Salaam University Press.

Msekwa, Pius. 2002. *Reflections on the First Multiparty Parliament, 1995–2000*. Dar es Salaam University Press Ltd.

Msekwa, Pius. 2006. *Reflections on the First Decade of Multiparty Politics in Tanzania*. Hanns Seidel Foundation

Msekwa, Pius. 2012. *The Story of the Tanzania Parliament*. P. Msekwa.

Mtei, Edwin. 2009. *From Goatherd to Governor*. Mkuki na Nyota Publishers.

Mudoola, Dan. 1988. 'Political Transitions since Idi Amin: A Study in Political Pathology'. In H. B. Hansen and M. Twaddle (eds), *Uganda Now: Between Development and Decay*. Currey. 280–298.

Mudoola, Dan. 1991. 'Institution-Building: The Case of the NRM and the Military 1986–9'. In M. Twaddle and H. B. Hansen (eds), *Changing Uganda: The Dilemmas of Structural Adjustment and Revolutionary*. Currey. 230–246.

Mueller, Susanne. 1981. 'The Historical Origins of Tanzania's Ruling Class'. *Canadian Journal of African Studies* 15 (3): 459–497.

Mugyenyi, Joshua. 1991. 'IMF Conditionality and Structural Adjustment under the NRM'. In M. Twaddle and H. B. Hansen (eds), *Changing Uganda: The Dilemmas of Structural Adjustment and Revolutionary Change*. Currey. 61–77.

Mukholi, David. 1995. *A Complete Guide to Uganda's Fourth Constitution: History, Politics and the Law*. Fountain Publishers.

Munishi, Gasper, and Asha Rose Mtengeti-Migiro. 1990. 'Rombo: The Dynamics of Election Organization in a One-Party Democracy'. In H. Othman, I. Bavu and M. Okema (eds), *Tanzania: Democracy in Transition*. Dar es Salaam University Press.

Museveni, Yoweri. 1997. *Sowing the Mustard Seed*. Macmillan.

Mushi, S. S. 1974. 'Elections and Political Mobilization in Tanzania'. In The Election study Committee University of Dar es Salaam (ed.), *Socialism and Participation: Tanzania's 1970 National Elections*. Tanzania Publishing House. 96–124.

Mutibwa, Phares. 1992. *Uganda since Independence: A Story of Unfulfilled Hopes*. Hurst.

Mutyaba, Michael. 2023. 'Uganda at 61: In his sunset years, Museveni tightens the noose'. *African Arguments*.

Mwakyembe, Harrison. G. 1986. 'The Parliament and the Electoral Process'. In I. Shivji (ed.), *The State and the Working People in Tanzania*. Dakar: CODESRIA. 16–57.

Mwansasu, Bismarck. 1974. 'The Selections of Candidates'. In The Election study Committee University of Dar es Salaam (ed.), *Socialism and Participation: Tanzania's 1970 National Elections*. Tanzania Publishing House. 139–164.

Mwansasu, Bismarck. 1979. 'The Changing Role of the Tanganyika African National Union'. In B. Mwansasu and C. Pratt (eds), *Towards Socialism in Tanzania*. Tanzania Publishing House. 169–192.

Mwapachu, Juma 2005. *Confronting New Realities: Reflections on Tanzania's Radical Transformation*. E&D Ltd.

Mwenda, Andrew. 2008. 'Musveni Hates Local Business'.

Nathan, Noah. 2019. *Electoral politics and Africa's urban transition: Class and ethnicity in Ghana*. Cambridge University Press.

Ndulu, Benno, and Charles Mutalemwa. 2002. *Tanzania at the Turn of the Century: Background Papers and Statistics*. World Bank.

Nel, Philip. 2005. 'Democratization and the Dynamics of Income Distribution in Low- and Middle-Income Countries'. *Politikon* 32 (1): 17–43.

Nijink, Lia, Shaheen Mozaffar, and Elisabete Azevedo. 2006. 'Parliaments and the Enhancement of Democracy on the African Continent: An Analysis of Institutional Capacity and Public Perception'. *The Journal of Legislative Studies* 12 (3–4): 311–335.

Njuba, Sam. 1991. 'Legal Adjustment to Revolutionary Change'. In H. B. Hansen and M. Twaddle (eds), *Changing Uganda: The Dilemmas of Structural Adjustment and Revolutionary Change*. Currey. 210–216.

Noble, Ben. 2020. 'Authoritarian Amendments: Legislative Institutions as Intraexecutive Constraints in Post-Soviet Russia'. *Comparative Political Studies* 53 (9): 1417–1454.

Nolutshungu, Sam. 1990. 'Fragments of a Democracy: Reflections on Class and Politics in Nigeria'. *Third World Quarterly* 12 (1): 86–115.

North, Douglass. 1990. *Institutions, Institutional Change and Economic Performance*. Cambridge University Press.

NRM. 1992. 'The NRM Ten-Point Programme'. In Y. Museveni (ed.), *What Is Africa's Problem?* NRM Publications. 279–282.

Nyagetera, Bartholomew. 1992. 'Reforming and Restructuring the Financial Sector in Tanzania'. In M. Bagachwa, A. Mbelle and B. Van Arkadie (eds), *Market Reforms and Parastatal Restructuring in Tanzania*. University of Dar es Salaam. 74–90.

Nyamsenda, Sabatho. 2018. 'Bulldozing Like a fascist? Authoritarian Populism and Rural Activism in Tanzania'. Emancipatory Rural Politics Initiative Conference, The Hague.

Nyamsenda, Sabatho and Michaela Collord. Forthcoming. 'Political Settlements Report, Dar es Salaam, Tanzania'. African Cities Research Consortium Working Paper.

Nyang'oro, Julius. 2011. *JK: A Political Biography of Jakaya Mrisho Kikwete, President of the United Republic of Tanzania*. Africa World Press, Inc.

Nyerere, Julius. 1963. 'Democracy and the Party System'. Tanganyika Standard. 1–27.

Nyerere, Julius. 1967. 'Groping Forward'. In *Freedom and Unity: Uhuru na Umoja*. Oxford University Press.

Nyerere, Julius. 1967. 'The Arusha Declaration'. Tanganyika African National Union. 1–26.

Nyerere, Julius. 1987. 'Kujitawala na Kujitegemea: Hotuba ya Mwalimu Julius K. Nyerere Mwenyekiti wa Chama cha Mapinduzi'. Meeting of the CCM NEC, Dodoma, Tanzania: CCM. Tanzania CCM. 1–26.

Nyirabu, Mohabe. 2002. 'The Multiparty Reform Process in Tanzania: The Dominance of the Ruling Party'. *The African Journal of Political Science* 7 (2): 99–112.

Nyirinkindi, Emmanuel, and Michael Opagi. 2010. 'Privatization and Parastatal Reform'. In F. Kuteesa, E. Tumusiime-Mutebile, A. Whitworth and T. Williamson (eds), *Uganda's Economic Reforms: Insider Accounts*. Oxford University Press. 355–382.

Ochieng, E. O. 1991. 'Economic Adjustment Programmes in Uganda, 1985–9'. In M. Twaddle and H. B. Hansen (eds), *Changing Uganda: The Dilemmas of Structural Adjustment and Revolutionary Change*. Currey. 43–60.

Odoki, Ben. 2005. *The Search for A National Consensus: The Making of the 1995 Ugandan Constitution*. Fountain Publishers.

Ofosu, George Kwaku. 2019. 'Do Fairer Elections Increase the Responsiveness of Politicians?' *American Political Science Review* 113 (4): 963–979.

Okafor, Obiora Chinedu. 2009. 'Remarkable Returns: The Influence of Labour-Led Socio-Economic Rights Movement on Legislative Reasoning, Process and Action in Nigeria, 1999–2007'. *Journal of Modern African Studies* 47 (2): 241–266.

Okumu, John, and Frank Holmquist. 1984. 'Party and Party–State Relations'. In J. Barkan (ed.), *Politics and Public Policy in Kenya and Tanzania*. Praeger.

Oloka-Onyango, Joseph. 2000. 'New Wine or New Bottles? Movement Politics and One-Partyism in Uganda'. In J. Mugaju and J. Oloka-Onyango (eds), *No-Party Democracy in Uganda: Myths and Realities*. 40–59.

Olson, David. 1994. *Democratic Legislative Institutions: A Comparative View*. Edited by A. P. I. P. Policy. M. E. Sharpe.

Omach, Paul. 2014. 'Peace, Security and Elections in Northern Uganda'. In S. Perrot, S. Makara, J. Lafargue, and M.-A. Fouere (eds), *Elections in a Hybrid Regime: Revisiting the 2011 Ugandan Polls*. Fountain Publishers, 348–371.

Opalo, Kennedy Ochieng. 2014. 'The Long Road to Institutionalization: The Kenyan Parliament and the 2013 Elections'. *Journal of Eastern African Studies* 8 (1): 63–77.

Opalo, Kennedy Ochieng. 2019. *Legislative Development in Africa: Politics and Postcolonial Legacies*. Cambridge University Press.

Opalo, Kennedy Ochieng. 2022. 'Leveraging Legislative Power: Distributive Politics and Committee Work in Kenya's National Assembly '. *Journal of Legislative Studies* 28(4): 513–532.

Opalo, Kennedy Ochieng. 2023. 'You Can't Eat Democracy'. *An Africanist Perspective*. Accessed 14 August 2023: https://kenopalo.substack.com/p/you-cant-eat-democracy.

Othman, H. 1994. 'Succession Politics and the Union Presidential Elections'. In R. S. Mukandala and H. Othman (eds), *Liberalization and Politics: The 1990 Elections in Tanzania*. Dar es Salaam University Press.

Paget, Dan. 2017. 'Tanzania: Shrinking Space and Opposition Protest'. *Journal of Democracy* 28 (3): 153–167.

Paget, Dan. 2019. 'The Authoritarian Origins of Well-Organised Opposition Parties: The Rise of CHADEMA in Tanzania'. *African Affairs* 118 (473): 692–711.

Paget, Dan. 2021a. Tanzania: The Authoritarian Landslide'. *Journal of Democracy* 32(2): 61–76.

Paget, Dan. 2021b. 'Mistaken for Populism: Magufuli, Ambiguity and Elitist Plebeianism in Tanzania'. *Journal of Political Ideologies* 26 (2): 121–141.

Palier, Bruno and Kathleen Thelen. 2010. 'Institutionalizing Dualism: Complementarities and Change in France and Germany'. *Politics & Society* 38 (1): 119–148.

Panebianco, Angelo. 1988. *Political Parties: Organization and Power*. Cambridge University Press.

Pedersen, Rasmus and Thabit Jacob. 2019. 'Political Settlement and the Politics of Legitimation in Countries Undergoing Democratisation: Insights from Tanzania'. Effective State-building and Inclusive Development Working Paper No. 124: 1–34.

Pengl, Yannick I., Philip Roessler, and Valeria Rueda. 2022. 'Cash Crops, Print Technologies, and the Politicization of Ethnicity in Africa'. *American Political Science Review* 116 (1): 181–199.

Pepinsky, Thomas. 2014. 'The Institutional Turn in Comparative Authoritarianism'. *British Journal of Political Science* 44 (3): 631–653.

Perrot, Sandrine, Sabiti Makara, Marie-Aude Fouéré, and Jérôme Lafargue. 2014. *Elections in a hybrid regime: Revisiting the 2011 Ugandan polls*. Fountain Publishers/IFRA.

Pierson, Paul. 2000. 'Increasing Returns, Path Dependence, and the Study of Politics'. *The American Political Science Review* 94 (2): 251–267.

Pitcher, Anne. 2012. *Party Politics and Economic Reform in Africa's Democracies*. Cambridge University Press.

Polsby, Nelson. 1968. 'The Institutionalization of the U.S. House of Representatives'. *American Political Science Review* 100 (4): 144–168.

Ponte, Stefano. 2004. 'The Politics of Ownership: Tanzanian Coffee Policy in the Age of Liberal Reformism'. *African Affairs* 103 (413): 615–633.

Pratt, Cranford. 1976. *The Critical Phase in Tanzania, 1945–1968: Nyerere and the Emergence of a Socialist Strategy*. Cambridge University Press.

Prunier, Gerard. 1995. *The Rwanda Crisis: History of a Genocide*. Columbia University Press.

Rahat, Gideon, and Reuven Hazan. 2001. 'Candidate Selection Methods: An Analytical Framework'. *Party Politics* 7 (3): 297–322.

Rakner, Lise, and Leonardo Rafael Arriola. 2015. 'Reconceptualizing African Party Systems: Explaining the Variation in Institutionalized Competition'. American Political Science Association, San Francisco. 1–26.

Randall, Vicky, and Lars Svasand. 2002. 'Party Institutionalization in New Democracies'. *Party Politics* 8 (1): 5–29.

Randall, Vicky, and Lars Svasand. 2002. 'Political Parties and Democratic Consolidation in Africa'. *Democratization* 9 (3): 30–52.

Reinikka, R., and J. Svensson. 2001. 'Confronting Competition: Investment, Profit and Risk'. In R. Reinikka and P. Collier (eds), *Uganda's Recovery: The Role of Farms, Firms, and Government.* World Bank. 207–234.

Remmer, Karen. 1997. 'Theoretical Decay and Theoretical Development: The Resurgence of Institutional Analysis'. *World Politics* 50 (1): 34–61.

Renno, Lucio, and Carlos Pereira. 2013. 'Effectiveness and Representation: Effects of Federal Deputies' Career Choice and Re-election'. In M. Mackinnon and L. Feoli (eds), *Representation and Effectiveness in Latin American Democracies: Congress, Judiciary And Civil Society.* Routledge. 75–90.

Resnick, Danielle. 2014. *Urban poverty and party populism in African democracies.* Cambridge University Press.

Resnick, Idrian. 1981. *The Long Transition: Building Socialism in Tanzania.* Monthly Review Press.

Reuss, Anna, and Kristof Titeca. 2017. 'Beyond Ethnicity: The Violence in Western Uganda and Rwenzori's 99 Problems'. *Review of African Political Economy* 44 (151): 131–141.

Reuter, Ora John. 2017. *The Origins of Dominant Parties: Building Authoritarian Institutions in Post-Soviet Russia.* Cambridge University Press.

Reuter, Ora John, and Thomas F. Remington. 2009. 'Dominant Party Regimes and the Commitment Problem: The Case of United Russia'. *Comparative Political Studies* 42 (4): 501–526.

Riedl, Rachel Beatty. 2014. *Authoritarian Origins of Democratic Party Systems in Africa.* Cambridge University Press.

Riker, William. 1980. 'Implications from the Disequilibrium of Majority Rule for the Study of Institutions'. *American Political Science Review* 74 (2): 432–446.

Roberts, George. 2022. *Revolutionary State-making in Dar es Salaam.* Cambridge University Press.

Rodan, Garry, and Kanishka Jayasuriya. 2012. 'Hybrid Regimes: A Social Foundations Approach'. In J. Heynes (ed.), *Routledge Handbook of Democratization.* Routledge. 175–189.

Rodney, Walter. 1980. 'Class contradictions in Tanzania'. In Haroub Othman (ed), *The State in Tanzania: A Selection of Articles.* Dar es Salaam University Press. 18–41.

Rodney, Walter. 2018. *How Europe Underdeveloped Africa.* Verso Books.

Ross, Michael. 2006. 'Is Democracy Good for the Poor?' *American Journal of Political Science* 50 (4): 860–874.

Rubongoya, Joshua B. 2007. *Regime Hegemony in Museveni's Uganda: Pax Musevenica.* Basingstoke: Palgrave Macmillan.

Saiegh, Sebastian. 2014. 'Lawmaking'. In S. Martin, T. Saalfeld and K. Strom (eds), *The Oxford Handbook of Legislative Studies.* Oxford University Press. 482–513.

Salih, Mohamed 2005. *African Parliaments: between Governance and Government.* Palgrave Macmillan.

Samoff, Joel. 1989. 'Popular Initiatives and Local Government in Tanzania'. *The Journal of Developing Areas* 24 (1): 1–18.

Samuels, David. 2002. 'Pork Barreling Is Not Credit Claiming or Advertising: Campaign Finance and the Sources of the Personal Vote in Brazil'. *The Journal of Politics* 64 (3): 845–863.

Sandbrook, Richard. 1972. 'Patrons, Clients, and Factions: New Dimensions of Conflict Analysis in Africa'. *Canadian Journal of Political Science/Revue canadienne de science politique* 5(1): 104–119.

Sandbrook, Richard, and Judith Barker. 1985. *The Politics of Africa's Economic Stagnation.* Cambridge University Press.

Sangmpam, S. N. 2007. 'Politics Rules: The False Primacy of Institutions in Developing Countries'. *Political Studies* 55: 201–224.

Sathyamurthy, T. V. 1975. 'The Social Base of the Uganda People's Congress, 1958–70'. *African Affairs* 74 (297): 442–460.

Saul, John. 1972. 'TANU and Economic Development'. In L. Cliffe and J. Saul (eds), *Socialism in Tanzania.* East African Publishing House.

Schattschneider, Elmer Eric. 1942. *Party Government*: Transaction Publishers.

Schatz, Sayre 1977. *Nigerian Capitalism*. University of California Press.

Schedler, Andreas. 1998. 'What is Democratic Consolidation?' *Journal of Democracy* 9 (2): 91–107.

Schedler, Andreas. 2002. 'The Nested Game of Democratization by Elections'. *International Political Science Review* 23 (1): 103–122.

Schuler, Paul. 2020. 'Position Taking or position ducking? A theory of public debate in single-party legislatures'. *Comparative Political Studies* 53(9): 1493–524.

Seawright, Jason, and John Gerring. 2008. 'Case Selection Techniques in Case Study Research: A Menu of Qualitative and Quantitative Options'. *Political Research Quarterly* 61 (2): 294–308.

Seeberg, Merete Bech, Michael Wahman, and Svend-Erik Skaaning. 2018. 'Candidate Nomination, Intra-Party Democracy, and Election Violence in Africa'. *Democratization* 25 (6): 959–977.

Sheingate, Adam. 2009. 'Rethinking Rules: Creativity and Constraint in the US House of Representatives'. In J. Mahoney and K. Thelen (eds), *Explaining Institutional Change: Ambiguity, Agency and Power*. Cambridge University Press. 168–203.

Shepsle, Kenneth A. 1989. 'Studying Institutions: Some Lessons from the Rational Choice Approach'. *Journal of Theoretical Politics* 1 (2): 131–147.

Shepsle, Kenneth A. 2002. 'Assessing Comparative Legislative Research'. In G. Loewenberg, P. Squire, and D. R. Kiewiet (eds), *Legislatures*. The University of Michigan Press. 387–399.

Shivji, Issa. 1976. *Class Struggles in Tanzania*. Heinemann Educational Books Ltd.

Shivji, Issa. 2013. 'Democracy and Democratization in Africa: Interrogating Paradigms and Practices'. *African Review* 40 (1): 1–13.

Shivji, Issa. 2021. 'The Dialectics of Maguphilia and Maguphobia'. *CODESRIA Bulletin Online* 13: 1–10.

Shivji, Issa, Saida Yahya-Othman, and Ng'wanza Kamata. 2020. *Julius Nyerere: A Biography* (vol. 3). Mkuki na Nyota Publishers.

Sigman, Rachel. 2023. *Parties, Political Finance, and Governance in Africa: Extracting Money and Shaping States in Benin and Ghana*. Cambridge University Press.

Sitta, Samuel, Willibrod Slaa, and John Cheyo. 2008. 'Bunge Lenye Meno: A Parliament with Teeth, for Tanzania'. Africa Research Institute.

Sklar, Richard. 1963. *Nigerian Political Parties: Power in an Emergent African Nation*. Princeton University Press.

Sklar, Richard. 1979. 'The Nature of Class Domination in Africa'. *The Journal of Modern African Studies* 17 (4): 531–552.

Slater, Dan. 2003. 'Iron Cage in an Iron Fist: Authoritarian Institutions and the Personalization of Power in Malaysia'. *Comparative Politics* 26(1): 81–101.

Smith, Benjamin. 2005. 'Life of the Party: The Origins of Regime Breakdown and Persistence under Single-Party Rule'. *World Politics* 57: 421–451.

Soares de Oliveira, Ricardo. 2015. *Magnificent and Beggar Land: Angola since the Civil War*. Oxford University Press.

Sommers, Marc. 2012. *Rwandan Youth and the Struggle for Adulthood*. University of Georgia Press.

Southall, Aidan. 1988. 'The Recent Political Economy of Uganda'. In H. B. Hansen and M. Twaddle (eds), *Uganda Now: Between Development and Decay*. Currey. 54–69.

Squire, Peverill. 1992. 'Legislative Professionalism and Membership Diversity in State Legislatures'. *Legislative Studies Quarterly* 17: 1026–1054.

Squire, Peverill. 1992. 'The Theory of Legislative Institutionalization and the California Assembly'. *The Journal of Politics* 54 (4): 1026–1054.

Stasavage, David. 2005. 'Democracy and Education Spending in Africa'. *American Journal of Political Science* 49 (2): 343–258.

Streeck, Wolfgang, and Kathleen Thelen (eds). 2005. *Beyond Continuity: Institutional Change in Advanced Political Economies*. Oxford University Press.

Steiler, Ilona and Chediel Nyirenda. 2021. 'Towards Sustainable Livelihoods in the Tanzanian Informal Economy: Facilitating Inclusion, Organization, and Rights for Street Vendors'. WIDER Working Paper, No. 2021/53.

Stokes, Susan, Thad Dunning, Marcelo Nazareno, and Valeria Brusco. 2013. *Brokers, Voters, and Clientelism: The Puzzle of Distributive Politics*. Cambridge University Press.

Strom, Kaare. 1997. 'Rules, Reasons and Routines: Legislative Roles in Parliamentary Democracies'. *The Journal of Legislative Studies* 3 (1): 155–174.

Sulle, Emmanuel. 2017. 'Social Differentiation and the Politics of Land: Sugar Cane Outgrowing in Kilombero, Tanzania'. *Journal of Southern African Studies* 43 (3): 517–533.

Svolik, Milan. 2012. *The Politics of Authoritarian Rule*. Cambridge University Press.

Swainson, Nicola. 1977. 'The Rise of a National Bourgeoisie in Kenya'. *Review of African Political Economy* 8 (1): 39–55.

Swainson, Nicola. 1980. *The Development of Corporate Capitalism in Kenya, 1918–1977*. University of California Press.

Swainson, Nicola. 1987. 'Indigenous Capitalism in Postcolonial Kenya'. In P. Lubeck (ed.), *An African Bourgeoisie: Race, Class and Politics in South Africa*. Yale University Press.

Tamale, Sylvia. 1999. *When Hens Begin to Crow: Gender and Parliamentary Politics in Uganda*. Westview.

Tambila, Kapwepwe. 2004. 'The Ups and Downs of the Tanzanian Parliament 1961–1994'. In R. S. Mukandala, S. S. Mushi, and C. Rubagumya (eds), *People's Representatives: Theory and Practice of Parliamentary Democracy in Tanzania*. Fountain Publishers Ltd. 46–72.

Tangri, Roger K., and Andrew M. Mwenda. 2003. 'Military Corruption and Ugandan Politics since the Late 1990s'. *Review of African Political Economy* 30 (98): 539–552.

Tangri, Roger K., and Andrew M. Mwenda. 2013. *The Politics of Elite Corruption in Africa: Uganda in Comparative African Perspective*. Routledge.

Tangri, Roger K., and Andrew M. Mwenda. 2019. 'Change and Continuity in the Politics of Government-Business Relations in Museveni's Uganda'. *Journal of Eastern African Studies* 13(4): 678–697.

Tanzania Electoral Monitoring Committee. 1997. 'The 1995 General Elections in Tanzania: Report of the Tanzania Electoral Monitoring Committee'. TEMCO.

Tanzania Election Monitoring Committee. 2006. 'The 2005 Elections in Tanzania: Report of the Tanzania Election Monitoring Committee'. TEMCO.

Tapscott, Rebecca. 2021. *Arbitrary states: social control and modern authoritarianism in Museveni's Uganda*. Oxford University Press.

Taylor, Keeanga-Yamahtta. 2016. *From #BlackLivesMatter to Black Liberation*. Haymarket Books.

Thelen, Kathleen. 1999. 'Historical Institutionalism in Comparative Politics'. *Annual Review of Political Science* 2: 369–404.

Therkildsen, Ole, and France Bourgouin. 2012. 'Continuity and Change in Tanzania's Ruling Coalition: Legacies, Crises and Weak Productive Capacity'. *DIIS Working Paper*. Copenhagen, Denmark: Danihs Institute of International Studies. 1–58.

Thioub, Ibrahima, Momar-Coumba, Diop, and Catherine Boone. 1998. 'Economic Liberalization in Senegal: Shifting Politics of Indigenous Business Interests'. *African Studies Review* 41 (2): 63–90.

Throup, David, and Charles Hornsby. 1998. *Multi-Party Politics in Kenya: The Kenyatta and Moi States and the Triumph of the System in the 1992 Election*. Ohio University Press.

Titeca, Kristof. 2014. 'The Commercialisation of Uganda's 2011 Election in the Urban Informal Economy: Money, Boda-Bodas and Market Vendors'. In S. Perrot, S. Makara, J. Lafargue, and M.-A. Fouere (eds), *Elections in a Hybrid Regime: Revisiting the 2011 Ugandan Polls*. Fountain Publishers. 178–207.

Titeca, Kristof, and Thomas Vervisch. 2008. 'The Dynamics of Social Capital and Community Associations in Uganda: Linking Capital and Its Consequences'. *World Development* 36 (11): 2205–2222.

Tordoff, William. 1977. 'Residual Legislatures: The Cases of Tanzania and Zambia'. *Journal of Commonwealth and Comparative Politics* 15 (3): 235–249.

Tordoff, William, and Robert Molteno. 1974. 'Parliament'. In W. Tordoff (ed.), *Politics in Zambia*. University of California Press. 197–241.

Tripp, Aili Mari. 1997. *Changing the Rules: The Politics of Liberalization and the Urban Informal Economy in Tanzania*. University of California Press.

Tripp, Aili Mari. 2010. *Museveni's Uganda: Paradoxes of Power in a Hybrid Regime*. Boulder, CO: Lynne Rienner Publishers.

Tripp, Aili Mari. 2010. 'The Politics of Constitution Making in Uganda'. In L. Miller (ed.), *Framing the State in Times of Transition: Case Studies in Constitution Making*. United States Institute for Peace. 158–175.

Tripp, Aili Mari. 2023. *Joan Wicken: A lifelong Collaboration with Mwalimu Nyerere*. Mkuki na Nyota Publishers.

Truex, Rory. 2014. 'The Returns to Office in a "Rubber Stamp" Parliament'. *American Political Science Review* 108 (2): 235–251.

Truex, Rory. 2020. 'Authoritarian Gridlock? Understanding Delay in the Chinese Legislative System'. *Comparative Political Studies* 53 (9): 1455–1492.

Tukahebwa, Geoffrey B. 1998. 'Privatization as a Development Policy'. In H. B. Hansen and M. Twaddle (eds), *Developing Uganda*. James Currey. 59–72.

Twaddle, Michael and Holger Bernt Hansen. 1998. 'The Changing state of Uganda'. In H.B. Hansen and M. Taddle (eds), *Deveoping Uganda*. James Currey. 1–18.

Twaweza. 2010. 'Did They Perform? Assessing Five Years of Bunge 2005–2010' In *Policy Brief*. Dar es Salaam. 1–16.

Upadhyaya, Radha and Edoardo Totolo. 2020. 'Financial Sector'. In Nic Cheeseman, Karuti Kanyinga, and Gabrielle Lynch (eds), *The Oxford Handbook of Kenyan Politics*. Oxford University Press. 465–481.

Utouh, Ludovik. 2018. *Uwajibikaji Ndani ya Kalamu Isiyokuwa na Wino*. Wajibu Institute of Public Accountability.

Uvin, Peter. 2002. 'Build-up to War and Genocide'. In J. Pottier (ed.), *Re-imagining Rwanda: Conflict, Survival and Disinformation in the Late Twentieth Century*. Cambridge University Press. 9–52.

Van Cranenburgh, Oda. 1990. *The Widening Gyre: The Tanzanian One-Party State and Policy towards Rural Cooperatives*. Eburon.

Van de Laar, A.J.M. 1972. 'Growth and Income Distribution in Tanzania since Independence'. In L. Cliffe and J. Saul (eds), *Socialism in Tanzania: An Interdisciplinary Reader*. East African Publishing House. 106–117.

van de Walle, N. 2001. *African Economies and the Politics of Permanent Crisis, 1979–1999*. Cambridge University Press.

van de Walle, N. 2003. 'Presidentialism and Clientelism in Africa's Emerging Party Systems' *The Journal of Modern African Studies* 41 (2): 297–321.

Van Donge, Jan Kees, and Athumani J. Liviga. 1986. 'In Defence of the Tanzanian Parliament'. *Parliamentary Affairs* 39 (2): 230–240.

Van Donge, Jan Kees, and Athumani J. Liviga. 1990. 'The 1985 Tanzania Parliamentary Elections: A Conservative Election'. In H. Othman, I. Bavu, and M. Okema (eds), *Tanzania: Democracy in Transition*. Dar es Salaam University Press. 1–21.

Van Velzen, H.U.E, and J.J. Sterkenburg. 1972a. 'The Party Supreme'. In L. S. Cliffe (ed.), *Socialism in Tanzania*. East African Publishing House.

Van Velzen, H.U.E, and J.J. Sterkenburg. 1972b. 'Stirrings in the Tanzanian National Assembly'. In E. A. P. House (ed.), *Socialism in Tanzania*. East African Publishing House. 249–263.

Van Vliet, Martin. 2014. 'Weak Legislatures, Failing MPs, and the Collapse of Democracy in Mali'. *African Affairs* 113/450: 45–66.

Vaughan, Sarah, and Mesfin Gebremichael. 2011. 'Rethinking Business and Politics in Ethiopia: The Role of EFFORT, the Endowment Fund for the Rehabilitation of Tigray'. Overseas Development Institute.

Verhoeven, Harry. 2012. 'Nurturing Democracy or into the Danger Zone? The Rwandan Patriotic Front, Elite Fragmentation and Post-liberation Politics'. In M. Campioni and P. Noack (eds), *Rwanda Fast Forward: Social, Economic, Military and Reconciliation Prospects*. Palgrave Macmillan. 265–280.

Vlassenroot, Koen, Sandrine Perrot, and Jeroen Cuvelier. 2012. 'Doing Business out of War. An Analysis of the UPDF's Presence in the Democratic Republic of Congo'. *Journal of Eastern African Studies* 6 (1): 2–21.

Vokes, Richard. 2016. 'Primaries, Patronage and Political Personalities in South-Western Uganda'. *Journal of Eastern African Studies* 10 (4): 660–676.

von Freyhold, Michaela 1979. *Ujamaa Villages in Tanzania: Analysis of a Social Experiment*. Heinemann.

Waliggo, John. 2001. 'The Main Actors in the Constitution-Making Process in Uganda'. In G. Hyden and D. Venter (eds), *Constitution-Making and Democratisation in Africa*. Africa Institute of South Africa. 43–68.

Wang, Vibeke. 2005a. 'The Accountability Function of Parliament in New Democracies: Tanzanian Perspectives'. CMI Working Papers: Chr. Michelsen Institute.

Wang, Vibeke. 2005b. 'Parliament as Machinery for Political System Control: The Inner Workings of Bunge Tanzania'. In M. Salih (ed.), *African Parliaments: Between Governance and Government*. Palgrave Macmillan. 183–200.

Wang, Vibeke, and Mi Yung Yoon. 2018. 'Recruitment Mechanisms for Reserved Seats for Women in Parliament and Switches to Non-quota Seats: A Comparative Study of Tanzania and Uganda'. *Journal of Modern African Studies* 56 (2): 299–324.

Wapakhabulo, James. 2001. 'Managing the Constitutional-Making Process in Uganda'. In G. Hyden and D. Venter (eds), *Constitution-Making and Democratisation in Africa*. Africa Institute of South Africa. 114–131.

Weaver, Vesla, and Gwen Prowse. 2020. 'Racial authoritarianism in U.S. demoracy'. *Science* 369(6508): 1176–1178.

Weghorst, Keith. 2022. *Activist Origins of Political Ambition: Opposition Candidacy in Africa's Electoral Authoritarian Regimes*. Cambridge University Press.

Weghorst, Keith, and Staffan. Lindberg. 2013. 'What Drives the Swing Voter in Africa?' *American Journal of Political Science* 57 (3): 717–734.

Whitfield, Lindsay, Ole Therkildsen, Lars Buur, and Anne Mette Kjaer. 2015. *The Politics of African Industrial Policy: A Comparative Perspective*. Cambridge University Press.

Widner, Jennifer. 1992. *The Rise of a Party-State in Kenya: From 'Harambee' to 'Nyayo!'*. University of California Press.

Wilkins, Sam. 2016. 'Who Pays for Pakalast? The NRM's Peripheral Patronage in Rural Uganda'. *Journal of Eastern African Studies* 10 (4): 619–638.

Wilkins, Sam. 2019. 'Capture the Flag: Local Factionalism as Electoral Mobilization in Dominant Party Uganda'. *Democratization* 26 (8): 1493–1512.

Wilkins, Sam. 2021. 'Subnational Turnover, Accountability Politics, and Electoral Authoritarian Survival: Evidence from Museveni's Uganda'. *Comparative Politics*, 54 (1): 149–173.

Wilkins, Sam, and Richard Vokes. 2016. 'The NRM regime and the 2016 Ugandan elections [Special Issue]'. *Journal of Eastern African Studies* 10(4).

Wilkins, Sam, and Richard Vokes. 2023. 'Transition, transformation, and the politics of the future in Uganda [Article Collection]'. *Journal of Eastern African Studies* 17(1–2).

Wilkins, Sam, Richard Vokes, and Moses Khisa. 2021. 'Briefing: Contextualizing the Bobi Wine Factor in Uganda's 2021 Elections'. *African Affairs* 120 (481): 629–643.

Williamson, Scott, and Beatriz Magaloni. 2020. 'Legislatures and Policy Making in Authoritarian Regimes'. *Comparative Political Studies* 53 (9): 1525–1543.

Wilson, Matthew Charles, and Joseph Wright. 2015. 'Autocratic Legislatures and Expropriation Risk'. *British Journal of Political Science* 47: 1–17.

Winters, Jeffrey, and Benjamin Page. 2009. 'Oligarchy in the United States?' *Perspectives on Politics* 7 (4): 731–751.

Wolf, Anne. 2023. *Ben Ali's Tunisia: Power and Contention in an Authoritarian Regime*. Oxford University Press.

World Bank. 1989. 'Sub-Saharan Africa: From Crisis to Sustainable Growth: A Long-Term Perspective Study'. World Bank.

Wright, Joseph. 2008. 'Do Authoritarian Institutions Constrain? How Legislatures Affect Economic Growth and Investment'. *American Journal of Political Science* 52 (2): 322–343.

Wu, Chung-li. 2001. 'The Transformation of the Kuomintang's Candidate Selection System'. *Party Politics* 7 (1): 103–118.

Wuhs, Steven. 2006. 'Democratization and the Dynamics of Candidate Selection Rule Change in Mexico, 1991–2003'. *Mexican Studies* 22 (1): 33–56.

Yoon, Mi Yung. 2008. 'Special Seats for Women in the National Legislature: The Case of Tanzania'. *Africa Today* 55 (1): 61–86.

Young, Crawford. 1966. 'The Obote Revolution'. *Africa Report.*

Young, Crawford. 2012. *The Postcolonial State in Africa: Fifty Years of Independence.* University of Wisconsin Press.

Zolberg, Aristide. 1966. *Creating Political Order: The Party-State of West Africa.* Rand McNally.

Unpublished dissertations and papers

Chachage, Chambi. 2018. 'A Capitalizing City: Dar Es Salaam and the Emergence of an African Entrepreneurial Elite'. Department of African and African American Studies, Harvard University, Cambridge, MA.

Cheeseman, Nic. 2006. 'The Rise and Fall of Civil-Authoritarianism in Africa: Patronage, Participation, and Political Parties in Kenya and Zambia'. Department of Politics and International Relations, University of Oxford, Oxford, UK.

Fisher, Thomas. 2012. 'Chagga Elites and the Politics of Ethnicity in Kilimanjaro, Tanzania'. University of Edinburgh.

Gray, Hazel, and Lindsay Whitfield. 2014. 'Reframing African Political Economy: Clientelism, Rents and Accumulation as Drivers of Capitalist Transformation'. In Working Paper Series 2014: Development Studies Institute, London School of Economics, London, UK. 1–32.

Hartmann, Jeannette. 1983. 'Development Policy-Making in Tanzania 1962–1982: A Critique of Sociological Interpretations', University of Hull, Hull, UK.

Humphreys, Macartan and Jeremy Weinstein. 2012. 'Policing Politicians: Citizens Empowerment and Political Accountability in Uganda'.

Jones, Will. 2014. 'Murder and Create: State Reconstruction in Rwanda since 1994'. Department of Politics, University of Oxford, Oxford, UK.

Kasfir, Nelson, and Hippo Twebaze. 2016. 'Performance and effectiveness of lawmaking and oversight: The 6th-9th Ugandan Parliaments'.

Nakamura, Robert, and John Johnson. 2003. 'Rising Legislative Assertiveness in Uganda and Kenya'. In *10th International Political Science Association World Congress.* Durban, South Africa. 1–29.

Odoki, Ben. 1997. 'The Constitution, Its Objective and the Role of Parliament'. In *Seminar for Parliamentarians.* Uganda International Conference Centre, Kampala, Uganda. 1–28.

Silwal, Ani Rudra. 2016. 'Three Essays on Agriculture and Economic Development in Tanzania'. University of Sussex.

Therkildsen, Ole. 2012. 'Democratisation in Tanzania: No taxation without exemptions'. In *Africa Studies Association Annual Conference.* New Orleans, LA. 1–27.

Tsubura, Machiko. 2014. 'Accountability and Clientelism in Dominant Party Politics: The Case of a Constituency Development Fund in Tanzania'. Development Studies, University of Sussex, Brighton, UK.

Twebaze, Hippo. 2014. 'Legislative Oversight of Security Sector in Transition Democracies: The Case of Parliament of Uganda (1986–2011)'. Makerere University, Kampala, Uganda.

van de Walle, N. 2009. 'The Democratization of Political Clientelism in Sub-Saharan Africa'. In *3rd European Conference on African Studies.* Leipzig, Germany. 1–17.

Index

For the benefit of digital users, indexed terms that span two pages (e.g., 52–53) may, on occasion, appear on only one of those pages.